Economists' Lives

Economists' Lives: Biography and Autobiography in the History of Economics

Annual Supplement to Volume 39
History of Political Economy

Edited by E. Roy Weintraub and Evelyn L. Forget

Duke University Press
Durham and London 2007

Printed in the United States of America
on acid-free paper. ISBN 978-0-8223-6683-6.
This is the 2007 supplement to
History of Political Economy, ISSN 0018-2702.

Contents

Introduction

E. Roy Weintraub and Evelyn L. Forget

In nonacademic bookstores, biographies and autobiographies are almost as common as romance novels or mysteries. People seem to like reading about other people's lives, perhaps imaginatively to project themselves into those lives or to otherwise engage with if not the rich, then the famous. In more specialized areas, however, like the history of science, biography has had to fight for a place. If the master trope of the history of science had been science's place in the Enlightenment project, its primary concern was to explain and contextualize the development of scientific knowledge: an individual scientist's life was interesting only to the extent that the knowledge products associated with it had lasting importance. If scientific knowledge grew in association with particular scientific communities and institutions, individuals necessarily fade into the background of that social history. It does, however, appear that the turn to the personal in the last quarter of the twentieth century, the understanding that knowledge is situated—a perspective widely shared among scholars in many disciplines—has removed some of the uneasiness about biography and life writing in the history of science. Individuals express their lives in science, and their science is an expression of their lives. As the historian

The editors wish to thank Duke University Press, Cathy Davidson (Duke's Vice Provost for Interdisciplinary Studies), Susan Roth (Duke's Associate Dean of Social Sciences), and Jean-Jacques Thomas (Directory of Canadian and North American Studies) for providing generous financial support for the 2006 *HOPE* conference.

History of Political Economy 39 (annual suppl.) DOI 10.1215/00182702-2006-035

Mary Terrall (2006, 313) has recently noted, "The historian conjures figures from these shadows, though not in the same way, or using the same techniques, as the novelist. Writing lives of individuals, retrieved and reconstructed from material evidence, also means writing about science itself, through the lived experience of its practitioners. Unfolding those faded letters and searching for the 'volatile and sentient forces' driving our subjects, we are led into the worlds of readers, spectators, institutions, collaborations, disputes, and all the other interactions that make up the life of science."

Historians of economics have been ambivalent about life writing. Should biography be a full partner to narrative histories of economics, as William Jaffé argued, or are such accounts irrelevant to the history of ideas, as George Stigler maintained? And what is to be the role of first-person accounts? We make use of autobiographical material in constructing our histories, but we have not, as a discipline, reflected on how and why that material was constructed and preserved, and how it ought to be read and interpreted by contemporary historians. We make use of interviews and oral histories in our reflections about biographical subjects, as we seek to understand those subjects' roles in the development of economics. But how are we to interpret such conversations and testimonies?

It is not sufficient to mimic the answers provided by historians of science. There are some complex differences between the history of economics and the history of science. Unlike historians of science, historians of economics do not stand "outside" the discipline they examine, and this leads to an increased familiarity with the lives of economists and thus both greater and lesser sensitivity to the contingencies of those lives. Autobiography is never very far from biography in the history of economics, and yet historians of economics have, for the most part, used those autonarrations sparingly in their own reconstructions. Although there are few biographies of economists that have engaged the popular imagination as, say, Richard S. Westfall's biography of Isaac Newton has, economists themselves have constructed biographies as part of their work as historians of economics.

Recognizing the increased volume of life-narrative studies becoming available through short biographies, long biographies, transcripts of conversations, and collections of short autobiographies, we decided that it was time to bring these materials more fully to the attention of historians of economics. Our initial call for papers asked variously about the treatment of autobiographical materials, the construction of heroes and villains, the relation between scientific biography and literary biography, concerns related to living subjects in recent history, and a number of other matters. We were very pleased with the large number of responses to that call, and the collection of papers that has finally emerged from the 2006 *HOPE* conference has opened a number of important areas for historians of economics to examine. The conferees were more diverse across disciplines than they had been at past *HOPE* conferences. Besides historians of economics, individuals represented literature, history, and sociology. The conference's subject matter, being new, meant that conferees did not have to engage with an individual's set-in-stone positions. Consequently, this *HOPE* conference involved participants' listening carefully to presentations, engaging with some new ideas, and collectively rethinking original papers in response to the work done at the conference itself. Put another way, this conference produced, if not a single shared perspective, at least deepened understandings about biographical and autobiographical writings in the history of economics among the participants themselves.

The volume opens with a discussion of the promise, and of the limits, of intellectual biography. Malachi Hacohen challenges us by asking whether biographers have learned the hard lessons that we ought to have learned during the 1970s and 1980s when biography languished in exile, no longer convincing intellectual historians that it could contribute to their project. Is the biography that has returned a humbler enterprise? Does it celebrate its strengths—the precision with which the situational logic of an individual life can illustrate the possibilities and limitations of creativity, and how collective structures can inform individual decisions—while acknowledging its limitations? Intellectual biography, Hacohen argues, can illustrate little about the evolution of bodies of discourse and their impact on the social and intellectual world within which individual thinkers pursue their life projects.

Jeremy Popkin also addresses the relationship between the self and the wider world in life writing. He asks what happens when an academic, someone who has spent a life immersed in a scholarly discipline searching for knowledge and understanding, writes an autobiography. Does the author's academic discipline matter to life writing? In particular, do the life stories constructed by economists differ from those of historians or literary critics? Popkin argues that all good academic work derives its energy from the unique passions of the scholar. Academic training, however, can be an instrument for self-knowledge. Academic biographies structure human lives in ways shaped by the disciplinary paradigms that authors use in their scholarship, to the point where it becomes almost impossible to separate a "true" self from the persona developed to achieve professional success.

The volume's second section addresses how economists use biographies in their intellectual projects. Roger Backhouse examines one of the more prolific genres of life writing in economics—collections of short biographies that, at their best, help us recognize that knowledge is the product of communities of economists. Perhaps by examining the lives and contributions of scholars beyond the few who merit long biographies, we can hope to understand something about the evolution of bodies of discourse. Robert Dimand considers the implications of demonizing and lionizing the great economists of the past, arguing that such unreflective celebration and vilification has benefits as well as costs. The creation of dramatic stories and larger-than-life characters has, perhaps, attracted at least some attention to an intellectual heritage that would, without such drama, be even more neglected by a present-minded discipline. As such, these stories—flawed as they are—serve as the occasion for new research and reflection. William Coleman examines similar themes in his essay, which reflects on his recent group biography of economists in Australian public life. As does Backhouse, Coleman asks what we can learn by writing "minor lives," and, like Backhouse, he concludes that group biographies may come closer to allowing us to understand the evolution of economics, which is a community product, than do individual biographies of great thinkers.

The third section looks at issues of narrative identity and the ways in which economists use life writing to create both individual and group identity. Paul John Eakin takes us back to the nineteenth century and asks how the changing economy might be reflected in the economic lives of ordinary people, a question wonderfully illustrated by Henry Mayhew's "little watercress seller." How does a child laborer in Victorian London understand her economic contribution, and are her insights systematically different from those proffered by twentieth-century autobiographers? Mike Reay picks up the same theme and asks how twentieth-century economists understand themselves as economists, and how that understanding is reflected in a set of interviews he did with American economists working in various academic and nonacademic settings. The identity of subcommunities of economists is no less interesting. What does it mean to be a "Chicago" economist or a "heterodox" economist? Ross

Emmett examines the first group, and Tiago Mata and Fred Lee the second, using similar strategies of interview and oral history.

Section 4 turns to a series of biographical studies of particular economists. Christine Théré and Loïc Charles conduct an archaeological dig on past biographies of François Quesnay, uncovering funeral orations, short eulogies published in academic journals, and longer biographies. They document how the mythmaking that is inevitable in some kinds of life writing is reinforced and preserved in more scholarly biographies, and ultimately leads to a picture of a life that would have been unrecognizable to his contemporaries, who better understood the context and, indeed, the tropes common to various period genres. Using Quesnay's life as a window into the eighteenth-century world of patronage, Théré and Charles present a rich and nuanced portrait of academic ambition. Jan-Otmar Hesse returns to a theme that is at least implicit in many of these works. What distinguishes an economist from other academics is that, in some cases and more often in earlier times, economists were not purely academics but made their lives and livelihoods outside universities. His study of L. Albert Hahn addresses the question of whether individuals' entrepreneurial undertakings help shape not only the identity they create for themselves but also ultimately their economic writing. Robert Leonard puts himself into the character of Oskar Morgenstern to reflect on equilibrium and mathematics in the 1920s. Does this blur the line between object and subject in biography, as some conference attendees argued, or does it merely reflect with greater honesty the unstable and permeable boundaries that always exist between biographer and subject?[1] Craufurd D. Goodwin and Patricia Laurence both reflect on the roles that community, the arts, and friendship played in the life and work of John Maynard Keynes. Goodwin notes that historians of economics are typically much less comfortable with wide-ranging investigations into the personal lives of their subjects than are biographers of political, cultural, or business figures. His essay reflects on some of the more puzzling aspects of Keynes's writing, such as his concern with how people should live their lives in advanced market economies. By examining Keynes's relationship with Virginia Woolf, whose impact on twentieth-century fiction was comparable with

1. Alone among the papers, Leonard's was previously published. The editors, in inviting Leonard to present the paper well after the "deadline," were impressed at the remarkable fit between Leonard's concerns and the emergent conference proceedings.

that of Keynes on economics, Goodwin asks whether Woolf might have had an impact on the development of Keynes's worldview and, as such, merit the attention of historians of economics. Laurence addresses a similar set of themes from a broader perspective, by reflecting on the Bloomsbury relationships that influenced Keynes's interest in the arts.

Section 5 contains the reflections of three well-known economic biographers on some of the larger questions of biography in the history of economics. Don Moggridge considers the use of autobiography in his biography of Harry Johnson. Bruce Caldwell, Friedrich A. Hayek's biographer, sends us a series of notes from the trenches—ideas that he confronted in his writing about one of the most contested lives in twentieth-century economics. Peter Groenewegen looks back not only on his writing of Marshall's biography but on the reactions of readers, reminding us that, inevitably, biography is not simply a conversation between the subject and the biographer but ultimately a conversation with the reader as well.

The volume ends with a personal reflection by Roy Weintraub that addresses many of the issues involved in life writing and reminds us of why this genre so successfully captures the attention of readers. Creating a life is, after all, the project with which we are all involved.

References

Terrall, M. 2006. Biography as Cultural History of Science. *Isis* 97:306–13.

Part 1
Stage Setting

Rediscovering Intellectual Biography—and Its Limits

Malachi Hacohen

Biography is back. Those who lived through the transformation of history, science studies, and literary criticism in the 1970s and 1980s may be surprised, as I am. During my graduate career, in the 1980s, biography practically vanished as a genre of professional historical writing. Social and cultural history, deploying methodologies borrowed from literature, anthropology, and cultural studies, were decidedly hostile to biography, especially when its subjects were elite thinkers. The history and philosophy of science took a cultural turn, too, and however methodologically varied their analyses of the formation of discourse were, biography was not part of them. Even in intellectual history, the predominant approaches dissolved both text and author into discourse, and language rather than the life was declared the appropriate subject matter. True, biography has always remained the preferred genre of popular historical writing, of military and political histories directed to broader public audiences. But, in the last decade, biography has returned with a vengeance in most fields of history. The 2006 *HOPE* conference, "Life Writing and the History of Economics," could not be timelier. Biography's potential and pitfalls need now be examined, in light of what we have learned through the long detour into the history of discourse.

My thanks to Joseph Agassi, Eric Brandom, Joel Revill, and the anonymous *HOPE* referee for their comments. In parts of this essay, I have used material (slightly revised) published in Hacohen 2000.

History of Political Economy 39 (annual suppl.) DOI 10.1215/00182702-2006-036

As a historian who made his reputation publishing an intellectual biography of the young Karl Popper, I might be expected to rejoice at having become a full-fledged citizen of the republic of historians after long years of preaching at the city's gate. But my joy is tempered because I am not sure that the hard lessons of exile have been learned. To be sure, historians experiment with writing biography, but, in some cases, there is little more than a gesture toward the methodologies of the linguistic turn. The new biographies do not always manifest consciousness of the difficulty of biography and commonly commit the same mistakes for which my generation had to endure a sojourn in the desert. Examples abound. To mention one relevant to this audience, I followed with interest the debate on Friedrich Hayek's "ambivalent anti-Semitism"—his high regard for Jewish friends contrasted with his occasional use of anti-Semitic stereotypes—in this journal and the electronic mailing lists, only to despair at the limits shown in constructing rich intellectual contexts that would make possible an intelligent conversation about ethnic prejudice (Reder 2000, 2002; Hamowy 2002; Weintraub 2003). If biography is to become useful to the history of economic ideas, it cannot be biography as commonly practiced before the 1980s.

It would be counterproductive to survey and criticize here recent biographies. A syllabus of errors has rarely reformed historical writing. Instead, I wish to retell some of the difficulties I encountered in writing the biography of Karl Popper, in approaching his autobiography, and in retrieving and reconstructing the contexts for his intellectual development. I wish to reaffirm the importance of biography in the history of ideas: it is indispensable for explaining intellectual change, for understanding the acquisition of new ideas. The situational logic of an individual life, the pursuit of which marks every good biography, enables historians to evaluate the reach of individual agency and the limits and possibilities for creativity. Without such precision, the history of ideas risks wooden uses of context and falsely coherent discourses, transgressions that the history of discourse has widely committed while criticizing traditional biography for them. But I also wish to show why traditional biography will not do and, furthermore, explain some of the limits of even the best biography. Since writing the young Popper's biography, I have moved to topics more properly falling within the history of discourse. Such a move, I show, has its costs. Biography engages collective structures, as institutions and discourses, in explaining the formation of the individual, but the individual remains the site for their interaction. In the history of discourse, the formation and impact of collective structures is at issue. The complexity of the explanatory models increases, and precision declines. Biographers, bound to regard the history of discourse as a product of multiple biographies done without the care possible in an individual one, can offer little help. These are the limits of biography.

Biography, Old and New: Shaping a Life

Biographers often inherit several narratives of their subject's life, ones created by obituaries, autobiographies, and, occasionally, previous biographies. They rarely leave them untouched. Popper's received narrative proved in need of an especially radical revision. It seemed as if history intervened repeatedly to distort his biography. A stranger in his homeland even before emigrating in 1937, Popper (1902–1994), a permanent exile, has become in the last two decades something of a national Austrian philosopher. Significantly, the centenary congress for his birth took place in Vienna. Still, although he was born and buried in Vienna, he is primarily known as a Western intellectual, an anticommunist prophet of Cold War liberalism. He first became famous for *The Open Society and Its Enemies* (1945). Written during World War II in Popper's New Zealand exile, the book was intended as a defense of democracy against fascism. The defeat of Austrian socialism and the collapse of Central European democracies were the major experiences informing his analysis. He saw himself as shaping a reform philosophy, an alternative to Marxism that would provide a platform for a united front of socialists and liberals in the postwar years. Instead, published on the eve of the Cold War, *The Open Society* became, with Popper's endorsement, an anticommunist manifesto and a charter of transatlantic liberalism. Popper's philosophy of science, exemplified best in *Logik der Forschung* (1935; translated in 1959 as *The Logic of Scientific Discovery*), went through a similar transformation. To be sure, it is commonly debated in the context of logical positivism and the Vienna Circle, whose politics was secular and cosmopolitan, ranging from liberal to radical socialist. But the circle's emigration, the postwar triumph of analytic philosophy in the Anglo-American academy, and the rebellion of the New Left against positivism in the 1960s transformed positivism, too, into a primarily Anglo-American philosophy with a conservative reputation. The "fugue of exile's disruptions" severed the thread connecting interwar Austria and the postwar Atlantic world, progressive Viennese politics and the Cold War (Bretenbach 1991, 81).

Popper developed his philosophy in dialogue with the circle, but he adamantly refused to take their linguistic turn. Against their platform for linguistic reform, he counterposed a revolutionary epistemology that rehabilitated philosophy, and even metaphysics, and made the search for "true" yet ever uncertain knowledge a compelling task. The circle regarded his work as contributing to their scientific philosophy and made publication of *Logik der Forschung* possible. The book appeared in the circle's famed series Schriften zur wissenschaftlichen Weltauffassung. Most discussions of Popper's philosophy of science in the immediate postwar period relied on the secondary reports of Vienna Circle émigrés. Popper protested to no end that he was their critic, not their friend, but his protests were in vain. What he called the "Positivist Legend" emerged.

Likewise, the reception of his political philosophy had little to do with its original intent. It was Red Vienna, not Soviet communism, that provided the grounds for his critique of Marx. When writing *The Open Society*, he knew next to nothing about the Soviet Union. He felt ambivalent about the Austrian Socialist Party, whose policies he deemed suicidal. Fascism, he thought, reflected a primeval urge to return to the closed "tribal" society, and Marxist mistakes prevented the working class from resisting effectively the fascist assault on democracy. Historians have corroborated much of his critique: socialist trust in the Marxist grand narrative was a major reason why the Austrian socialists did not take up arms early enough to defend parliamentary democracy. Popper proposed a united front of socialists and liberals to combat the prospective resurgence of fascism in postwar Central Europe. Within two years of the publication of *The Open Society*, he discovered that he had actually written the platform for the postwar Cold War consensus in the West, a consensus that legislated for the welfare state and mobilized to contain communism.

Popper was the foremost philosopher to carry the progressive Viennese legacy into the postwar era. In his critiques of the Vienna Circle and Red Vienna, he confronted the philosophical and political problems of the Viennese late Enlightenment (*Spätaufklärung*), and the interwar crises of scientific reason and Central European democracy. Refashioning the fin de siècle progressive legacy, he drew novel visions of liberal science and politics, imagining utopian scientific and political communities engaged in the pursuit of truth and reform. He made critical debate the acid test of political and scientific rationality. Establishing a free public sphere as the *conditio sine qua non* of the open society, he innovated on a familiar liberal motif, shared by thinkers as different as Immanuel Kant, Germaine de Staël, François Guizot, John Stuart Mill, and Jürgen Habermas.

My intellectual biography restored Popper to fin de siècle Vienna and interwar Central Europe, the vanished world of the assimilated Jewish intelligentsia. By historicizing Popper, I hoped to recover the legacy of progressive and socialist Vienna for the post–Cold War world. It proved a difficult task. Having begun my work in the mid-1980s, I faced major difficulties in reconstructing Popper's intellectual biography. I first considered him a member of the postwar liberal cohort, but quickly discovered that two foundational texts, *The Open Society* (1945) and *The Poverty of Historicism* (1944–45), made no sense to me as a historian when read in the Cold War context. The issues and figures that the books addressed belonged in a radically different milieu, and the popular Cold War reception overran significant textual resistance. To understand the origins of Popper's political philosophy, one had to go back to interwar Vienna. This was easier undertaken than done. A young generation of Austrian scholars, usually on the left and on the margins of Austrian universities, was only then beginning to turn out the wonderful works that, in the past two decades, have recovered interwar Viennese culture. Popper's archives were not available yet, and his 1974 *Autobiography*, anachronistic on some issues, scarce in historical detail on others, proved less helpful than I had hoped. I interviewed Popper once, for four hours, and he was kind and hospitable, but he did not remember very well the interwar years and seemed reluctant to talk about them. I read his 1928 dissertation and his articles, published from 1925 to 1931, in two organs of the Austrian school reform movement. They made it clear that the *Autobiography* could not have accurately described his intellectual progress, but, touching on unfamiliar problems and contexts, they left me as much in the dark as before. There was no choice but to follow leads in Popper's works and *Autobiography*, delve into interwar Viennese culture and politics, and reconstruct the institutional and discursive contexts relevant to his work from scratch.

I soon recognized that I was writing as much a book on interwar Viennese culture as on Popper. Biography opened a window to intellectual milieus that repeatedly surprised me with their richness, sophistication, and creativity. Interwar Vienna, capital of a tiny republic, could not compete with Hapsburg Vienna for social and political splendor, but it was its intellectual match. As in fin de siècle years, intellectual innovation took place mostly in circles on the academy's margins, not at the university itself. The economic base was, however, thinner, as the socialist municipality only partially substituted for lost private funds. With limited resources, in a tense political atmosphere suffused with anti-Semitism, these circles created much of what the postwar Atlantic world would recognize as its own art history, economics, jurisprudence, mathematics, music, philosophy, political theory, sociology—and the list is by no means complete. Popper worked on the margins of these circles. Always a stranger in his homeland, he saw more presciently than most Austrian intellectuals what was in store for Central Europe and left early in 1937 for New Zealand, joining the intellectual migration that enriched the Anglo-American academy and turned Vienna into an intellectual province (Bailyn and Fleming 1969; Stadler 1987–88; Stadler and Weibl [1993] 1995).

The various pieces of the biographical puzzle gradually fell into place. The picture that formed was surprising. It sharply diverged from both the autobiographical self-portrait and the familiar Cold War polemicist and disgruntled positivist. Whence, I wondered, the divergence? The disjunction between interwar Central Europe and the postwar Atlantic world surely formed part of the explanation, but it seemed insufficient. The reception of other émigrés' works did not seem to raise as many problems. Further coincidences, I discovered, complicated the Popper reception. The sequence of publication of his English works upset the chronology of their formation and accentuated the chasm between the contexts of formation and reception. Until 1957, "The Poverty of Historicism," his treatise on planning and social science methodology, was buried in wartime issues of the journal *Economica*. Until 1959, when *Logik der Forschung* appeared in English, his philosophy of science was known primarily through hearsay. His three-volume *Postscript to the Logic of Scientific Discovery*, written in the 1950s, remained unpublished until the early 1980s. Until his archives opened in November 1990, his early manuscripts were inaccessible even to researchers. Much of the evidence for his intellectual trajectory was unavailable for a long time and, when it became available, seemed to speak to concerns widely different from those he developed later in life.

Popper regarded his 1920s work on psychology and pedagogy as immature, made few references to it until his *Autobiography* ([1974] 1976), and was reluctant to have others read it (Popper 1925, 1927, 1928, 1931). In 1929 he moved from cognitive psychology to the logic of science. His geometry thesis, signaling the move, became accessible only when his archives opened. His first book, *Die beiden Grundprobleme der Erkenntnistheorie*, written between 1930 and 1932, remained unpublished until 1979. It should finally come out in English in the next few years. Reading *Grundprobleme*, one sees Popper's novel vision of science emerging from his critique of Kant and his epigones, Jakob Fries and Leonard Nelson. *Logik der Forschung* radically compressed this critique and, then, to make things worse, took a quarter of a century to appear in English. During the time that elapsed, Popper's philosophy came to form part of logical positivist discourse. The positivists knew little and cared nothing about Fries and Nelson, and Popper himself forgot about them. (He mentioned them in Popper 1962, 2–10, and [1974] 1976, 74–75, but it is not clear that he was fully cognizant of the role they played in his intellectual development. Compare Popper 1979, sec. 11, and 1935, secs. 25, 29.) His published work seemed to obscure, rather than illuminate, the intellectual transformations that he had undergone as a young intellectual.

Popper helped the confusion by first omitting historical signposts from his work, then reconstructing his intellectual autobiography in a manner that concealed most turns and dead ends. Already when writing "The Poverty of Historicism" in New Zealand, he reshaped Central European discourses so as to make them relevant also to Western Europe, rarely mentioning Viennese intellectuals and seldom referring to Central European *Methodenstreiten*. He had conceived of "Poverty" before he left Europe, wrote a draft in New Zealand before the war, and rewrote most of the work for publication in 1944–45, after he had already completed *The Open Society*. Most people read "Poverty" only when it was published as a book, dedicated to the victims of Nazism and communism. As it came out the year after the Soviet repression of the Hungarian and Polish uprisings, and Popper had the reputation of Marx's foremost critic, it became another contribution to the Cold War. Many of Popper's arguments made little sense in this context—but no other existed. A book formed at three intervals, in between cultures, with moving targets of criticism and few historical markers represented a nightmare for the historian seeking to identify its "original" aims.

My intellectual biography of the young Popper was the first scholarly account of his life. In the boundless literature on his ideas, there was not, at the time, one historical monograph. (Now there are a few more—albeit not biographies—and a few more in the making.) Popper's breadth of interests would not have deterred historians, who often find they have to write about fields in which they have less than adequate competence. It is rather that, with Popper, one did not quite know where to begin. Virtually everyone who knew him recognized that one had to go back to interwar Vienna, but outside Austria, the interwar Viennese milieu was not well known. Not surprisingly, Austrian scholars and those Popper students reading German were responsible for the few attempts at historical study of Popper. They produced work that was most helpful for my own.

Young Austrian scholars took advantage of the Second Republic's effort, beginning in the 1980s, to reclaim the interwar cultural heritage and proclaim Popper, an eternal exile who escaped the country for his life, an "Austrian philosopher." With remarkable energy, they have painstakingly reconstructed the life of fin de siècle and interwar Central European networks, thereby throwing light on the context for Popper's work. They recognized Austrian socialism as the crucial context for Popper's political philosophy. Using evidence yielded by the opening of the archives of the Vienna Circle and its affiliates, they emphasized Popper's ambivalent relationship to the circle (Dvorák 1986; Stadler 1997, chap. 10; Wallner 1985). The Popper archives opened in 1990. While the archives contain only limited personal material, they still convey a vivid picture of the person, with all his eccentricities, anxieties, and moods. Archives of Viennese intellectuals kept opening in the 1990s, and they included illuminating correspondence not only with Popper but also about Popper, rendering a fuller picture of his place in Viennese and Central European debates. I capitalized on these fortunes to produce the first monograph on his work by an intellectual historian.

Popper aptly called his *Autobiography* an *intellectual* autobiography. It is the history of his ideas, his progress from one philosophical problem to another. Precious little of the person and the context found its way into the work. For all of its clarity, simplicity, and elegance of style, the *Autobiography* frustrates the historian's effort to identify the debates and people Popper engaged in his work. It can sometimes be misleading. Popper imposed the telos of his mature philosophy on his intellectual development. His progress from youth politics to psychology in the 1920s to the logic of science in the 1930s to the open society during World War II seems linear. The "rationality of scientific revolution" dominates the narrative. Only the theories that withstood the test of time and criticism—above all, Popper's own criticism—made it into the *Autobiography.* He projects a coherence of philosophy and life that seems almost unworldly. It conceals the plurality of directions in which his thought developed, the intellectual impasses, the options foreclosed, and the decisive turning points. His autobiography dehistoricized his life and philosophy.

Readers may trace in my complaints against Popper's *Autobiography* the post-structuralists' grievances against biography as such. Biography, they believe, presumes the author's stable identity. As the subject, or the self, is discursively constructed, even alterably performed, deconstruction of identity seems a more promising strategy than biographical assemblage, or unification. Biography also seems to imply a linear narrative of life rather than plurality of directions, coherence of experience rather than multiplicity of contexts, teleology rather than contingency. In my view, however, historiography, biography included, moves between stability and change, unity and dispersal, determinance and indeterminance, either radical position rendering it impossible or superfluous. The post-structuralists have appropriately put the fear of premature coherence in the heart of every methodologically aware historian, but they have also rendered problematic, even illegitimate, modes of scholarship, intellectual biography among them, that I am eager to recommend. I may be able, however, to arbitrate some of the post-structuralist complaints by explaining why my own biography is not open to the objections I raise against Popper's *Autobiography.*

We commonly tell stories of our lives with particular purposes in mind. Already in the early 1930s, Popper used his biography to argue a priority claim on nonfoundationism against the Vienna Circle. He had, however, little time or inclination in interwar years to take a longer view of his life. A young philosopher in search of recognition, convinced that he had a revolutionary message, he was absorbed in his projects. Only after the war, when he became a leading Atlantic philosopher, did he begin systematic reflection on the history of his ideas. By the early 1950s, he had solved many of his philosophy's thorny problems. He was fighting the prevalent "positivist" reading of his work, determined to show that, intellectually, he owed nothing to the circle. He was also beginning to have private priority disputes with his students, the philosophers Joseph Agassi and Paul Feyerabend. His recollection of his early intellectual life was no longer vivid. The past was traumatic, not only on account of fascism and exile but also because his progress was a story of repeated emotional crises, radical shifts between elation and depression. He endeavored to present his own development as a model for the growth of knowledge. As a result, he produced an anachronistic account of his intellectual development, reading his later philosophy back into the interwar years. Initially, I suspected either amnesia or a willful distortion, but neither seems necessary to explain his account (and neither is likely). Autobiographical anachronism is common, and Popper's memory failure may not even be as surprising as I still occasionally find it.

Popper's main story line for the interwar years runs as follows. After a brief youthful engagement with communism in 1919, he rejected it. Responding to the corroboration of Albert Einstein's relativity theory in a major experiment the same year, he demarcated science from pseudoscience through testability: Marxism and psychoanalysis were not testable, hence pseudosciences, Newtonian and Einsteinian physics were testable, hence scientific (although they may be "wrong"). His explorations in psychology in the early 1920s led him to reject the prevailing empiricist and behaviorist doctrines and overthrow induction, the view that science progressed by generalizing particular observations into laws. Rather, science progressed through conjectures and refutations, offering theories (laws) that went beyond experience, then subjecting them to criticism and tests. In 1929 he realized that his solution to the two problems, demarcation and induction, actually converged into a revolutionary view of science. Scientists and philosophers used induction to demarcate science because they had no better criterion of demarcation. He did—testability. He also recognized that arguments he sought to make in psychology were best made in the logic of science. His philosophy of science emerged from his psychology. In the later 1930s he began applying his philosophy of science to politics. From 1919 on, he had been elaborating fundamentally the same philosophy (Popper [1957] 1963, 33–59).

This is not the way things happened. Popper formulated neither the induction nor the demarcation problem before 1930, and his intellectual breakthrough in the logic of science required that he renounce his previous research program for psychology as "psychologism." He also gained more than he was willing to acknowledge from his encounter with the Vienna Circle. All the same, the 1950s set the road map for Popper's *Autobiography.* He settled on a narrative that clarified, to him and others, the significance of his experiences as a young Viennese intellectual. That the narrative did little justice to his intellectual confusion during the 1920s did not matter.

Not all was lost—yet. When Paul Arthur Schilpp, editor of the noted Library of Living Philosophers, told Popper in May 1963 that a volume was planned on his philosophy, Popper enthusiastically responded, "I have actually started writing my autobiography" (Schilpp to Popper, 7 May 1963; Popper to Schilpp, 12 June 1963, Popper Papers [334, 2]). (Each Schilpp volume began with an autobiography, followed by contributors' critical essays, to which the philosopher replied.) But Popper had difficulties writing. In the following years, he produced a number of outlines (which the archives contain) and wrote occasional fragments that he hoped would eventually find their place in the *Autobiography* (Popper Papers [134, 4, 6]). His outlines included references to Viennese intellectuals, political events, and books about which we hear nothing later in the drafts, and even less in the published version. Had he carried out his original plans, we would have had a different autobiography from the one we possess. But he did not. He sensed that the *Autobiography* was his great chance to shape his image and legacy, and he had great expectations for public recognition, yet he was reticent about speaking of himself and revealing the life behind his philosophy. "I find it greatly embarrassing to write my intellectual autobiography. So far, arguments were the very life of what I have written." "It is more interesting to go on trying to solve problems than to look back on one's failures. . . . there is too much material, and too little confidence that it will interest anybody." "It takes such an effort to write one's intellectual autobiography" (fragments of the *Autobiography*, Popper Papers [134, 4]).

Returning to the Vienna of his youth, a vanished world, Popper also recollected personal losses. "Ghosts walk Vienna's streets," he told the philosopher John Watkins, his student (personal communication with Watkins, 8 March 1996). He now had to converse with the ghosts. He was always frightfully busy, and so, faced with an unpleasant and seemingly unmanageable task, he procrastinated writing his autobiography. In January 1967 he began seeing his way through the dark, happily reporting to Watkins that he had discovered that a youthful dispute that he had had with his father was actually over essentialism: he had rejected the notion that words, or definitions, had an essential meaning and were something other than conventional instruments, malleable with context (note to John Watkins, 19 January 1967, Popper Papers [134, 4]). Popper began writing about essentialism, rather apologetically, as a digression, emphasizing that the terms he was using had not been available to him as a youth. Both the apologies and the caveats gradually disappeared. With growing confidence, he discovered a series of early philosophical problems (one, the problem of infinity, at the age of eight) and extended the digressions, as well as discussions of his current theories, until they constituted the bulk of the text. He reported to Schilpp that he was writing a "philosophical autobiography." If the extant drafts are evidence enough, he spent more time on the early sections, to World War I, than on the rest. He did most of the writing during the spring and summer of 1969 (Schilpp to Popper, 31 December 1968, 6 June, 4 August, and 20 September 1969; Popper to Schilpp, 12 June, 23 July 1969, Popper Papers [134, 4, 6, 8–9, 11, 12]). Pressed for time, writing with lightning speed, he latched on to a narrative of philosophical problems. "Earlier generations," he said gleefully, "used texts as their point of departure. . . . Nowadays, one starts with a problem-situation, a problématique" (fragment, Popper Papers [134, 4]).

Once Popper turned his life into a story of intellectual progress, he was in familiar territory. He had ready-made models for the history of philosophy and science. He may have not thought over their methodology yet, but he had long favored problem-oriented historical narratives. Already in his 1929 geometry thesis, he modeled his history of geometry on Max Born's *Einstein's Relativity Theory* (1924). Born began with classical mechanics, moved to Newtonian mechanics, optics, and electrodynamics, and ended with Einstein's relativity. He outlined each theory and explained how discoveries in related fields problematized it, thereby creating conditions for the next scientific advance. Popper adopted this explanatory model, used it whenever he discussed scientific progress, and now applied it to his autobiography. He thought the result a major success. Where he had no biographical narrative before, he now had one that wonderfully shaped his life into an unending quest for growing knowledge, endowing it with supreme philosophical significance. Greatly heartened, he elaborated further, in several essays, on the relationship between intellectual history and the "logic of the situation," his method for constructing social science models. In the 1980s he urged Bill Bartley to adopt a problem-focused narrative for his planned Popper biography.

Born's explanatory model was powerful. It represented the traditional history of ideas, explaining their development by focusing on tensions in theories and thinkers' efforts to resolve them. It is a crucial intellectual history method, and I have argued elsewhere that, despite being neglected in recent years, it must be recovered (Hacohen 1996). But it has limits. The problem-situations that thinkers face are not solely theoretical but reflect a variety of contexts—political, social, cultural. The art of intellectual history is coordinating internal (theoretical) and external (contextual) explanation. Leonard Krieger, the previous generation's brilliant intellectual historian, let the theoretical explanation run its course until a theory reached a crisis, its logic breaking down, then permitted other contexts to explain its transformation. This, however, constrains historical explanation, or "historicization." The theoretical problem-situation is rarely closed to history. Theories, texts, and authors respond to "history" at all times, historical changes translating into theoretical tensions and new problems.

It is tempting to describe my intellectual biography of Popper as historicizing the antihistoricist thinker par excellence, but that would be misleading. Popper's critique of historicism has little to do with historicization. He distinguished between "historicism" (*Historizismus*) and "historism" (*Historismus*). The first entailed "inexorable historical laws," the latter the "historical dependence of our opinion" (Popper 1957, 3; 1945, 2:196). The first was a dangerous theory, the major subject of his political critique; the latter was nebulous. He thought that *Historismus* contained an "undeniable but rather trivial kernel of truth" and usually reflected conservative resistance to scientific endeavors to rationalize the world (Popper 1945, 2:242–43). His stance against *Historismus* depended, however, on the historicization in question. He opposed the social determination of ideas but not the use of social context to explain the formation of ideas. He himself produced wonderful historical scholarship on Plato, classical Athens, and the philosophy of science. His conclusions were controversial, but his manner of relating text, biography, and contexts was exemplary, showing sensitivity to literary clues, psychology, institutions, and intellectual development.

Indeed, by reworking models that Viennese economists had built to explain market situations and agents' decisions, Popper (1957, secs. 31–32; 1972; [1963] 1994; [1969] 1994) developed a mode of historicization—"situational logic." He suggested that we account for theoretical advances (or theoretical "moves" thinkers made) by constructing the problem-situation, then explaining the solution as a response to the problem. This disposes of determinism. Agents "move." Problem-situations explain the relative constraints under which they operate. The extent of freedom varies from one situation to another. Admittedly, Popper was inclined toward an "internalist" philosophical explanation: the intellectual problem-situation was the one he considered most valuable. He was suspicious of sociological and psychological explanations and usually used them to delegitimize opponents or to explain philosophical failures, that is, to clarify the reasons why thinkers did not see things right or failed to make the correct moves. There was something undignified about historicization. One psychologized and sociologized failure, not success. This was an unnecessarily defensive move. Popper argued, at the same time, that ideas' origins have nothing whatsoever to do with their validity. Intersubjective criticism was the criterion for acceptance, not freedom from prejudice (of whatever sort), which, in any case, was impossible. If his criterion for "objectivity" is accepted, historicization poses no threat to universal validity. Popper could have cast his contextual net wider.

I attempted to do so in my intellectual biography of Popper. This is not to suggest that Popper would have approved of my biography. To explain his intellectual formation, I called on contexts that he considered irrelevant—above all, the assimilated Jewish intelligentsia—and on others that he had overlooked, or diminished, in his autobiography (Hacohen 1999, 2006). I rehistoricized the life that he dehistoricized. My aim was not only to provide a fuller and more accurate account and recover a rich culture that vanished but also to rescue the young Popper for the present, to see how the adventurous socialist who revolutionized the philosophy of science and formed a compelling vision of the open society could help us rethink our problems today. I believe that my biography and mode of historicization are not open to the charge of premature closure of authorial identity and formative experience. I constructed Popper's identity from historical materials, not presupposed it, and assembled multiple contexts to create the problems that he addressed without reducing his philosophy to a unitary context. I emphasized the changing contexts, was attentive to the constant remaking of the self, and did not privilege continuity or unity. I endeavored to show that an intellectual biography was possible after post-structuralism. Individuals may be socially (and discursively) shaped, and their biographies, as a student wrote me, "nothing other than the local study of the intersecting discourses that make up the individual subject," but they provide superb sites for analysis of discursive interaction. Rumors of the death of the author and the eclipse of experience are greatly exaggerated.

I proved right in ways I did not expect. My Popper biography received a warm reception and few, if any, challenges from the methodological innovators of recent decades. Most recognized my biography as part of the linguistic turn and, I gather, as compatible with their own historical writing. Surprisingly, recent years have witnessed the resurgence of biographies that are oblivious to the literary character of biographical narrative. Even when their authors are aware of the literary shaping of a life, they seem predisposed to relinquish the patient construction of contexts that would permit arbitration of conflicting claims. I offer Popper's *Autobiography* as a cautionary tale and my biography of Popper as evidence that the endeavor to arbitrate historically claims about the shape of a life is not hopeless.

The History of Discourse and the Limits of Biography

Biography's return should not obscure its limits. However well done, it has a narrow reach: it cannot answer most queries about the formation and influence of discourse. Its virtues are real: by constructing the problem-situations that individuals, or a small group of thinkers, faced, historians have had the greatest success in explaining the range of options available to them and the political and intellectual moves they make (Skinner [1969] 1989). Robert Leonard's (1995, 1998) essays on the Central European context for the emergence of game theory are one example of the use of this method in the history of economic ideas. Biography can determine with some precision the influence of a particular discourse on the shaping of a thinker. But biography can rarely do the opposite: effectively assess the role of an individual, a group, or a theory in the shaping of a tradition. Discourse usually lacks any single site for its formation—the sites are many and variegated. The analysis of formation requires more expansive generalization, involving greater risks of premature closure and false unity. Charting the trajectory of a discourse against a background of social change and major events, historians often treat it as a unity. They bracket as irrelevant both "anomalies" and biographical information relating to the agents articulating the discourse. Broad discursive change has proved too complex, or elusive, for explanation in detail. These are, respectively, the limits of biography and of the history of discourse.

To be sure, historians of discourse have constructed social and cultural contexts to explain discursive shifts, but moving between agents and discourse to explain paradigmatic change, locating moments when individual utterances seem to create a discursive shift, remains problematic. The models explaining a paradigmatic shift are complex, involving more variables than biography. Only a combination of good method and good fortune (and much patience) allows for precise determination of moments of change. The alternative, pursued by most historians, is to reduce the model's complexity by diminishing the role of individuals and precipitously closing the discourse, that is, treating it as a unified entity. Turning collective constructs, such as discourse, state, and society, into individual agents, they restore a manageable logic of the situation. This reflects less a carelessness or laziness and more a recognition of what is possible. By drawing broadly the parameters of discourse against major social transformations and political events, historians are able to aptly theorize discursive changes as, say, responses to social crises. The theory's broad brush may adequately respond to a general question, but it could also reflect reduced content: anomalies are explained away with ad hoc theories (special conditions), and the historian quickly discovers that the anomalies are more interesting (content rich) than the theory. These are the hazards of the history of discourse.

They need, however, to be confronted because the formation and influence of discourses (or traditions) remain major historical concerns, and influence is even trickier to track and measure than formation. Historians wish to know the role discourses had in shaping beliefs, even practices, of large social strata, institutions, and, at the end of the day, the course of events. The difficulties methodological individualists encounter when they move from biographies to discourse, from individuals to institutions, are universally shared (by historians and economists alike). Institutions and traditions represent, in part, the unintended consequences of the interaction of individuals. At the same time, they constrain individual action. Social collectives thus have a modus operandi of their own, and methodological individualists concede as much by speaking of the "quasi-existence" of institutions (even if they insist that they be explained, in the last analysis, through individuals' interaction) (Popper [1962] 1976, 103; Agassi 1960, 1975; Jarvie and Matzner 1998, esp. 353–54, 365–80). How does one transform interacting individuals into an institution, or a tradition, which, in turn, modifies the individuals' behavior? Could interactive models mediate between individuals and institutions and move between micro and macro analysis? Perhaps, but, as I pointed out above, they are exceedingly complex. The problems know no easy or obvious solutions.

I have encountered them in my recent work. From Popper's biography I have moved to the history of the Central European Jewish intelligentsia, an artifact of modernity—of Enlightenment, Jewish emancipation, and the nation-state. The acceptance of Jews as virtually equal citizens in the modern nation-state triggered paradigmatic changes in Jewish and Christian discourses and created new dilemmas, crucial to contemporary debates on multiculturalism. I have sought to trace these changes in Jewish and Christian discourses through the transmutation of the typology of Jacob and Esau, the two biblical brothers vying for their father's legacy.

Jews and Christians have been retelling the biblical story of the rivalry of Jacob and Esau for more than two millennia. Each claimed Jacob's legacy and decried the other as Esau. For Jews, Esau has become a symbol for all non-Jews, seeking to undermine Jacob, Israel, the Chosen People. An eternal Jew confronted an eternal Christian. But emancipation debates in Central Europe, from the 1780s to the 1860s (when Germany and the Hapsburg monarchy granted political rights to Jews), encouraged Christians and Jews to rewrite the old story or, alternatively, repress it. The rise of ethnonationalism, and especially of racial anti-Semitism, in the 1880s in Central Europe (and the Zionist response) reinforced traditional stereotypes. Jacob's and Esau's unremitting hostility seemed reconfirmed by social reality. This did not mean, however, an end to experimentation with the typology. Both the struggle against fascism and, later, the Jewish-Arab conflict in the Middle East occasioned creative responses among the Jewish and German intelligentsia that revolutionized the typology.

Such a history of discourse presents different problems from biography. For one, the reach of the discourse is historically far wider, and the historian cannot possibly devote the same attention, given to the subject of a biography, to each moment in the history. The situational logic obtaining in a biography may remain valid for each moment in the formation of the discourse, but biographical or prosopographical details are not always significant enough for the discourse's formation to interest the historian. Historians usually opt to set up the logic of the situation with fewer parameters shared by a greater number of agents, that is, they denude individuals of their peculiarities for the sake of a coherent discourse. It would be wishful thinking to assume that nothing gets lost: individual originality may get lost, and generalization proceeds on less firm grounds. A decline in scholarly precision as a result of the historian's reduced capacity for detailed work is common. I myself opted for focusing on representative biographies and setting them against the background of the discourse, in the formation of which they participate. This hybrid of the two genres, biography and history of discourse, provides no miracle solution: the biographies cannot be as meticulous as I hoped my Popper biography would be, and I do not altogether escape the risks of the shortcuts of the history of discourse. But, if the history of a discourse is to be written, that is the price to be paid.

The question of the diffusion of discourse appears both more crucial and less tractable in the history of discourse than in biography. Philosophers may disagree about Popper's influence, and the reach of his philosophy among the educated public is tricky to trace, but there are established procedures and resources for adducing evidence to support claims of influence: academic and journalistic citations, translations and sales, and so forth. The question of Popper's influence also seems less important than that of his contribution. Having traced the formation of his philosophy, I could assume I had accomplished my major task. With Jacob and Esau, the question of the discourse's permeation among larger strata is of paramount importance, and reliable sources are few and far between. Tracking the discourse becomes a matter of luck and, possibly, speculation.

Even trickier is the question of the discursive shaping of social behavior: In what ways did popular conceptions of the other, held by Jews and Christians, shape attitudes and actions? Did they expand or foreclose possibilities for Jewish integration, or did they merely register (as symptoms) the state of Jewish-Christian relations, or perhaps neither? It is only the rare and fortunate coincidence of discursive and practical change in local cases that provides a chance for arbitrating the question. Setting the local cases against a discursive and practical background known in lesser detail, the historian may then endeavor to establish a trend. More often, the historian can show the conjunction of discourse and practice but has to leave the causal question open. The temptation to call on theory to settle the question is great but ought to be resisted: one need not hold to a radically antideterminist view of history to recognize that particular relationships are contingent, or at least escape historiographical control. No theory can help circumvent the lack of evidence or the unmanageable complexity of the model required to answer questions of influence. Insights from psychology and sociology are welcome in understanding the logic of the situation, but they provide no shortcut.

The obvious generalizations—such as that Jewish narratives of reconciliation promoted and responded to emancipation, whereas reification of traditional stereotypes promoted exclusivity and accompanied the rise of anti-Semitism and Zionism—do not take us far and are refuted repeatedly: historical contingency allows for agents defying discursive trends and imagining an alternative to reality. Both for its genius and for what it tells us about the anxieties and aspirations of people at the time, the alternative that bucks the trend is of great interest to intellectual historians. If this were not enough, the ironies and paradoxes of history become especially apparent as the unintended consequences of discourse and social action come into play: the triumph of emancipation discourse triggers racial anti-Semitism, the Jew as a modernizer turns from a figure of emancipation discourse (Roscher 1878; Penslar 2001, 144–58) into an anti-Semitic one (Sombart [1911] 1951). Having failed to provide tools for the history of discourse, the biographer still celebrates a victory.

The logic of the situation obtaining for individual biography and the history of discourse is the same, but the questions they pose, the answers they provide, and the agents they involve diverge. Biography is an essential and viable genre in the history of economic ideas and can best answer questions concerning the formation of economic theory. Properly executed, it has overcome post-structuralist doubts and adequately responded to post-structuralist queries. It remains an essential methodological component, a stage, in the history of economic discourse, too, but it cannot answer the broader and perhaps more weighty historical questions broached by the latter, relating to the triumph of economic paradigms and their historical influence. To answer such questions, we often give up on the detail and precision of biography. At this stage of my career, the questions I pursue in the history of the Central European Jewish intelligentsia require that I do so. I have not given up on biography, but it has become part of a larger project, which biography alone cannot address.

References

Agassi, Joseph. 1960. Methodological Individualism. *British Journal of Sociology* 11:244–70.

———. 1975. Institutional Individualism. *British Journal of Sociology* 26:144–55.

Bailyn, Bernard, and Donald Fleming, eds. 1969. *The Intellectual Migration*. Cambridge, Mass.: Harvard University Press.

Born, Max. 1924. *Einstein's Relativity Theory*. Translated by Henry L. Brose. London: Methuen.

Bretenbach, Breyten. 1991. The Long March from Hearth to Heart. *Social Research* 58:69–83.

Dvorák, Johann. 1986. Karl Popper und die Wissenschaft von der Geschichte in der Epoche des Faschismus. In *Versuche und Widerlegungen: Offene Probleme im Werk Karl Poppers*, edited by K. Müller, F. Stadler, and F. Wallner. Vienna: Geyer.

Hacohen, Malachi. 1996. Leonard Krieger: Historicization and Political Engagement in Intellectual History. *History and Theory* 35:80–130.

———. 1999. Dilemmas of Cosmopolitanism: Karl Popper, Jewish Identity, and "Central European Culture." *Journal of Modern History* 71:105–49.

———. 2000. *Karl Popper, 1902–1945—the Formative Years: Politics and Philosophy in Interwar Vienna*. New York: Cambridge University Press.

———. 2006. From Empire to Cosmopolitanism: The Central European Jewish Intelligentsia, 1867–1968. *Simon Dubnow Institute Yearbook* 5:117–34.

Hamowy, Ronald. 2002. A Note on Hayek and Anti-Semitism. *HOPE* 34:255–60.

Jarvie, Ian, and Egon Matzner, eds. 1998. Situational Analysis. Special issue, *Philosophy of the Social Sciences* 28.3.

Leonard, Robert. 1995. From Parlor Games to Social Science: Von Neumann, Morgenstern, and the Creation of Game Theory, 1928–1944. *Journal of Economic Literature* 33:730–61.

———. 1998. Ethics and the Excluded Middle: Karl Menger and Social Science in Interwar Vienna. *Isis* 89:1–26.

Penslar, Derek J. 2001. *Shylock's Children: Economics and Jewish Identity in Modern Europe*. Berkeley: University of California Press.

Popper, Karl. Papers. Hoover Institute Archives, Stanford University, Stanford, Calif.
——. 1925. Über die Stellung des Lehrers zu Schule und Schüler. Gesellschaftliche oder individualistische Erziehung? *Schulreform* 4:204–8.
——. 1927. "Gewohnheit" und "Gesetzerlebnis" in der Erziehung. *Hausarbeit* submitted to the Pädagogisches Institut, Vienna. In Popper Papers (12, 11).
——. 1928. Zur Methodenfrage der Denkpsychologie. PhD diss., University of Vienna.
——. 1929. Axiome, Definitionen und Postulate der Geometrie. 2 vols. Popper Papers (4, 6).
——. 1931. Die Gedächtnispflege unter dem Gesichtpunkt der Selbsttätigkeit. *Die Quelle* 81:607–19.
——. 1935. *Logik der Forschung: Zur Erkenntnistheorie der modernen Naturwissenschaft.* Vienna: Julius Springer.
——. 1944–45. The Poverty of Historicism, I, II, III. *Economica* 11–12:86–103, 119–37, 69–89.
——. 1945. *The Open Society and Its Enemies.* 2 vols. London: Routledge.
——. 1957. *The Poverty of Historicism.* London: Routledge.
——. 1959. *The Logic of Scientific Discovery.* Translated by Karl Popper. London: Hutchinson.
——. 1962. Julius Kraft: 1898–1960. *Ratio* 4:2–10.
——. [1957] 1963. Science: Conjectures and Refutations. In *Conjectures and Refutations*, by Karl Popper. New York: Basic Books.
——. 1972. On the Theory of the Objective Mind. In *Objective Knowledge*, by Karl Popper. Oxford: Clarendon.
——. [1962] 1976. The Logic of the Social Sciences. In *The Positivist Dispute in German Sociology*, by Theodor Adorno et al. Translated by Glyn Adey and David Frisby. London: Heinemann.
——. [1974] 1976. *Unended Quest: An Intellectual Autobiography.* La Salle, Ill.: Open Court.
——. 1979. *Die beiden Grundprobleme der Erkenntnistheorie.* Edited by Troels Eggers Hansen. Tübingen: Mohr.
——. 1981–82. *Postscript to the Logic of Scientific Discovery.* 3 vols. London: Hutchinson.
——. [1963] 1994. Models, Instruments, and Truth. In *The Myth of the Framework*, by Karl Popper. London: Routledge.
——. [1969] 1994. A Pluralist Approach to the Philosophy of History. In *The Myth of the Framework*, by Karl Popper. London: Routledge.
Reder, Melvin W. 2000. The Anti-Semitism of Some Eminent Economists. *HOPE* 32:833–56.
——. 2002. Reply to Hamowy's Note on Hayek and Anti-Semitism. *HOPE* 34:261–72.
Roscher, Wilhelm. 1878. Die Juden in Mittelalter. *Ansichten der Volkswirtschaft* 2:321–54.

Skinner, Quentin. [1969] 1989. Meaning and Understanding in the History of Ideas. In *Meaning and Context: Quentin Skinner and His Critics*, edited by James Tully. Princeton, N.J.: Princeton University Press.
Sombart, Werner. [1911] 1951. *The Jews and Modern Capitalism*. Translated by M. Epstein. Glencoe, Ill.: Free Press.
Stadler, Friedrich, ed. 1987–88. *Vertriebene Vernunft*. 2 vols. Vienna: Jugend und Volk.
——. 1997. *Studien zum Wiener Kreis*. Frankfurt: Suhrkamp.
Stadler, Friedrich, and Peter Weibl, eds. [1993] 1995. *Vertreibung der Vernunft: The Cultural Exodus from Austria*. 2nd ed. New York: Springer.
Wallner, Friedrich. 1985. Popper und die österreichische Philosophie. In *Karl Popper—Philosophie und Wissenschaft: Beiträge zum Popper-Kolloquium*, edited by Friedrich Wallner. Vienna: Braumüller.
Weintraub, Roy. 2003. Prejudice and the History of Economics: A Minisymposium. *HOPE* 35:685–86.

Is Autobiography Anti-academic and Uneconomical? Some Thoughts on Academic Autobiography

Jeremy D. Popkin

One could make a good case that the writing of an autobiography is an activity deeply antithetical to the values of serious academic research, whether in economics or any other discipline. Autobiographies, or so the romantic image of the genre would have it, are flamboyant assertions of individuality and subjectivity, whereas serious scholarly endeavor, at least in the social and natural sciences, is often collective, and its results are supposed to be unaffected by researchers' private interests and emotions. In popular culture, particularly in the United States, the past few decades have established themselves as an "age of memoir," but academia likes to pride itself on marching to its own drumbeat. The fact that so many respectable academics have published narratives of their own lives in the past few decades might be taken as a worrisome sign that the barbarians and their cult of celebrity have broken through the walls of the ivory tower. Economists might try to comfort themselves with the belief that their discipline's bastions still stand. At the conference where the essays in this volume were originally delivered, several participants quoted the emphatic declaration of George Stigler: "Science is a social enterprise, and those parts of a man's life which do not affect the relationship between that man and his fellow scientists are strictly anti-scientific. When we are told that we must understand a man's life to understand what he really meant, we are being invited to abandon science" (cited in Moggridge 2003). Meant as

History of Political Economy 39 (annual suppl.) DOI 10.1215/00182702-2006-037

a critique of the energy devoted to biography, Stigler's comment clearly implied that autobiographies, too, should be of no real interest to serious students of economics.

The insidiousness of autobiography is demonstrated, of course, by the fact that in 1985 Stigler himself capitulated to it, becoming the author of a volume titled *Memoirs of an Unregulated Economist.* Reading Stigler's memoir, however, suggests that when academics engage in autobiography, it is not only the values of academia that are at risk. Stigler's memoir hardly fits the popular notion of an autobiography. Readers are given a bare outline of the author's family origins and his childhood, and hardly any other information about any of the nonprofessional aspects of his life. What Stigler tells us about his professional career is mixed with impersonal reflections about the discipline of economics. And yet Stigler's book does meet the basic requirements for inclusion in the category of life narrative. It tells a story of its author's life, if not perhaps a very full one; but no autobiography is all-inclusive. There is little reason to fear that its author has veered off into the domain of fiction, and most of the statements Stigler makes about his life could be verified if there was any reason to doubt his claims.

Are academic memoir authors like Stigler subverting the literary genre of autobiography by showing that it can contain, and indeed must extend its aegis to, texts that lack almost all the attractions we normally associate with it, particularly a sense of emotional connection between reader and author? Does *Memoirs of an Unregulated Economist* reveal that autobiography is not necessarily the individualistic enterprise it pretends to be? Stigler's book appears to have been written not so much because its author felt a strong desire to share the details of his life with readers but because the institutions of academia pressured him to do so. *Memoirs of an Unregulated Economist*, along with the memoirs of Herbert Simon, forms part of a series of scientists' memoirs subsidized by the Alfred P. Sloan Foundation, with the announced purpose of promoting public appreciation of the scientific enterprise. In agreeing to contribute to this series, Stigler may well have thought he was acting more for the discipline of economics than for himself. The inclusion of economists in a series whose first contributor was the distinguished nuclear physicist Freeman Dyson was a sign of the discipline's acceptance as a true science. Stigler's memoir thus suggests that autobiographies can be as much social products as individual enterprises and that they can perform many functions besides that of expressing their author's personality. The case of *Memoirs of an Unregulated*

Economist shows that a study of academic autobiography may force us to revise our notions of what autobiography is and why it exists.

Academic autobiography, as the discussions at the 2006 *HOPE* conference made clear, is only one of many forms of academic life writing. It coexists with a number of other genres, including biography, whether full-length, short, or group; diaries; collections of correspondence; and forms such as the eighteenth-century *éloge*, or academic eulogy, which are hard to classify in modern terms. Autobiography and memoir are distinguished from any of the various forms of biography by the fact that the subjects of such personal stories are also their authors. Consequently, the claims for attention that autobiographers make are more controversial than those put forward for their subjects by biographers: first-person authors are inherently suspect of excessive egoism. Their projects differ from diary and letter writing because those forms of life writing are normally undertaken without a broader audience in mind. Diaries and letters also do not involve the same conscious effort of retrospection that autobiography and memoir require, so that these more private and personal forms of self-narration do not raise the same issues of memory and narrative structure. Finally, autobiography and memoir are literary genres whose practitioners are not confined to academia: academics who engage in such projects know that they are inviting comparison both with literary classics and with popular best sellers. For all of these reasons, academic autobiography poses some special issues that are distinct from those raised by other forms of academic life writing.

I first began to take a scholarly interest in the issues posed by academic autobiography about fifteen years ago, when I read *Essais d'ego-histoire*, a volume of autobiographical essays by well-known French historians. It was not the first time I had encountered a personal memoir by a university scholar: my father, a well-known philosophy professor, had published such an essay in a Festschrift volume dedicated to him several years earlier (Popkin 1988). The family discussions about some of the facets of his private life he had chosen to discuss had shown me the difficult issues such projects could raise. The preface to the French volume I stumbled on a few years later immediately alerted me to the fact that some people thought that academic autobiography had broad philosophical significance. The volume's instigator, the publisher and historian Pierre Nora, asserted that his colleagues' personal essays reflected a major shift of epistemological paradigms. All had been trained in an era when the prevailing definition of "scientific" knowledge was knowledge of the world or of human affairs that was objective and independent of the lives of those investigating it. Historians, Nora (1987, 5, 6) wrote—but his words could have applied to most other academic disciplines as well—were taught "to lose themselves in their work, to disguise their personality behind their knowledge, to take refuge behind their notecards." But, he claimed, the intellectual developments of recent decades had taught a different lesson. By the 1980s it was impossible not to recognize that an admission of "the direct, intimate and very personal connection" that scholars had with their subjects was more convincing than "vain protestations of objectivity."

The questions raised by the Nora volume showed me that academic autobiographies continue a debate that goes back at least to the eighteenth-century Italian philosopher Giambattista Vico, himself the author of an autobiography (Verene 1991). Challenging the paradigm of objective scientific understanding that had emerged from the Scientific Revolution, Vico asserted that human beings can fully understand only what they themselves have experienced and created. He thus argued that the social sciences were a better model of knowledge than the natural sciences. At the end of the nineteenth century, the German philosopher Wilhelm Dilthey, in his critique of positivism, put autobiography squarely at the center of epistemological debates. He argued that an observer who could combine both internal and external perspectives on human experience could achieve deeper insights than anyone else and that autobiography is "the highest and most instructive form in which the understanding of life confronts us" (Dilthey [1914] 1962, 85). Nora's presentation of his colleagues' essays used them to put this debate in modern terms and to suggest that the true test of a scholar's insight is whether he or she can understand his or her own life.

I soon discovered that these *essais d'ego-histoire* were part of a broader phenomenon. Such publications are rapidly becoming more common, both among historians and among academics in other fields, in the United States and elsewhere. This proliferation has been linked to contemporary developments in philosophy and literary theory, but my researches led me to a number of older academic autobiographies as well and made me suspicious of the notion that the genre is simply a current fad. I also discovered that academic autobiographies come in many forms, from tightly disciplined collections of parallel lives such as the Nora volume to utterly unconstrained memoirs venturing into the most unexpected crannies of their authors' lives. I also learned that, if I were going to pursue the subject seriously, I would have to go beyond the comfortable confines of my own discipline and learn something about theory in fields such as literature, philosophy, sociology, and anthropology. I discovered that there are scholars, like the deconstructionist literary critic and, as we now know, Nazi collaborator Paul de Man (1979), who denounced the enterprise of autobiography as the most fraudulent form of literature, an attempt to pass off words on paper for what they could never be: an accurate representation of truth about the world. And there were those, such as James Olney (1972), Philippe Lejeune (1989), and Paul John Eakin (1985, 1992), who admitted the literary characteristics of the genre and its similarities to the writing of fiction, but who remained convinced that the autobiographer's *will to truth* was an essential characteristic of the genre, setting it off from other forms of literature.

As I pursued my inquiry and wrote a book on historians and autobiography, I came to realize that academic autobiographies not only are of interdisciplinary interest but are a way to get at issues of general human significance (Popkin 2005). Not every person writes a memoir, and even fewer publish one, but the impulse to look back and try to find coherence in one's personal life story is widespread. Paul John Eakin, one of the most acute critics of the genre, sees the autobiographical impulse as a "third and culminating phase in a history of self-consciousness" comparable with the acquisition of language in early childhood and the development of a distinct notion of the self as an individual in childhood and adolescence. "The impulse to write autobiography is but a special, heightened form of that reflexive consciousness which is the distinctive feature of our human nature," Eakin concludes, and he has recently expanded his argument to suggest that telling stories about our lives is in some sense a biological imperative, part of "the human organism's homeostatic regulatory activity" (Eakin 1985, 9; 2005, 3). The academic autobiography, written by an author trained to reflect explicitly on the problems involved in telling a true story, holds the promise of providing special insights into the meaning of this widely shared human impulse.

Although theorists of autobiography may be theoretically willing to include academics' autobiographies in their purview, they have rarely chosen such texts for extended analysis. In general, these scholars have preferred to write about autobiographical texts composed by figures from the "real world." Most often we encounter criticism of the autobiographies of canonical literary figures such as Goethe, or of contemporary texts like Maxine Hong Kingston's *The Woman Warrior*, that have managed to straddle the line between serious and popular literature. In recent years there has been an upsurge in attention to autobiographical texts by "outsiders," people normally denied literary representation of any kind and presumably innocent of any suspicion of the pitfalls inherent in the genre—peasants, African Americans, immigrants (Lejeune 1989; Olney 1980). A few autobiographical texts by contemporary academics have begun to attract critical attention and to show up on class reading lists, but a suspicion of collective narcissism or even incest hangs over such initiatives. For academic scholars to spend their working time producing diligently footnoted discussions of each other's life stories would simply confirm accusations that professors are too absorbed in their own petty concerns.

Some critics have suggested that academic autobiographies are not worth discussing because they are inherently inferior specimens of the genre of autobiography itself. Forced to read one example, a grumpy reviewer asked, "Who cares about the confessional outpourings of an academic historian whose horizon is bounded by grants-in-aid, tenure anxieties, and scholarly articles?" (Eby 1969, 650). Philippe Lejeune, known for his catholic sympathies with many variants of life writing, found his patience exhausted by the productions of his fellow intellectuals. "I am often confused by the naiveté and the simplicity of mind that takes hold of people who are nevertheless intellectually gifted, and who have acquired a reputation in literary, psychological, or philosophical areas, when they take it into their head to talk about their own life. Not only does critical sense vanish, and they no longer estimate very well what might interest other people . . . but it especially surprises me that they themselves might be interested in what they are relating," he wrote in one of his early essays (Lejeune 1989, 235). In a review of my book on historians' autobiographies, Allan Megill argues that a genre of autobiography defined by its authors' professional identities is bound to be superficial, since such commitments, made voluntarily and relatively late in life, cannot have the genuinely existential impact on consciousness that ethnic or religious identity does. "It is a matter of existential priority: in other words, we need to ponder the question, How deep an aspect of the self is 'being a historian'?" he asks (Megill 2006, 482). Uninteresting academic life narratives run the risk of undermining the prestige of academia in general, by exposing scholars as ordinary people, no more fit to tackle the great issues of human life than anyone else, and incapable of expressing themselves as effectively as the popular authors whose memoirs make the best-seller lists.

One can certainly find on any library's shelves academic autobiographies that fit this stereotype—as well as equally unreadable autobiographies by politicians, movie stars, and other "real world" authors. Whether the proportion of boring and superficial memoirs by academics is higher than that among authors from other categories remains an open question. As for the question of how deep a stratum of self is engaged in professional identity, one can reply that if substantial numbers of people are prepared to devote most of their adult lives to academic careers and then write personal memoirs in which they identify themselves as sociologists, philosophers, or scholars of literature, this would seem to indicate a considerable investment of psychic resources. The notion that those aspects of identity that we are born into or acquire in childhood are necessarily more profound and meaningful than those we may choose to develop in later life reflects assumptions about human life that deserve to be debated, rather than taken for granted, and academic autobiographies, precisely because they address these issues so clearly, may be important resources for such a discussion.

If we admit that the academic life is a respectable subject for autobiography, does it make any difference what discipline an academic autobiographer belongs to? There are numerous examples of scholars who have worked in more than one discipline, and one could argue that it would be more reasonable to see all these texts as examples of the more general phenomenon of intellectual autobiography. It is true that in my research on autobiographies written by historians, I did not find unmistakable markers that always distinguish such texts from those by academics in other disciplines, or from autobiographies by nonacademics. Historians may be somewhat more inclined than others to draw attention to the documentation underlying their autobiographies and to pay attention to the historical context of their lives, but at best these are statistical tendencies rather than hard-and-fast rules, and there are certainly narratives that are less concerned with these issues than some autobiographies by outsiders to the profession. Nevertheless, it is clear that most, although not all, historian-autobiographers see the fact that they are historians as a major facet of their identities, and my unsystematic reading in autobiographies by members of other disciplines suggests that this is true of them as well.

Historians who write about the development of their vocation are usually quite insistent about the special qualities of that discipline that attracted them. They frequently discuss the moment when they chose history as a defining moment in their lives, one that both reflected certain aspects of their personalities and had the effect of shaping them in certain ways. I suspect that further research would show this to be true for authors from other disciplines as well; it is certainly the case for the authors of some of the most widely discussed texts of recent years, such as Alice Kaplan's *French Lessons* (1993) and Pierre Bourdieu's *Esquisse pour une auto-analyse* (2004). It is, of course, true that modern academic autobiography grows out of an older tradition of intellectual autobiography, and that the authors of such classic texts as Augustine's *Confessions* and John Stuart Mill's *Autobiography* can hardly be assigned to specific disciplines. The division of knowledge along disciplinary lines is a fact of modern intellectual life, however, despite valiant efforts to promote interdisciplinarity. Academic autobiographies are in fact, in my opinion, one of the best ways to understand how this situation has come into being and what it means to the men and women in academia.

The recognition of the important connections between history, historians, and autobiography proposed in my book is not meant to claim a privileged place in the canon of academic personal narrative for the members of my own scholarly field. Rather, this case study of the relations between history and autobiography should provoke new interest in the connections between autobiography and other disciplines. History and autobiography do share a joint project, the reconstitution of the past, but that is only one aspect of life writing. Literary studies, through its concern with narrative technique and structure and with the uses of language; psychology, sociology, and anthropology, because of their interest in the formation of the self; philosophy, through its preoccupation with consciousness; and even the natural sciences—"bios" is part of both "autobiography" and "biology"—all intersect with autobiographical writing in ways that are potentially as interesting as those of history. Economics, too, deals with issues that every individual confronts on a personal level—we all have to earn a living and balance our checkbooks—as well as raising philosophical questions about human rationality and the extent of our ability to shape our own destinies. Autobiography is inherently a polymorphous enterprise. It intersects not only with history but with the concerns of many other academic disciplines and has the potential to reveal important aspects of each of them.

As it happens, economists' autobiographies had not figured into my research until I received the invitation to address the 2006 *HOPE* conference. Roy Weintraub's invitation immediately left me pondering two questions: Do economists write autobiographies? And are these *academic* autobiographies—that is, do their authors see themselves and their lives as having been shaped in significant ways by their commitment to an academic discipline? Inasmuch as I was a visiting scholar at Princeton when I was writing my conference paper, I made a crude effort to answer the first question by typing "economists" and "autobiography" into the Princeton University online library catalog and came up with ten results, of which eight are published volumes in English that fit conventional definitions of autobiography. This is in the same range as many other academic disciplines. Princeton's library catalog yielded eight comparable entries for sociologists, seventeen for psychologists, eight for physicists, and three for anthropologists. On the other hand, however, a search for "historians" and "autobiography" produced fifty results, including not only individual autobiographies and collective volumes of autobiographical essays but also theoretical literature about the relations between history and autobiography.

A visit to the library shelves in the region of call number HB119, the Library of Congress's classification for books in the subject category "Economists—United States—Biography," produced some additional data. In the first place, a quick survey identified nine items that clearly should have been in the online list but were not, including the memoirs of John Kenneth Galbraith, Herbert Simon, and George Stigler. (Two of these did surface in a search for "Memoirs—Economists"; none of the texts cataloged as autobiographies came up in this search.) So much for reliance on computerized catalog searches! Like the titles returned by the computer search, all these volumes were by men. (Deirdre McCloskey's *Crossing* [1999] is shelved under a different classification.) Interestingly, from the point of view of a scholar of historians' autobiographies, these autobiographical publications were heavily outnumbered by biographies, whereas an investigation of the shelves devoted to "Historians—United States—Biography" showed that biographies are at best more or less equal in number to first-person accounts. Contemporary economists such as Milton Friedman, Galbraith, and Paul Samuelson are the subjects of multiple studies, a status enjoyed among American historians by only one figure, Henry Adams, a historian who died almost a century ago and who is now chiefly celebrated because of his autobiography rather than his contributions to historical scholarship.

Both Princeton's online catalog and this brute-force search of the shelves turned out to be misleading, however, because neither revealed the existence of a number of volumes of short autobiographical essays, itemized in recent articles by Donald Moggridge (2003) and Roy Weintraub

(2005). Whereas full-length autobiographies by self-identified economists are relatively few, the number of economists who have contributed to these collections is impressive: Moggridge counted no less than 198 of them. Collective enterprises of this sort are common in a number of academic disciplines—they finesse the problem of vanity by allowing authors to present themselves as writing at someone else's invitation, and they look less like idiosyncratic personal projects competing in the general literary marketplace and more like contributions to scholarship (Popkin 2001)—but the ratio of such short efforts to longer single-author life stories seems to be unusually high in economics. The reason for the multiplication of these publications in the past two decades is clear: they are widely seen as valuable materials for reconstructing the history of economic ideas. They thus reflect less the subjective concerns of their authors than the collective concerns of the community of historians of economics. Nevertheless, even if the stated reasons for the proliferation of first-person publications by economists are more "scientific" than the justifications cited by members of other disciplines, the timing of the phenomenon—first evident at the end of the 1970s, with a marked rise in publications during the 1990s—suggests that economists have been as much affected as members of other disciplines by the current "age of memoir."

Comparing the content and characteristic themes of economists' autobiographies with those of other academics is a project that will have to wait until someone awards me a generous research grant. I did, however, undertake a small controlled experiment in this area. To be specific, I indulged my historian's penchant for going back into the past by reading a two-volume collection of economists' autobiographical essays published in Germany in the 1920s as part of a large multidisciplinary series of academic autobiographies: Felix Meiner's (1924, 1929) *Die Volkswirtschaftslehre der Gegenwart in Selbstdarstellungen* (*Present-Day Economics in Self-Portraits*). Most of the contributors to this collection—Eduard Bernstein, Karl Diehl, Irving Fisher, Heinrich Herkner, Karl Kautsky, Robert Liefmann, Achille Loria, Franz Oppenheimer, Heinrich Pesch, Edwin R. Seligman, Camillo Supino, Leopold von Wiese, and Julius Wolf—are forgotten today, but the collection has the advantage of being comparable to the two volumes of historians' autobiographical essays in the same series, edited by Sigfrid Steinberg (1925), with which I was already familiar. As a crude measure of these economists' prominence, six were either the subject of entries in the *Encyclopedia of the Social Sciences* (1930) or else contributed to it (Seligman was the general editor of the work). Several others would presumably have been included in that work except that they were still living. Seven of the twelve were in the *International Encyclopedia of the Social Sciences* (1968), but only one was in the *International Encyclopedia of the Social and Behavioral Sciences* (2001). Curiously, only a single one of these encyclopedia entries over the years refers readers to its subject's autobiographical contribution to the Meiner collection.

One may object that the contributors to both projects, all born in the second half of the nineteenth century, lived in a world so different from the present day that a comparison between the two collections is irrelevant to the contemporary situation, but my reading of them suggests that this is not entirely the case. They do indeed reflect an earlier era—I was struck, for example, by the number of economists who had had to spend long periods in sanatoriums at a relatively young age, a reminder of the changes that medical progress has made in everybody's lives—but they also seem to reflect some enduring differences between members of these two disciplines.

The most significant differences I noted in these two collections of autobiographical essays are the economists' far greater connection with that famous "real world" about which historians speculate but which they rarely encounter and, perhaps somewhat contradictorily, the great importance of theory in economists' lives, as opposed to those of historians. Since the samples involved are small—sixteen historians, twelve economists—sociological analysis of the authors' backgrounds yields only suggestive results. Nevertheless, it is clear that more economists than historians had fathers who were in commerce or manufacturing and that more historians came from households connected to the learned professions. Whereas historians typically remember their childhood selves as enthusiastic readers, these economists more typically recall watching what went on in their fathers' factories or businesses. Most economists undertook university studies, but whereas this was the only route to a professional career open to historians, there are some exceptions among the economists. The contrast is most emphatic when it comes to recounting their adult careers, however. The sixteen historians in the collection were all lifelong academics. Research and teaching structured their lives, which were lived in a relatively closed academic environment. They might engage in other activities, notably politics, but even an event as massive as the revolution following Germany's defeat in 1918 did not wrench them out of their universities.

The economists, however, are a completely different kettle of fish. Here we find authors active in banking, politics, journalism, business, nonprofit foundations, and government as well as academia, and many who moved back and forth from one activity to another. Whereas the historians were all sure that "historian" was in fact the term that best described them, these authors were much less wedded to the notion of themselves as economists. The two German Social Democratic Party leaders included in the collection—Eduard Bernstein and Karl Kautsky—were probably rarely labeled that way, and the more academically inclined Leopold von Wiese preferred to think of himself as a sociologist. All the contributors were so thoroughly involved with the world around them that the editor, Felix Meiner (1929, 2:v), explained the five-year delay between the publication of the first and second volumes in the collection by the fact that his contributors had to give priority to "tasks of such immediate importance" as dealing with hyperinflation, the problem of reparations, and the rebuilding of European infrastructure after the Great War before they could fulfill their commitments to him. Although the issues of the day have changed, the tendency of leading economists to move back and forth between academia, business, and government, while historians remain cloistered in their universities, seems remarkably similar. As J. A. Kregel (1989, 2:xvii) wrote in introducing a collection of short autobiographical essays by contemporary economists, "If one were to search for a unifying aspect of the careers of the authors of these essays an obvious candidate would be their extensive experience in government or business." One consequence of this is that many economists' autobiographies are less purely "academic" than those of their colleagues in many other disciplines, and indeed some of the recent American ones fall into the category of celebrity memoirs. The irrationally exuberant $8.5 million that a publisher is rumored to have offered Alan Greenspan for his memoirs is not likely to be matched soon by any historian.

The other contrast between historians and economists revealed by the Meiner volumes is somewhat at odds with this engagement with social and political reality. This is the economists' concern with theory. Whereas the historians in Meiner's collection normally integrated their narratives into a single chronological account of their major research projects and their shifts from job to job, the economists usually produced bifurcated essays, starting with a short *Lebenslauf* and then shifting to a discussion of the theoretical issues that had most concerned them. Whereas the historians in the Meiner collection were often content to indicate the subject area of their research, without making much effort to explain their specific contributions to the field, the economists were concerned to define their unique contributions to the discipline and to argue against opponents. This has continued to be true in contemporary economists' memoirs, which tend to be justified in terms of their potential "useful role in the history of economics" (Moggridge 2003, 599). Methodological issues loomed much larger in the contributions to Meiner's volumes on economists than in those devoted to historians, who tended to write as if there was only one universally accepted way of doing history. The result is that the economists' essays depicted a discipline riven by disagreements, whereas their historian colleagues projected the image of a group of scholars each pursuing his own interests and rarely crossing a competitor's path.

Even this brief glimpse at economists' memoirs thus suggests that economics has a distinctive relationship to the genre of autobiography, reflecting the fact that the discipline of economics interacts with the worlds of business and politics in a way that most other academic disciplines do not, and that theoretical disputes play a large role. At the same time, however, autobiographers who identify themselves as economists do not cut themselves off completely from the sphere of abstract ideas and the pursuit of knowledge. Writing for the Meiner collection in 1929, Edwin R. Seligman (1929, 2:144) concluded that his concerns had always been balanced between "the making of historical and comparative connections, theoretical analysis, and practical application." More than sixty years later, Herbert Simon also framed his autobiography as the story of a person divided between the "scientist and teacher" and "the science politician" engaged in world affairs. In between those two domains, however, Simon (1991, xviii) also promised to make room for the story of "the private person: of growing up, of love and family and friends and travel and leisure": in other words, for the realm of what we would normally call the autobiographical.

Since George Stigler's aversion to biographical research has helped frame this discussion, I would like to conclude by returning to it briefly. Like the contributions to the Meiner collection, Stigler's memoirs appeared as part of a collective project, the Alfred P. Sloan Foundation series, even though they were published, like the other titles in the series, as a separate volume. The series itself began in 1979, just as the age of memoir was dawning in both popular and academic culture. The unsigned preface to the first of the series's volumes justified the project as a way to overcome the difficulties of explaining modern science to a wider audience. The details of scientific research might have become too esoteric to be communicated to a lay audience, but autobiographical narratives could convey the message that science "is quintessentially human" (Dyson 1979, vii). Stigler's volume, one of two economists' lives included in the series so far (the other is by Simon), is at the more impersonal and antiliterary end of a spectrum whose other extreme is represented by the biologist François Jacob's *Statue Within* ([1987] 1988), an intensely emotional narrative with echoes of such texts as Jean-Paul Sartre's *Les mots*. Nevertheless, as I have argued earlier, Stigler's book still remains within the boundaries of the autobiographical genre.

Stigler's life story, as he constructs it, is a classic example of how traditional academic memoirs serve to affirm both American values and those of the university world. Like most American academics, Stigler was in no sense born to be a professor. His parents were immigrants from Central Europe in the period before World War I, and Stigler grew up in the American hinterland, in the state of Washington. Stigler describes himself as a casual student through college who assumed that he would go on to a business career; only the difficulty of finding a job in 1931 led him to enter graduate school. "Only gradually did economics begin to appear to me to be an intellectual discipline worthy of full-time study in its own right rather than as a plausible introduction to a life in business," he writes. He pays tribute to several inspiring teachers who helped stimulate him and to student colleagues whom he claims taught him more than his professors. He also realizes that historical circumstances helped make him part of a cohort of young economists who would profoundly reshape the discipline. Given the conditions of the Great Depression, "large numbers of the best graduate students entered economics because it was the discipline grappling with what seemed to be society's most urgent problem." In academia he found a milieu whose unique virtues and limitations apparently suited him. "Universities cater to more highly specialized human beings than most other callings in life. If X is a great mathematician, he will be more or less silently endured even though he dresses like a hobo, has the table manners of a chimpanzee, and also achieves new depths of incomprehensibility in teaching. . . . That is less true in most other callings because in the normal progression of his or her career, an entrepreneur or a cleric or a bureaucrat or a lawyer must display a larger variety of talents to succeed" (Stigler 1985, 15, 51, 31).

Although young people who later became historians often interpreted the lessons of the Depression and of America's national mobilization during

World War II as arguments in favor of activist government, Stigler and his fellow economists of the "Chicago school" drew the opposite conclusion. He spent a short period in Washington, D.C., during the New Deal, working on projects that were never implemented, and saw what he considered sound economic principles ignored during the war, when he worked for the Office of Price Administration. "My role in our work was so modest," he writes, "that my claim must be that I did not aid the enemy." Although economists are more likely than most academics to be recruited into public service, Stigler's own experience and his observation of his colleagues' behavior convinced him that, as a general rule, they are better off sticking to research and teaching. "A political career must eventually lead an economist at very best to a strained and artificial position. He must be silent on, or at most cautiously critical of, policies he deplores, such as the minimum wage law or acts of protectionism. He must support policies which are not so much wrong as ridiculous" (62, 135).

Although Stigler makes some critical judgments about both American society and academia based on his personal experiences, he warns readers that his life was basically undramatic and that they will find little tension in his narrative: "I have been treated generously by my fellow economists. There is no anger and little complaint in this account of a half century in American economics." He is well aware that academia is no utopia, but when he mentions its shortcomings, he normally does so through general observations rather than descriptions of personal experience. He writes that "I should not exaggerate the virtuous single-mindedness of the university's search for scholarly ability," acknowledges "the strenuous competition that pervades the scholarly disciplines," and debunks romantic notions about genius and creativity: "Important individual advances and bold gambles are so tiny a fraction of scientific work, however, as to be comparable to the crust on the tip of the iceberg. Scientific research is a market process, differing vastly in form but little in substance, from the comparable activities of grocers or manufacturers of computers" (xi, 31, 33, 84). He does provide one specific account of how academic feuds can poison scholars' lives, but the example he describes involved two of his teachers rather than himself personally.

George Stigler was undoubtedly a talented and influential economist, but it is fair to say that he wrote a rather uninteresting autobiography. Probably the exercise was antipathetic for him: as I have shown, he did not think much of the biographical approach to the history of economics. The most interesting question about *Memoirs of an Unregulated Economist* is why it was published at all. One can see that an academic memoir like Stigler's serves to reaffirm the virtues of the academic discipline and institutions that made the author's career possible. Despite the negative characterization of American politics implicit in Stigler's remark about the fate of economists who commit themselves to it, his story also affirms the basic values of American society, in which a child of immigrants like himself could make a prestigious career on the basis of his abilities. There is a certain irony in the fact that Stigler's career in economics was devoted, as the title of his memoir indicates, to defending the virtues of the unregulated free market, whereas one may doubt that market demand alone would have justified the publication of his bland and not particularly interesting life story. The appearance of *Memoirs of an Unregulated Economist*, made possible by support from a private foundation, shows how academia generates mechanisms to produce published life stories that reinforce its values. Whether these mechanisms also work to ensure that anyone reads such conventional memoirs is another question.

Even a quick and superficial examination of the relations between economics and life narrative thus suggests that the differences between academic disciplines do affect the kinds of life stories that their practitioners produce. In particular, economists' ambition to present their discipline as a "hard" science, based on objective laws that are independent of human subjectivity, leads them to view the inherently subjective project of autobiography differently from those disciplines in which interpretation is accepted as an essential aspect of knowledge. Even a relatively "unautobiographical" text like Stigler's reminds us, however, that the lessons we can hope to learn from economists' life stories are not entirely divorced from those that emerge from other forms of academic autobiography. Despite Stigler's reticence, one can sense that there was a real personal passion behind his commitment to his discipline and that circumstances had some effect on his career. Some economists may resist these conclusions, but others are willing to embrace them. As Michael Szenberg (1992, ix), one of the most active proponents of autobiography among economists, has put it, that discipline's indifference to autobiography has meant both that it has "neglect[ed] the role of personal and social factors in the formation of economic discourse" and that it has refused to acknowledge the energy that comes from reading about other people's lives. In the second of his three volumes of autobiographical essays, Szenberg was able to enlist no less a luminary than Paul Samuelson (1998) to preach the virtues of the reading and writing of economists' life stories. At least some economists thus seem willing to join colleagues from other academic disciplines in embracing the possibility that autobiographical writing, rather than undermine the status of their discipline, as Stigler warned, might instead enrich it and help demonstrate its place as one of the many forms of human creativity.

Economists have, then, contributed to academia's embrace of autobiography as a legitimate genre. In doing so, however, they have demonstrated, as I suggested at the beginning of this essay, that the inclusion of academic autobiography in the purview of autobiography studies requires us to modify some prevalent assumptions about the characteristics of first-person writing. Most economists' memoirs, at least to date, have been relatively impersonal and devoid of the emotional and subjective elements that are often regarded as inherent to such writing. The vast majority of them have appeared in collective volumes, which are, as I have argued, one of academic autobiography's distinctive contributions to autobiographical literature. Finally, it is clear that the main force driving the multiplication of economists' autobiographical essays comes from the working of mechanisms built into the structure of economics as a discipline, not from the psyches of its individual members. Economists' autobiographies, like academic autobiographies in general, thus raise questions about the relationship between individualism and a literary genre that is often assumed to be the quintessential expression of personal identity.

References

Bourdieu, Pierre. 2004. *Esquisse pour une auto-analyse.* Paris: Raisons d'agir.

De Man, Paul. 1979. Autobiography as De-Facement. *Modern Language Notes* 94:919–30.

Dilthey, William. [1914] 1962. *Pattern and Meaning in History: Thoughts on History and Society*, edited by H. P. Rickman. New York: Harper and Row.

Dyson, Freeman. 1979. *Disturbing the Universe.* New York: Harper and Row.

Eakin, Paul John. 1985. *Fictions in Autobiography: Studies in the Art of Self-Invention.* Princeton, N.J.: Princeton University Press.

———. 1992. *Touching the World: Reference in Autobiography.* Princeton, N.J.: Princeton University Press.

———. 2005. Living Autobiographically. *Biography* 28:1–15.

Eby, Cecil. 1969. Review of *Historian's Quest*, by Gabriel Jackson. *Book Review Digest*, 19 October, 650.

Jacob, François. [1987] 1988. *The Statue Within: An Autobiography.* Translated by Franklin Philip. New York: Basic Books.

Kaplan, Alice. 1993. *French Lessons.* Chicago: University of Chicago Press.

Kregel, J. A., ed. 1989. *Recollections of Eminent Economists.* 2 vols. New York: New York University Press.

Lejeune, Philippe. 1989. *On Autobiography.* Translated by Katherine Leary. Minneapolis: University of Minnesota Press.

McCloskey, Deirdre. 1999. *Crossing: A Memoir.* Chicago: University of Chicago Press.

Megill, Allan. 2006. Review of *History, Historians, and Autobiography*, by Jeremy D. Popkin. *Biography* 29:481–85.

Meiner, Felix, ed. 1924, 1929. *Die Volkswirtschaftslehre der Gegenwart in Selbstdarstellungen.* Leipzig: Felix Meiner Verlag.

Moggridge, D. E. 2003. Biography and the History of Economics. In *A Companion to the History of Economic Thought*, edited by Warren J. Samuels, Jeff E. Biddle, and John B. Davis. Malden, Mass.: Blackwell.

Nora, Pierre. 1987. *Essais d'ego-histoire.* Paris: Gallimard.

Olney, James. 1972. *Metaphors of Self: The Meaning of Autobiography.* Princeton, N.J.: Princeton University Press.

———. 1980. Autobiography and the Cultural Moment. In *Autobiography: Essays Theoretical and Critical*, edited by James Olney. Princeton, N.J.: Princeton University Press.

Popkin, Jeremy D. 2001. Coordinated Lives: Between Autobiography and Scholarship. *Biography* 24:781–805.

———. 2005. *History, Historians, and Autobiography.* Chicago: University of Chicago Press.

Popkin, Richard H. 1988. Intellectual Autobiography: Warts and All. In *The Sceptical Mode in Modern Philosophy: Essays in Honor of Richard H. Popkin*, edited by Richard A. Watson and James E. Force. Dordrecht: Nijhoff.

Samuelson, Paul A. 1998. Foreword to *Passion and Craft: Economists at Work*, edited by Michael Szenberg. Ann Arbor: University of Michigan Press.

Seligman, Edwin R. 1929. Edwin R. Seligman. In *Die Volkswirtschaftslehre der Gegenwart in Selbstdarstellungen.* Vol. 2. Leipzig: Felix Meiner Verlag.

Simon, Herbert A. 1991. *Models of My Life.* New York: Basic Books.

Steinberg, Sigfrid, ed. 1925. *Die Geschichtswissenschaft der Gegenwart in Selbstdarstellungen.* 2 vols. Leipzig: Felix Meiner Verlag.

Stigler, George J. 1985. *Memoirs of an Unregulated Economist.* New York: Basic Books.

Szenberg, Michael, ed. 1992. *Eminent Economists: Their Life Philosophies.* Cambridge: Cambridge University Press.

Verene, Donald. 1991. *The New Art of Autobiography: An Essay on the Life of Giambattista Vico Written by Himself.* Oxford: Clarendon.

Weintraub, E. Roy. 2005. Autobiographical Memory and the Historiography of Economics. *Journal of the History of Economic Thought* 27:1–11.

Part 2
Varieties of Economists' Biographies

Lives in Synopsis: The Production and Use of Short Biographies by Historians of Economics

Roger E. Backhouse

> Brevity is the soul of wit.
> —Shakespeare, *Hamlet*

> To preserve . . . a becoming brevity—a brevity which excludes everything that is redundant and nothing that is significant—that, surely, is the first duty of the biographer.
> —Lytton Strachey, *Eminent Victorians* (1918)

The starting point for many writers on the genre of biography is Lytton Strachey's *Eminent Victorians*, which took as its target the "standard" biographies of the Victorian era:

> It is perhaps as difficult to write a good life as to live one. Those two fat volumes, with which it is our custom to commemorate the dead—who does not know them, with their ill-digested masses of material, their slipshod style, their tone of tedious panegyric, their lamentable lack of selection, of detachment or design? They are as familiar as the *cortège* of the undertaker, and wear the same air of slow, funereal barbarism. (Strachey 2003, 6)

I am grateful to Bradley Bateman, Philippe Fontaine, Bruce Caldwell, and the editors of this volume for helpful advice on earlier drafts of this essay, and to Steven Durlauf and Morgen Witzel for sharing with me their ideas on this topic.

History of Political Economy 39 (annual suppl.) DOI 10.1215/00182702-2006-038

Strachey's blanket denunciation of the Victorian era is no doubt grossly unjust. As the age that produced Thomas Carlyle's essays and Leslie Stephen's *Dictionary of National Biography*, it should perhaps be called the age of the biographical sketch. To suggest that Victorian biographies typically extended to "two fat volumes" was, of course, an exaggeration, but even such memorials provided the material from which Strachey could, through careful plagiarism and judicious selection, construct his own portraits of the age (Sutherland 2003; Gittings 1978, 34; Bell 1989, 54). It does, however, provide a useful starting point in considering a genre that has recently proliferated, namely, short biographies of economists.[1] Strachey was a close friend and inspiration for the economist whose work forms the starting point of this essay, John Maynard Keynes. Strachey's attitude toward biography also provides a useful peg on which to hang a discussion of what might be expected from short biographies, in economics or elsewhere.

Strachey saw his tasks as being to write brief lives of his subjects, selecting material from longer lives so as to expose: it was explicitly *not* to be complimentary. Implicitly, given the above quotation, he thought that short biographies should be stylish, detached, and well designed. Following Strachey, Brian Harrison (2003), former editor of the *Oxford Dictionary of National Biography* (*ODNB*), the recent successor to the original *Dictionary of National Biography* (*DNB*), has claimed that short biographies focus on the heart of a life story rather than bury it in a large volume, and that the requirement of brevity increases the motive for a biographer to provide the surprising insight. Shorter biographies, he argues, are not necessarily inferior to longer ones. Newspaper obituaries often aim to convey the character of a life, perhaps starting, in the manner of a journalist covering a cricket match, with an account of the most memorable episode, which is then built up into an account of the life as a whole. Of course, not all short biographies even aim at these goals. Some, such as *Who's Who in Economics* (Blaug and Vane 2003), are no more than chro-

1. The nearest to a definition of a short biography that I will be employing is one that does not occupy an entire volume, or even the major part of one, but appears as part of a collection. Thus I exclude the short biographies of John Maynard Keynes produced by Donald Moggridge (1976) and Robert Skidelsky (1996), on the grounds that these are complete volumes, albeit very slim ones. I also exclude Mehrling 1997 on the grounds that its three biographies are each too substantial and, besides, three biographies do not comprise enough of a collection. Keynes's essay on Marshall, on the other hand, is included, as are biographical entries in dictionaries or encyclopedias, however long. This may seem slightly arbitrary, but it isolates an important group of short works.

nologies of basic facts, which might be provided by the subjects themselves or compiled by an outsider.[2]

Going beyond the individual life, short biographies provide the opportunity for what Harrison describes as "proportion." Some lives are more interesting than others, a fact that can be reflected much more readily in the space allocated by the editor of a volume such as the *DNB* than by "full-length" biographies where the scope of a biography is dictated by a range of factors other than the importance of the subject, most notably the availability of source material, the time available to the biographer, and his or her commitment. According to this criterion, we should pick out those collections of lives, such as the *DNB*, *The Biographical Dictionary of British Economists* (*BDBE*) (Rutherford 2004), or the biographical entries in reference works such as general encyclopedias or *The New Palgrave: A Dictionary of Economics* (Eatwell, Milgate, and Newman 1987; Blume and Durlauf forthcoming) as offering something different from collections of lives where no such criterion is employed.[3] It may be going too far to say that short biographies enable us to see the "average" economist (prosopography or bibliometrics may be needed for that), but they do enable us to come closer to that goal. Knowledge belongs to communities, and, even if a small number of individuals are responsible for setting the agenda, it is rarely possible to understand ideas without ranging more widely beyond those economists who merit long biographies.

Keynes and Schumpeter

Keynes's writings on biography illustrate the Bloomsbury group's interest in the genre.[4] It is thus not surprising that his essays reflect many of the concerns and attitudes of his friend Strachey. Keynes explores his subjects' family backgrounds and psychology. Thus his essay on Thomas Malthus gives significant space to the friendship between Malthus's father,

2. Throughout, this essay excludes any consideration of *auto*biography, as raising a different set of issues. For a list of the many recent collections of short autobiographical essays, as they then existed, see Backhouse and Middleton 2000, ix–x.

3. I should declare an interest, as one of the supervising editors of the *BDBE* (and author of a dozen entries) and as an associate editor of the second edition of the *NPDE*, though without responsibility for any biographical entries.

4. Though I have made a few modifications in the light of discovering them, I wrote the first draft of this section unaware of the discussion of Keynes by Walker (1985) and of Schumpeter by Shionoya (1997, 279–92). Walker places much greater emphasis on Keynes's evaluations of his subjects' work.

Daniel, and David Hume and to the extent of Malthus's contact with Jean-Jacques Rousseau: given the position Malthus was to take in his *Essay on Population*, the Rousseau connection has a significance over and above its influence on the type of education that Daniel Malthus provided for his son, Robert. Though Keynes does not explore this side of Malthus's work as extensively as some recent historians would, he locates Malthus squarely in the politics of the period and in the radicalism of his father's associates and many of his friends. Names such as William Paley, Thomas Paine, Samuel Taylor Coleridge, and Percy Bysshe Shelley are prominent, which might surprise readers who think of Malthus as the bridge between Adam Smith and David Ricardo.

The same can be said of the other essays Keynes wrote on people whom he considered to be economists.[5] Much attention is paid to the "stock" from which they came, to family background, to individual psychology, and to religion. In learning about these, we learn much about struggles with authority. Malthus was not simply arguing against the radicals William Godwin and Paine but was questioning the radical environment, inspired by Rousseau, in which his father lived. Alfred Marshall and Mary Paley were both reacting against strict, even "despotic," evangelical parents. Yet Marshall did not fully escape:

> The nearest objects of his [Marshall's father's] masterful instincts were his family, and their easiest victim his wife; but their empire extended in theory over the whole of womankind. . . . Heredity is mighty, and Alfred Marshall did not altogether escape the influence of the parental mould. An implanted masterfulness towards womankind warred in him with the deep affection and admiration which he bore to his own wife, and with an environment which threw him in closest touch with the education and liberation of women. (Keynes 1972, 162)

It is tempting to speculate that Keynes might have seen the early death of William Stanley Jevons's parents as having spared him the need to rebel in the family sphere as well as in the economic! Of course, not everyone fell into this category, but there are enough cases to show the Strachean parallels. Herbert Foxwell was not, as far as we know, rebelling against parents, but, as Keynes describes, he was bitter about Marshall's prejudice against his approach to economics, which, so Foxwell believed, resulted in his failure to advance in the Cambridge academic hierarchy.

5. By placing them under that category in *Essays in Biography*.

Above all, there are parallels with Strachey's use of irony. This point can be made only by quotation. The previous account of Marshall's attitudes toward women could easily have been written by Strachey, as could any of the following passages, chosen more or less at random. Consider Keynes's (1972, 234) discussion of Mary Paley's father.

> But what a very odd, and sometimes terrible, thing are strict principles! Why can an age only be great if it believes, or at least is bred up in believing, what is preposterous? The Simeonite rector's beliefs were so strict that he could not even be intimate with any neighbouring clergyman.

Skepticism about ethical rules, religious doubts, and the absurdity of much of Victorian society come together in three short sentences, any one of which, by itself, is highly pointed. Jevons's use of statistics has nothing to do with ethics or religion, but Keynes's denunciation of it is expressed in equally dismissive language.

> The virus, however, had entered into his system. No one who has once deeply engaged himself in coincidence-fitting of this character will easily disembarrass himself of the enquiry. (124)

It is, no doubt, significant that, with the exception of Malthus, the figures Keynes discusses are personally known to him or known to those in whose circles he moved, Jevons having taught Foxwell and having communicated with Marshall. Even Malthus was another Cambridge economist and connected, through William Paley, with those whom Keynes knew.[6] This will have helped in acquiring the impressive range of primary sources, including much correspondence, on which his essays are based. Closeness to his subjects may, in some ways, have blunted his critical faculties, as in his acceptance of many of Marshall's claims about his own work. However, in providing a sympathetic account of Foxwell, Keynes was implicitly criticizing Marshall. Like Foxwell, Keynes would later rebel against Marshall's exaggerated respect for Ricardo. He writes of Foxwell's influence in having changed Marshall's mind on several issues. On Jevons, Keynes's admiration was tempered by methodological differences and by criticism inherited from Marshall. Similarly, though Keynes admired Malthus (and was to praise him even more highly in the *General Theory*), he did not share Malthus's conservatism—Bloomsbury was far from the

6. More generally, Walker (1985, 185) has argued that his essays were vitiated by being closely tied to British economics.

near-socialist radicalism against which Malthus was reacting, but both were questioning established authority.

These essays are all focused on economists' lives, with discussion of their works being almost always in the context of these lives. A partial exception is Keynes's essay on Henry Cunynghame, where a fairly conventional account of the life, ending with the remark "such men as Cunynghame are the honour and glory of the British Civil Service" (Keynes 1972, 300),[7] is followed by a list and analysis of his "contributions to economics," which bears no relation to that life. Perhaps this is natural for someone whose career was mostly spent outside academic economics and whose work was primarily mathematical. In the essay on Frank Ramsey, whose work on taxation and savings Keynes (1972, 335) described as "one of the most remarkable contributions to mathematical economics ever made,"[8] Keynes evinces no interest at all in the life: Ramsey is a philosopher and logician. Perhaps the origin of this essay in a book review is part of the explanation. Equally, it could be that the differences in their outlooks on life (in relation to homosexuality) made the task of considering his life too difficult, especially when Keynes wanted to praise Ramsey after his death. It could also be argued that what Keynes most admired about Ramsey was the power of his logical analysis, and this meant that consideration of Ramsey's life was not important.

Where Keynes focused on Cambridge and on those within his fairly immediate circle, his great rival, Joseph Schumpeter, extended his reach much more widely, both in *Ten Great Economists* (1997) and in the biographical sketches provided in his *History of Economic Analysis* (1954).[9] Comparison is valuable because Schumpeter represents a perspective on biography that is very different from that of Keynes. It is the more forceful because many of the circumstances surrounding his essays were close to those of Keynes: all the subjects in *Ten Great Economists* were, with the exception of Marx, personally known to him;[10] many were economists he admired; and a significant number of the essays were obituaries. However, there are striking differences. Where Keynes focuses on individual psy-

7. Perhaps this is intended ironically, but I see no reason to think that this is the case.

8. In posthumous editions of *Essays in Biography*, Ramsey is variously listed among "Economists" and "Friends."

9. Mark Perlman's introduction to Schumpeter 1997 has been particularly helpful for this part of the essay. As noted above, had I seen it in time, Shionoya 1997 would have been equally useful.

10. This ignores those discussed briefly in the appendix, whose inclusion was not due to Schumpeter himself.

chology and upbringing, Schumpeter spurns this. At one point, he even argues that life and scientific achievements are hard to relate to each other.

> The great difficulty of a biography like this [Keynes on Marshall] consists in making one connected whole of its two elements, disposition of a life and exposition of scientific achievements, which are so refractory to being welded together. (Schumpeter 1933, 654)

Instead of exploring the personal, Schumpeter saw biography as "the art of focussing an epoch and an environment in the story of an individual" (652). His real interests lay, as the opening chapters of the *History of Economic Analysis* make clear, in the relationships between society, ideology, and science. Biography might provide a way into these broader themes, but he did not share Bloomsbury's interest in the individual and psychology for their own sake. It is also possible that, in neglecting the personal in his essays on great economists, Schumpeter was showing, by example, the way he wanted future generations to treat him; he wanted his own private life to remain private.

What was of interest to Schumpeter were the achievements of his subjects. Writing of Carl Menger, he claimed that biographical details were not needed "to lend fame to Menger's name," the basis for which was a single decisive achievement that revolutionized economic theory (Schumpeter 1997, 81). Schumpeter's interest lies in what he describes as "Menger's *scientific* personality" (81; emphasis added), which can be explained not by psychology but by the environment out of which Menger came. That environment is sketched in a one-paragraph summary on the emergence of a market economy. From there Schumpeter goes on to the reasons, located in German intellectual history, why Menger's rapid success was quickly followed by defeat. In the case of Léon Walras, Schumpeter provided more biographical detail, giving a short factual sketch of his life and then jumping to an assessment of his main achievement. After that, he offered a brief account of the background to Walras's work and an evaluation of where it led. Similarly, Schumpeter outlines Vilfredo Pareto's life to locate him in an intellectual context that is different from that of the "Anglo-American tradition." It is social context, not individual psychology, that matters.

Schumpeter's discussion of Marshall was posed as an answer to the claim that Marshall's economics would pass away, as had that of Adam Smith and John Stuart Mill. His response was that Marshall's work possessed "a peculiar quality which effectively resists decay" (Schumpeter

1997, 93). Marshall was thoroughly evolution-minded, and this pervaded his theoretical work. Schumpeter painted his work as grounded in "an economic sociology of nineteenth-century English capitalism" (94) that was based on a firm understanding of economic history. In contrast with this, Marshall's theory was likely to be less enduring, for it was a static theory, being used to represent phenomena that were inherently dynamic. Schumpeter went on to criticize the acknowledgment Marshall gave to the "great impersonal ally" to whom he owed much—mathematics.

In all these remarks, Schumpeter could be seen as laying the foundations for assessing his own work.[11] He judges economists primarily according to whether they created a new vision, finding such in the work of, for example, Marx, Walras, and Marshall. This was a criterion according to which Schumpeter himself comes out rather well. Furthermore, he reads Marshall as laying the foundations for his own work (dynamic, evolutionary change) yet criticizes him for using a theoretical framework that was inadequate because it was static. Several of the essays can be seen as setting the record straight: Eugen von Böhm-Bawerk, Keynes, and Wesley Mitchell were all economists with whom Schumpeter's relations were, in one way or another, strained.[12]

In reviewing Keynes's *Essays in Biography*, Schumpeter praised the book where it adopted an approach similar to his own. For example, he praised Keynes's account of Malthus for conjuring up the milieu of the past out of which the *Essay on Population* came, yet criticized Keynes for not making some of the judgments that he would have made: Malthus's statements on the need for unproductive consumption were "patently wrong," and Keynes gave a distorted picture of Francis Ysidro Edgeworth through neglecting his work on monopoly, international trade, and taxation (Schumpeter 1933, 653, 655).

One might also sense Schumpeter's rivalry with Keynes in his account of what makes for good biography. He readily conceded what he called Keynes's "Kunstverstand," his understanding of art, describing him as "an artist of very high rank" (Schumpeter 1933, 652), picking out illustrations of his brilliance. However, this should, no doubt, be read against Schumpeter's obsession with "scientific" analysis. He also argues that good biography requires someone with a vision of an epoch, which can "vibrate through the pages," and who is "master of all the walks of life and ways of

11. In contrast, many of Keynes's biographical essays had been written before he knew what his main work in economics would be.

12. See Perlman's remarks in Schumpeter 1997, x–xi.

thinking of his hero" (652). Keynes's Bloomsbury vision of the epoch in which he lived can be seen in his biographies, but perhaps not so clearly as Schumpeter's shines through the ones he wrote. In writing about Marx the sociologist, Marx the economist, and Marx the teacher, Schumpeter was using a classification that emphasized the breadth of Marx's vision, but also one that could have been used for himself.

Schumpeter's *History of Economic Analysis* is renowned for containing numerous biographical vignettes (Shionoya [1997, 285] claims to have counted around three hundred of them). Though less important figures are covered in footnotes, some are in the text, such as his account of Marshall, though here all we find on his life is a bibliography preceded by the remark that his portrait had been "painted with unsurpassable brilliance by Lord Keynes" (Schumpeter 1954, 834). Perhaps this technique, of citing the praise of others, was used to avoid having to praise himself when he did not regard that person at all highly. However, the most vivid short lives are in the footnotes. Quotation is necessary to give their flavor.

> John A. Hobson (1858–1940), who had the good fortune to establish himself as an archheretic in the heyday of Marshallian supremacy and to survive into a time in which this had become a badge of honor, was in many respects a very interesting man—vital, versatile and aggressive. He was an educated man—in the sense of having had a classical education—and an emotional radical, a combination that is responsible for much of the English social-science literature of that time. In economics he was self-taught in a wilful way that made him both able to see aspects that trained economists refused to see and unable to see others that professional economists took for granted. He . . . was by no means averse to the comfortable explanation that his Marshallian opponents were actuated by an inquisitional propensity to crush dissent, if not by class interest: the possibility that, owing to his inadequate training, many of his propositions, especially his criticisms, might be provably wrong and due to nothing but failure to understand never entered his head, however often it was pointed out to him. (Schumpeter 1954, 832–33 n. 5)

This is a brilliant summary—unfair, but characterizing many of Hobson's characteristics with great precision. In its account of someone's psychology, it would be worthy of Strachey.[13] For another example, take

13. Shionoya (1997, 286) argues that Schumpeter admired Strachey's short biographies, so that the similarity in style may not be coincidental.

Schumpeter's account of Alexander Hamilton, a figure "so familiar to the reader that it would be absurd to tell him who and what Hamilton was": "He was one of those rare practitioners of economic policy who think it worth while to acquire more analytic economics than that smattering that does such good service in addressing audiences of a certain type" (199 n. 9). This concisely summarizes all Schumpeter feels he needs of Hamilton's life for the type of history he is constructing. Another example is his summary of Colbert.

> Jean Baptiste Colbert (1619–83), of bourgeois origin, was a civil servant who rose to be minister of finance. . . . He was an honest, able, and energetic administrator who knew how to raise money, intimidate creditors, improve administrative and accounting methods, stimulate industry, . . . There is no reason to extol his achievement, especially to see in him the oversized champion of some great principle. (148 n. 5)

Or take the portrait of Cairnes, who is portrayed as a significant underachiever.

> John E. Cairnes's (1823–75) career—if career is indeed the word to be used—as a research worker, writer, academic teacher, and, though behind the scenes, politician, was marred by ill health, the obvious reason why he failed to fill to the full the measure of his great ability. (533 n. 7)

In all these cases, Schumpeter has expressed a clear judgment on the individual's life.

Vignettes—of Career, Life, and Work

Few would consider a "who's who" entry, giving basic biographical information, perhaps submitted by the subject himself or herself, to be interesting as biography, however indispensable such works may be to biographers. However, such work (including among others Blaug and Vane 1999; Arestis and Sawyer 2001; Hagemann and Krohn 1999) shades almost imperceptibly into what may be usefully termed vignettes, of a few hundred words, and from there into short and then longer biographies. The closest to the who's who format is perhaps Howard Vane and Chris Mulhearn's *Nobel Memorial Laureates in Economics: An Introduction to Their Careers and Main Published Works* (2005). It is written to a formula, each entry starting with basic biographical information on the economist's life and career before proceeding to discuss his main works. Though bereft of insights into individual psychology or the epiphanies in the subjects' lives (cf. Denzin 1989, 70–71), the entries interpret. Merely to make a judgment that, for example, "Stigler will be remembered first and foremost for his pioneering work in industrial organisation and economic regulation" is to interpret, something not affected by its reflecting the judgment of present-day practitioners of the subject.

Mark Blaug's two volumes, *Great Economists before Keynes* (1989) and *Great Economists since Keynes* (1985), arguably take interpretation a stage further, even though each economist receives no more than three, and in some cases only one, page of text. For example, in the discussion of Jevons, alongside the biographical skeleton and academic career, we find pointers to important stages in his intellectual development: Jevons's early interest in social questions, the consequences of the failure of the family business, and his consciousness of being a revolutionary. The next entry, on Richard Jones, locates him among his Cambridge friends, William Whewell and John Herschel, explaining Jones's commitment to the inductive method. It then points out how this worked out in his writing on property and social institutions, justifying the claim that he should be seen as an early institutionalist.

Economic Thought since Keynes, by Michel Beaud and Gilles Dostaler (1995, 3), exhibits a similar willingness to supplement basic biographical details and lists of selected publications with analyses of its subjects' "contributions to economic thought." Both the choice of authors (150, compared with 100 in Blaug's volume covering the same period) and the interpretations reflect Beaud and Dostaler's perspective, which favors unorthodox economists, including many Marxists and radicals whom Blaug does not include. The unusual aspect of their dictionary of major contemporary economists is that it is preceded, in the same volume, by an outline of the history of economic thought since Keynes, which provides a clear indication of the perspective that underlies their selection of economists such as Samir Amin, Paul Baran, Charles Bettelheim, Krishna Bharadwaj, and others whom Blaug neglects (and would almost certainly have neglected even had he included an additional fifty economists). More selective in its coverage than Blaug's or Beaud and Dostaler's volumes is Steven Pressman's *Fifty Major Economists* (1999), which runs from Thomas Mun to Robert Lucas. Possibly because so few economists are covered, the selection is largely conventional and the treatment fairly neutral, combining brief lives with outlines of the economists' work.

A volume that does focus on lives is Geoff Harcourt's *Post-Keynesian Essays in Biography* (1993). Quite apart from its title, much in this volume echoes Keynes on biography. Its focus is economists whom Harcourt knew personally; it was written on the assumption that a person's ideas cannot be understood apart from his or her life. Memoirs and obituaries are mixed with articles that look further back. As with Keynes, all the biographies are written with great affection. The essays are, of course, colored by Harcourt's post-Keynesian perspective, with the result that critical questions that others might wish to ask are not always answered, but what is missing when the volume is compared with Keynes is the ironic Bloomsbury style that Keynes uses even when talking about economists close to him (though even he did not maintain that when talking about a very close friend such as Ramsey).

Perhaps paradoxically, the problems with defining what constitutes a biography grow as short biographies become longer. An early example is the two-volume *Pioneers of Modern Economics in Britain* (O'Brien and Presley 1981; Greenaway and Presley 1989). The fifteen chapters all begin with a section titled "Introduction—Biographia," which presents material comparable with that discussed in the previous volumes. The additional space available is devoted not to expanding the biographical coverage but to discussing the subjects' works. In some cases, such as John Creedy's analysis of Edgeworth's role as editor of the *Economic Journal*, or David Collard's discussion of A. C. Pigou, the essays take us further into their subject's life and its relation with his work, but in many, one feels that providing the basic bibliographic facts is no more than a courtesy before the serious business of analyzing the subject's writings. Similar remarks can be made about *Twelve Contemporary Economists* (Shackleton and Locksley 1981), *American Economists of the Late Twentieth Century* (Samuels 1996), *Italian Economists of the Twentieth Century* (Meacci 1998), or *European Economists of the Early Twentieth Century* (Samuels 1998, 2003). Some contain interesting vignettes of economists' lives, often drawing on more substantial biographies, but others focus entirely on textual exegesis or else provide a formal, and unrevealing, account of the life that barely goes beyond a who's who entry, albeit written more elegantly. In some cases, what one finds are expositions of the economists' work, without any suggestion that the author considers biography to have any bearing on it. Such essays may be of value, but they are hardly biography, even, to use an abused term, intellectual biography. These volumes are edited collections where, in many cases, the approach depends on the individual contributor, and as a result what might be called short biographies are mixed together with essays whose authors have no interest in their subjects' lives, even though the volumes' titles often imply that they are about economists rather than about their works.

The *BDBE*, to be followed by a similar work on American economists, opens by comparing John Hicks's and Keynes's approaches to biography. Rutherford (2004, vii) points out that Hicks "tended to concentrate on an economist's theoretical achievement," while Keynes provided "vivid portraits" before analyzing the economic thought. Rutherford went on to express the hope that the *BDBE* would "be more in the spirit of Keynes the biographer." Many entries achieve this goal, though there is inevitably great variety, which is instructive to explore in some detail, as it illustrates some general features and problems of this type of work. The length of entries was set by the editor, reflecting his or her judgment about the subject's importance.

As an example, take the second edition of the *New Palgrave*.[14] As table 1 shows, the large majority of economists receive entries that are between 500 and 2,000 words, the mode being 750 words. Entries that are much shorter include ones where there is simply little to be said or because the subject is judged a marginal figure (e.g., Daniel Defoe is conventionally regarded as much less important in the history of economics than in English intellectual life more generally). At the other extreme, Ricardo, Edgeworth, Walras, Smith, Marshall, Marx, and Keynes have entries of 12,000 words or more. These have in common the facts that they are on historical figures considered important to the long-term evolution of economics, on whom substantial critical literature exists. All are written by people who have written much larger studies of their subjects.

Similar remarks could be made about the *BDBE*. It comprises 611 entries, for which the commissioned lengths were up to 600 words (50 percent); 600 to 2,500 words (40 percent); and 2,500 to 4,000 words. Especially with the shortest entries, entries will normally have come near the maxima of these ranges. The large number of short entries reflects the many minor figures who are covered. Their inclusion is not "neutral," for they are frequently applied economists whose work was better known in nonacademic circles.

Of course, the courtesies needed to recruit a large team of biographers mean that these figures should be interpreted with heavy qualifications.

14. This count is based on the "expected commissioned length" as of 10 March 2006. The final distribution may end up being slightly different, though little of substance is likely to change.

Table 1 Distribution of Lengths of Biographies in *The New Palgrave Dictionary of Economics*

Length	Number
250 or less	9
251–500	21
501–1,000	240
1,001–2,000	108
2,001–5,000	68
5,001–10,000	28
10,001 or more	7

Editors can try to persuade, but in the last resort they cannot force delivery. There are inevitably circumstances where, faced with the choice of accommodating a potential author and having him or her opt out, they will sometimes choose the former. The result may be that subjects whose biographers stick to editors' deadlines get shorter entries than those whose biographers are less economical with words and persuade the editors that the material is worth the additional space. In a second edition, the constraints are greater still. As Don Patinkin had died in the interim, the editors of the *New Palgrave* did not have the option of asking him to revise the 27,000-word entry on Keynes in the first edition, so they chose to retain it unchanged rather than either replace it or have someone else revise it.

There are clearly radical differences between writing short biographies and long ones. Whereas writing a long biography is frequently the result of immersing oneself in a life, short ones typically involve much less intense engagement with the subject.[15] Perhaps a more important difference is the availability of materials. Few will commit to a long biography unless there is a substantial archive of materials from which the life can be constructed: as a result, many potential subjects fail to receive the biographical attention that might be thought due. There is simply not enough material to work on. The result is that many short biographical essays focus on the skeleton derivable from the public records, or birth, education, career, and death,

15. It has been suggested that the proliferation of short biographies results from the fact that they can be produced at extremely low cost to the writer and therefore constitute an easy way to expand one's CV. There is probably truth in this, but on the other hand there is the low prestige, and hence low benefits, from writing them. The great variety found within the literature, in terms of length, approach, and quality, no doubt reflects a great variety of motives underlying the writing process.

perhaps with marriage and other life events included, supplemented by a publications list. However, even in a six-hundred-word dictionary entry, it is usually possible to go beyond this, usually starting from obituaries in national newspapers. There are few economists on whom nothing has been published; even where archives are either nonexistent or inaccessible, given the resources available, it is possible to build up a picture of the subject, using simple methods of historical and literary criticism to sift through inconsistent or incomplete accounts. This provides a context against which published work can be analyzed.

From there, biographies extend to figures on whom much more has been published, where the writer is surveying and interpreting biographical data and interpretations of the subject's work, selecting material that makes sense of the economist's life.[16] This may be informed directly by acquaintance with archival evidence, or it may rely on such evidence only indirectly, drawing on those who have based their writings on it. However, the constraints of space and the need to paint, as it were, with a broad brush mean that such evidence is unlikely to be prominent. The effects of compression in this way are perhaps best illustrated by considering short biographies by biographers who have already published longer studies of their subjects, and asking what happens to a biography when its length is severely constrained.[17]

A Long One Shrunk?

Referring to her biography of William Morris and the entry that she subsequently wrote for the *ODNB*, Fiona MacCarthy wrote,

> There was the technical challenge of reducing a life on which I had expended 300,000 words [and seven years] down to a narrative of just 7,000. The epic had to be recast as the short story. I enjoyed the paring down, the concentration on the essentials. In the end I felt that the article was better than the book.[18]

16. Strachey's *Eminent Victorians* would fit in here, though one hopes that modern examples will plagiarize and distort through selective use of sources less than he did. After comparing one of Strachey's paragraphs with an earlier biography, his editor concluded that, though Strachey had significantly enlivened the style, "any student doing this in a Ph.D. thesis . . . would be flunked for plagiarism" (Sutherland 2003, xiv).

17. An interesting exercise would be to see whether there are discernible differences between short biographies that are written en route to a more substantial biography and ones written after the latter. This has not been attempted here.

18. Quotation from undated Oxford University Press advertising leaflet on the *ODNB*.

So what are the relations between short biographies of economists and long ones?

By the standards of full-length biographies, *The Political Economy of Robert Lowe* (Maloney 2005) is hardly long, at 146 pages of text, but the *BDBE* offers only a single page (plus bibliography). However, despite the title, Maloney's work is a biography, exploring the events of Lowe's life and their relation to his economics. In Maloney's *BDBE* entry we are introduced to the personal circumstances that explained much of Lowe's career and attitudes—his education and early career in Australia, and the Australian parliament, and the failing eyesight, doctors' advice for which explained some of his actions. Maloney offers a concise summary of Lowe's ideology, which involved "defining liberalism as the doctrine that no one class in the country should be made tributary to another class" (Rutherford 2004, 698).

Maloney's book can be seen as amplifying the appraisal offered in the *BDBE* entry, not as doing anything different. Some remarks in the latter, though offering clear comments on Lowe's psychology and politics, turn out to be severe understatements. Lowe's "roughness and sarcasm" hardly does justice to his ability to offend, which the book documents in detail, thereby explaining one reason why he was such a maverick. The *BDBE* entry about Lowe being willing to compromise on laissez-faire is correct and is an important theme in the book; however, it pales in comparison with the remark that Lowe "stands out as a particularly vivid example of a Benthamite coming to terms with the increased power of the nineteenth-century state. The coming to terms, however, had mostly been at Lowe's own idiosyncratic speed" (Maloney 2005, 3). What is left out are any pointers to Lowe's rapidly changing, even oscillating, opinions on matters such as commercial treaties that left many of his contemporaries (and even some readers of the biography) bewildered. This along with the position that now seems incredible, of being simultaneously a politician and an anonymous leader-writer for the *Times*, are surely aspects that merited discussion even in a short biography. Lowe's belief in the universality of economic doctrines, his belief that political economy was essentially complete, his anti-relativism, and his denial that sociology even existed, all discussed in the *BDBE*, go a long way to explain John Stuart Mill's remark that "some 'friends' of political economy were its own worst enemies" (Rutherford 2004, 698). The book, however, suggests that there may have been much more behind this view: had Lowe been simply a pragmatic liberal in matters of policy, Mill's remark would have cut much less deeply.

Maloney's *BDBE* entry was written while he was working on the longer biography. This may explain why the latter not only develops the themes further but significantly refines the argument: perhaps, when writing the short biography, he had not developed fully the judgments that characterize the long one. It is also possible that, in writing the one-page entry, Maloney felt constrained by the genre to present an account that was unquestionably fair to Lowe and therefore refrained from making statements that might have been taken as more damning than intended when shorn of more detailed explanation.[19] Either way, the short biography signals clearly, if with much understatement, what is to come in the long one.

In contrast, Peter Groenewegen wrote his *BDBE* entry on Alfred Marshall after his long (eight-hundred-page) biography, *A Soaring Eagle* (1995)—see Groenewegen, this volume. The concision is done by parceling off the life in two paragraphs of basic factual information. Observing that "Marshall's major claim to fame is his work on economics" (Rutherford 2004, 739), Groenewegen then proceeds to a broadly chronological analysis of his publications. We are told of Marshall's early translation of Mill into mathematics and about the *Economics of Industry*, written with Mary Paley Marshall, a book that Groenewegen argues is more important than it is sometimes taken to be. We are then led through the history of the *Principles* and to Marshall's later works. There is a substantial discussion of *Industry and Trade*. After that, Groenewegen analyzes the content of Marshall's economics, focusing on the various fields to which he contributed.

Using the benchmarks of Keynes and Schumpeter, this account is much closer to Schumpeter, though without his attention to background. Groenewegen clearly decided that, for a dictionary of economists, Marshall's published work was important, believing that the reader needed to be told what that work comprised and what its value was. This is in dramatic contrast with *A Soaring Eagle*, which offers a meticulously detailed account of Marshall's life, his relationships with friends and colleagues, the creation of the Cambridge economics degree in Cambridge, and of "Cambridge economics" itself. That, however, is clearly not what Groenewegen thinks is important for a dictionary of economics. Marshall's lifelong rivalry with Henry Sidgwick is not mentioned, and neither are his engagements (or lack of them) with utilitarianism and biology. The life itself, and hence the vast bulk of *A Soaring Eagle*, seems strangely irrelevant. Historiographically, the two biographies are very different.

19. In all cases, I assume that the character of the dictionary entry was not dictated by the editor but was chosen by the author.

Like Groenewegen's short biography of Marshall, Bruce Caldwell's *New Palgrave* biography of Friedrich Hayek followed on from *Hayek's Challenge* (2004), a biography on which Caldwell had been working for many years, an account of which is provided in Caldwell, this volume. Its opening paragraphs offer a clear and wonderfully concise summary of the key aspects of Hayek's career that he wants economists to hear: "Hayek had the good fortune of repeatedly being in the right place at the right time, crossing paths with some of the century's most brilliant economists and thinkers . . . but it was usually with the wrong ideas, at least from the perspective of most of his contemporaries."[20] The story moves from fin de siècle Vienna, through the London School of Economics (LSE), Hayek's encounters with Keynes, the socialist calculation debate, and postwar debates over socialism and planning in the postwar order. Hayek then moved to the United States, and Chicago, close to Milton Friedman, who was a central figure in key developments in postwar economics. Hayek was perceived as saying the wrong things, in that he got the worse of his exchanges with Keynes in the 1930s, he was on what was considered the losing side of the socialist calculation debate, and his warnings failed to stem the move toward central planning. Even at Chicago, he was not part of the economics department: though Hayek and Keynes might agree on politics, their styles of doing economics were poles apart.

Caldwell's abridged biography follows the long one faithfully, tracing the sequence of projects in which Hayek was engaged. In this we discover the processes that led from one project to the other, rendering what might appear to be great diversity into a logical path: Hayek's journey, to cite the title of the book's middle section, had what Caldwell clearly considers a compelling rationale. His reward was that, eventually, he was vindicated by the fall of the Soviet system, the demise of Keynesianism, and the triumph of free market capitalism. He may have been saying things his contemporaries did not want to hear, but so much the worse for them. These themes are covered in the chapters that constitute the core of *Hayek's Challenge*. Clearly, detail is lost, but the long account provides the justification for the shorter one, and the shorter one a sharper account of what is being said in the longer one. But is the account changed in any significant way?

20. Quotations are from an unpublished typescript, provided by Caldwell; hence the absence of page references.

The context provided by Carl Menger, Max Weber, the *Methodenstreit*, and early-twentieth-century disputes over positivism and historicism is passed over in the short biography. No attempt is made to root Hayek's thinking in this phase of intellectual history, one that the reader of *Hayek's Challenge* might have thought Caldwell considered foundational for what came afterward. Not for Caldwell either the social background that Schumpeter emphasized or Keynes's psychological analysis, with the result that the shorter account leaves the intellectual origins of Hayek's work in the air. This fits with the emphasis on the good fortune of being in the right place at the right time. Given this, the lack of discussion of Hayek's personality makes sense, though it raises questions about what the biography is explaining.

At the other end, Caldwell's Hayek entry in the *New Palgrave* misses out on a long epilogue delving into methodology. Presumably the reason is that in the *New Palgrave* entry, Caldwell believes he is addressing a different audience. The epilogue, which he describes as more personal than the rest of the book, returns to the debates over positivism and methodology with which Caldwell (2004) has been concerned since his first book. This is a significant change. To present Hayek's intellectual biography shorn of, for example, discussions of either Hayek's engagements with positivism or his relations to Popper is to change the story: in *Hayek's Challenge*, positivism is both the starting point and the end point, and Hayek, whose career was bound up with positivism, crops up throughout the story.[21] Though this would be an exaggeration, there would be an element of truth in saying that Caldwell's shorter biography presents Hayek as less German, and more Anglo-American, viewing his work in the light of modern concerns.

Caldwell describes *Hayek's Challenge* as an intellectual biography. Though one may question whether this is the appropriate approach for an intellectual biography,[22] the term implies an approach that is focused on Hayek's series of projects, and it explains Caldwell's lack of concern with aspects of Hayek's life that would have interested other students of Hayek. Neither the short nor the long biography, for example, mentions Hayek's

21. "Legal positivism" makes one appearance in the *NDBE* entry, and there is a reference to Hayek's having helped bring Popper to LSE. That is all.

22. See the assessment made by Moggridge (2004). Caldwell's response to this is that up till shortly before publication, the subtitle was to have been *F. A. Hayek and the Limits of Social Science*, which is perhaps a more accurate description of the book's approach.

important liaison with Antony Fisher, whose Institute of Economic Affairs directly and indirectly helped promote the cause of free markets. This side of Hayek, the political activist, is not Caldwell's concern. Neither are the details of Hayek's personal life.

Gordon Fletcher's *Understanding Dennis Robertson: The Man and His Work* (2000) is very different. It is a story of a man tormented by personal doubts, rooted in his upbringing and problems involved in coming to terms with his sexuality. His intellectual isolation after his break with Keynes was tied up with a sense of isolation resulting from his ending up at Trinity rather than King's College. Not only was he isolated from where the crucial intellectual developments were taking place, but he was in an environment much less congenial, given his homosexuality. The resulting torments, to establish which Fletcher interweaves Robertson's personal biography with analysis of his literary output, placing great emphasis on Lewis Carroll's "Alice" books from which Robertson regularly quoted, are central to the life recounted in the book.

Fletcher's *BDBE* entry, on the other hand, passes over this side of Robertson's life, no more than hinted at through reference to the lateness of his admission to the "Apostles" and an intimate homosexual affair in the late 1920s. This is not to say that the personal is missing in the shorter biography. Far from it. Robertson's approach to economics is linked to his "complex personal makeup" (Rutherford 2004, 1026),[23] and there is a concise explanation of how his personality influenced both his early engagements with Keynes and his later reaction against Keynesianism. The entry does discuss Robertson's work, though intertwining it with his very active life in a way that makes it hard to summarize. An interesting touch is that it ends, out of chronological sequence, with Robertson's business cycle theory, his monetary economics, and his *Banking Policy and the Price Level* (1926), a book that Fletcher describes as "seminal," citing the importance Keynes attached to it. Robertson's work has been shown to arise out of his life.

The aim of these remarks is not so much to appraise these biographies, long and short, though doing so is inevitable. All, in their own ways, are skilled products by biographers who are captivated by their subjects and who have greatly enhanced our understanding of them. Rather, it is to show that going from a long biography to a short one does not involve simply portraying the same life more concisely, leaving out the details

23. If the longer biography is correct, this is even more of an understatement than Maloney's summary of Lowe's interpersonal skills.

on which the interpretation rests. The interpretation changes. It may be that a shorter biography is aimed at a different audience, focusing on what that audience is likely to consider important (Caldwell 2004 and Groenewegen 1995). It may be that biographers exercise greater discretion in discussing material that might be misinterpreted without more detailed context (Maloney 2005 and Fletcher 2000). There is also what the biographer learns after the first production is committed to publication. Perhaps there is no such thing as a "neutral" condensation: even if the biographer is attempting to summarize, without changing the interpretation, simply leaving out details whose effects on the reader cannot be anticipated may mean that its meaning, a product of communities comprising readers and the writer, is inevitably liable to change.

What Are the Questions?

Stefan Collini (2005), reviewing the *ODNB*, pointed to its greater inclusiveness compared with the original *DNB*. It had become more democratic, less a catalog of "the great and the good." In this, it reflected changing expectations that, over the preceding three or four decades, had been reflected in the publication of volumes aimed at "making good" its deficiencies: biographical dictionaries of radicals, feminists, businessmen, philosophers, and even economists. In the same way, within economics, there have been many specialist volumes. The editors of *A Biographical Dictionary of Women Economists* (Dimand, Dimand, and Forget 2000, xv) started with the suspicion that "there had been more women contributing to the development of our discipline than economists knew about," a suspicion that was proved more than justified as they uncovered more and more women economists who had long been overlooked: apart from the general problem that women have often worked in fields to which historians have paid less attention (often applied fields), and the fact that in some cases their gender was not clear from their publications, there has been a tendency to overlook women. Harcourt (1993) focuses attention on biographies relevant to post-Keynesian economics. Arestis and Sawyer (2001) cover "dissenting" economists or, what King (1988) called, perhaps somewhat confusingly, "economic exiles." Genuine exiles are cataloged and their movements analyzed in Hagemann and Krohn 1999.

Though it may not have been conceived for this purpose, the *BDBE* served to correct the record provided by more selective collections of biographies in a more subtle way. More selective collections, even ones containing as many economists as the *NPDE* or the *ODNB*, inevitably focus on economists who fall into one of four categories: they are regarded as important in conventional histories of the subject; they are distinguished in other fields (perhaps politics or literature) as well as working in economics; they have been honored by bodies such as the Nobel Foundations; or they are contemporaries (usually recently deceased) who are respected by their surviving peers. The *BDBE*, in including almost anyone who had published something on economics, cast its net much more widely, including people who, though they might once have fallen into the last category, no longer fall into any of them. They published work that engaged the attention of contemporaries but engages economists no longer.

Of what use are such lives to economists, beyond that which attaches to directories such as who's who or the membership lists of the American Economic Association? One is that, as was mentioned above, they come closer to telling us about the "average" economist—of telling us what past economics was "really" like, placing those whose names endured longer in an appropriate context. In addition, they can be useful in defining the networks that are important to the creation of economic ideas. Obituaries frequently tell, in a way that directories rarely do, of those with whom economists worked, who influenced them, and where they fit into a wider picture. In some cases these networks are important in suggesting patterns in an otherwise inchoate mass of ideas that do not fit into conventional canons. In others, they are of interest in themselves: there exist historical questions about those networks for which short biographies can provide the answer.[24]

Conclusion

Keynes and Schumpeter offer two styles of writing a short life. Though Keynes's lives were more obviously "biographical," Schumpeter can also be seen as placing lives in context—as writing lives in a different way. It is tempting to argue that much of the subsequent literature follows Schumpeter, with his greater focus on analysis of what economists wrote. However, that is to ignore Schumpeter's focus on sociology and context, which differentiates his approach from many recent analyses of economists' contributions to the subject. Paradoxically, such work has prolifer-

24. Backhouse 2005, which analyzes economists in Parliament, is centered on an analysis of the biographies of economist members of Parliament from the *BDBE*.

ated at the same time as historiographical fashions have moved away from what Schumpeter chose to call the filiation of economic ideas. However, this may be due to the increased focus on the twentieth century. Not only has the advent of modern "professional" economics possibly changed the relation between biographical or social background and economic ideas, it is more true than ever that the emergence of new ideas is the product of communities of economists and that picking out individuals is harder.[25] As a result, the links between individual biographies and the emergence of ideas may be weaker. It becomes harder to summarize an era through an individual, as Schumpeter wanted to do.[26]

Short biographies are, perhaps necessarily, different from long ones, even by the same writer. They are obviously no replacement for more substantial works. However, they are important: they introduce economists of whom, for various reasons, more substantial lives will never be written and, at their best, encapsulate more clearly than a large volume the essence of a life as seen by the biographer. Not only do they enforce what has been called "the discipline of brevity," but insofar as they mitigate "the romantic individualism of conventional biography," they may offer perspectives that would otherwise not be available (Walter 2006, 321, 335–36). Of course, not all short lives achieve this: some are hardly lives at all. What makes for a good one? Schumpeter wrote that the biographer must have a vision that "vibrates" through the pages. He had such a vision, and it vibrates though the pages of *Ten Great Economists*. Blaug's *Great Economists* volumes are to some extent similar: even if they do not exhibit a single vision in the same way, they are enlivened by his willingness to make bold judgments.

References

Arestis, P., and M. Sawyer. 2001. *A Biographical Dictionary of Dissenting Economists*. 2nd ed. Cheltenham, U.K.: Elgar.

Backhouse, R. E. 2005. Economists in Parliament in Britain, 1848–1914. In *Economists in Parliament in the Liberal Era, 1848–1920*, edited by M. E. L. Guidi and M. Augello. Aldershot, U.K.: Ashgate.

25. Note that this claim is completely different from the view criticized by Porter (2006, 315), that the personal lives of professional scientists should have no bearing on their work. It is that the larger scale and greater integration of the relevant communities may have altered the significance of individuals' biographies.

26. It is worth noting that T. W. Hutchison (1953) found this true of the interwar period, reflected in the different organization of his material.

Backhouse, R. E., and R. Middleton, eds. 2000. *Exemplary Economists*. Vol. 1. Cheltenham, U.K.: Elgar.
Beaud, M., and G. Dostaler. 1995. *Economic Thought since Keynes*. Cheltenham, U.K.: Elgar.
Bell, M. 1989. Lytton Strachey's Eminent Victorians. In *The Biographer's Art: New Essays*, edited by J. Meyers. London: Macmillan.
Blaug, M. 1985. *Great Economists since Keynes*. Brighton: Wheatsheaf Books.
———. 1989. *Great Economists before Keynes*. Brighton: Wheatsheaf Books.
Blaug, M., and H. Vane. 2003. *Who's Who in Economics*. 4th ed. Cheltenham, U.K.: Elgar.
Blume, L. E., and S. N. Durlauf, eds. Forthcoming. *The New Palgrave Dictionary of Economics*. 2nd ed. Basingstoke, U.K.: Palgrave Macmillan.
Caldwell, B. 2004. *Hayek's Challenge: An Intellectual Autobiography of F. A. Hayek*. Chicago: University of Chicago Press.
Collini, S. 2005. Our Island Story. *London Review of Books*, 20 January.
Denzin, N. K. 1989. *Interpretive Biography*. London: Sage.
Dimand, R., M. A. Dimand, and E. L. Forget, eds. 2000. *A Biographical Dictionary of Women Economists*. Cheltenham, U.K.: Elgar.
Eatwell, J., M. Milgate, and P. Newman. 1987. *The New Palgrave: A Dictionary of Economics*. London: Macmillan.
Fletcher, G. A. 2000. *Understanding Dennis Robertson: The Man and His Work*. Aldershot, U.K.: Elgar.
Gittings, R. 1978. *The Nature of Biography*. London: Heinemann.
Greenaway, D., and J. R. Presley, eds. 1989. *Pioneers of Modern Economics in Britain*. Vol. 2. London: Macmillan.
Groenewegen, P. D. 1995. *A Soaring Eagle: Alfred Marshall, 1842–1924*. Aldershot, U.K.: Elgar.
Hagemann, H., and Claus-D. Krohn, eds. 1999. *Biographisches Handbuch der deutschprachigen wirtschaftswissenschaftlichen Emigration nach 1933*. Munich: Saur.
Harcourt, G. 1993. *Post-Keynesian Essays in Biography*. London: Palgrave Macmillan.
Harrison, B. 2003. British Biography, Large and Small. *History Compass* 1.
Hutchison, T. W. 1953. *A Review of Economic Doctrines, 1870–1929*. Oxford: Clarendon Press.
Keynes, J. M. 1972. *Essays in Biography*. Vol. 10 of *The Collected Writings of John Maynard Keynes*. London: Macmillan.
King, J. E. 1988. *Economic Exiles*. London: Macmillan.
Maloney, J. 2005. *The Political Economy of Robert Lowe*. London: Palgrave Macmillan.
Meacci, F. 1998. *Italian Economists of the Twentieth Century*. Cheltenham, U.K.: Elgar.
Mehrling, P. G. 1997. *The Money Interest and the Public Interest: American Monetary Thought, 1920–70*. Cambridge, Mass.: Harvard University Press.
Moggridge, D. 1976. *Keynes*. London: Fontana.

———. 2004. Review of *Hayek's Challenge*, by Bruce Caldwell. http://eh.net/pipermail/hes/2004-July/002473.html.
O'Brien, D. P., and J. R. Presley, eds. 1981. *Pioneers of Modern Economics in Britain*. London: Macmillan.
Porter, T. M. 2006. Is the Life of the Scientist a Scientific Unit? *Isis* 97:314–21.
Pressman, S. 1999. *Fifty Major Economists*. London: Routledge.
Rutherford, D., ed. 2004. *The Biographical Dictionary of British Economists*. Bristol: Thoemmes.
Samuels, W. J. 1996. *American Economists of the Late Twentieth Century*. Cheltenham, U.K.: Elgar.
———, ed. 1998. *European Economists of the Early Twentieth Century: Studies of Neglected Thinkers of Belgium, France, the Netherlands, and Scandinavia*. Vol. 1. Cheltenham, U.K.: Elgar.
———, ed. 2003. *European Economists of the Early Twentieth Century: Studies of Neglected Continental Thinkers of Germany and Italy*. Vol. 2. Cheltenham, U.K.: Elgar.
Schumpeter, J. A. 1933. Review of *Essays in Biography*, by J. M. Keynes. *Economic Journal* 43:652–57.
———. 1954. *History of Economic Analysis*. New York: Oxford University Press.
———. 1997. *Ten Great Economists*. London: Routledge.
Shackleton, J. R., and G. Locksley. 1981. *Twelve Contemporary Economists*. London: Macmillan.
Shionoya, Y. 1997. *Schumpeter and the Idea of Social Science*. Cambridge: Cambridge University Press.
Skidelsky, R. 1996. *Keynes*. Oxford: Oxford University Press.
Strachey, L. 2003. *Eminent Victorians*. Edited by J. Sutherland. Oxford: Oxford University Press.
Sutherland, J. 2003. Introduction to *Eminent Victorians*, by L. Strachey. London: Heinemann.
Vane, H., and C. Mulhearn. 2005. *Nobel Memorial Laureates in Economics: An Introduction to Their Careers and Main Published Works*. Cheltenham, U.K.: Elgar.
Walker, D. A. 1985. Keynes as a Historian of Economic Thought: The Biographical Essays on Neoclassical Economics. *HOPE* 17.2:159–86.
Walter, J. 2006. The Utility of Short Lives. *Biography* 29.2:329–37.

The Creation of Heroes and Villains as a Problem in the History of Economics

Robert W. Dimand

When historians lionize or demonize economists, they bring attention to figures who might otherwise be less noticed in a present-minded discipline; but such lionizing and demonizing also shapes and filters how economists' contributions are understood and the extent and manner in which these contributions can influence, inspire, or suggest subsequent developments. John Maynard Keynes was a hero in Germany, where *The Economic Consequences of the Peace* (1919) was received enthusiastically, yet a villain in France. Though logically unrelated to the issue of demand management, this influenced how *The General Theory* was received in the two countries. One of the most hostile reviews of *The General Theory* was written by the son of Georges Clemenceau's interpreter at the peace conference, who later wrote *The Carthaginian Peace, or the Economic Consequences of Mr. Keynes* (Mantoux 1952). Another hostile reaction to *The General Theory* came from Jacques Rueff, who had clashed with Keynes over the German transfer problem. Joseph Schumpeter raised this issue in *Capitalism, Socialism, and Democracy* ([1942] 1987), when he proposed treating Karl Marx seriously as an economic theorist and social scientist rather than as an infallible prophet or a subversive menace. The present essay explores both the consequences of the creation of heroes and villains in economics (with attention to parallel phenomena in other social and behavioral sciences) and the causes of the phenomenon.

One source of demand for heroes is that the proponents of new intellectual developments, like the newly eminent in other contexts, look for

History of Political Economy 39 (annual suppl.) DOI 10.1215/00182702-2006-039

respectable genealogies comparable to those of their established rivals and seek affirmation by invoking great names as allies and precursors. Those wishing to present their work as an innovation worthy of notice, a revolutionary (or counterrevolutionary) break with the preceding bad old days, also have an incentive to construct a caricature of the villainous thinkers and doctrines they are overthrowing—the hard-hearted pre-Keynesians who assumed continuous full employment and the misguided Keynesians who demanded boundless budget deficits and wanted to produce lots of inflation to trick people into working more than they really want.

Another source of demand for heroes is that historians of economics, otherwise hard-pressed to compete for the discipline's attention (let alone respect), emphasize anniversaries and local affinities (Adam Smith in Scotland, Knut Wicksell and the Stockholm school in Sweden, Irving Fisher at Yale, the Chicago school) as occasions for conferences and publications, with an inevitably celebratory tone, but with the consequences of sponsoring the creation of scholarly works and of educating economists who otherwise would not pay attention to the field's past. Thus the coincidence of the seventieth anniversary of Keynes's *General Theory* with the centenary of his only visit to Siena provides the occasion for a Siena bank to support an International Economic Association conference in Siena titled "Keynes's *General Theory* after Seventy Years."

The production of heroes and villains provides a dramatic focus and convenient symbolism useful in policy debates and especially in the teaching of economics, where it is a convenient mnemonic device to associate a theory with the name of one person and where the pressure for simplification promotes such identification and caricature. Such celebration and denunciation distort understanding and divert inquiry, as simplifications of use in introducing students to a subject become ingrained, yet also contribute to the advancement of knowledge by providing stimulus for investigation, reflection, and critical debate that would not otherwise occur. The process both helps and hinders intellectual history, creating difficulties for historical research that otherwise might never be undertaken, supported, or noticed.

Brave Bad Men, Untarnished Knights, and Heroes of Their Own Dispatches

The historian and statesman the Earl of Clarendon, seeking in exile to understand the convulsions of his time, characterized Oliver Cromwell as "a brave bad man." Such explanations of displeasing events have seemed convenient or satisfying to economists on occasion, yet, as with Cromwell, they obscure the full story. According to Murray Rothbard (1972, 159–60), "Ralph Hawtrey proved to be one of the evil geniuses of the 1920s. . . . Hawtrey was the main inspiration for the stabilization resolutions of the Genoa Conference of 1922." Rothbard conceded that the idea of a stable price level might be useful during a boom to sound-money advocates opposing inflation, but warned that it would interfere with the necessary deflation to restore the economy's health after a boom. While condemned by Rothbard for advocating interference with free markets, Hawtrey (director of financial inquiries at the British Treasury from 1919 to 1945) was also subjected by Keynesians to the opposite criticism for taking a do-nothing stance toward prolonged unemployment, exemplified by the 1929 Treasury White Paper critiquing Lloyd George's public works proposal (Hawtrey was away as a visiting professor at Harvard while the White Paper was written, but had contributed to the intellectual climate in which it was composed). He has been used as a foil for Keynes. Thus Lawrence Klein (1947, 45–46) concludes that Hawtrey, in his Macmillan Committee testimony about crowding out of private investment by expansionary fiscal policy, "must have been working with assumptions of Say's Law and/or full employment," and observes a few pages later that "Hawtrey believed that an easy-money policy could stimulate any revival" (53). Instead of linking the two passages on the effectiveness of monetary policy and ineffectiveness of fiscal policy to deduce an implicit assumption of interest-inelastic money demand rather than of full employment, Klein only remarks (without recalling that seven pages earlier he had noted Britain's return to the gold standard at the prewar parity as a constraint on an easy-money policy), "It is hard to see how an economist who lived in England through the 1920's could support such a theory" (53). Caricaturing Hawtrey as either the evil genius of stable prices or as an unenlightened pre-Keynesian blindly assuming full employment amid high unemployment clouded understanding of the policy and analysis he offered, as happens in other cases of demonizing an economist.

Some economists have been, as Norman Mailer was described, the heroes of their own dispatches. Sébastien Le Prestre de Vauban, author of treatises on fortification as well as taxation and one of Louis XIV's marshals, began the genre of autobiographies of economists with his memoirs, of which the first four volumes appeared more than a century after his death (see also Vauban 1839, a much shorter work, and Paret 1986). John R. Commons, Milton and Rose Friedman, John Kenneth Galbraith, Benjamin Higgins, Alvin Johnson, Charles Kindleberger, Mary Paley Marshall, John Stuart Mill, Lionel Robbins, Herbert Simon, Thomas Sowell, George Stigler, and Barbara Wootton have all written autobiographical books, as have less familiar but also interesting and significant economists from Vincent Bladen and James Mavor to Eleanor Lansing Dulles and Scott Nearing (see Moggridge, this volume). Many more have written autobiographical essays (e.g., Backhouse and Middleton 2000), including those solicited by the *American Economist* and, in the cases of Nobel laureates, the Lives of the Laureates lecture series at Trinity University of San Antonio (Breit and Hirsch 2004). Inevitably, as in Akira Kurosawa's movie *Rashomon*, participants see things from their own point of view and are most conscious of events at which they were present or which directly affected them, rather than of related developments involving others, even with the less egotistical autobiographers. Winston Churchill expressed confidence that history would judge him leniently, since he intended to write that history himself. Recollections of distant events dim or change with time, revelations are selective, and scores are settled, sometimes by omission, as when Adam Smith made a point of refuting Sir James Steuart's views without citing Steuart. These considerations should not, but sometimes do, cause surprise. They are outweighed by the benefit to scholarship of receiving the knowledge and insights of participant-observers. Also, several of the books (not so often the essays) are entertaining as well as informative. From Kindleberger's *Life of an Economist* (1991, 65), one learns that when Kindleberger was on the nominating committee of the American Economic Association, the committee took note that no Canadian, Southerner, or woman had ever been AEA president, and thereupon resolved to look for a suitable Canadian, eventually selecting Harold Innis as AEA president for 1952.

Another, related source of heroes is that biographies of economists are often commissioned to be written by their admiring disciples and younger disciples. Roy Harrod's biography of John Maynard Keynes and the *Economic Journal* memorial articles on Alfred Marshall by Keynes and on Keynes by Austin Robinson come readily to mind, but the genre goes back to Condorcet's *Vie de Turgot*. There have also been biographies of Richard Whately and Sir William Ashley by their daughters, and of Irving Fisher by his son (as, among Whig historians, Lord Macaulay's life was written by his nephew, Sir George Otto Trevelyan, whose life was written by his son George Macaulay Trevelyan).

There certainly are examples of sustained scholarly accounts of someone the author finds profoundly antipathetic, for instance, Steve Fuller's *Thomas Kuhn: A Philosophical History for Our Times* (2000), witty, erudite, insightful, but also an extended diatribe with such chapter titles as "Kuhnification as Ritualized Political Impotence." Malice can be energizing: Will Blythe's account of the Duke-UNC basketball rivalry is titled *To Hate Like This Is to Be Happy Forever* (2006). Critical distance can be a bar to engagement: according to Donald Walker's introduction to William Jaffé's essays on Léon Walras, Jaffé, translator of Walras's major work and editor of his correspondence, was unable to write his long-promised definitive biography of Walras because he was unable to warm to Walras's personality. Commissioned studies by admirers, begun in sympathy and admiration, need not be uncritical. The psychologist Leslie Hearnshaw gave the memorial address at Sir Cyril Burt's funeral and was then invited by Burt's sister to write an authorized biography. Hearnshaw 1979, the definitive unmasking of Burt as a wholesale fabricator who invented fictitious coauthors (and fictitious authors for laudatory reviews of his own books) and an entire spurious data set of identical twins raised separately (having lost a real, but unspectacular, data set in the wartime bombing of London, Burt needed to keep publishing as he tried to hang on to the department and journal he had founded beyond the retirement dates he had set), was published with the full backing of Burt's pained but undaunted sister. Richard Herrnstein and Charles Murray (1994, 11–12), attempting to rehabilitate Burt's reputation and data set in *The Bell Curve*, were reduced to pretending that Hearnshaw's book did not exist and attributing the allegations against Burt to left-wing journalists.

An economist or other scholar can be portrayed as a villain because of disapproval of the person's political and social views beyond his or her professional writings, as Herrnstein and Murray (1994) unconvincingly claim to be the case with Burt, and as with the Web site devoted to a running critique and denunciation of Paul Krugman's *New York Times* columns, with Paul Samuelson's place on President Nixon's enemies list (which cited Samuelson for his *Newsweek* columns), and with the abuse and misrepresentation that Thomas Sowell (2000) has experienced. The Veritas Foundation's *Keynes at Harvard: Economic Deception as a Political Credo* (Dobbs 1969), an over-the-top excoriation of Keynesianism as Fabian socialism (equated with communism), denounced John Neville Keynes, Alfred Marshall, Knut Wicksell, Joseph Schumpeter, and the

Rockefellers as socialists. (The first edition of this curious work had nine printings, with 140,000 copies.) Samuelson's introductory textbook has been excoriated for its pro-state, antimarket bias by Mark Skousen (1997) and for its anti-state, promarket bias in Marc Linder's *Anti-Samuelson* (1977, abridged from 4 volumes in Danish). The lionization of Jeffrey Sachs by those who share his vision of how to eradicate poverty in developing countries is the other side of the process.

But the examples of Sir Cyril Burt and of T. D. Lysenko, the tyrant of Soviet agronomy and suppressor of Soviet genetics (Joravsky 1970), serve to remind us that sometimes scholars are portrayed as villains because they have done something villainous. Beyond their negative contributions to the advancement of knowledge, Burt's fake data contributed to Britain's 11+ exams by pretending to show that intelligence is innate and largely inherited, so that those who test poorly at age eleven are unsuited for advanced education, and Lysenko supported his Lamarckian arguments by having his critics imprisoned or liquidated. There have been actions and positions taken by prominent economists that, to say the least, pose problems for celebrants: Vilfredo Pareto's acceptance of a Senate seat from his former student Benito Mussolini, John Commons's anti-immigration *Races and Immigrants in America*, Fisher's (1997, vol. 14) eugenics and his (unfounded) claim of responsibility for the racist Immigration Restriction Act of 1924, Joan Robinson's naively enthusiastic books on the Great Leap Forward and the Great Proletarian Cultural Revolution, Sidney and Beatrice Webb's embrace of the Soviet Union in the late 1930s (after a lifetime of upholding social democracy against communism), and, in the exceptional case of Professor António Salazar of the University of Coimbra, four decades as a semifascist dictator, presiding over domestic repression and colonial wars. Salazar aside, the instances just cited were distinguishable from the main scholarly contributions of each of these scholars, unlike Burt, Harrison, or Lysenko.

Economics has, however, produced at least one undeniable villain (although he has left no mark as an economist): Professor Dr. Franz Six, dean of the economics faculty at the University of Berlin (as such, the academic superior of Heinrich von Stackelberg, who also accepted at least honorary rank in the SS). Professor Six was sentenced at the Nuremberg war crimes trials to twenty years' imprisonment for his role in the SS Einsatzgruppen (mobile killing squads) in Russia, but was released after four years. He had been designated to head the Reich Central Security Office (RSHA, including the Gestapo, Criminal Police, and Security Service) in Britain after the anticipated success of Operation Sea Lion, with a Special Search List of 2,300 people to arrest, a list that did not neglect British economists (Shirer 1960, 782–84).

Respectable Ancestries and Straw Men

The newly eminent in learned disciplines, like the newly rich or freshly ennobled, look to acquire ancestors suitable to their new station. Thus the new millionaires of America's Gilded Age bought family portraits from English aristocratic houses, a group of mid-nineteenth-century English artists proclaimed themselves the Pre-Raphaelite Brotherhood, and the Chancellor of the Exchequer to King James I of England proudly bore the name Sir Julius Caesar. Some retrospective identification with past economists is lightly held: Robert Lucas "once thought of myself as a kind of Austrian, but Kevin Hoover's book persuaded me that this was just a result of my misreading of Hayek and others" (interview in Snowdon and Vane 2005, 274). Despite Roy Harrod's efforts to talk Keynes out of what Harrod regarded as a tendentious glorification of fools, Keynes constructed a new intellectual ancestry for himself in *The General Theory*, a "brave army of heretics" stretching back from Silvio Gesell and the underconsumptionist John Hobson through Thomas Robert Malthus to the mercantilists. Keynes used this excursion into intellectual history to provoke those such as A. C. Pigou whom he lumped together with their predecessors back to Ricardo as classical upholders of Say's law. Eli Heckscher, whose classic (and proclassical) treatise on mercantilism provided Keynes with much material, replied indignantly to what he saw as Keynes's twisting of his research, but the ensuing reappraisals of mercantilism added to knowledge. More seriously and at vastly greater length, Karl Marx in *Theories of Surplus Value* ([1862–63] 1963–71) and Eugen von Böhm-Bawerk in *Capital and Interest* each rewrote the history of past theorizing about the source and amount of the return to ownership of capital in terms of how successful past economists had been in approaching the true theory that the historian had expounded (not of course the same true theory in the two works). Earlier, Pierre Samuel du Pont, later du Pont de Nemours, gave a triumphalist, heroic account of physiocracy in "On the Origin and Progress of a New Science" ([1768] 2003), with a tone comparable to that of other physiocrats who ranked François Quesnay's *Tableau économique* with the invention of writing. Such treatment of past thought as imperfect attempts to achieve the present way of thinking afflicts many fields, not just economics: Daniel Boorstin (1941, 428, 426) lamented "the subservience of legal historian to practicing lawyer," such that "the classifications found in legal textbooks and treatises have become the classifications for the material of legal history." The distinctive feature of the reinterpretations of the history of economics by Marx, Böhm-Bawerk, and Keynes is that, in casting themselves as heroes, they portray the past of their discipline as imperfect attempts to achieve their own personal innovation in theory. Böhm-Bawerk's dismissal in *Capital and Interest* of Turgot as holding a land fructification theory of interest, despite having previously presented a seminar paper on Turgot's justification of interest on the ground that a good at a future date is not the same commodity as the same good now, illustrates the hazards of rereading past writers from the standpoint of present heroic innovation (see Rothbard's *New Palgrave* article on time preference, and Peter Groenewegen's edition of Turgot). Groenewegen reminds us at this conference that Marshall, who particularly disapproved of Böhm-Bawerk's treatment of Turgot, set a competition for his students to find such distortions in Böhm-Bawerk's discussions of earlier economists.

Such discovery of ancestors is selective and contested: if "classical economist" means anything, David Ricardo was one, but neoclassical, new classical, and neo-Ricardian have different meanings. Ricardians, denying that government debt is part of net wealth, have no more in common with neo-Ricardians, inspired by Piero Sraffa, than the American school of free-market Austrian economists have in common with the neo-Austrian capital theorists of Europe, and perhaps less than new Keynesians share with Post Keynesians. Invoking Ricardo as a respectable ancestor for debt neutrality or alternatively for a Sraffian reconstruction of price determination with a role for demand conditions places one in the illustrious company of someone who cannot be excluded from the mainstream of economics. This is achieved at the cost of not stressing that Ricardo's statement of debt neutrality is followed by his explanation of why he did not think it held in practice or, in the Sraffian instance, of turning attention away from the marginal analysis in Ricardo's theory of differential rent and from the emphasis of mutual gains from exchange in Ricardo's numerical example of comparative advantage.

Idols of the Tribe: Local Heroes

Not only do individual economists (or scholars in other disciplines) look for respectable ancestors of their theories, but the economists (or other social, behavioral, or natural scientists) of a particular university or country celebrate their local heroes. This leads to a focus on the work of particular past economists with whom the present economists might not have identified except for the local connection, but it also leads to study and remembrance of at least a fragment of the discipline's intellectual heritage by economists who might otherwise take little note of works published before (and in some cases, also those published after) they themselves were in graduate school. The *Scandinavian Journal of Economics* or the *Scottish Journal of Political Economy* would be unlikely to welcome papers in the history of economic thought, were it not for a sense of retrospective identification with Wicksell and the Stockholm school of macroeconomics or with Adam Smith and the Scottish tradition in political economy, respectively. It would be most out of the ordinary for the director of the Cowles Foundation for Research in Economics, a mathematical economist specializing in general equilibrium with incomplete markets, to coedit, and contribute to, a conference volume on the work of a long-dead economist, except that the conference celebrated the contributions of Irving Fisher (Dimand and Geanakoplos 2005). James Tobin taught the Yale economists to appreciate their local hero: when Tobin arrived in New Haven from Harvard in 1950 (three years after Fisher's death), he found that the Yale community, like the general public, remembered Fisher more for having been very quotably wrong about the stock market in October 1929 than for his scientific achievements. A slightly earlier conference (with some overlap of participants) was held to mark the fiftieth anniversary of Fisher's death by the Irving Fisher Gesellschaft, a German society on monetary economics founded by Fisher's research assistant, the late Hans Cohrssen (Leaf and Monissen 1999).

Anniversaries combined with local heroes are particularly fertile as occasions for conferences, conference volumes, and special issues of journals, attracting the attention of economists beyond the history of economic thought to the message of a past master. Thus the bicentenary of the 1796 birth of John Rae, the pioneering capital theorist, theorist of endogenous growth and technical change, and proponent of the infant industry argument for tariff protection and subsidies, attracted the interest of economists both in his native Scotland and in Canada, where he wrote his major work (Hamouda, Lee, and Mair 1998). The anniversary years and recognition as local heroes are fortuitous but can help renew appreciation of important economists who had, for extended periods, received relatively little attention.

The 1983 centenary of Marx's death and the births of Keynes and Schumpeter was especially productive of scholarly activity of high quality, involving not only scholars of the history of economic thought but also leading economic theorists, as was also true of the 1976 bicentenary of *The Wealth of Nations*, the 1990 centenary of Marshall's *Principles of Economics*, and the bicentenary of Smith's death. Cambridge celebrated Marshall and Keynes, Scotland celebrated Smith, although smaller festivities honoring the work of these worldly philosophers also occurred elsewhere. Traditionally, the claims made at these gatherings for the uniqueness, validity, and significance of the local hero's contribution are slightly overstated, for as Dr. Johnson noted, one is not speaking upon oath in a eulogy. Nonetheless, good research gets written, published, and noticed that otherwise would not have been carried out, thoughts are stimulated, and economists, both the eminent ones invited to the celebrations and others who listen or read, are to some extent educated.

Lest we be too casual in dismissing the commemoration of anniversaries, recall that when Václav Havel "announced that he had scheduled the arrival of the West German president for 15 March, the same day as Hitler's invasion of Prague in 1939—one of the reporters noted that Havel 'liked anniversaries,' whereupon Havel immediately corrected him. 'No,' he told him, 'I did not say that I "liked anniversaries." I spoke about symbols, metaphors and a sense of dramatic structure in politics'" (Klima 1994, 64). So also in economics do symbols, metaphors, and a sense of dramatic structure aid memory and understanding.

The celebration of local heroes can be an example of what the title of Hobsbawm and Ranger 1983 terms the invention of tradition. Traditions and heroes provide cohesion and a sense of community to groups, including groups of academic researchers. The most fiercely contested rediscovery or invention of local heroes is the Chicago oral tradition of monetary economics, acclaimed in Friedman 1956. Don Patinkin challenged the existence of this in essays eventually collected in Patinkin 1981, arguing that, while Friedman and students certainly drew on such past Chicago contributions as Henry Simons on rules versus authorities in monetary policy, crucial aspects of Friedman's approach (notably money demand as a portfolio choice) stemmed from Keynes 1936 rather than from any Chicago source. David Laidler (in essays reprinted in Laidler 2003, chaps. 10 and 11) found two of the three characteristics by which Friedman characterized Chicago monetary economics of the 1930s to have also appeared outside Chicago in the analysis of Harvard economists Allyn Young and Lauchlin Currie, and of the British Treasury economist Ralph Hawtrey, who as a visiting professor in 1928–29 took over Young's Harvard teaching (Young had moved to the London School of Economics), with Young's student Currie as his assistant. George Tavlas (1997, 1998) responded vigorously to Laidler, insisting on the distinctiveness and continuity of the Chicago tradition. This controversy is notable for its intramural aspect: among those doubting the uniqueness and continuity of the Chicago tradition, Patinkin's entire university education was at the University of Chicago, Laidler is a firmly established Friedman-style monetarist (as distinct from new classical economist), and Johnson ([1971] 1978, 1972) was teaching at the University of Chicago when he questioned Friedman's account of the tradition.

1776, 1936, and All That: Simplification and Memory

Steve Fuller (2000, xi) charged that "Thomas Kuhn famously updated [the] elitist myth of humanity's collective quest by associating the great paradigmatic thresholds in the history of science with the names of revolutionary geniuses who set the pace for lesser worthies. 'Newton,' 'Lavoisier,' and 'Einstein' appear in Kuhn's own text as the originators of paradigms. 'Darwin' and other luminaries of the biological and social sciences have since been added by Kuhn's admirers." Such identifications were common long before Kuhn, and one reason for them is that Sir Isaac Newton, Antoine-Laurent Lavoisier, Albert Einstein, and Darwin, and also Adam Smith and Keynes, did in fact achieve works of synthesis and of original thought that stood out from the writings of their predecessors and contemporaries and made an impact on those working in their fields.

But another reason is pedagogical: textbooks and lectures aimed at students who are studying economics or biology, chemistry or physics or psychology, rather than studying the history of the subjects, attach names to theories and tell a bit of the history of theories to make the theories interesting and memorable to students. Attaching someone's name to a concept or model is a useful mnemonic device: the Slutsky equation; Roy's identity;

Divisia, Paasche, Laspeyres, and Fisher indexes; Allais and Ellsberg paradoxes; Fisher diagram; Gini coefficient; Lorenz, Engel, and Laffer curves; Bayes rule; Phillips curve; and Edgeworth box are easier to learn and remember with names attached, even if many more have heard of Roy's identity than could identify René Roy. The Brouwer fixed-point theorem and the Kakutani fixed-point theorem are so named not just to honor those who first stated them but also to make it easier to recall which is which. Long lists of names and subtle distinctions among individual contributions and points of view will not serve the pedagogical purpose. Leopold von Ranke's dictum *wie es eigentlich gewesen*, even if its attainment was imaginable (consider a map on a scale of one to one), would be beside the point for the use of names and potted histories in the textbooks that shape the vague impression of a discipline's past held by those working in the discipline, far more than it is shaped by books and articles specifically about the history of the discipline. Such convenient labels also convey unequivocally to the student the impression that the person whose name is attached to the concept had done a Good Thing, in the sense of *1066 and All That* (Sellar and Yeatman 1930) and of Martha Stewart.

One consequence of the pedagogical limit of one name per concept is to overlook Mertonian multiple discoveries, the actual or apparent independent discoveries of identical or closely related concepts, such as the appearance of the classical theory of rent in separate pamphlets by Malthus, Sir Edward West, Robert Torrens, and Ricardo in London in February 1815; or the independent demonstrations by Phillip Wicksteed in 1888 and Fisher in 1892 that a measurable utility function exists if a person's utility function is additive in its arguments; or presentations of the kinked demand curve for oligopoly by Paul Sweezy and by R. L. Hall and C. J. Hitch, both in 1939 (Merton 1973; Stigler 1982, chap. 9). John Hobson and Albert Mummery, Charles Bickerdike, Thomas Nixon Carver, Ralph Hawtrey, and Albert Aftalion expressed the accelerator theory of net investment in some form before John Maurice Clark's 1917 statement of the theory attracted general attention, while the attribution of comparative advantage to Robert Torrens in 1815 or David Ricardo in 1817 is still hotly debated in *HOPE*. The shorthand phrase "Cobb-Douglas production function" is useful in getting students to remember the multiplicative production function, a purpose not assisted by telling them that Knut Wicksell used that function in a review article in Swedish in 1924, four years before Charles Cobb and Paul Douglas published their article (Wicksell's priority was recorded as early as Schumpeter 1954, 1042).

Not only are multiple independent discoveries (simultaneous or not) obscured by the need for a single memorable name to attach to a concept, so is the more general fact that scholars and scientists interact, building on and responding to each other's contributions. Milton Friedman (1957, ix) was clear, generous, and emphatic in explaining how the permanent income hypothesis of consumption emerged from intellectual exchanges among a group of economists: "Miss Reid, with characteristic enthusiasm, persistence, and ingenuity, proceeded to put to a critical test the hypothesis that had been evolving out of the conversations [between Friedman, Rose Director Friedman, Margaret Gilpin Reid, and Dorothy Stahl Brady]. When it seemed to be passing the test with flying colors, she pressed me to write up the underlying theory, so that she could refer to it in a paper presenting her conclusions. This book is the result, and though my hand held the pen, and though I am fully responsible for all its defects, it is in essential respects a joint product of the group, each member of which not only participated in its development but read and criticized the manuscript in its various stages." Similarly, in his Nobel lecture, Franco Modigliani (1985, 262) agreed that "the highly imaginative analysis of Margaret Reid . . . was an important source of inspiration, both for the Life Cycle and for the roughly contemporaneous Permanent Income Hypothesis (PIH) of Milton Friedman (1957)." However, if only one name becomes attached to a concept, it will be the name of the person who held the pen or made the largest (or most noticeable) contribution. Textbooks (and the Nobel committee) attributed the permanent income hypothesis to Friedman and the life cycle hypothesis to Modigliani, no matter how clear those two Nobel laureates were about the valuable roles of others (but Reid did become a Distinguished Fellow of the AEA in 1980, the first woman so chosen). Friedman and Modigliani tried to draw attention to the thick history of their subject (of course, not all leading theorists do so), but there is no useful role for that in the consumption function chapter of an intermediate macroeconomics textbook. Another factor is the far greater attention by textbooks and histories of economics to theorists than to empirical researchers such as Brady and Reid, and perhaps also a correlation between gender and visibility. David Laidler's *Fabricating the Keynesian Revolution* (1999), placing Keynes's *General Theory* in the context of interwar theorizing about monetary equilibrium, economic fluctuations, and the causes and remedies of unemployment, stands as a formidable protest against the implicit representation in economics textbooks (other than those specifically about the history of the subject) of the history of economics as a series of revolutionary advances by isolated, heroic geniuses. Similarly, Schumpeter (1954, 184) insisted that "the fact is that the *Wealth of Nations* does not contain a single *analytic* idea, principle, or method that was entirely new in 1776," although "Smith was no doubt equal to the task of co-ordinating them without further help from anyone" (183). It is convenient to treat Smith in textbooks and lectures (for economics courses other than those in history of economic thought) as if he created all the elements of his system of theory and policy by himself in 1776, although at least some students may wonder that laissez-faire, often used as a shorthand summary of Smithian policy, does not sound Scottish (see Clark 2003).

The purposes of the present do not only manufacture heroes through the pedagogical convenience of attaching a single name to a theory. There is also an incentive to construct retrospective straw men to be defeated by heroes. The concept of mercantilism as "the mercantile system of political economy" (as distinct from variegated pamphlets or actions of assorted German cameralists, English merchants lobbying for special privileges, and French administrators such as Colbert) was formulated by Smith in *The Wealth of Nations* as a systematization of all that he did not like about the preceding two centuries of public policy and economic argument. Smith made mercantilism more unified and systematic than it had ever been before, so that he could ridicule and overthrow it. The emergence of the field of evolutionary biology involved treating Darwin and Darwinism as heroic, Lamarck and Lamarckism as villainous. Adopting the "as if" methodology of Milton Friedman, Harry Johnson ([1971] 1978, 186) asked in his Ely lecture,

> suppose I wished to start a counter-revolution against the Keynesian revolution in monetary theory, how would I go about it—and specifically, what could I learn about the technique from the revolution itself? To pose the question this way is, of course, to fly in the face of currently accepted professional ethics, according to which purely scientific considerations and not political considerations are presumed to motivate scientific work; but I can claim the protection of the "as if" methodology against any implication of a slur on individual character or a denigration of scientific work.

Both the Keynesian revolution and the monetarist counterrevolution benefited from "the existence of an established orthodoxy which is clearly inconsistent with the most salient facts of reality, and yet is sufficiently confident of its intellectual power to attempt to explain those facts, and in its efforts to do so exposes its incompetence in a ludicrous fashion" (186). Johnson held that existing, pre-Keynesian monetary theory could have adequately analyzed the British unemployment of the 1920s and 1930s as the result of misguided monetary policy and a fixed, overvalued exchange rate. Nonetheless, "eminent British economists sought to explain mass unemployment as a consequence of the satiation of real human wants. . . . Other economists viewed the depression as punishment justly visited upon enterprises and individuals for past sins of speculation and erroneous micro-economic decision making" (187). Other essays by Johnson (in Johnson and Johnson 1978) make clear that the first explanation refers to Dennis Robertson's Macmillan Committee testimony in 1930, and the second to Hayek 1931 and Robbins 1934. Keynesian economics was similarly unable to analyze inflation, according to Johnson ([1971] 1978), who made no mention of his 1958 claim that Keynes's *How to Pay for the War* provided a better framework for analyzing inflation than did the quantity theory (see Dimand 2001).

The second requirement for a successful intellectual revolution or counterrevolution "was the production of an apparently new theory that nevertheless absorbed all that was valid in the existing theory while so far as possible giving these valid concepts confusing new names" (Johnson [1971] 1978, 194). Like Patinkin (1981), Johnson saw Friedman's 1956 restatement of the quantity theory of money as a generalization of Keynes's concept of liquidity preference, not a rejection of Keynes in favor of an earlier Chicago oral tradition of monetary theory, since Keynes had been, in 1936, the first to explicitly write money demand as a function of aggregate income and the interest rate and, like Friedman but unlike Chicago monetarists of the 1930s, treated money demand as a portfolio choice among assets. Johnson (1972, 60) held that "the starting point was a restatement of the quantity theory of money as a capital-theoretic formulation of the demand for money, absorbing the best ideas of Keynes and Irving Fisher, and involving neither of the two assumptions that had been the gravamen of Keynesian ridiculing of previous versions of the theory—the assumptions that the economy naturally tends towards the condition of full employment, which was declared to be a matter of supply response not properly belonging to monetary theory, and that the velocity of circulation is a parametric constant subject to arbitrary variations, which was replaced by the assertion that velocity is a behavioral functional relationship of a few variables that have to be appropriately measured." (If "full employment" is replaced by "natural rate of unemployment," the first assumption would later be reaccepted by monetarist and new classical economists.)

Johnson ([1971] 1978, 197–98) decried "the invention of a Chicago oral tradition that was alleged to have preserved understanding of the fundamental truth among a small band of initiated through the dark years of the Keynesian despotism. . . . There was no lonely light constantly burning in a secret shrine on the Midway, encouraging the faithful to assemble in waiting for the day when the truth could safely be revealed to the masses: the candle was made, and not merely lit, only when its light had a chance of penetrating far and wide and attracting new converts to the old-time religion." Even George Tavlas (1998, 217–18), insisting on Friedman's roots in a continuing Chicago tradition, accepts "an element of truth" in Friedman's indebtedness to Keynesian liquidity preference and claims no more than that "Friedman's transmission mechanism was . . . part Keynes and part 1930s Chicago" (perhaps because, as Robert Leeson has pointed out, Keynes's *Treatise on Money* was part of what was taught at Chicago in the 1930s).

Johnson also saw Keynes's marginal efficiency of capital as, like Fisher's rate of return over costs, no more than a renamed marginal product of capital, granting that Keynes placed more emphasis than his predecessors on the uncertainty of expected returns and less on physical productivity. Such confusions help a new theory satisfy "the third criterion for success, a degree of difficulty of understanding just sufficient to deter the old and to challenge and reward the young, and hence to open the avenues of professional advancement for the ambitious" (Johnson [1971] 1978, 195). Further, a successful theory is one that provides employment for budding econometricians by giving them an empirical relationship to estimate such as the Keynesian consumption function or a stable money demand function: "Moreover, since intelligent young men and women will persevere until they succeed in finding statistical validation of an allegedly important theoretical relationship, and will then interpret their results as evidence in favor of the theory that originally suggested the relationship, their efforts will inevitably be extremely favorable to the theory in question" (196).

Conclusion

Schumpeter (1954, 481) noted that "Keynes's partiality for Malthus, though morally admirable—for those are few who extol a forerunner and Keynes believed Malthus to have been a forerunner of his—went to lengths that are not much less unreasonable than was Marx's hatred. And right from the publication of the *Essay on Population* to this day, Malthus had the good fortune—for this *is* good fortune—to be the subject of equally unreasonable, contradictory appraisals. He was a benefactor of humanity. He was a fiend. He was a profound thinker. He was a dunce." Why did Schumpeter consider these portrayals as hero or villain (such as Marx and Keynes received themselves) to be good fortune? These "passionate appraisals" showed that Malthus's work had "stirred people's minds" (481). Lionizing and demonizing Malthus or Marx or Keynes (or Samuelson or Friedman or Krugman), however distorting it may be, is more productive than apathy. The distortions can be extreme, as with Allan Chase's *Legacy of Malthus: The Social Costs of the New Scientific Racism* ([1977] 1980), an otherwise informative historical exposé of the American eugenics movement (awarded the Anisfield-Wolf Award in Race Relations) disfigured by a conviction that scientific racism must somehow stem from Malthus and that, because Edwin Chadwick wished to improve sanitary conditions through government action, he and Malthus must have been enemies (see also Meek 1953 for Marx's attacks on Malthus). Overly enthusiastic readings of Malthus as a premature Keynesian have failed to notice that Malthus did not distinguish a decision to save from a decision to invest and so did not analyze the forces that bring saving into equality with planned investment. Nonetheless, these treatments of Malthus as villain or hero indicated that people cared enough to think about him and about the issues he raised, as when Keynes, revising an earlier paper on Malthus for inclusion in his *Essays in Biography*, was moved to think about the question of effective demand, or when Charles Darwin and Alfred Russel Wallace were (independently of each other) inspired to think about natural selection after they had read Malthus on population.

As with Malthus, so it is with other villains and heroes, including local heroes. The process of demonizing and lionizing produces one-sided, selective readings, the fabrication of intellectual revolutions led by the heroes overstating discontinuities with caricatures of past orthodoxies, or the construction of invented traditions establishing continuity with real or imagined respectable orthodoxies of the past. "An exaggerated veneration for an exceptional individual poses an insidious temptation," warns Lucy Hughes-Hallett in her recent *Heroes: Saviours, Traitors, and Supermen* (2005). "It allows worshipers to abnegate responsibility, looking to the great man for salvation or for fulfillment which they should more properly be working to accomplish for themselves" (as quoted in Scott 2005). But the creation of heroes and villains has also served a function for the history of economics, attracting attention to an intellectual heritage that would otherwise be even more neglected by a present-minded discipline than it otherwise is, and provides occasion and stimulus for research and reflection as well as for unreflective celebration and vilification. This conclusion should not shock economists: it only states that an activity that continues to be carried on must have some benefits, not just costs.

References

Backhouse, R., and R. Middleton, eds. 2000. *Exemplary Economists.* 2 vols. Cheltenham, U.K.: Elgar.

Blythe, W. 2006. *To Hate Like This Is to Be Happy Forever: A Thoroughly Obsessive, Intermittently Uplifting, and Occasionally Unbiased Account of the Duke–North Carolina Basketball Rivalry.* New York: HarperCollins.

Boorstin, D. 1941. Tradition and Method in Legal History. *Harvard Law Review* 54:424–36.

Breit, W., and B. Hirsch, eds. 2004. *Lives of the Laureates: Eighteen Nobel Economists.* 4th ed. Cambridge, Mass.: MIT Press.

Chase, A. [1977] 1980. *The Legacy of Malthus: The Social Costs of the New Scientific Racism.* Reprint, Urbana: University of Illinois Press.

Clark, H., ed. 2003. *Commerce, Culture, and Liberty: Readings on Capitalism before Adam Smith.* Indianapolis: Liberty Fund.

Dimand, R. 2001. Harry G. Johnson as a Chronicler of the Keynesian Revolution. *American Journal of Economics and Sociology* 60.3:667–91.

Dimand, R., and J. Geanakoplos, eds. 2005. *Celebrating Irving Fisher: The Legacy of a Great Economist.* Malden, Mass.: Blackwell.

Dobbs, Z. 1969. *Keynes at Harvard: Economic Deception as a Political Credo.* 2nd ed. West Sayville, N.Y.: Probe Research.

Du Pont de Nemours, P. S. [1768] 2003. On the Origin and Progress of a New Science. In Clark 2003.

Fisher, I. 1997. *The Works of Irving Fisher.* Edited by W. J. Barber. 14 vols. London: Pickering & Chatto.

Friedman, M., ed. 1956. *Studies in the Quantity Theory of Money.* Chicago: University of Chicago Press.

———. 1957. *A Theory of the Consumption Function.* Princeton, N.J.: Princeton University Press.

Fuller, S. 2000. *Thomas Kuhn: A Philosophical History for Our Times.* Chicago: University of Chicago Press.

Hamouda, O. F., C. Lee, and D. Mair, eds. 1998. *The Economics of John Rae.* London: Routledge.

Hayek, F. A. 1931. *Prices and Production.* London: Routledge.

Hearnshaw, L. S. 1979. *Cyril Burt, Psychologist.* Ithaca, N.Y.: Cornell University Press.

Herrnstein, R. J., and C. Murray. 1994. *The Bell Curve: Intelligence and Class Structure in American Life*. New York: Free Press.

Hobsbawm, E., and T. Ranger, eds. 1983. *The Invention of Tradition*. Cambridge: Cambridge University Press.

Hughes-Hallett, L. 2005. *Heroes: Saviours, Traitors, and Supermen*. Toronto: Viking Canada.

Johnson, E. S., and H. G. Johnson. 1978. *The Shadow of Keynes*. Chicago: University of Chicago Press.

Johnson, H. G. 1972. *Inflation and the Monetarist Controversy*. Amsterdam: North-Holland.

———. [1971] 1978. The Keynesian Revolution and the Monetarist Counter-revolution. In Johnson and Johnson 1978.

Joravsky, D. 1970. *The Lysenko Affair*. Cambridge, Mass.: Harvard University Press.

Keynes, J. M. 1919. *The Economic Consequences of the Peace*. London: Macmillan.

———. 1936. *The General Theory of Employment, Interest, and Money*. London: Macmillan.

Kindleberger, C. P. 1991. *The Life of an Economist*. Cambridge, Mass.: Blackwell.

Klein, L. R. 1947. *The Keynesian Revolution*. New York: Macmillan.

Klima, I. 1994. *The Spirit of Prague and Other Essays*. London: Granta Books.

Laidler, D. 1999. *Fabricating the Keynesian Revolution: Studies of the Inter-War Literature on Money, the Cycle, and Unemployment*. Cambridge: Cambridge University Press.

———. 2003. *Macroeconomics in Retrospect: The Selected Essays of David Laidler*. Cheltenham, U.K.: Elgar.

Leaf, H.-E., and H. G. Monissen, eds. 1999. *The Economics of Irving Fisher*. Cheltenham, U.K.: Elgar.

Linder, M., with J. Sensat. 1977. *Anti-Samuelson*. 2 vols. New York: Urizen Books.

Mantoux, E. 1952. *The Carthaginian Peace, or The Economic Consequences of Mr. Keynes*. New York: Scribner's Sons.

———. [1937] 1977. Mr. Keynes' "General Theory." Translated by P. Cortney and H. Hazlitt. In *The Critics of Keynesian Economics*, edited by H. Hazlitt. 2nd ed. New Rochelle, N.Y.: Arlington House.

Marx, K. [1862–63] 1963–71. *Theories of Surplus Value*, 3 pts. Translated by E. Burns and S. Ryazanskaya. Moscow: Progress.

Meek, R. L., ed. 1953. *Marx and Engels on Malthus*. London: Lawrence and Wishart.

Merton, R. K. 1973. *Sociology of Science*. Chicago: University of Chicago Press.

Modigliani, F. 1985. *Life Cycle, Individual Thrift, and the Wealth of Nations*. Stockholm: Nobel Foundation.

Paret, P., ed. 1986. *Makers of Modern Strategy from Machiavelli to the Nuclear Age*. Princeton, N.J.: Princeton University Press.

Patinkin, D. 1981. *Essays on and in the Chicago Tradition*. Durham, N.C.: Duke University Press.

Robbins, L. 1934. *The Great Depression*. London: Macmillan.

Rothbard, M. 1972. *America's Great Depression*. Los Angeles: Nash.

Schumpeter, J. A. 1954. *History of Economic Analysis*, edited by E. B. Schumpeter. New York: Oxford University Press.

———. [1942] 1987. *Capitalism, Socialism, and Democracy*. 6th ed. London: Unwin Paperbacks.

Scott, C. 2005. No Man Is a Hero to His Hallett. *Toronto Globe and Mail*, 5 November.

Sellar, W. C., and R. J. Yeatman. 1930. *1066 and All That: A Memorable History of England, Comprising All the Parts You Can Remember, including 103 Good Things, 5 Bad Kings, and 2 Genuine Dates*. London: Methuen.

Shirer, W. L. 1960. *The Rise and Fall of the Third Reich*. New York: Simon and Schuster.

Skousen, M. 1997. The Perseverance of Paul Samuelson's *Economics*. *Journal of Economic Perspectives* 11.2:137–52.

Snowdon, B., and H. R. Vane. 2005. *Modern Macroeconomics: Its Origins, Development, and Current State*. Cheltenham, U.K.: Elgar.

Sowell, T. 2000. *A Personal Odyssey*. New York: Free Press.

Stigler, G. J. 1982. *The Economist as Preacher and Other Essays*. Chicago: University of Chicago Press.

Tavlas, G. 1997. Chicago, Harvard, and the Doctrinal Foundations of Monetary Economics. *Journal of Political Economy* 105.1:153–77.

———. 1998. Was the Monetarist Tradition Invented? *Journal of Economic Perspectives* 12.4:211–22.

Vauban, S. 1839. *Abrégé des services du maréchal de Vauban, fait par lui en 1703*. Edited by A. Augoyat. Paris.

The Group Life as a Genre of Economists' Life Writing

William Coleman

This essay explores the lessons of writing a "group life" of economists: *Giblin's Platoon: The Trials and Triumph of the Economist in Australian Public Life* (Coleman, Cornish, and Hagger 2006). This book tells the story of the personal and intellectual bond between four men who dominated economic thought, policymaking, and institution building in Australia over the three decades up to 1950: L. F. Giblin (1872–1951), J. B. Brigden (1887–1950), D. B. Copland (1894–1963), and Roland Wilson (1904–1996).

Giblin's Platoon illustrates both the possibilities of and the challenges faced by the group life as a genre of life writing in the history of economics. Its research also raises questions about the various and alternative grounds for writing the lives of economists and how the group life may provide another ground.

A Brief History of Their Group Life

The key figure of the group at hand, L. F. Giblin, was born in Tasmania in 1872, the son of the colony's premier, chief justice, and treasurer. Educated at University College, London, between 1890 and 1892, Giblin appears to have formed there a friendship with Edward Garnett, whose son, David ("Bunny"), was later to provide Giblin with an entrée to Bloomsbury. At

The author is indebted to the comments of Roger Backhouse, Robert Dimand, Susan Howson, and Roy Weintraub.

History of Political Economy 39 (annual suppl.) DOI 10.1215/00182702-2006-040

King's College, Cambridge, between 1892 and 1896, Giblin secured a senior optimes in the mathematical tripos. After more than a decade of roving through remote corners of the British Empire, he returned to England in 1916 as Captain Giblin, where he met and befriended John Maynard Keynes at Charleston. At about this time Private Brigden, while recuperating in an Oxford hospital from wounds suffered on the Western Front, was being befriended by Edward Cannan and F. Y. Edgeworth. With the benefit of their patronage, Brigden undertook and secured a BA at Oxford in economics and jurisprudence. In 1919, Giblin was appointed to the council of the University of Tasmania, where he secured the appointment of James Brigden to the faculty of commerce and the promotion of Douglas Berry Copland to professor of that faculty. Copland and Giblin then coaxed a very bright but very uncertain seventeen-year-old Roland Wilson to undertake a bachelor of commerce. Later Giblin, Copland, and Brigden managed to persuade this "reluctant young man" (Wilson 1976) to undertake further study outside Australia: a DPhil at Oxford, followed quickly by a PhD at Chicago, under Jacob Viner.

Within a short spacc of timc "thc platoon" produccd thrcc publications that provided important insights into international economics: *Capital Imports and the Terms of Trade* (Wilson 1931), *Australia, 1930* (Giblin 1930), and *The Australian Tariff* (Brigden et al. 1929). The remainder of their careers, however, lay in public service, and those careers may be considered to constitute the arrival of the economist in Australian public life. Giblin secured Wilson's entry as the first economist into the Australian public service proper and Brigden as the first economist to head a government department (the Department of Social Services). During the 1930s and 1940s the four designed and saw implemented "fiscal equalization" within the Australian federation, smoothed Australia's reluctant entry into the International Monetary Fund, reformed her gimcrack public administration, educated her treasurers in Keynesian public finance, and successfully championed the inclusion in the United Nations Charter of a pledge to full employment.

The Importance of Being Important

The elements above are the skeleton of a tellable tale. But they may seem to lack the ingredient that is normally expected of any monograph-length biography that will contribute to the history of economics: exceptional achievement within economics. As typically understood, the biographer's task is to record and, it is to be hoped, explain in some measure the special achievement of the subject. But all four figures in this biography are, at least in terms of the history of economic thought, minor figures. So in embarking on *Giblin's Platoon* the authors were, as historians of economics, put to reflect: what is it about these figures that makes them worth writing about at length? More generally, under what circumstances might minor figures warrant life writing? Or, to put it differently, by what means can minor figures become interesting? There are a number of commonly used means available to biographers.

Reflected glory. One common means by which minor figures are afforded interest is through their association with the glorious. Thus Nelly Ternan becomes interesting, not only during her association with Charles Dickens but also before and after it. Similarly, we become interested in Lydia Keynes "as an important person in her own right and of special interest as the woman who shared Keynes' life" (Butlin 1951, 96). "Reflected glory" is a source of interest in *Giblin's Platoon*: it records its subjects' extensive relations with Viner, Cannan, Edgeworth, J. A. Schumpeter, and above all Keynes. Whatever Keynes does is interesting, and Keynes crops up in eight of the book's ten chapters: meeting each of the four, conferring with them, disagreeing with them, and (in the midst of the Depression) seriously disappointing them.

The defect of reflected glory as a rationale for biography is that to make some figure worthy of biography by virtue of association to some source of glory really requires that the association be important to the source of glory. And from the point of view of intellectual history, it seems doubtful that a significant intellectual relationship was successfully sustained between Giblin and Keynes, despite the distinct personal sympathy between the two. Intellectually, they were separated by a gulf: Keynes was a theorist, and Giblin was an empiricist. Keynes had no interest in Giblin's work on the multiplier or protectionism (Coleman, Cornish, and Hagger 2006, 96–103).

Flattering analogy. Another means of conferring interest on a minor figure is latching a major reputation on to a minor one: thus Taussig becomes "America's Marshall" (Schumpeter 1954b). Might Giblin be pronounced Australia's Irving Fisher? There are some parallels in the two stories. Their dates are similar (1867–1947 vs. 1872–1951); both were raised as Congregationalists; both suffered the loss of a father before maturity; both were eugenicists; both studied mathematics before entering economics; both were quantitative and empirical (Giblin was Australian academia's sole member of the Econometric Society during the 1930s). But the authors of *Giblin's Platoon* recoil at such a comparison. And we did so because these supposedly flattering analogies are actually diminishing rather than heightening. One might aspire to be Venezuela's greatest novelist. But who wants to be Venezuela's Dickens?

Not minor, neglected. Another approach is to increase the subject's significance by arguing that he or she is not so much a minor figure as a neglected figure (see, e.g., Fletcher [2000] on Robertson). We move, in other words, into the territory of revaluations. *Giblin's Platoon* engages in revaluations. The authors have explored some connections between the four's theorizing and theorizing of greater recognition. We contend that in the late 1920s the four made three memorable forays into international economics, which in two cases had significant ramifications.

The Export Multiplier

Authoritative accounts of the multiplier's genesis have, for many years, granted that Giblin, with the assistance of Copland and Brigden, developed a version of "the multiplier" before Richard Kahn (Wright 1956; Dimand 1988; Moggridge 1993).[1] Giblin's version—which had imports as the only leakage and exports as the only injection—was published in April 1930 as *Australia, 1930*, fifteen months before the Cambridge multiplier was in print and several months before the Cambridge multiplier was conceived, in the summer of 1930. Giblin, Copland, and Brigden deployed their multiplier concept throughout the early years of the Depression. Indeed, they deployed it to predict the magnitude of the Depression. On 16 September 1929, five weeks before the Wall Street crash, Brigden spoke in Sydney to the conservative Constitutional Association on the economic position of Australia and foretold the approaching calamity with striking prescience. Using a multiplier of two, he predicted that the recent reduction in export prices and capital inflow spelled a fall in Australian national income in 1930 "at least equal to 10 percent" (Coleman, Cornish, and Hagger 2006, 96–103).

But the question for historians of economics is, is Giblin's multiplier part of the story of Keynesian economics?

1. Giblin's closest contestant for priority is Jens Warming (Boserup 1969). For pre-1914 anticipators, see Wright 1956, Goodwin 1962, and Hegeland 1954.

The history of Keynesian economics would seem to reply, no. Although Giblin's priority is conceded, his multiplier is largely ignored in the historiography of Keynes's *General Theory.* Thus Don Patinkin (1982, 1993, 1994) in his various studies of the birth of the multiplier never mentions Giblin. Robert Skidelsky's biography of Keynes mentions Giblin's multiplier only once—and only by implication, in a footnote.[2]

This position seems just, for there is no positive evidence that Keynes or any of his circle read, or were even aware of, Giblin's multiplier.[3] Nevertheless, given Giblin's close links to Keynes and King's College, it is legitimate to speculate about the possibility of a connection. It is intellectually legitimate to be tantalized by the fact that King's College library does contain a copy of *Australia, 1930.* Giblin himself sent it, and it arrived in June 1930.[4]

Nevertheless, in the absence of any further evidence, the historian of economic thought should record the two multipliers as "doubletons."

"The Second Terms of Trade"

Roland Wilson's *Capital Imports and the Terms of Trade of 1931,* published with the good offices of Giblin and Copland, planted an acorn that grew into a decent-sized oak. In this study Wilson began a thread of discussion of the relations between capital inflows and the price of tradables to nontradables, which was to culminate in the 1970s with notions of the Dutch Disease and the Gregory Thesis.

The starting point of Wilson's book is the impact of capital flows on the relative price of exportables and importables: the familiar "terms of trade." However, Wilson's interests led him to examine the impact of capital flows on a "second" relative price: the relative price of tradables and nontradables. The impact of capital flows on this "second terms of trade" seems to have been previously uninvestigated. Wilson's analysis began with the observation that capital inflow amounted to a transfer of purchasing power from the lender country to the borrower country. As the borrower country's propensity to consume the borrower country's nontradables would surely exceed the lender country's propensity to consume the borrower's

2. Dimand (1988, 105–8) does give a detailed treatment of Giblin's multiplier.

3. The only positive evidence for any awareness of Giblin's multiplier at Cambridge is in the 1933 doctoral dissertation of Ronald Walker, an Australian student at St. John's, Cambridge, that drew on Giblin's multiplier (Cairncross 1998).

4. The King's College copy of *Australia, 1930* records that it was "Presented by the Author."

nontradables, this shift in purchasing power toward the borrowing country must increase the demand for its nontradables, and so their price relative to tradables.

It was Australian economists who were to cultivate Wilson's insight into the second terms of trade, especially Trevor Swan (1918–1989), who was appointed in 1950 as the foundation professor in economics at the Research School of Economics at the Australian National University (ANU), after Wilson had declined the position. In early 1950s Canberra, the new professor was in regular contact with the now senior mandarin of the Treasury. The first fruit of Swan's cultivation of Wilson's thesis was the Swan diagram (Swan [1955] 1963), which demonstrated how, in a neo-Keynesian context, capital inflows would necessitate an appreciation in the value of services (i.e., nontradables). Wilfred Salter (1929–1963), at the ANU's Research School in Social Sciences (RSSS) from 1956 until 1959, recast the same ideas in neoclassical form in the Salter diagram (Salter 1959). But the most significant revival came with Swan's return to the public stage in the early 1970s, after some "difficult years," with his "Overseas Investment in Australia: 'Treasury Economic Paper No. 1'" in the *Economic Record*.

> This paper might be labelled No. 2, for the first on the subject was published by Roland Wilson in 1931 . . . [when] . . . he disputed and overturned the established views on capital imports and terms of trade held by Taussig, Viner, Keynes. . . . An important condition for running such a [current account] deficit . . . is that our domestic costs and prices should rise relative to the prices of importables and exportables. This truth . . . is the one asserted against the previous orthodoxy by Roland Wilson. (Swan 1972, 282)

The key application of the notions that Swan had cultivated was now about to take place, in the Gregory Thesis. Trained in international economics, R. G. Gregory had joined the RSSS in 1971. In his paper "Some Implications of the Growth of the Mineral Sector" (Gregory 1976), he pressed a simple but socially significant implication of Wilson's thesis: that an increase in the value of nontradables would cause a reduction in production and incomes in the import-competing sector. The paper resonated sharply with current events. Booming values in the prices of fuels during the 1970s and 1980s and the associated inflows to develop them had raised the prospect of deindustrialization. The ideas were given wide currency by Max Corden (Corden and Neary 1982) using the Salter diagram, which Corden had had a hand in devising.

The "Australian Case for Protection" and the Stolper-Samuelson Theorem

Brigden, Giblin, and Copland were coauthors of a semiofficial monograph of 1929, *The Australian Tariff: An Economic Enquiry*, which was to advance an "Australian Case for Protection" that was to "set off an analytical controversy that has helped shape the discovery of what has come to be known as modern international trade theory" (Samuelson 1981, 147; see also Cain 1973; Manger 1981; Irwin 1996).

One landmark in the modern theory of international trade was the 1941 proof of Wolfgang Stolper and Paul Samuelson that higher tariffs would unambiguously increase real wages if the country's import-competing sector had a higher labor–capital labor ratio than the export-competing sector. The old protectionist notion that "protection protects high wages" seemed suddenly to have a solid theoretical foundation. The *Enquiry* of 1929 seems highly significant here because it had grated certain authorities in neoclassical trade (such as Jacob Viner) by plainly contending that higher protection *did* increase real wages.

The argument behind the *Enquiry*'s contention was first advanced by Brigden (1925). In Brigden's model, labor is assumed to operate with diminishing marginal productivity in food, but with constant marginal returns in manufactures. Given this, increasing tariffs on manufactures will not reduce the marginal productivity of labor in manufactures (by assumption) and so will not reduce the wage in terms of manufactures. However, with manufactures now more valuable in terms of food, there is reallocation of labor from food and toward manufactures. The marginal product of labor in food is thereby increased. The upshot is that the manufactures wage is unchanged, and the food wage is increased. The utility of the worker (i.e., the "standard of living") must rise, as long as the worker consumes some nonzero quantity of food. As the *Enquiry* distinctly asserted, on its first page, in Australia's present circumstances, free trade would lower her "standard of living."

The *Enquiry* was widely reviewed but little heeded. It seems to have been preserved from oblivion by an attempt to ensure its oblivion. Karl Anderson (1938) sought to comprehensively dispose of the Australian case for protection in a paper in the *Quarterly Journal of Economics.* Marion Crawford Samuelson (1939) advanced a riposte to Anderson's attempted rebuttal of the report. In referring to the "Australian case," M. C. Samuelson never mentions names or publications. P. A. Samuelson (1981, 151) later wrote, "With great probability, M. C. had never read the 1929

Report." Samuelson (1981, 153) merely says, noncommitally, she "may have" read Copland's 1931 summary of the *Enquiry*.

In 1941 Samuelson wrote with Stolper, and Marion as amanuensis, "Protection and Real Wages" (Stolper and Samuelson 1941). The authors review the literature on this issue, the great bulk of which is hostile to the thesis that protection increases real wages, and refer to some previous arguments that have a similarity with Brigden's.[5] The authors do not refer to the *Enquiry*, and Samuelson later stated that he did not read it. In the conclusion he suggests the Australian economy may be illustrative of the Stolper-Samuelson theorem and refers the reader without any further explication to the papers of Copland, M. C. Samuelson, and Anderson.

What is to be concluded? It is helpful to make a distinction between the *thesis* of the case and the *argument* of the case. We contend the Australian-case-for-protection *argument* had no significance for the development of "modern trade theory." First, Paul Samuelson had not read the *Enquiry*. Second, Samuelson was, in any case, already aware of the older literature coming to conclusions that resembled those of the *Enquiry*. Third, and most important, the *Enquiry* was irrelevant to the argument of modern trade theory, as "modern" trade theory turns on the mobility of capital between sectors, but capital and its mobility is totally ignored in the *Enquiry*.[6] Nevertheless, it is plausible that the case's *thesis* was significant for the development of modern trade theory. In the expectant and restless atmosphere of postwar theorizing, the *Enquiry* aired, with the help of commonplace economic principles and empirical evidence, the notion that protection increased real wages, a notion that was effectively defended from one line of criticism by M. C. Samuelson. A possibility had materialized. In P. A. Samuelson's (1987, 241) own words: "I at least had very much in mind at the time of the Stolper-Samuelson investigations the definitive 1939 findings by Marion Samuelson that verified the correctness of the 'Australian case for the tariff.'"

Alternative Rationales for Biography

But whatever the four contributed to theory, nobody would describe Giblin, Brigden, Copland, or Wilson as "theorists" by vocation. They had some

5. That marginal productivities might be such that a tariff reduction could reduce real wages had been previously anticipated in 1887 in the *Principles of Political Economy* of Henry Sidgwick. For further discussion, see Coleman, Cornish, and Hagger 2006, 64.

6. Brigden's case may be considered a "degenerate" special case of the Stolper-Samuelson economy, where the import-competing sector has no capital requirement at all.

bright ideas that they pursued so far, but not far enough. It appears that a rationale for writing their lives in terms of exceptional achievement is still lacking.

When Everybody Is Somebody . . .

One response to this lack is to repudiate exceptional achievement as a criterion for life writing. This might be done by rejecting exceptional achievement as conventionally conceived. This rejection would begin with the insistence that importance always rests, at bottom, on some value judgment, and value judgments are notoriously heterogeneous.

One way to put the implication of value heterogeneity is to assert that "all heroes are local heroes." Every city has its own god, every tribe its own fetish. Some heroes may pretend to be universal, but in truth, values are so heterogeneous that that is only pretense. In this mosaic of contrary values, everyone is big, and no one is big, at the same time.

Is such a position tenable? Values may be so fragmented as to make it so. And there is sufficient fragmentation of values such that some putative universal heroes are subject to controversy. To give a drastic example, Keynes was very differently esteemed in France and Germany in the interwar period. In the postwar period, different valuations across the Atlantic were brought out by the publication of the third volume of Skidelsky's biography of Keynes. One person's hero is another person's villain (Dimand, this volume).

Nevertheless, it is doubtful if values are so fragmented among historians of economic thought that all heroes are local heroes.

"Not Histories, but Lives"

Another way to discard the exceptional achievement criterion would be to substitute a different theory of the subject matter of biography. An alternative statement of biography's purpose would be the delineation of some valuable individuality. This might be called the Plutarchian theory of biography. "My intention is not to write histories, but lives" (Plutarch [ca. 75] 1973).[7] In this view, the test and triumph of the biographer's art consists of the full communication of the subject's individuality. If the biographer

7. "My task is to dwell on actions that illuminate the workings of his soul . . . a chance remark or joke may reveal far more of a man's character than the mere feat of winning battles. . . . I leave to others the story of his greatest struggle" (Plutarch [ca. 75] 1973, 252).

does not get the subject's personality right, then the biography has failed. Or, if the subject's personality only suddenly peeps through when the subject is quoted, then the biographer has not done well. That is why the previous biographical study of Giblin, *Giblin: The Scholar and the Man* (Copland 1960), does not, for all its merits, quite succeed. It does not bring out the singularity—the oddness—of Giblin.

The key point is that special achievement is not essential to warrant biography under this rationale, as special achievement does not necessarily imply a valuable individuality. Indeed, it might be held "special achievement" is by itself almost unrewarding to contemplate. The sheer brilliance of the prodigy, for example, excites more "wonder" than "admiration." It is the person, not the achievement, that seems great. Thus, even a lack of achievement may win our respect. Failure—tragic failure—can win our interest and sympathy, and have grandeur about it. Heroism lies more in the attempt than succeeding in the attempt. A valuable individuality does not necessarily imply special achievement.

Under the Plutarchian view of biography, the justification of doing some person's life lies in the personality of that person: one that wins our sympathy, or admiration, or at least holds some sort of allure. Consider Elizabeth Gaskell, who wrote what was, for many years, considered to be the authoritative biography of Charlotte Brontë. "Gaskell's major concern [in writing her biography of Brontë] is with the representation of a friend whom she admired, rather than public figure" (Shelston 1977, 58). Gaskell's own rationale for the biography was that "leaving all authorship aside her character as a woman was unusual to the point of being unique" (Gaskell, cited in Shelston 1977, 58). Gaskell the novelist did not require some special achievement from her characters to judge them worth writing about. And Gaskell the biographer, it seems, did not require some special achievement from Brontë to judge her worth writing about.

Giblin certainly warrants a biography under the Plutarchian criterion. His massive and mysterious personality is enough to transfix one's attention. As one reviewer of Giblin's posthumous *The Growth of a Central Bank* said, "I found myself increasingly absorbed in Giblin at the expense of interest in the Commonwealth Bank" (Bopp 1952, 383).

Yet there is a difficulty in using "fascinating personality" as the occasion of life writing. Acquaintance can be disenchanting. The very wideness of modern biographers' investigations brings within its net the totality of the person, and parts of that totality are, inevitably, not pleasing. This difficulty can be illustrated with Keynes. It is awkward to learn that

Keynes had the "habit of calling all Indian students, no matter how well he knew their names, as 'Darkie'" (Butlin 1951), which is neither courteous nor very amusing. His enthusiasm for eugenics is today received suspiciously. Keynes's ridiculous paean to Soviet communism in 1936 is at best . . . ridiculous (see Coleman 1992). His ill-considered remarks about totalitarianism in the foreword to the French edition of the *General Theory*, and the ugly comments of Keynes that Skidelsky logs in the last volume of his biography, make for difficult digestion.

There are similar difficulties in simply setting out to write a tribute to Giblin. To spit on the carpet is an unattractive habit. His misogyny is off-putting. His relish for the company of boys would today be instantly (and no doubt rightly) diagnosed as pederastic in foundation. His (fitful) eugenicism seems racist. His potential, as late as 1937, to soften his expressions of repugnance to Nazism with some indulgent remarks about the same is disappointing.[8]

There are several responses to the difficulty of maintaining the subject's charm in the face of investigations of the totality of his or her personality.

1. It is a psychological truism that fascination may survive acknowledgment of objectionable characteristics. Edward Gibbon Wakefield was a scoundrel, but as one memorialist records, "Almost everyone who met Wakefield commented on the fascination of his personality" (Fairburn 1990, 573). One enemy declared that the only way to resist Wakefield was to hate him intensely. Those who have not succeeded in hating him intensely may find him interesting despite his failings.
2. Alternatively, it might be maintained that biographies are not about "great persons" but about the greatness that lies within some person. To record and explain that greatness is the task of the biographer, not to record the ungreat. The great person who is only great does not exist—granted—but that does not matter. The defect, in this view, of the genuinely balanced biography—say, Robert Rhodes

8. The far-from-perfect state of humanity has provided rich meat for a kind of biography that is the opposite of the tribute: the debunking biography. Mother Teresa (Hitchens 1995), Bertrand Russell (Monk 1996), and Winston Churchill (Cannadine 2005) have all received the treatment. In the routine of debunking, the researcher excavates the subject's insane relatives; exposes his or her dubious favorites; details his or her selfishness, hypocrisy, and cruelty; and (very commonly in mid-twentieth-century subjects) records his or her credulous responses to Soviet or fascist propaganda.

James's (1970) biography of Churchill's life before 1939—lies in its very balance. We are not interested in a truly comprehensive view of Churchill, but only in his elements of greatness.

3. Finally, the appeal of individuality might be rejected as a totally inadequate foundation of biography. To have done something remarkable, to have achieved something significant: that makes you fit for a biography, and nothing else is required. We do not expect a genius to be a nice man, and do not really care. That Dickens was "abominably cruel" to his wife and "tyrannical" to his children (Orwell 2003) will hardly disqualify him as a subject of biography. We write and read biographies about Shakespeare because of his plays, without any concern for Anne Hathaway and that "second best bed."[9]

The Group Life

Having exhausted unsuccessful motivations for writing the life of Giblin's four, we come to the factor that does make them worthy of a biography: they were a group. They were not just a string of friends or colleagues. There was a close bond between them. This is the stuff of a good story.

It is the interest we have in groups—their formation, progress, ties, and tensions—that have made group lives attractive to authors and readers. Perhaps literary lives have proved most fertile, as in *The Knox Brothers* by Penelope Fitzgerald, *Bloomsbury* by Quentin Bell, or the numerous literary groups whose life has been told by Humphrey Carpenter, especially *The Inklings: C. S. Lewis, J. R. R. Tolkien, Charles Williams, and Their Friends* (Carpenter 1978; see also Carpenter 1987, 1989, 2002).

But group lives have also been written in diplomacy—*The Wise Men: Six Friends and the World They Made: Acheson, Bohlem, Harriman, Kennan, Lovett, McCloy* (Isaacson and Thomas 1986), *Milner's Young Men: The "Kindergarten" in Edwardian Imperial Affairs* (Nimocks 1968)—and intellectual/political elites: *The Souls* (Abdy and Gere 1984) and *The Guardsmen: Harold Macmillan, Three Friends, and the World They Made* (Ball 2005). And they have also been written in science: *The Brotherhood*

9. But the quest for discovering who "really" wrote Shakespeare's plays may betray a hunger for a more satisfying personality behind the plays than William Shakespeare seems to provide.

of the Bomb: The Tangled Lives and Loyalties of Robert Oppenheimer, Ernest Lawrence, and Edward Teller (Herken 2002).

The titles reinforce the earlier point about the interest that lies in groups. For we see in these titles C. S. Lewis, Acheson, Macmillan, Oppenheimer, mostly major figures. Why not just write about Lewis? Because the group structure adds something. The group is interesting because it is a group.

Plot in Group Biographies

The dramatic structure of a group life presents both difficulties and possibilities.

In terms of structure, individual biography has one particular merit: an individual's life has a fairly unambiguous beginning and an end. But in a group life there are several lives—several birth dates and several death dates—and the beginning and ending of the group is difficult.

But in the place of the birth there is in a group biography what we might call the "forge": the place where the group is "born." This could be a family, a university, the army. It might not even be a place but a historical context that supplies a unique, common experience that unites those who share it. This is where we speak of a "generation."

In the case of Giblin's platoon there was a forge: a tiny provincial university—the University of Tasmania—where all four came together, between 1922 and 1924. Copland was appointed in 1917, then Giblin arrived in 1919, the pair of them hiring Brigden and persuading Wilson to enroll in the university (instead of the local Cadbury concern) in 1922.

There was also a distinct historical context for the platoon. The Great War greatly changed their lives. Between them the four could count two enlistments and one attempted enlistment, two younger brothers killed, four wounds, the permanently damaged physical health of Giblin, and the biographer's suspicion—only a suspicion—of lingering gunshot-wound neurosis in Brigden. And it was the war that had brought them together, in Tasmania. Copland arrived in Tasmania from New Zealand, to replace a pacifistic lecturer (Herbert Heaton) who had been driven to resign by jingo sentiment. The war had badly damaged Giblin's previously promising political career and introduced him to Keynes and, by example, the possibility of a new career as "public servant/public intellectual." Brigden's wound had sent him by freak chance to a hospital in Oxford and thereby opened a door that was previously locked. As Brigden told Copland, "Up to the War I hadn't much luck, rather the contrary. . . . but since some strange benefactor of a Bosche . . . sent a piece of German lead through me I haven't been able to stop it" (Coleman, Cornish, and Hagger 2006, 24).[10]

After the forge, what next? Can a group life obtain a plot, beyond a mere congerie of episodes? Stories seem more available for individual biography. Consider one popular plot:

> The young prince driven out of his rightful inheritance by evildoer; in exile has some adventures in which he proves his natural merits; returns, destroys the evildoer and assumes rightful inheritance.

This is the plot of Hamlet. It is the plot of the Lion King. It is, in considerable measure, the plot of Keynes's life, at least as implied by Skidelsky; a hypothetical interpretation may go as follows.

> Keynes is the brilliant heir expectant of British economics; he is "betrayed" [Skidelsky's word] by the Treaty of Versailles. He experiences a nervous breakdown. He then banishes himself with "The Economic Consequences of the Peace." In exile he honorably battles the restoration of the gold standard; then achieves a brilliant victory over Treasury, and the Bank of England, and classical economics. In a renewed national crisis he is summoned to assume his birthright at Treasury, the Bank of England, and the House of Lords. His victory culminates with the contest with Harry Dexter White; a contest, which, in Skidelsky's telling, is a matter of St. George duelling a necromancer in the secret service of the forces of evil. In this last climactic sword fight, in the moment of his ascendancy, Keynes dies, killed in fact.

Can there be the same sort of successful plotlines for group lives?

One sometimes powerful plot for a group life may be summarized thus: leader meets followers—followers lose leader—followers keep on "following" all the same. In this group story there is one key, overarching figure who collects the others, who accept his leadership for some mission. The key figure then dies. But he somehow lives on, with the followers

10. One of Giblin's memorialists recorded: "It was in Tasmania during his middle age (1919–29) that Giblin exercised a wide influence upon his generation, and this phase will provide a biographer with deeply interesting, if illusive, material" (Reynolds ca. 1951). "The postwar generation in Hobart was as mentally adrift and unadjusted as elsewhere throughout the world. The high hopes of brighter new worlds as preached by the starry-eyed patriots, which had taken fathers and elder brothers to Gallipoli and Flanders, did not eventuate. Old pre-war Hobart, and Tasmania for that matter, seemed by 1921 to be slipping back into the outlook of the depression years of the eighteen nineties. . . . For those with eyes, he [Giblin] gave new horizons, quite literally" (Reynolds ca. 1951, cited in Coleman, Cornish, and Hagger 2006, 39).

spreading his message. The one towering example of this plot is the Gospel narrative of Jesus and the disciples. There is more to the Gospel story than this group story, but the group story is certainly in there, and almost integral.

Giblin's Platoon fits such a plot. There is one overarching powerful figure, L. F. Giblin. After appropriate portents in his youth of things to come, he collects around him in his maturity a group of persons, two of whom confess a frankly filial submission to him; together they undertake feats. But Giblin dies. At his funeral he is compared by one disciple to Socrates. Another, Roland Wilson, remarks, "The curious thing is that in my mind he was so 'indestructible' that his physical passing makes little difference" (cited in Coleman, Cornish, and Haggen 2006, 207). Giblin is dead, but he is not really dead. A few weeks later Wilson—handpicked by Giblin years before—becomes the secretary to the Treasury, and a quarter century later he declares of Giblin, "A man of stature and personality can hardly be said to die" (Wilson 1976).

The Promise of the Group Life History in the History of Economics

The upshot of this essay has been to focus attention on the existence of one genre of biography—the group life. The question that remains unresolved is how extensive are the opportunities for exploiting this genre within the history of economics?

I think the answer depends on how narrowly "group" is conceived. If we think of a "group" as something close to a "partnership," then I suspect that opportunities exist, but are not many. It might be questioned if there are many groups so closely connected as to constitute a partnership. Several literary group lives have seemingly lacked that strength of bond. Of Carpenter's many group lives, the literary group of the greatest intensity was "The Inklings," ostensibly built around Lewis, Tolkien, and Charles Williams. But that triplet existed for only six years. And, as Carpenter freely allows, Tolkien never cared for Williams; he considered him an intruder.

But there are some possibilities in economics worth investigating. We have the genuine and extraordinary partnership of Marx and Engels that has been studied "intellectually" (Carver 1993) but not intellectually *and* personally.

The physiocrats constitute another possibility. They possessed a key figure and a "group mentality." "They . . . always acted as a group, praising one another, fighting one another's fights, each member taking his share in group propaganda" (Schumpeter 1954a, 223). They therefore may prove a good and unexploited opportunity for a group life, despite being intensively researched as individuals.

A third possibility is the triplet of William Whewell (1794–1866), Richard Jones (1790–1855), and Charles Babbage (1791–1871). These three "socially aware" Tories befriended each other in Cambridge, drawn together in part by a common scientific and political mission.

But I think the possibilities of group lives are greater if we turn to groups that were less than near partnerships. Economics is full of "schools" and "circuses" and "colloquia." The benefit of the group life here might not be so much to tell the story of the group organism but to better understand the individuals who make up the school, the circus, the colloquia. For the group life promises to reduce the distortion that an individual life history inevitably brings to that history of that individual life. One major economist who has been the subject of repeated biographical inquiry can illustrate: Keynes. As one biographer of Keynes has commented, "A biography . . . distorts one's subjects" by "concentrating on one person no matter how much one adds of the 'times'" (Moggridge 1993, xxv). In a similar vein, an acquaintance of Keynes complained of Roy Harrod's biography, "that one could have wished for a clearer view of Keynes the boy and the man in terms of his relation with his family. It is clearly Harrod's principle that all other persons mentioned in the book shall be referred to only in some specific action to Keynes, which has the curious result of making Keynes seem from earliest boyhood a lonely figure, than which nothing could be more false" (Butlin 1951, 97).

References

Abdy, Jane, and Charlotte Gere. 1984. *The Souls*. London: Sidgwick & Jackson.

Anderson, Karl L. 1938. Protection and the Historical Situation: Australia. *Quarterly Journal of Economics* 53.1:68–104.

Ball, Simon. 2005. *The Guardsmen: Harold Macmillan, Three Friends, and the World They Made*. HarperPerennial.

Bell, Quentin. 1968. *Bloomsbury*. New York: Basic Books.

Bopp, Karl R. 1952. Review of *The Growth of a Central Bank*, by L. F. Giblin. *Journal of Economic History* 12.3:303.

Boserup, Mogens. 1969. A Note on the Prehistory of the Kahn Multiplier. *Economic Journal* 79.315:667–69.

Brigden, J. B. 1925. The Australian Tariff and the Standard of Living. *Economic Record* 1.1:29–46.

Brigden, J. B., D. B. Copland, E. C. Dyason, L. F. Giblin, and C. H. Wickens. 1929. *The Australian Tariff: An Economic Enquiry*. Melbourne: Melbourne University Press.

Butlin, S. J. 1951. Review of *The Life of John Maynard Keynes*, by R. F. Harrod. *Economic Record* 27.1:95–98.

Cain, Neville. 1973. Political Economy and the Tariff: Australia in the 1920s. *Australian Economic Papers* 12.2:1–20.

Cairncross, Alec. 1998. *Living with the Century*. Fife: Lynx.

Cannadine, David. 2005. *The Aristocratic Adventurer*. London: Penguin.

Carpenter, Humphrey. 1978. *The Inklings: C. S. Lewis, J. R. R. Tolkien, Charles Williams, and Their Friends*. London: Harper Collins.

———. 1987. *Geniuses Together: American Writers in Paris in the 1920s*. London: Unwin Hyman.

———. 1989. *The Brideshead Generation: Evelyn Waugh and His Friends*. London: Weidenfeld and Nicolson.

———. 2002. *That Was the Satire That Was: Beyond the Fringe, the Establishment Club, Private Eye*. London: Phoenix.

Carver, Terrell. 1993. *Marx and Engels: The Intellectual Relationship*. Brighton, U.K.: Wheatsheaf Books.

Coleman, William. 1992. Keynes and Communism. *Salisbury Review* 11.2:10–13.

Coleman, William, Selwyn Cornish, and Alf Hagger. 2006. *Giblin's Platoon: The Trials and Triumph of the Economist in Australian Life*. Canberra: ANU E Press.

Copland, D. B. 1931. A Neglected Phase of Tariff Controversy. *Quarterly Journal of Economics* 45.2:289–308.

———, ed. 1960. *Giblin: The Scholar and the Man*. Melbourne: Cheshire.

Corden, Max, and J. Peter Neary. 1982. Booming Sector and De-industrialisation in a Small Open Economy. *Economic Journal* 92.368:825–48.

Dimand, Robert W. 1988. *The Origins of the Keynesian Revolution*. Cheltenham, U.K.: Elgar.

Fairburn, Miles. 1990. Wakefield, Edward Gibbon, 1796–1862. *Dictionary of New Zealand Biography*. Wellington: Allen & Unwin.

Fletcher, Gordon. 2000. *Understanding Dennis Robertson: The Man and His Work*. Cheltenham, U.K.: Elgar.

Giblin, L. F. G. 1930. *Australia, 1930*. Melbourne: Melbourne University Press.

Goodwin, C. D. 1962. Alfred de Lissa and the Birth of the Multiplier. *Economic Record* 38.81:74–93.

Gregory, R. G. 1976. Some Implications of the Growth of the Mineral Sector. *Australian Journal of Agricultural Economics* 20.2:92–102.

Hegeland, Hugo. 1954. *The Multiplier Theory*. Lund, Sweden: C. W. K. Gleerup.

Herken, Gregg. 2002. *Brotherhood of the Bomb: The Tangled Lives and Loyalties of Robert Oppenheimer, Ernest Lawrence, and Edward Teller*. New York: Holt.

Hitchens, Christopher. 1995. *The Missionary Position: Mother Teresa in Theory and Practice*. New York: Verso.
Irwin, Douglas A. 1996. The Australian Case for Protection. In *Against the Tide: An Intellectual History of Free Trade*. Princeton, N.J.: Princeton University Press.
Isaacson, Walter, and Evan Thomas. 1986. *The Wise Men: Six Friends and the World They Made: Acheson, Bohlem, Harriman, Kennan, Lovett, McCloy*. New York: Simon and Schuster.
Manger, Gary J. 1981. The Australian Case for Protection Reconsidered. *Australian Economic Papers* 20.37:193–204.
Moggridge, D. E. 1993. *Maynard Keynes: An Economist's Biography*. London: Routledge.
Monk, Ray. 1996. *Bertrand Russell: The Spirit of Solitude*. London: Cape.
Nimocks, Walter. 1968. *Milner's Young Men: The "Kindergarten" in Edwardian Imperial Affairs*. Durham, N.C.: Duke University Press.
Orwell, George. 2003. *Orwell: The Observer Years*. London: Atlantic Books.
Patinkin, Don. 1982. *Anticipations of the General Theory? And Other Essays on Keynes*. Oxford: Blackwell.
——. 1993. On the Chronology of the General Theory. *Economic Journal* 103.418:647–63.
——. 1994. Mr Meade's Relation, Kahn's Multiplier, and the Chronology of the General Theory: Reply. *Economic Journal* 104.426:1143–46.
Plutarch. [ca. 75] 1973. *The Age of Alexander: Nine Greek Lives*. Translated by Ian Scott-Kilvert. Harmondsworth, U.K.: Penguin.
Reynolds, John. ca. 1951. *L. F. Giblin: A Plea for an Adequate Biography and Some Tasmanian Incidents*. Ingamells Collection, Flinders University Library, Adelaide, Australia.
Rhodes James, Robert. 1970. *Churchill: A Study in Failure, 1900–1939*. London: Weidenfeld and Nicolson.
Salter, W. E. G. 1959. Internal and External Balance: The Role of Price and External Expenditure Effects. *Economic Record* 35.2:226–38.
Samuelson, Marion Crawford. 1939. The Australian Case for Protection Reexamined. *Quarterly Journal of Economics* 54.1:143–51.
Samuelson, Paul A. 1981. Summing Up on the Australian Case for Protection. *Quarterly Journal of Economics* 96.1:147–60.
——. 1987. Joint Authorship in Science: Serendipity with Wolfgang Stolper. *Journal of Institutional and Theoretical Economics* 143.2:235–43.
Schumpeter, J. A. 1954a. *A History of Economic Analysis*. New York: Oxford University Press.
——. 1954b. *Ten Great Economists from Marx to Keynes*. London: Allen & Unwin.
Shelston, Alan. 1977. *Biography*. London: Methuen.
Sidgwick, Henry. 1887. *The Principles of Political Economy*. London: Macmillan.
Stolper, Wolfgang F., and P. A. Samuelson. 1941. Protection and Real Wages. *Review of Economic Studies* 9.1:58–73.

Swan, T. [1955] 1963. Longer Run Problems of the Balance of Payments. In *The Australian Economy: A Volume of Readings*, edited by H. W. Arndt and W. M. Corden. Melbourne: Cheshire.

——. 1972. Overseas Investment in Australia: "Treasury Economic Paper, No. 1." *Economic Record* 48.122:282–85.

Wilson, Roland. 1931. *Capital Imports and the Terms of Trade: Examined in the Light of Sixty Years of Australian Borrowings*. Melbourne: Melbourne University Press.

——. 1976. L. F. Giblin: A Man for All Seasons. *Search* 7.7:307–14.

Wright, A. L. 1956. The Genesis of the Multiplier Theory. *Oxford Economic Papers* 8.2:181–93.

Part 3
Autobiography and Identity

The Economy of Narrative Identity

Paul John Eakin

In the winter of 1849–50, at work on his ambitious project to chronicle the lives of London's working poor, Henry Mayhew interviewed an eight-year-old girl selling watercresses in the streets of the East End. "The poor child," he writes, "although the weather was severe, was dressed in a thin cotton gown, with a threadbare shawl wrapped round her shoulders. She wore no covering to her head, and the long rusty hair stood out in all directions." The child's account of herself opens as follows:

> "I go about the streets with water-creases, crying, 'Four bunches a penny, water-creases.' I am just eight years old—that's all, and I've a big sister, and a brother and a sister younger than I am. On and off, I've been very near a twelvemonth in the streets. Before that, I had to take care of a baby for my aunt. No, it wasn't heavy—it was only two months old; but I minded it for ever such a time—till it could walk. . . . Before I had the baby, I used to help mother, who was in the fur trade; and, if there was any slits in the fur, I'd sew them up. My mother learned me to needle-work and to knit when I was about five. I used to go to school, too; but I wasn't there long. I've forgot all about it now, it's such a time ago." (Mayhew [1861–62] 1968, 151)

The historian Carolyn Steedman ([1986] 1987, 136), drawing on her own research into the lives of working-class girls to examine this child's bleak story, claims that such children learn at an early age to know their places in

History of Political Economy 39 (annual suppl.) DOI 10.1215/00182702-2006-041

an economic system: "Her labour functioned as a description of herself—or rather, she used it as a description of what she knew herself to be . . . a worker, a good and helpful little girl, a source of income. *In this situation her labour was not an attribute, nor a possession, but herself*; that which she exchanged daily for the means of livelihood, for love, and food and protection" (emphasis added).[1] Thinking about Mayhew's little watercress seller, whose sense of her identity was informed by a stark "economic vision" (Steedman [1986] 1987, 135), prompts me to pose a series of questions to historians of economics working on life writing.

Most of the historians of economics presenting papers at the *HOPE* conference in 2006 were writing biographies of some kind, while a few were concerned with autobiography, and a few with oral history. That is to say, in one way or another almost all of the participants were reconstructing, creating, collecting, or otherwise studying someone else's character and life story. Their subjects, in turn, like the watercress girl, were also once engaged in a work of self-fashioning, as indeed all of us necessarily are. There is a common concern with identity, then, that underwrites these projects, bringing into play some historical and economic questions that I want to pursue: what model of self, what model of life story, did the subjects of these life narratives embrace? Moreover, did they have what Steedman calls an "economic vision" of themselves as persons? And were economic forces involved in constructing those models of self and story? I should make clear that I mean nothing mysterious in this talk of models. Despite our illusions of autonomy and self-determination—"*I* write my story, *I* say who I am"—we do not invent our identities out of whole cloth. Instead, we draw on the resources of the cultures we inhabit to shape them, resources that specify what it means to be a man, a woman, a worker, a person in the settings where we live our lives.

It is easy enough to posit that we draw on models of identity as we go about the business of making our selves, whether in our lives or in writing about them; it is much more challenging, however, to specify how this process works. In what follows I want to approach this problem by way of narrative identity. I begin by arguing that we are all of us embedded in what I call a narrative identity system. In this section my approach to the economy of narrative identity rests on the following definition of *economy*, taken from the *American Heritage Dictionary*: "The functional arrange-

1. For nineteenth-century working-class children's sense of "economic selfhood," see Steedman 1982, 110–31.

ment of elements within a structure or system." Then I consider whether this narrative identity system is inflected by economic conditions. In this second section I invoke *economy* in the sense (from the same dictionary) of "the economic system of a country or area," "a system for the management and development of resources." Specifically, I ask two complementary questions: do people understand themselves and their lives in economic terms, and do economic circumstances shape the terms in which people understand themselves and their lives? In effect, I want to explore the possibility of a connection between identity formation and the processes defining persons engaged in an economic system.

Narrative Identity and the Narrative Identity System

Insofar as the *HOPE* conferees were all concerned with life histories, they were making, recovering, or investigating narratives of identity, so it is worth considering the implications of the phrase "narrative of identity." In fact, the relation between narrative and identity is much closer, more dynamic, than this formulation suggests, for narrative is not only a literary form, a convenient envelope to contain a story, but part of the fabric of lived experience. In presenting my notion of narrative identity, I am proposing that narrative is not merely *about* self but in some profound way a constituent part *of* self—of the self, I should be careful to add, that we express in self-narrations, for narrative is not coextensive with all of selfhood, given the many kinds of self and self-experience.

Life writing in its various forms presents us with the subject's self as product, as text, whereas in what follows I consider self as process. The psychologist Ulric Neisser (1988) has identified at least five kinds of selfhood, involving physical, social, and mental contexts. One of these selves, the extended self, the self moving through time, is the primary subject of autobiographical discourse. It is this self, the consciousness we have of possessing a continuous identity across time, that is my focus in this essay. According to Neisser, by the age of three, children are aware of themselves "as existing outside the present moment, and hence of the extended self" (47). As Paul Ricoeur has taught us, narrative is especially suited to registering the impact of time and change central to this mode of self-experience. Consequently, the extended self takes the form of a narrative identity, and identity narratives serve as the medium for displaying that self in interpersonal encounters.

Phrases such as "identity narrative" and "self-narration" run the risk of sounding rather abstract and even clunky, so I should pause to emphasize what is involved in the habitual, everyday practice of talking about ourselves. When we meet each other, we dole out the stories of our lives in bits and pieces. What do these pieces look like? Consider the "Portraits of Grief," brief evocations of those killed at the World Trade Center on September 11, 2001, that were published in the *New York Times* in the weeks and months that followed. There were usually a dozen or more of them on the page, with a banner headline across the top announcing some of the headings of the individual profiles, as, for example, this one from 17 November 2001: "A Taste for Fine Wine, a Seeker of Good Deals, and Fun on Halloween." The header for each piece features some leading characteristic, a kind of capsule identity or microstory: "The Gadget Guru," "A Motorcycle for a Ring," "Always Time for Golf." The short paragraphs that follow, touching on personal qualities, habits, favorite activities, and plans, highlight life plots now left incomplete. Ironies and fateful choices abound, as they do in any life. I think that these loose narrative fragments give a good idea of the ephemeral identity material we draw on when we present ourselves to others, and this is not surprising, for the portraits were generated in conversations between reporters and those close to the deceased. These informal biographical portraits display with striking immediacy the scraps of identity narrative that make up all forms of self-narration and life writing. In the "Portraits of Grief" pages we see, cumulatively, a veritable anthology of the models of identity and life story current in our culture. In characterizing these "portraits" as "loose," "informal," and "fragmentary," I mean to suggest just how close they are to the *spoken* exchanges in which we transact our narrative identities; none of the conventional categories in which biography in its various forms is *written* apply—the "Portraits of Grief" are not obituaries or vignettes, and so forth. Their novelty is precisely a consequence of the ordinariness of the identity material they present, an ordinariness that accounts for the fact that there was no preexisting written genre to capture it—why, indeed, should this material be preserved? What we say about ourselves in passing is usually swept away, the detritus of discourse, and it takes a rupture in the normal unfolding of everyday life to bring it into view and remind us of its value as identity's bedrock.

In "Against Narrativity," the philosopher Galen Strawson (2004, 439) has dismissed the idea of narrative identity as merely an "intellectual fashion," part of a narrative turn across a broad spectrum of academic disciplines. To the contrary, we are embedded in a narrative identity system whether we like it or not.[2] Our social arrangements—in the United States, at any rate—require self-narration as the occasion demands, and the identity narratives we produce, delivered piecemeal everyday, establish for others our possession of normal, functioning identities. This claim that we are players willy-nilly in a narrative identity system may seem surprising and counterintuitive, given that we doubtless believe that we talk about ourselves both freely and spontaneously. Don't we conduct our lives, after all, in a culture of democratic individualism?

To begin with, the habitual, daily performance of self-narration tends to mask the fact that we participate in a rule-governed system; after years of practice, we operate on automatic pilot, we know the identity protocols by heart. The working of the system becomes visible, however, when memory fails and narrative competence collapses, or when self-narration is deliberately refused. Then the link between identity narrative and normality becomes manifest. As Kay Young and Jeffrey Saver (1995, 7) put it bluntly in their study "The Neurology of Narrative," "Individuals who have lost the ability to construct narrative have lost their selves." (I would amend this statement to read "have lost their selves *for others*," for it could well be that modes of selfhood survive the collapse of normal identity's twin supports, memory and narration.) We can test their view against our own experience, for most of us have encountered individuals whose memories and narrative competence have been impaired by injury, disease, or failing powers—it is an increasingly common occurrence in an aging population such as our own. "She was not herself today," we say of the elderly relative who scarcely seemed to recognize us; we don't need to explain, for everyone knows what we mean.

The refusal of self-narration offers an equally revealing if rarer insight into the operation and social significance of narrative identity. William Chaloupka (1996) uses the case of Hood River "John Doe" to illustrate Michel Foucault's understanding of the link between the individual and the apparatuses of state power. Here was a man, arrested for stealing a car, who refused to tell the police in Hood River, Oregon, anything about himself, even his name. Training a Foucauldian lens on this otherwise minor episode, Chaloupka concludes that "the act of autobiographical telling has roots and functions crucial to the operations of contemporary power" (378). John Doe's refusal to identify himself disrupted customary grids of

2. For a critique of Strawson, see Eakin 2006.

identity processing, making them instructively visible as a result. The bafflement of the police in dealing with this anomalous situation points up how the judicial system normally functions. According to a local paper, John Doe "would probably have been out of jail already had he cooperated with authorities." "Without a past," the paper comments, "no one could determine if Doe was a risk to flee the area" (Chaloupka 1996, 373). John Doe was eventually identified by his father, who had seen a picture of his son circulated by the police. "Soon after his name was discovered," Chaloupka reports, "[he] was sentenced to ninety days in jail and was promptly released on probation, as he had already served far more than ninety days" (388).

Whether we are considering contrarian John Doe or our forgetful elders, lapses in identity narration generate consequences, including possible confinement in prisons or long-term care facilities. These consequences confirm that the interpersonal exchange of self-narrations is a rule-governed regime and that the rules are enforced. Others police our performance, and it is also true that we do this policing ourselves. We monitor and judge what others tell us (we exchange glances, we may even roll our eyes); we determine that our interlocutor is "not tracking," has "lost it," and so forth. The psychologist John Shotter (1989, 141) claims that our participation in what I am calling a narrative identity system is governed by social accountability: "What we talk of *as* our experience of our reality is constituted for us very largely by the *already established* ways in which we *must* talk in our attempts to *account* for ourselves—and for it—to the others around us. . . . And only certain ways of talking are deemed legitimate" (141). The analyses of Chaloupka, Foucault, and Shotter sensitize us to the presence of social constraint in the exercise of self-narration; our sense of autonomy, of total control, is something of an illusion when it comes to talking about ourselves.

How do we know how to play this narrative identity game? Training in self-narration begins early, and the fact that it does testifies to our tacit complicity in the working of the system. We introduce our children to the practice of making identity narrative during an unusually rich phase of early child development in which the child's newly acquired language and narrative skills combine with temporal awareness and a nascent sense of social accountability to lay the foundations of autobiographical memory. This training takes the form of what psychologists call the child's "memory talk," homely little stories that parents and caregivers coach us to tell about ourselves. The early materials of these collaborative efforts in making a life story are slight, to be sure—a walk around the block, activities at nursery school, a trip to the zoo—but they provide practice nonetheless for longer, solo flights of self-narration in the time to come. In these parent-child conversations, "children learn the conventionalized narrative forms that eventually provide a structure for internally represented memories" (Fivush and Reese 1992, 115). Describing this process of socialization, Robyn Fivush (1988, 280–81) offers this memorable formulation of the give-and-take between awareness of self and autobiographical memory: "The self-concept and memories of past experiences develop dialectically and begin to form a life history. The life history, in turn, helps organize both memories of past experiences and the self-concept." Children learn not only that they are expected to be able to display to others autobiographical memories arranged in narrative form; they learn what is tellable as well.

Cumulatively, whatever it is that we are acts as a kind of magnet or nucleus attracting particles of life story that we can—and that we do when prompted—fashion into the forms of life narrative that we recognize as autobiography. By the time we reach adulthood we know how to deliver a suitably edited version of our stories as the occasion requires. For the most part, we are not left to our own devices when we talk about ourselves, for protocols exist for many of the kinds of self-narration we may need to engage—in churches, in courtrooms, in meetings of Alcoholics Anonymous, and so forth. Institutions even produce manuals stipulating the kinds of stories they want us to tell.

I don't think that the process of adult self-narration has attracted anything like the research devoted to the child's practice of "memory talk." Perhaps this is to be expected, for on the face of it we might well ask what more we could learn about an activity so familiar that we perform it without thinking. Yet if we follow the lead of Michel de Certeau, everyday practices of any sort are likely to be rule-governed, and self-narration proves to be no exception. This, at any rate, is what Charlotte Linde discovered when she investigated a particular form of "life story," the vocational accounts offered by white, middle-class professionals in answer to the question, "What do you do?" Linde (1993, 3) concludes that the notion of narrative identity is so deeply rooted in our culture that it functions as a criterion for normality: "In order to exist in the social world with a comfortable sense of being a good, socially proper, and stable person," she comments, "an individual needs to have a coherent, acceptable, and constantly revised life story." Such an expectation is culture-specific: as Linde sees it, we happen to live in a culture that subscribes to "the idea that we 'have' a life story, and that any normally competent adult has one." Following Clifford Geertz, she presents narrative identity as "part of the interpretive equipment furnished to us by our culture" (20).

What, specifically, does using this equipment require? The ability to construct a narratively coherent life story. Narrative coherence, Linde argues, derives from principles of causality and continuity, and, once again, it is culture that supplies what she calls "coherence systems," "cultural device[s] for structuring experience into socially sharable narrative" (163). Freudian psychology, Marxism, feminism, most religious faiths—Linde points to these as examples of large-scale sources of narrative coherence. I am struck by the connection Linde makes between narrative self-presentation and normality. She claims that an individual's refusal to supply an appropriate answer to the question "what do you do?" will appear "anomalous and, eventually, sinister" (53). Our performance of self-narration, then, takes place in an environment of social convention and constraint. Having mastered its rules and developed a repertoire of stories about ourselves, we tend—at least socially—to merge with them: in this sense our stories are our selves. Two caveats: what we think we are, of course, is doubtless not identical to what we say. Moreover, returning to the consequences for the individual of narrative incapacity and memory loss, I would not want to assent to the proposition that the de-storied person has become de-selved. As I observed earlier, there are many modes of self and self-experience, more than any self-narration or autobiography could relate

Individualism and Economic Value

So far I have been considering identity formation as a narrative process, as a social process, as an everyday process. Now I want to ask whether economic forces shape the model of individualism that underwrites narrative identity and its representation in life writing.[3] In posing this question, I continue to engage the possibility that determinism—in this case economic—lurks at the heart of a model of the person that we more usually associate with values of freedom and autonomy. To what extent are the selves we think we are and the life stories we think we have lived the

3. In recent years, students of autobiography have become increasingly aware of the importance of relational identity as a characteristic manifestation of individualism, which is often associated with a more distinctly autonomous kind of identity.

product of our position in an economic structure? Recall Carolyn Steedman's assessment (1987, 136) of Henry Mayhew's little watercress-seller: "Her labour functioned as a description of herself—or rather, she used it as a description of what she knew herself to be." The terrain is slippery here, as Steedman's equivocal formulation suggests: the child is equivalent to her work, or, alternatively, the child *uses* her work to articulate "what she knew herself to be." How to discriminate agency from conditioning in this matter of identity? As Steedman's account of the child's sense of self implies, and as I mean to show in the discussion that follows, we never experience economic forces in a simple and transparent way.

The historian Karl J. Weintraub (1975, 847) attributes the rise of Western autobiography at the end of the eighteenth century to two key developments, "the recognition of a strong historical dimension of all human reality" and "a modern mode of self-conception as an individuality."[4] In 1992 I speculated that this new attention to life story and individuality was linked to the rise of bourgeois capitalism. "Modern autobiography," I wrote, "seems to have emerged concurrently with—and is perhaps a symbolic manifestation of—people's acquisition of a distinctly personal space in which to live, rooms of their own, in which, according to architect Witold Rybczynski, the bourgeois values of privacy, intimacy, and 'home' could flower" (Eakin 1992, 100–101). Rybczynski (1986, 35) claims that shifts in the design of domestic space in places like seventeenth-century Protestant Holland led to "the emergence of something new in the human consciousness: the appearance of the internal world of the individual, of the self, and of the family."

This connection between person and property has remained a constant in thinking about individualism from the seventeenth century to the present day. In the early modern period, for example, according to C. B. Macpherson (1962, 3), European political theory from Thomas Hobbes to John Locke features "possessive individualism," which posits the individual "as an owner of himself." Two centuries later, in the United States, Samuel D. Warren and Louis D. Brandeis ([1890] 1984, 85) make a similar link between person and property when they base their concept of the

4 Ariès [1960] 1962, Stone 1977, Taylor 1989, Trilling 1972, Weintraub 1975, and others address the gradual emergence of the concept of modern individuality from 1500 to 1800. All of these commentators concur in affirming the existence of a distinctive kind of selfhood in the modern period, although they assign various dates to its emergence. By the time of Rousseau's *Confessions*, the stage was set for the novel exhibition of interiority as a value. "I have displayed myself as I was," Rousseau ([1781] 1967, 17) announces grandly; in writing his autobiography he has "resolved on an enterprise that has no precedent."

individual's right to privacy and hence the right to "an inviolable personality" on "the right of property in its widest sense." Do we, then, own our selves and the stories of our lives? Privacy, property—is it capitalism that accounts for the potentially jarring linkage of inner states to material possessions? Richard A. Posner's ([1978] 1984, 338) economic theory of privacy, for example, pits privacy and prying against each other as two competing "economic goods" in a world where—he claims—"few people want to be let alone." One might well think otherwise, for current debates about a woman's right to choose, about a terminally ill patient's right to die, suggest that many Americans believe that the right to privacy and the individual's liberty it supports are threatened. Economic prosperity may have generated the possibility of rooms of one's own, and selves and lives to lead in them, as Rybczynski proposes, but in the present age in which persons can be marketed as commodities, modern individuality may be under attack. The demand for personal information and the technology that makes it easy to get are hard to withstand. Despite the aura of self-determination (as in "self-made man") that we associate with individuality, does this model of the person obscure the extent to which people in the modern state are subject in the very core of their identities to economic and political pressures beyond their control?

Pursuing this connection between identity and economy, I want to return to the pair of related questions I asked at the outset: Do individuals see themselves in economic terms? And do economic forces inflect the terms in which people think of themselves and their lives? As to the first of these questions, all sorts of evidence supports the view that economic factors play an important role in people's self-conceptions—Mayhew's little watercress-seller would be only an obvious and salient example. As Charlotte Linde's research suggests, we are conditioned in professional life to be ready to answer the question "what do you do?"; any failure to answer appropriately, she asserts, would place our normality in question. What we do, moreover, can seem to make up a very large part of what we are. Economic value infuses the "successful" life that Benjamin Franklin has modeled indelibly for generations of Americans in his autobiography. It is hard to escape the spell of the success story in the United States. I have to say that when I started graduate school, I felt keenly that my choice of an academic career was a disappointment to my father, an investment banker. Although he never said so, I felt sure that for him college teaching was second best; it lacked the economic and social standing of what he thought of as "the professions."

Social esteem and self-esteem—they can pair in uncomfortable ways in a world where cash is the measure of worth. I spent my career in a large state institution where salaries were public information by law, and I know that colleagues studied the compensation schedules to learn how their work—and they themselves—were valued by the institution. While the slippage between work and self in these questions of value has always struck me as telling, not everyone's work experience will confirm the conflation of occupational and personal identities that I have been describing, and not everyone, moreover, participates directly in the world of work. Obviously, gender will affect these identity questions in complex ways as well, but I would argue that no one is free from awareness of class in the Western societies where individualism remains a key value. In the United States, for example, from the end of the nineteenth century to the present day, class has been a major preoccupation of our novelists—I am thinking of Edith Wharton, Theodore Dreiser, F. Scott Fitzgerald, John Dos Passos, and William Faulkner, of John O'Hara and John Cheever, and later on of John Updike and Philip Roth.

It is the second of my questions, whether economic conditions shape the models we draw on in forging a sense of identity, that strikes me as especially pertinent for historians of economics working on life writing to consider. The anthropologist Marianne Gullestad (1996, 10), for example, claims that "global capitalist modernity has put autobiography, morality, and self-fashioning into the foreground in new and forceful ways." To test the truth of such an observation, we need to bridge the gap Gullestad posits between "the ways in which ideal life courses and identity categories are constructed by the state, the market, and the mass media, on the one hand," and "how people in their everyday lives construct themselves as subjects, on the other" (306). Anthropologists, including Gullestad, have drawn on a line of inquiry associated with Clifford Geertz to conceptualize the relation between culture and the individual in terms that apply usefully to life writing: what are our cultural resources, they ask; what is the conceptual equipment we think with? And where does this equipment or toolkit come from, how is it transmitted to us?[5] If we accept Gullestad's assertion that there is a connection between globalization and individualism, it then becomes a challenge to understand how identity formation unfolds as part of a larger, informing economic structure and the cultural processes it sets in motion.

5. See, for example, Geertz 1973 and Bruner 1990.

For one instructive formulation of the interface between the individual and culture, consider the philosopher Ian Hacking (1996, 59) on the emergence of the "meta-concept" of normality, which he identifies as "one of the most understudied phenomena of the industrial and information-theoretic worlds in which we lived and live." Hacking asserts that the Industrial Revolution ushered in a paradigm shift in the Western concept of the person: "During the nineteenth century, the idea of normal people displaced the Enlightenment ideal of Human Nature" (59).[6] Citing Foucault's investigation of the "constitution of subjects" (Hacking 1986, 226), Hacking directs our attention to the curious phenomenon of "making up people": "Social change creates new categories of people, . . . new ways for people to be. People spontaneously come to fit their categories" (223). Bureaucrats, statisticians, and social observers of various kinds create categories of persons; individuals in their everyday lives embody categories. Hacking (1995, 370) proposes the notion of a feedback loop to describe this process of classification and embodiment in action: "New sorting and theorizing induces changes in self-conception and in behaviour of the people classified. Those changes demand revisions of the classification and theories, the causal connections, and the expectations. Kinds are modified, revised classifications are formed, and the classified change again, loop upon loop." The historian of economics might ask whether the play of categories that Hacking describes is a characteristic manifestation of societies at a certain stage of capitalism.

"New sorting and theorizing induces changes in self-conception and in behaviour of the people classified"—thinking about the interplay between theorists and ordinary citizens in this matter of identity categories, I find myself recalling the work of the great twentieth-century sociologist David Riesman, who believed that models of identity in a culture emerge in response to large-scale social forces. In *The Lonely Crowd* Riesman presents a vision of a United States undergoing unprecedented social change in the years following the Second World War, a change manifested in a major shift in national "character" types from the "inner-directed" model that earlier generations of Americans had internalized to a new "other-directed" model of the person (Riesman, Denney, and Glazer 1950). "Inner-directed" for Riesman meant that "*the source of direction for the individual is 'inner' in the sense that it is implanted early in life by the elders and directed toward generalized but nonetheless inescapably destined*

6. See note 4 for parallel claims about the emergence of the modern concept of the person.

goals" (15; emphasis in original). "*What is common to all other-directeds*," by contrast, "*is that their contemporaries are the source of direction for the individual—either those known to him or those with whom he is indirectly acquainted, through friends and through the mass media*" (22; emphasis in original). What interests me in Riesman's analysis is the correlation he makes between particular "character" types and population phases in modern Western history (14, 26). Riesman charts the emergence of the inner-directed individual from the Renaissance onward as the dominant character type in the West against the backdrop of a society "characterized by increased personal mobility, by a rapid accumulation of capital (teamed with devastating technological shifts), and by an almost constant *expansion*: intensive expansion in the production of goods and people, and extensive expansion in exploration, colonization, and imperialism" (15).[7] For Riesman, then, economic forces play no small part in configuring social structure and the models of character that individuals internalize in the work of self-fashioning. While Riesman himself displayed a keen awareness of the potential for reductiveness in the character categories he deployed in *The Lonely Crowd* (6–7), they certainly achieved a wide currency in the 1950s. When people I knew in those years referred to someone as "other-directed," for example, they were invoking precisely the kind of labeling, of modeling of the person, that Hacking sees as part of the endless spooling of identity categories in response to social change.

Can life writing in its various forms shed light on this making up of persons? Marianne Gullestad points the way in her study, *Everyday Life Philosophers: Modernity, Morality, and Autobiography in Norway* (1996). Drawing on a corpus of autobiographies gathered in a national contest in Norway, she maps the cultural sources of self and life story available to her subjects. The forms of lives, she argues, are transmitted not only through story as such but also through value. Working over her autobiographers' narratives with patience and tact, she teases key value words back to their origins in everyday discourse, discourses spoken in schools and churches and especially in families. "Kari," for example, one autobiographer whom Gullestad studies, notes a shift in identity models from "being of use," a formulation characteristic of her own 1950s childhood that she linked to the idea of obedience, to "being oneself," a model she proposes

7. Again, see note 4 for parallel claims about the emergence of the modern concept of the person.

for her daughter's formation forty years later (285–86). Kari's struggle with being herself confirms the importance of what Gullestad calls "categories of belonging," including "kinship, home, locality, nationality, and religion" (292), which help define "anchorage points for the self" (285). Being oneself, for example, may now function as a primary value in contemporary Norway, but as Kari's story suggests, individuals may be obliged to find this self in order to be it. Building on Gullestad's key insight that value is a repository of form, I have argued elsewhere (in Eakin 1999) that latent in the discourses used to express values are metaphors for self and life story, rudiments of plot and character that individuals draw on as they live their lives and—sometimes—write them. Gullestad's study of the transmission of values shows how social institutions are *experientially* linked to the individual: "Values," she urges, "do not only exist as explicit notions, but may also be reproduced in subtle ways through embodied practices in everyday life" (265). Sensitizing us to recognize these "embodied practices" that make up the texture of the quotidian, Gullestad puts us in a good position to recognize how identity formation functions as cultural process.

I have tried to situate identity formation and the everyday narrative practices associated with it in the context of the cultures in which they unfold. More specifically, I believe that what I have been calling the narrative identity system functions as it does at least in part because of its place in a larger economic structure. When Foucault links autobiographical telling and contemporary power, when Gullestad connects individualism and globalization, I think they both identify how models of self and life story intersect with large-scale historical forces, but they reach contrasting conclusions about the individual's agency in the playing out of cultural process. Their claims prompt this question: culture dwells in us for sure, but how does it dwell? Think back to the example of Mayhew's little watercress-seller: we have the eight-year-old child's story pretty much as she told it, I am convinced; we read her story, however, under the heading "Watercress Girl," slotted into the double columns of volume 1 of Mayhew's magisterial four-volume survey of the working class, *London Labour and the London Poor*; the watercress-girl narrative in its turn is placed under the rubric "Street-Sellers of Green Stuff," one of the major categories of "Sellers" who make up Mayhew's "Street-Folk." The child's story functions as a building block in Mayhew's ambitious program of classification, namely, "A Cyclopedia of the Condition and Earnings of Those That Will Work, Those That Cannot Work, And Those That Will

Not Work." The isolated individual and her story, then, contained in the larger structure of an economic system. How to read the evidence?

Focusing on the site of autobiographical telling—specifically, of testimony in a judicial setting—William Chaloupka (1996, 389), as I suggested earlier, invokes Michel Foucault's dark vision of individualism as a disciplinary practice of the state: "Hood River John Doe's expressive silence—his temporary escape from identity—briefly illuminates how power now works, how successfully it captures and rearranges the seemingly simple, unproblematic fact of having an identity and expressing it." Is Chaloupka's resisting John Doe so much of an exception? As for me, although I am chastened by Foucault's insight into the workings of power, I side nonetheless with the less deterministic views of Marianne Gullestad and Ian Hacking, for example, who read the exchange between individuals and the social structures they inhabit as a dialogic, give-and-take process. "People live their lives and tell their stories," Gullestad (1996, 32) writes, "within socially structured conditions, but their actions and stories also have a potentially transformative impact on 'society.'" Even the little watercress-seller gets to have her say.

References

Ariès, Philippe. [1960] 1962. *Centuries of Childhood: A Social History of Family Life*. Translated by Robert Baldick. New York: Random House.

Bruner, Jerome. 1990. *Acts of Meaning*. Cambridge, Mass.: Harvard University Press.

Certeau, Michel de. 1984. *The Practice of Everyday Life*. Translated by Steven F. Rendall. Berkeley: University of California Press.

Chaloupka, William. 1996. (For)getting a Life: Testimony, Identity, and Power. In *Getting a Life: Everyday Uses of Autobiography*, edited by Sidonie Smith and Julia Watson. Minneapolis: University of Minnesota Press.

Eakin, Paul John. 1992. *Touching the World: Reference in Autobiography*. Princeton, N.J.: Princeton University Press.

——. 1999. Autobiography and the Value Structures of Ordinary Experience: Marianne Gullestad's *Everyday Life Philosophers*. In *Making Meaning of Narratives*, edited by Ruthellen Josselson and Amia Lieblich. The Narrative Study of Lives 6. Thousand Oaks, Calif.: Sage.

——. 2006. Narrative Identity and Narrative Imperialism: A Response to Galen Strawson and James Phelan. *Narrative* 14:180–87.

Fivush, Robyn. 1988. The Functions of Event Memory: Some Comments on Nelson and Barsalou. In *Remembering Reconsidered: Ecological and Traditional Approaches to the Study of Memory*, edited by Ulric Neisser and Eugene Winograd. New York: Cambridge University Press.

Fivush, Robyn, and Elaine Reese. 1992. The Social Construction of Autobiographical Memory. In *Theoretical Perspectives on Autobiographical Memory*, edited by Martin A. Conway, David C. Rubin, Hans Spinnler, and Willem A. Wagenaar. Dordrecht, The Netherlands: Kluwer Academic Publishers.

Geertz, Clifford. 1973. *The Interpretation of Cultures*. New York: Basic.

Gullestad, Marianne. 1996. *Everyday Life Philosophers: Modernity, Morality, and Autobiography in Norway*. Oslo: Scandinavian University Press.

Hacking, Ian. 1986. Making Up People. In *Reconstructing Individualism: Autonomy, Individuality, and the Self in Western Thought*, edited by Thomas C. Heller, Morton Sosna, and David E. Wellbery. Stanford, Calif.: Stanford University Press.

———. 1995. The Looping Effects of Human Kinds. In *Causal Cognition: A Multidisciplinary Debate*, edited by Dan Sperber, David Premack, and Ann James Premack. Oxford: Clarendon Press.

———. 1996. Normal People. In *Modes of Thought: Explorations in Culture and Cognition*, edited by David R. Olson and Nancy Torrance. Cambridge: Cambridge University Press.

Linde, Charlotte. 1993. *Life Stories: The Creation of Coherence*. New York: Oxford University Press.

Macpherson, C. B. 1962. *The Political Theory of Possessive Individualism: Hobbes to Locke*. Oxford: Clarendon Press.

Mayhew, Henry. [1861–62] 1968. *London Labour and the London Poor*. 4 vols. New York: Dover.

Neisser, Ulric. 1988. Five Kinds of Self-Knowledge. *Philosophical Psychology* 1:35–59.

Posner, Richard A. [1978] 1984. An Economic Theory of Privacy. In *Philosophical Dimensions of Privacy: An Anthology*, edited by Ferdinand David Schoeman. Cambridge: Cambridge University Press.

Ricoeur, Paul. 1984–88. *Time and Narrative*. 3 vols. Translated by Kathleen McLaughlin and David Pellauer. Chicago: University of Chicago Press.

Riesman, David, Reuel Denney, and Nathan Glazer. 1950. *The Lonely Crowd: A Study of the Changing American Character*. New Haven, Conn.: Yale University Press.

Rousseau, Jean-Jacques. [1781] 1967. *The Confessions*. Translated by J. M. Cohen. Reprint, Harmondsworth, U.K.: Penguin.

Rybczynski, Witold. 1986. *Home: A Short History of an Idea*. New York: Viking.

Shotter, John. 1989. Social Accountability and the Social Construction of "You." In *Texts of Identity*, edited by John Shotter and Kenneth J. Gergen. London: Sage.

Steedman, Carolyn Kay. 1982. *The Tidy House: Little Girls Writing*. London: Virago.

———. [1986] 1987. *Landscape for a Good Woman: A Story of Two Lives*. New Brunswick, N.J.: Rutgers University Press.

Stone, Lawrence. 1977. *The Family, Sex, and Marriage in England, 1500–1800*. New York: Harper.

Strawson, Galen. 2004. Against Narrativity. *Ratio* 17:428–52.

Taylor, Charles. 1989. *Sources of the Self: The Making of the Modern Identity.* Cambridge, Mass.: Harvard University Press.

Trilling, Lionel. 1972. *Sincerity and Authenticity.* Cambridge, Mass.: Harvard University Press.

Warren, Samuel D., and Louis D. Brandeis. [1890] 1984. The Right to Privacy. In *Philosophical Dimensions of Privacy: An Anthology*, edited by Ferdinand David Schoeman. Cambridge: Cambridge University Press.

Weintraub, Karl J. 1975. Autobiography and Historical Consciousness. *Critical Inquiry* 1:821–48.

Young, Kay, and Jeffrey L. Saver. 1995. The Neurology of Narrative. Paper presented at the Modern Language Association convention, New York.

Using Autobiographical Statements to Investigate the Identity of American Economists

Mike Reay

Social life necessarily involves expectations about who people are and how they are likely to behave. Some of these expectations are formally codified and enforced—for example, in legally binding job requirements—but others involve much looser ideas or images of what people playing a particular role do, what they know, and what their character should be (see Goffman 1959; Berger and Luckmann 1966). The importance of these role expectations has been recognized at least implicitly by historians of American economics exploring the influence of the "scientific" status of the discipline, that is, ideas about what makes an economist a neutral scientist rather than a political advocate, historian, or artist (see, e.g., Furner 1975; Yonay 1998; Mirowski 1989, 1991; Weintraub and Mirowski 1994). However, these explorations have focused primarily on elite academic debates, so relatively little is known about the images and expectations influencing economists more generally in their dealings with the public, their professional activities, and their personal lives.[1]

The research in this essay was supported by NSF Dissertation Improvement Grant SBR-9731162. The author would also like to acknowledge the indispensable support of Andrew Abbott, Gary Herrigel, Jeff Biddle, Elyse Shuk, and an anonymous reviewer for *HOPE*. Thanks also to all the subjects who so graciously gave their time for this project, to the participants of the 2006 *HOPE* conference, and especially to Evelyn Forget and E. Roy Weintraub. Quotations from the interviews are cited by interview number.

1. Consideration of nonelite and nonacademic economists seems to be somewhat rare in the history of economics, although some authors do engage in it to some extent (see, e.g., Ruggles

History of Political Economy 39 (annual suppl.) DOI 10.1215/00182702-2006-042

The following discussion aims to improve this situation by exploring the public, professional, and personal identity images affecting a wide range of academic and nonacademic economists working in the United States at the end of the twentieth century. The evidence comes from fifty-two face-to-face interviews recorded by the author—a sociologist—between June 1999 and July 2000, with economists working in a wide variety of jobs around Chicago and Washington, D.C.[2] The interviews aimed to get the subjects talking informally and open-endedly about four general topics: their activities as professional economists, the role of abstract theory in their work, their experiences in training, and the nature of economics as a science. The data are thus self-reports of attitudes and beliefs, plus brief autobiographical statements, that is, more extended stories of personal experiences.

Such self-reports and autobiographical statements lead a rather conflicted existence in American sociology. They are often treated as indications of "objective" phenomena such as events, social conditions, and psychological states, or typical sequences thereof (Schaeffer and Presser 2003; Laslett 1999). But they are sometimes treated instead as indications of "subjective" phenomena such as common genres of expression, socially accepted "vocabularies" of motives, and situation-specific strategies of self-presentation (Potter and Mulkay 1985; Linde 1993). The following analysis tries to bring these two approaches together by treating the inter-

1970; Barber 1985, 1996; Bassi 1989; Biddle 1998; Colander 2003; Siegfried and Stock 2004; Stock and Hansen 2004). Far more common, of course, are narratives of the lives of particular elite academics or investigations of nonelites that nevertheless focus only on academics (Katouzian 1980; Goodwin 1980; Burkhardt and Canterbery 1986; Tarascio 1986; Klamer and Colander 1990) or on nonacademic activities typically engaged in by elite visitors (Allen 1977; Coats 1980, 1981, 1986).

2. Twenty of the interviewees were academics, from eight different economics departments and six business programs. Thirty-two were nonacademics, from twelve different parts of the federal government, two think tanks, two major international organizations, five financial institutions, and six other private sector organizations. The academics were selected randomly from departmental listings, although half were selected to be members and half nonmembers of the American Economic Association. The nonacademics were randomly selected from two professional association membership directories, the 1997 AEA directory and the 1998 National Association for Business Economics directory. All subjects were selected to have been practicing for around twenty years, having finished their highest degree during the period 1978–82. The overall response rate of selected and eligible subjects was fairly high: fifty-two out of sixty-seven, or nearly 78 percent. The interviews lasted on average an hour and ten minutes. The shortest was fifty minutes, the longest around two hours. Whenever an interview is quoted below, an identifying code number will be given so that readers can see the variety of subjects used to support the various observations.

view transcripts sometimes as indicators of objective events or consciously held attitudes (e.g., involvement in particular work tasks or appreciation of current peer-review standards), but other times as evidence of the subjective behavior of economists in an interview setting (e.g., using particular metaphors). There is no single logic to how this is done; it is opportunistic and leaves the reader to consider in each case the viability of the interpretation. The proposed justification for this is that the subjective and objective elements in self-reports are so inherently intertwined that it is impossible to state fixed methods for correct interpretation (cf. Bertaux and Kohli 1984; Zussman 1996). Just as the rhetorician Charles Bazerman (2004, 321) says of simultaneously analyzing speech acts and the genres through which they are expressed, one can engage only in an ongoing "bootstrapping operation" of comparing multiple statements, using assumptions from each kind of phenomenon to support claims about the other. In the case of self-reports, this means using assumptions about subjective biases when judging assertions about objective facts, and assumptions about objective conditions when assessing subjective expressions.

At each level of analysis—public, professional, and personal—the discussion suggests that there was a surprisingly heterogeneous collection of images relevant to economists' identity, distributed unevenly both across space (i.e., different social groups and different practical situations) and across time (i.e., different stages of people's lives). These elements of identity varied widely in their accuracy and even their mutual consistency, but because of their practical separation they could be effectively "insulated" from each other and subsequently formed a somewhat flexible "tool kit" of plausible identifiers that could be mixed and matched by both economists and laypeople. Furthermore, this tool kit was far from dominated by the ideal of the rigorous academic scientist, even though this image prevailed in elite academia and during early professional socialization. The discussion closes with some suggestions about how this finding might be useful to historians of economics of this and other periods.

Public Images

When treated as indications of objective events, states, and attitudes, the interviews reveal a number of clues as to how noneconomists saw economists. When subjects were asked "how do people react when you tell them you're an economist?" they responded that most people had an undeveloped or inaccurate picture of what economists do. Around one-quarter of the subjects in fact reported people having little or *no* image or experience of economists:

> I don't think people know what economists do, by and large, and they don't understand economics . . . whereas, you know, they have a very crisp idea of what doctors and lawyers do. Probably some fraction of the time they've dealt with doctors and lawyers, although they don't like to. But people just don't deal professionally with economists. (no. 15)

> [My recreational sporting colleagues] look at me as a bit of a curioso.
> M: What do they think you do?
> Well, that's what they ask me: "What do you *do*?" (no. 27)

This kind of reaction was less common in D.C., where, as one subject noted, there were "probably more economists per square foot than anywhere else in the world [so] it's likely that I'm not the first economist they've ever met" (no. 6). But this still did not mean that people there had an *accurate* picture of economics. In fact, the commonest reaction mentioned in all locations was some kind of generalization from a small subset of economists—those involved in macroeconomic forecasting or stock market prediction:

> I have a brother who is in that sense a *real* economist because he works for a brokerage firm and appears on television and prognosticates about what's going to happen with interest rates. I think that's most people's conception of what economists do. . . . That's the typical man-on-the-street perception [laughs]. (no. 29)

> Most of them think of macro, and God help them they sometimes ask me for stock investment advice, which is a *big* mistake [laughs].
> M: Do you give it?
> Oh sure! [laughing] Why not?! But most people won't have any idea of what we do. I think the majority of economists deal in the micro area. (no. 10)

It is worth noting here that very few subjects encountered outright hostility to what they supposedly did. As one government economist insisted, "I don't *hide* it. I don't get a *negative* reaction. . . . I don't get a letdown from telling them I'm an economist" (no. 4). But one subject did bemoan college experiences in which people accused economics of being immoral:

> I care about pollution, I care about hunger, I care about fixing those sorts of problems and that's why I'm interested in economics. But there was just the assumption that it was, you know, "cold cash, blah blah blah." (no. 34)

College was, however, more commonly cited as one place where people got their misleading impressions of economics—both positive and negative:

> I've had people say, "Ooh, I took that in college, and I *hated* it." I get that. But I've had some people who were really interested when they took it, and, you know, I'll be at a social occasion and they'll want a treatise on current monetary policy. (no. 12)

Another suggestion was that the impressions of laypeople might come simply from their everyday experience of related activities. "I've always sort of jokingly said that anyone who feels they can balance a checkbook thinks he knows economics [laughs]" (no. 36). It also seems as if public images were influenced disproportionately by particularly prominent individuals, even when those individuals were not in fact representative. Several subjects, for example, noted glumly the fame of then chairman of the Federal Reserve Board Alan Greenspan. As one said, "A large segment of the population can identify him as one of the top economists, although he's mainly a finance person [laughs]" (no. 44). On top of this misleading superstar effect, public impressions of particular economists were clearly filtered by the interests of media personnel and the incentives embodied in media organizations. Unfortunately, these interests and incentives could again foster false impressions, this time of simplicity and overconfidence:

> The economists who get quoted in the press are the people who give answers, give the flip answer, who are willing to overstep their limits. . . . I've had other economists, really very good people, tell me they never get quoted because they're not willing to speak with a flourish. (no. 15)

The very formatting of television was in fact seen by some to affect the impression given of economics: "On TV—everything has to be simplified too much. . . . On some of the talk shows it's a little better. But usually on the TV news, it has to be shortened. You *never* get the essence of an issue" (no. 44).

One thing all this suggests is that public images of economists may have been inaccurate simply because experience with the discipline was unevenly "distributed" throughout American society. Direct interaction with actual economists was rare, so although it clearly went on somewhere, it was "insulated" from most people's daily lives and hidden from their view. Inaccurate stereotypes could easily persist in such an environment, with knowledge of the activities of economists coming only through selective channels at particular times (e.g., during college) and in particular places or situations (e.g., watching television news).

Many interviewees suggested, however, that they could partly manage these kinds of persistent misperceptions by invoking *nondisciplinary* identifiers closer to the direct experiences of laypeople. More than one-third of the academics, for example, mentioned how they could reduce confusion by referring in some way to their role as professor. However, some subjects also noted that this strategy worked only if it emphasized the *teaching* aspect of academic jobs. The notion of research work was much less familiar to the public:

> They're trying to figure out what you do [when not in class], and when you say "research," well, that doesn't mean anything. And at some point, you just get so tired of trying to explain it that sometimes you just say, "Well, I play tennis and golf, and just goof around." (no. 11)

Of course, most government and business economists did not have the option of claiming to be teachers. As one commented wistfully,

> It's not really that well recognized as a profession. If I said, "I'm an economist and I teach at this university," then that's easier to digest. But the idea of an economist who is not teaching, I think, is pretty unfamiliar to most people. (no. 30)

On the other hand, many nonacademics could refer instead to the type of organization or the specific agency where they worked. About one-third of the subjects mentioned things along the lines of "usually, I say I'm an economist and I work for the X division of the Agency" (no. 42). Again, the results of this varied with the nature and public visibility of the organization involved:

> When I tell them I work on antitrust cases for the Agency, they don't really know what that means. In fact, if you tell them you work for the

> Agency, they almost instantly think you work on X [laughs], and the Agency doesn't have anything to do with that actually. (no. 23)

> I guess the biggest problem I have now is trying to explain what the Agency does; it's such an obscure agency and does such obscure work that most people have never heard of it and don't really have a clue of what it does. And I just say I'm an economist with the government, and deal with X. (no. 12)[3]

Overall then, public images of economists seemed to be characterized not only by shortcomings and misperceptions but also by heterogeneity. In a world of unevenly distributed knowledge and insulated experiences, different people had different inaccurate images of economics, and different economists could themselves invoke various identity elements from what amounted to a "cultural tool kit" (Swidler 1986) to present a positive public image. As I show below, these same features of distribution, insulation, and heterogeneity also seemed to characterize identity images *within* the economics profession.

Professional Images

Objective evidence from the interviews suggests that economists are initially socialized into seeing "real" economists as elite academic scientists, but that over time they progressively pick up other impressions of what characterizes their professional life.

The general lack of a public image clearly meant that economists at this time typically first encountered their discipline during higher education. Around 80 percent of both the academics and the nonacademics claimed that their introduction to economics came only in college or later, primarily because until then they had no idea what the subject was about:

> How could you always want to be an economist? It's just a small profession, you don't know what it is. You didn't have it in high school, how can you possibly know? (no. 22)

3. Interestingly enough with respect to distributed and insulated images, the policy area "X" is the same thing in these last two quotes. In other words, the first subject complains that his agency is mistaken for the other's, while the other complains that no one has heard of his agency or has any idea about what it does.

Across this blank slate, college and graduate school seemed then to inscribe an official picture of real economics based on a strictly hierarchical system of elite academic research within orthodox "scientific" traditions. As past observers have recognized, academic economics in the United States is strongly influenced by a small number of top departments that dominate high-status publications, meetings, funding, and the training of the next generation of professionals (Day 1989; Barbezat 1992; Hinshaw and Siegfried 1995; Scott and Mitias 1996). Many also suggest that this system filters down to the level of formal training as a fairly strictly enforced conformity to, and unthinking acceptance of, currently dominant, purely academic work. In the opinion of one particularly scathing critic, "Graduate students are taught to jump through . . . hoops," "play mental ping-pong," and engage in "neoscholastic obeisance to the liturgy" of abstract models that "constrain economic actors to behave like puppets" (Shubik 1970, 410, 415–16; see also Leontief 1982; Klamer and Colander 1990; Krueger 1991; Brenner 1992).

The legacy of this socialization could be seen in the number of interviewees at low-ranked and nonacademic institutions who at some point—before, during, or after the actual taped discussion—suggested that they were not real economists. Overall, around one-quarter of academics and nonacademics alike indicated some surprise at being included in the study, despite the fact that they clearly made a living as economic experts. They worried that they might be "uninteresting" or "irrelevant," because of their atypical lack of involvement in or disagreement with the orthodox academic research literature.[4]

Despite this legacy of training, however, there was also much in the interviews to imply that experienced professionals had learned over time to see "being an economist" as involving much more than the official stereotype. When they were asked about the unique contributions of economics to society, the most important things learned during training, and what current graduate students needed to know, they painted a much broader, more heterogeneous picture of "core" defining skills and habits picked up in different places and at different career stages. At the simplest level, "what economists know" was typically thought to involve a fairly basic set of

4. A study of British health economists in the 1980s came across the same phenomenon, with one investigator suggesting a strong contrast with his experiences studying natural scientists: "It wasn't like this when I studied physicists. You never got physicists saying 'well actually I'm not really a physicist'" (Ashmore, Mulkay, and Pinch 1989, 120).

insights and practical techniques, such as instinctively considering costs as well as benefits, focusing on incentives and decision maximization, assuming that prices respond to supply and demand, and acknowledging opportunity costs. These skills were often condensed into the notion of "thinking like an economist," something that could not be learned from texts alone but had to be picked up by actually doing research or absorbing it from others in an almost apprentice-like manner. Hence "being able to watch people close up, who are really good, kind of go through the process of getting from point A to point B is just incredibly important" (no. 15).

Most importantly, acquiring this core set of skills was not thought to be synonymous with learning to conform to elite research standards. One subject suggested, for example, that after his experience at graduate school, "the first thing I learned I guess is that it's a terrible way to learn economics. And after I came out of graduate school I was *not* an economist. It took me about five years to learn economics after graduate school, 'til I thought like an economist" (no. 43). Nearly one-fifth of both academic and nonacademic subjects also echoed prominent criticisms of academic economics by suggesting that one thing their training did not include enough of was knowledge relevant to the real world: "I didn't really see much [laughs] in the relevance of what I did as a student . . . and in the beginning I would argue that it *hurt* me" (no. 7). "The weakest part of *any* economics program today I think is the dependency on abstraction, and the divorce from real economic activity" (no. 51). Furthermore, about half the academics and more than three-quarters of the nonacademics made some kind of reference to the professional irrelevance and excessive formalism of most elite academic research. And when economists were asked "what does economics as a profession most need?" the commonest answer from academics as well as nonacademics was reform of the publications-based academic system:

> I think [it would help] if you could get more economists that would be willing to address questions that are difficult to answer, as opposed to setting it up so that you've sort of got a trick shot in pool; you set everything up, and then you solve it. (no. 35)

Without such reform, there would be continuing tension between conforming to the elite academic image and doing economics properly:

> I guess the advice I find myself giving most is to think about what's important. You want to divorce yourself from the literature-driven exercise, where authors x, y, and z did this, this, and that, and I'm going to do

this because it's the natural follow-up. But really step back and think about what makes a difference, what's important. And what do you think is really going on? That's sort of what good economics is about, trying to figure out what's going on, not just putting another notch in your belt because you got another publication. (no. 15)

Subjects also mentioned features beyond the core that could help define an effective economist. The two most important were communication and interpersonal skills:

Looking back on graduate school, I wish I had learned how to write [laughs], or the importance of that. . . . I think that's the thing in graduate school, since there's so much obsession with technique, you don't learn how to write. If anything, your writing deteriorates. (no. 39)

The important things in life aren't from graduate training or professional training anyway. The important things in life are learning to deal with people. And I'm not sure how much you can expect a graduate Ph.D. program to teach you how to play the politics of an institution you're in, assuming you're not self-employed. . . . The key is how to deal with people, and that is not taught. That is learned by making bad mistakes and how you dealt with them in the past. (no. 22)

It is hardly surprising then that both academics and nonacademics perceived the danger of graduate students becoming too absorbed in the official image:

I think they should be realistic about what their job is going to be, and try to acquire skills and tastes in grad school consistent with what that job is going to be. And many of them, they're not going to be able to get a job as an economic methodologist, . . . and they do themselves a disservice to think they will. . . . Most jobs are applied. (no. 26)

Most of the professors you're working with, what they want you to do when you leave there is to go get a job in a university somewhere. They don't want you to take a job working in the government, working for a corporation, or even working for the World Bank, or the Fed, or something. . . . So . . . I think just by osmosis [academia] becomes what you think you want. (no. 21)[5]

5. All of this seems generally consistent with David Colander's (2003, 15) finding that as economists gain job experience they put increasing importance on such things as "a broad knowledge of the economics literature" and "a thorough knowledge of the economy."

Transcending this initial state of insulation from other viable identities seemed contingent on breaking down the barriers of practical insulation between academic and various other professional experiences:

> When you were in grad school you are entirely inside the academic world. So *success* is defined as going to a good university. . . . [but] before I went to graduate school, I worked at the Agency, and watched, and so I knew about the applied world. . . . And while I was in graduate school, I was doing consulting, working with one of our rivals. . . . So I was aware that there were other paths as well; I knew that it wasn't academics or nothing. (no. 30)

Even within the profession, then, images of what it is to be an economist were heterogeneous and distributed over space and time. Starting from more or less a blank slate in college, economists were explicitly encouraged to think of the real economist in terms of academic research. But over time, and with experience in various situations beyond grad school, many developed a much richer and more multifaceted sense of what makes a *real* real economist. And again there seemed to be a tool kit of several commonly used identifiers, such as facility with the core, the ability to communicate, and political skill. As I show next, a similar situation also seemed to characterize the interviewees' more personal expressions of identity.

Personal Images

One indication of how the interviewees perceived themselves at a more intimate, personal level comes from a rough, subjective interpretation of their answers to the first question in the interview, "What do you do?" The idea here is that identity images might be reflected to some extent in the objects mentioned—organizations, functions, fields, titles, and so on—and even in the pronouns and verbs used. The results again suggest a number of different elements involved, distributed to some extent unevenly between academics and nonacademics. For example, the percentage of subjects referring to some kind of organizational unit was similar for academics and nonacademics—around one-half—but the nonacademics were more likely to refer to their *subunit* within their organization, suggesting perhaps that their self-conception was more dependent on their particular institutional location.

A clearer difference between academics and nonacademics was that the basic use of "we" was much lower among the former—hardly any versus more than one-third among nonacademics—apparently indicating again that in some sense the self-conception of nonacademics was more group or organization based. Other differences in identification were that nonacademics were much more likely to mention their practical function (teaching, vetting policies, providing information, etc.) and their position of authority and responsibility. The few subjects who started with their *general* professional identifier "economist" were all nonacademics, but academics were more likely to start by announcing their *subfield* of specialization, which is still a professional rather than organizational identifier.[6]

A related interview question that might also have some bearing on identity concerned work enjoyment. When they were asked what they most liked about their jobs, most academics and nonacademics mentioned specific tasks, mainly teaching and researching for academics, and contemplating policy issues for nonacademics. But nonacademics were more likely than academics to mention real-world connections and influence as well as interaction with their work colleagues, which reinforces the idea that they were more organizationally or functionally identified than their academic counterparts:

> Being close to policymaking sometimes, having at least the image—I get cynical sometimes—[laughs] the *image* of influencing it, the image of being at the table or something like that, is also sorta fun. So we'll meet a minister of something or other and get to put your two cents in. Whether it has any influence on *anything*, I really don't know, but you have a sense that you're there. So that's also satisfying in a way. As long as you don't expect to change the world too much on your own. (no. 19)

Generally speaking however, it seemed as if the nonacademics did not have completely *different* sources of satisfaction from the academics, so much as a more even *spread* across various sources potentially available in any job, such as writing, interacting with colleagues, learning new things, and organizing group projects. In fact, more than one-quarter of the nonacademics, compared with less than one-tenth of the academics, explicitly identified with the variety of satisfactions involved in their job. As one subject put it,

6. For somewhat similar findings with respect to other professions, see Wallace 1995, Mueller and Lawler 1999, and Finley, Mueller, and Gurney 2002.

> There are several different types of satisfaction, . . . preventing bad things from happening, . . . the recognition of others that you've done something good. And . . . I get a reasonable amount of satisfaction when I do something generally of an academic nature, you know, deliver a paper at a conference, publish a paper in a journal, or a chapter in a book. . . . I also find it interesting and satisfying to interact with decision makers in the private sector . . . having a chance to really see as an outsider how the business works. . . . on those occasions when I've had line responsibility for a particular proceeding I have gotten satisfaction from bringing it to a conclusion and having the Agency adopt a final decision. . . . And I guess also I get sort of a social satisfaction just from the colleagues of mine. (no. 37)

What this suggests is that once again the positive self-identity of economists may have involved several resources that could be combined or substituted for each other without stepping beyond the boundaries of the image "professional economist." *Social* distribution and insulation could again have been involved here, preventing the most jarring conflicts between people emphasizing different elements, but the same structuring of awareness may also have been present at a *cognitive* level, allowing potentially contradictory elements to coexist. One intriguing indication of this is that even when interviewees were explicitly skeptical of the "official" image of academic scientist, they still in some way held on to it.

As noted above, there was widespread doubt that elite academic standards were "the" essence of economics, and many interviewees were reluctant to explicitly embrace the image of "science" or "scientist." When they were asked "are you a scientist; is economics a science?" only about one-third of the academics and nonacademics said yes, and of these, only two academics and two nonacademics failed to add some kind of qualification. The rest seemed fairly ambivalent:

> People ask me if I'm a scientist, I'd say, "No, I'm an economist." However, that doesn't mean I don't think it's rigorous, and I think it's as rigorous as science, many sciences, and many scient*ists*. It's actually in some ways—in a lot of ways—more like engineering than science. (no. 40)[7]

7. One must of course consider the effect of interview context on these kinds of self-report, although it seems somewhat unlikely that the respondents were completely dissembling or criticizing a part of their identity that in most other contexts was absolutely crucial. One must also consider the wording of the question in terms of "science" rather than "social science." It seems likely that most respondents would have accepted that economics is a social science or

But as noted above, some subjects still implicitly relied on the official identity when they doubted that they were real economists. This continuing legacy of training could also be seen in another kind of subjective evidence from the interviews: laughter. To appreciate this, it is necessary to consider a long-proposed explanation of laughter: that it is caused by a contradiction between reality and ideals. In the classic formulation of Arthur Schopenhauer (1958, 91),

> the phenomenon of laughter always signifies the sudden apprehension of an incongruity between . . . a concept and the real object thought through it, and hence between what is abstract and what is perceptive.

Applying this to the case at hand, one can argue that if economists at some level still held to the ideal academic-scientific image of the profession, or had it mentally close at hand in any situation, they might have laughed spontaneously when describing realities that contradicted it. As many of the preceding quotes illustrate, this seemed to be precisely the case. Further examples were as follows:

> Sometimes you get to the point of wondering [laughs] at least from the nonacademic point of view, do the academics really . . . have they ever gone into a bank, and found out what a bank does [laughing]? (no. 16)

> We had a seminar here this year. Somebody who had the third most downloaded paper at the end, and it was a terrible paper, and a great title [laughs]. So . . .
> M: I guess they had the word "sex" in the title.
> Almost as good. It had the word "hedging" in the title [laughs]. (no. 19)

> Economists know one thing; demand slopes down. Everything else is obfuscation of that point [laughs]. (no. 20)

> Within microeconomics there's a bit more unanimity [than in macro], . . . whether we're *right* or not who knows [laughs]. (no. 21)

What this suggests is that the academic image of economics persisted within the minds of professionals, but tended to be insulated from images that contradicted it, causing the professionals momentary problems only

---

even that economics is the *most* scientific of the social sciences (cf. Colander 2003, 9). But it is interesting that when the question was framed in the more absolute terms, the kinds of things that many economists said suggest that "most scientific of the social sciences" may not be particularly high praise.

in relatively unusual situations such as laying out their opinions and experiences in a recorded interview. Identities constructed using the tool kit of personal identifiers did not therefore have to be seamless and consistent, merely stable with respect to what a particular economist typically did and thought about at different times and in different situations. To paraphrase the social psychologist George Herbert Mead (1962, 142), for economists of this generation a multiple personality was in a sense normal.

One final indication of this cognitive structuring was the fact that despite commitment to the intuitive "core" skills of economics, very few of the interviewees seemed to use that core when explaining and commenting on their own life stories. To look for this kind of effect, the interview transcripts were searched for the use of economic theory–based metaphors applied to things not directly related to economics.[8] Out of a list of fifty root phrases, academics mentioned on average 5.46, while nonacademics mentioned slightly more, 5.81.[9] The pattern was similar for the average total number of mentions of any of the fifty: 8.8 for academics and 9.6 for nonacademics. This does not seem particularly high for conversations lasting on average an hour and ten minutes, especially given that most of the metaphors used were ones perhaps commonly applied by anyone living in a capitalist society, such as market, value, skill, choice, decision, and personal preference. An example of this kind of borderline use was the subject who stated the following:

> I don't think we're well organized, both as a discipline or as a marketing entity by any means, to have that kind of influence, and I think the values are really not so much on a lot of the nuts and bolts applied work that really is important to understand. (no. 39)

More clearly esoteric uses were phrases such as "I understand we use [publishing] as the signaling mechanism. So I appreciate that aspect, but to me it's a very inefficient equilibrium" (no. 11), and "we had people that

8. It did not seem sensible to mark the use of economics terms when subjects discussed more or less economic matters, or matters for which economic phrases are definitely commonly used by laypeople. Examples of the latter were talk of job "markets" and the "cost" of living.

9. The phrases marked in the various forms they appeared—given appropriate usage—were as follows: demand, preference, comparative advantage, margin, opportunity cost, equilibrium, market, elastic, price, supply, demand, maximum, minimum, rational, efficient, incentive, benefit, diversify, expectation, distribution, value, shortage, cheap, decision, choice, depreciate, capital, trade, reward, expense, portfolio, sell, stochastic, skill, scarce, resource, normative, cost, substitute, division of labor, produce, information, input, output, risk, competition, zero-sum, premium, option, and buy.

would train for theory that had far less math than I do, and it's *silly* because it's not their comparative advantage" (no. 26). But while it seemed possible that these were more often used by academics, they were actually so infrequent that there was really no reliable pattern. Perhaps surprisingly to many critics of economics, even "market," "cost," "supply," and "demand" were seldom used when discussing nominally noneconomic matters. It seems therefore that by this crude measure economists had not absorbed their expertise to the point of exhibiting a blanket "occupational psychosis," that is, a professional identity so dominant that they were "incapable of understanding other ways of describing things, even in their private lives" (Feyerabend 1978, 50). In other words, they could limit their use of core skills to particular parts of their lives and switch off their economic way of thinking in others.

Overall, then, the interviews contain several suggestions that, even at the level of personal identity, images of "the economist" were heterogeneous and structured by distribution and insulation. Individuals working in different settings could form a variety of positive self-images from a tool kit of possible elements, even when some of those elements were somewhat logically incompatible. Partly as a result of this, it seems, ideals of the academic scientist picked up during training neither completely dominated economists' identities nor fell apart in response to other, contradictory images.[10]

Conclusion

The preceding discussion suggests how autobiographies and self-reports can reveal interesting information despite the logical difficulty of separating their objective content from subjective forms of expression. It treated the interview transcripts sometimes as evidence of situations, sequences of events, or explicitly stated beliefs and attitudes, and sometimes as indications of unconscious dispositions and styles of talking. This kind of analysis must inevitably "bootstrap" its dual interpretations, but the discussion tried to support its claims by comparing multiple autobiographical reports and looking for general patterns in the statements of economists working in a wide variety of institutional settings.

10. This is perhaps similar to Michèle Lamont's (2000) finding that working-class identity in France and the United States involves more than just comparison with upper-class standards and that it varies according to local situations and resources.

The aim of the interpretation was to discover something about the identities of economists working in the United States at the end of the twentieth century. Its main finding in this respect was the heterogeneity and distribution of positive images of "economist," and the images' potential spatial, temporal, and cognitive insulation from each other. Rather than there being a single image, there seemed to be a cultural tool kit of possible identifiers available to economists and laypeople at all three levels of analysis: public impressions, internal professional standards, and personal identity. These elements could be combined in multiple ways to produce both negative and positive images, not all of them reducible to the ideal of economists as academic scientists producing abstract formal knowledge.

There are several ways this basic finding might be useful to historians of economics. At the level of public images it suggests that there are major problems with focusing too much on internal disciplinary debates. What laypeople see and think of economics—and hence presumably how disposed they are to support the profession—does not seem to hinge solely on the difference between neutral scientist and political advocate, at least in this particular historical setting. Of course, intellectual historians may not be interested in sources of legitimation and social support, but insofar as they are, they would certainly benefit from looking beyond what elite economists themselves say within their own professional arena.

At the level of that professional arena itself, the analysis clearly reconfirmed the existence of a powerful ideal of abstract academic science in late-twentieth-century American economics. However, it also suggested that commitment to this ideal was both more limited and more subtle than is typically acknowledged. The balance between scientific standards and other ideals of what makes a good economist is a socially complex phenomenon, and historians interested in the discipline's professional institutions might benefit from considering in more depth the distribution and insulation of multiple images even within a dominant orthodoxy. The idea of distribution and insulation over time might also be useful here, suggesting as it does that changes in commitment over the course of a career are normal and may follow predictable patterns within a given historical setting.

Finally, at the level of personal images the analysis might again be useful to historians primarily because of what it reveals to be normal and predictable. If its claims about cognitive structuring are correct, one would fully expect economists to make contradictory self-presentations at different times and in different places, perhaps even within single utterances. This does not make their personal testimonies worthless as sources of information, but it does mean that those testimonies should seldom be expected to form single coherent narratives. The lives of economists make as much sense as those of anyone else, but historians of economics might want to look for that sense less in grand overarching personal ideologies and more in the perfectly normal fragmented, and situation-specific, ways their subjects imagine their identities.

References

Allen, William R. 1977. Economics, Economists, and Economic Policy: Modern American Experiences. *HOPE* 9:48–88.

Ashmore, Malcolm, Michael Mulkay, and Trevor Pinch. 1989. *Health and Efficiency: A Sociology of Health Economics*. Philadelphia: Open University Press.

Barber, William J. 1985. *From New Era to New Deal: Herbert Hoover, the Economists, and American Economic Policy, 1921–1933*. New York: Cambridge University Press.

———. 1996. *Designs within Disorder: Franklin D. Roosevelt, the Economists, and the Shaping of American Economic Policy, 1933–1945*. New York: Cambridge University Press.

Barbezat, Debra A. 1992. The Market for New Ph.D. Economists. *Journal of Economic Education* 23:262–76.

Bassi, Laurie J. 1989. Special Study to Interview Nonacademic Employers of Economists. Unpublished manuscript, American Economic Association Commission on Graduate Education in Economics.

Bazerman, Charles. 2004. Speech Acts, Genres, and Activity Systems: How Texts Organize Activity and People. In *What Writing Does and How It Does It: An Introduction to Analyzing Textual Practices*, edited by Charles Bazerman and Paul Prior. Mahwah, N.J.: Erlbaum Associates.

Berger, Peter L., and Thomas Luckmann. 1966. *The Social Construction of Reality: A Treatise in the Sociology of Knowledge*. New York: Anchor.

Bertaux, Daniel, and Martin Kohli. 1984. The Life Story Approach: A Continental View. *Annual Review of Sociology* 10:215–37.

Biddle, Jeff. 1998. Institutional Economics: A Case of Reproductive Failure? In *From Interwar Pluralism to Postwar Neoclassicism*, edited by Mary Morgan and Malcolm Rutherford. *HOPE* 30 (supplement): 108–33.

Brenner, Reuven. 1992. Macroeconomics: The Masks of Science and Myths of Good Policy. In *Educating Economists*, edited by David Colander and Reuven Brenner. Ann Arbor: University of Michigan Press.

Burkhardt, Jeffrey, and E. Ray Canterbery. 1986. The Orthodoxy and Professional Legitimacy: Toward a Critical Sociology of Economics. *Research in the History and Methodology of Economics* 4:229–50.

Coats, A. W. 1980. The Culture and the Economists: Some Reflections on Anglo-American Differences. *HOPE* 12:588–609.

——, ed. 1981. *Economists in Government: An International Comparative Study.* Durham, N.C.: Duke University Press.

——, ed. 1986. *Economists in International Agencies: An Exploratory Study.* New York: Praeger.

Colander, David. 2003. The Aging of an Economist. Discussion Paper 03–04, Middlebury College, Department of Economics.

Day, Colin. 1989. Journals, University Presses, and the Spread of Ideas. In *The Spread of Economic Ideas*, edited by David Colander and A. W. Coats. Cambridge: Cambridge University Press.

Feyerabend, Paul K. 1978. From Incompetent Professionalism to Professionalized Incompetence—the Rise of a New Breed of Intellectuals. *Philosophy of the Social Sciences* 8:37–53.

Finley, Ashley P., Charles W. Mueller, and Cynthia A. Gurney. 2002. Organizational and Professional Commitment in Professional and Non-Professional Organizations: The Case of Nurse Doctorates. *Research in Social Stratification and Mobility* 20:325–58.

Furner, Mary O. 1975. *Advocacy and Objectivity: A Crisis in the Professionalization of American Social Science, 1865–1905.* Lexington: University Press of Kentucky.

Goffman, Erving. 1959. *The Presentation of Self in Everyday Life.* Garden City, N.Y.: Doubleday.

Goodwin, Craufurd D. 1980. Toward a Theory of the History of Economics. *HOPE* 12:610–19.

Hinshaw, C. Elton, and John J. Siegfried. 1995. Who Gets on the AEA Program? *Journal of Economic Perspectives* 9:153–63.

Katouzian, Homa. 1980. *Ideology and Method in Economics.* New York: New York University Press.

Klamer, Arjo, and David Colander. 1990. *The Making of an Economist.* Boulder, Colo.: Westview.

Krueger, Anne O. 1991. Report of the Commission on Graduate Education in Economics. *Journal of Economic Literature* 29:1035–53.

Lamont, Michèle. 2000. *The Dignity of Working Men: Morality and the Boundaries of Race, Class, and Immigration.* Cambridge, Mass.: Harvard University Press.

Laslett, Barbara. 1999. Personal Narratives as Sociology. *Contemporary Sociology* 28:391–401.

Leontief, Wassily. 1982. Academic Economics. *Science* 217:104–5.

Linde, Charlotte. 1993. *Life Stories: The Creation of Coherence.* New York: Oxford University Press.

Mead, George Herbert. 1962. *Mind, Self, and Society from the Standpoint of a Social Behaviorist.* Chicago: University of Chicago Press.

Mirowski, Philip. 1989. *More Heat Than Light: Economics as Social Physics, Physics as Nature's Economics.* New York: Cambridge University Press.

——. 1991. The When, the How, and the Why of Mathematical Expression in the History of Economic Analysis. *Journal of Economic Perspectives* 5.1:145–57.

Mueller, Charles W., and Edward J. Lawler. 1999. Commitment to Nested Organizational Units: Some Basic Principles and Preliminary Findings. *Social Psychology Quarterly* 62:325–46.

Potter, Jonathan, and Michael Mulkay. 1985. Scientists' Interview Talk: Interviews as a Technique for Revealing Participants' Interpretative Practices. In *The Research Interview: Uses and Approaches*, edited by Michael Brenner, Jennifer Brown, and David Canter. New York: Academic.

Ruggles, Nancy D., ed. 1970. *Economics*. Englewood Cliffs, N.J.: Prentice Hall.

Schaeffer, Nora Cate, and Stanley Presser. 2003. The Science of Asking Questions. *Annual Review of Sociology* 29:65–88.

Schopenhauer, Arthur. 1958. *The World as Will and Representation*. Vol. 2. Indian Hills, Colo.: Falcon's Wing Press.

Scott, Loren C., and Peter M. Mitias. 1996. Trends in Rankings of Economics Departments in the U.S.: An Update. *Economic Inquiry* 36:378–400.

Shubik, Martin. 1970. A Curmudgeon's Guide to Microeconomics. *Journal of Economic Literature* 8:405–34.

Siegfried, John, and Wendy Stock. 2004. The Market for New Ph.D. Economists in 2002. *American Economic Review* 94.2:272–85.

Stock, Wendy, and W. Lee Hansen. 2004. Ph.D. Program Learning and Job Demands: How Close Is the Match? *American Economic Review* 94.2:266–71.

Swidler, Ann. 1986. Culture in Action: Symbols and Strategies. *American Sociological Review* 51:273–86.

Tarascio, Vincent J. 1986. The Crisis in Economic Theory: A Sociological Perspective. *Research in the History of Economic Theory and Methodology* 4:283–95.

Wallace, Jean E. 1995. Organizational and Professional Commitment in Professional and Nonprofessional Organizations. *Administrative Science Quarterly* 40:228–55.

Weintraub, E. Roy, and Philip Mirowski. 1994. The Pure and the Applied: Bourbakism Comes to Mathematical Economics. *Science in Context* 7:245–72.

Yonay, Yuval. 1998. *The Struggle over the Soul of Economics: Institutionalist and Neoclassical Economists in America between the Wars*. Princeton, N.J.: Princeton University Press.

Zussman, Robert. 1996. Autobiographical Occasions. *Contemporary Sociology* 25:143–48.

The Role of Oral History in the Historiography of Heterodox Economics

Tiago Mata and Frederic S. Lee

In recent years, we have witnessed in the history of economics a remarkable increase in the publication of biographies, autobiographies, biographical dictionaries, collections of interviews, and oral histories (surveyed in Forget 2002 and Moggridge 2003). For the history of heterodox economics,[1] the trend has been the collection of brief autobiographical testimonies and biographical entries into dictionary volumes (Harcourt 1993; Arestis and Sawyer [1992] 2000; Backhouse and Middleton 2000). This literature comprises simple narratives, exclusively concerned with the professional life of individuals, typically stringing together an author's contributions to reveal a unifying intellectual mission.

We thank the participants at the 2006 *HOPE* conference for their critical engagement with our essay; in particular, we have greatly benefited from the comments of an anonymous referee and from the suggestions of this volume's editors, E. Roy Weintraub and Evelyn Forget. Tiago Mata has benefited from a travel grant from the Central London Research Fund to conduct interviews with American radical economists and from a postdoctoral fellowship from the Economic and Social Research Council (U.K.) for the writing of this essay. We owe a special debt of gratitude to the radical economists who spoke to us about their economics and politics, in particular Laurie Nisonoff, Nancy Wiegersma, Herbert Gintis, Michael Zweig, John Weeks, and Barry Bluestone.

1. The term *heterodox economics* refers in a collective sense to various heterodox approaches and paradigms, such as Austrian, feminist, Marxian, Post Keynesian, and radical economics; to the community of heterodox economists who engage in and across the paradigms; and to the development of an alternative economic theory and policy that draws from the various heterodox approaches.

History of Political Economy 39 (annual suppl.) DOI 10.1215/00182702-2006-043

The flood of testimonies and short biographies has so far had a modest impact on the arguments of historians of heterodox economics. For instance, the most recent and significant work in the history of Post Keynesian economics, *A History of Post Keynesian Economics since 1936* by John E. King (2002), makes only passing reference to life history details despite its author's conversations with Post Keynesians about their working lives (King 1995). In King's comprehensive intellectual history, biographical materials appear sparingly, never exceeding a paragraph, serving only to introduce his cast of characters. These materials convey information about nationality and education, not unlike what one would find on the first page of a CV or in a short entry to a biographical dictionary (King 2002, 18, 35–36, 105, 110, 114, 125, 185). The only biographical resource used recurrently by King is A. P. Thirwall's (1987) biography of Nicholas Kaldor, from which King (2002, 49–50, 63, 76) draws to support a running commentary on Kaldor's political and policy commitments and to explain his theoretical dilettantism.

We wish to distinguish our approach to the history of heterodox economics from earlier contributions, where "it was the ideas that were paramount. Anything uniquely personal about the author of the ideas—passions, idiosyncrasies, or even 'vision'—was considered irrelevant" (Forget 2002, 231). We do not propose a history of heterodox theory, which has already been partially accomplished,[2] but a history of the heterodox community that provides the social basis for theory development.[3] We seek to get at the social relationships and agency that ensured that heterodox economists could do research and publish in heterodox economics, could teach it, and could engage in professional and activist heterodox activities.

Our essay addresses the problem of how life histories can be used to write the history of heterodox economics as a history of communities of scholars. Our contention is that social relationships are not easily discerned from the professional writings of scholars. Instead, we suggest that the sites for this evidence are a variety of dispersed personal media, locked away in private correspondence or in the unspoken memories of the participants. In

2. See, for example, Howard and King 1989, 1992; King 2002; and Hodgson 2004.

3. We speak here of community instead of network. We acknowledge that the term *network* is favored by the sociology of knowledge literature, but since we wish to address dimensions that are sometimes lost in sociological and semiotic analysis, such as emotional, trust, and personal ties between historical subjects, the concept of community seems more adequate.

our research we have considered published testimonies; conducted "oral history interviewing" (Morrisey 1998); and solicited from participants their written memories of particular events.[4] We are not biographers, as we do not seek from these materials to build an account of a life. Instead, we have used life histories as a record of the making of relationships of identity and difference in the heterodox community (Peacock and Holland 1993; Watson 1976).[5]

Reflective statements by historians of economics on life histories have tended to focus on the failings of memory (Moggridge 2003, 597; Tribe 1997; Weintraub 2005). It has often been remarked that memory weighs, distorts, and displaces events, particularly in "life history interviews" where the recollection of dates or sequences of events are ostensibly shown to be unreliable (Portelli 1991). If our concern is with fact, then one may invoke Carlo Ginzburg's (1992) description of the practice of history as akin to detective work. It is only by being attentive to many clues and details that the mysteries of the past may be uncovered, and one should seek multiple sources of evidence as checks to the informant's memory. It is unlikely that a formula can be devised to replace the historian's judgment. History is a craft that cannot be fully formalized, and one must rely on the unscientifically sounding "instinct, insight and intuition" (Ginzburg 1992, 125).

It is when autobiographical testimonies are made to do more than recover past events that they begin to yield insights that no other evidential source can match.[6] Both the written testimony and the life history interview are "the construction and expression of one's subjectivity. To ignore or exorcise subjectivity, as if it were only a noxious interference in the pure data, is ultimately to distort and falsify the nature of the data themselves" (Portelli 1997, 80). We propose to look at how heterodox economists have constructed the narrative of their lives (Portelli 1998). As Paul John Eakin (this volume) argues, self-narration is our culture's privileged resource to experience selfhood and locate it in the cultural

4. Each of these materials poses particular problems. For instance, oral sources need to be studied differently from written ones, to consider the nature of orality and the study of pauses—see the overview provided in Portelli 1991.

5. Our aim is akin to that of Mike Reay's (this volume). Reay studies the multiple and heterogeneous "images" or "identities" economists may hold in relation to their profession, expressed in statements about what economists "know" or "do." Our emphasis is on how one such self-image, the radical one, was historically constituted.

6. The papers collected in the volume edited by Robert Perks and Alistair Thomson (1998) forcefully make this point.

landscape. Far from polluting historical discourse, the subjective discourse of the participants is an invaluable resource for historical and ethnographic research.

In the remainder of this essay we illustrate how we believe subjectivity, expressed in interviews and testimonies, can be used for the history of heterodox economics communities. Our case study is on radical economics, and we begin section 1 with a brief account of the founding of the Union for Radical Political Economics (URPE). Then, we illustrate how life histories can be used to uncover the formation of identity between heterodox economists. Our material refers to the first crucial years of URPE's growth in creating a radical community. In the second section, we address a silence of the written record. Through the 1970s, URPE was subject to a series of schisms that were not registered in print. Life histories are the only entry point to study these troubling times. The essay concludes with a discussion of what it means to use life histories to make visible what is invisible.

1. Life Histories and the Creation of the Radical Economics Community

Heterodox economic theories and communities of heterodox economists have existed in the United States throughout the twentieth century. However, as a result of repression by McCarthyism, the pre-1950s heterodoxy seemed doomed and, as a corollary, that the history of heterodoxy had run its course. Yet from the 1960s communities of Marxist-radical, institutional, Post Keynesian, and social economists were created anew, without clear lines of descent both intellectual and social from the earlier heterodoxy (Lee 2000, 2004a, 2004b). The historian is thus posed with a striking discontinuity, and the problem of accounting for the formation of these new heterodox entities ex nihilo.

URPE was formed at a five-day conference held at Ann Arbor, Michigan, from 4 to 8 September 1968.[7] "It was attended by a small group of twelve graduate students and faculty members, all of whom were affected and influenced by the civil rights movement, Vietnam War, feminist movement, and the New Left" (Lee 2004a, 187–88). Meetings between radical faculty members and students in economics preceded the founding of URPE. These meetings are difficult to chronicle, for they left no written

7. Members are often referred to as "URPErs."

records. From the memory of participants these seemed to have been frequent and informal, and mainly organized from the University of Michigan (186–87).

The preliminary contacts between radicals are insufficient to account for the remarkable and immediate increase in URPE's membership. In December 1968, three months after its formal creation, the first issue of its *Newsletter* reported a total membership of three hundred paying members and an even more impressive mailing list of eight hundred names (Bluestone 1969, 5). How were the twelve graduate students and young faculty from the Ann Arbor meeting able to achieve such a success?[8] The argument of this section is that an answer can be given only with resort to the detail of life histories and to the subjectivity they evince.[9]

If we survey the published autobiographical testimonies of radical economists, it is striking to find that although they refer to the 1960s as a crucial formative period for their research commitments, there is only brief mention of URPE. Most of these autobiographical entries become an occasion to review a life work of a radical economist and to reveal connections between what may appear to be diverse interests and contributions. Such intellectual reflections are usually performed to the detriment of more private aspects of a life. Recurrent in these narratives is the reference to the "political ferment" of sixties' social movements, said to have fundamentally shaped radicals' political convictions and directed their interests in scholarship (Sherman [1992] 2000, 604; Reich [1992] 2000, 578).

Some of these autobiographical testimonies are more revealing, such as that of Samuel Bowles. Bowles ([1992] 2000) begins his life narrative by retelling how in his first year teaching introductory economics his students challenged him on the curriculum's social relevance. He adds, "They continued to press me, but they were leaning on an open door. It was 1965" (Bowles [1992] 2000, 73).[10] For Thomas Weisskopf ([1992] 2000,

8. The rise in membership was sustained through the early 1970s—from 1969 to 1972 membership increased 40 percent a year (Historical Profile of URPE 1976).

9. For this and the following section we draw on a set of over twenty interviews collected by Mata with radical economists for an ongoing project on the history of radical economics. These were all one- to two-hour interviews collected in close accordance with the precepts set by oral historians and "life history interviewing" (see Thompson 1988 and Seldon and Pappworth 1983).

10. The mid-1960s is often identified as the tipping point for the formation of a critical-radical consciousness among the young economics faculty. For another instance, "From 1966 on it became increasingly difficult to persuade oneself that public service in the US would have any positive effect on issues of poverty, social justice, civil rights and peace" (Foley [1992] 2000, 182).

710), the critical experience that radicalized his views on economics was research work in planning India's economic development; he became disillusioned "about the relevance of mainstream economics." URPE appears in these narratives as a late-sixties phenomenon, to which these leading radical figures proudly claim ownership as founding members (Bowles [1992] 2000, 75; Gordon [1992] 2000, 250; Weisskopf [1992] 2000, 710; Reich [1992] 2000, 578; Sherman [1992] 2000, 604).

Inasmuch as the lives contained in the available (auto)biographical collections are those of the generally recognized leaders of the radical community, they may provide us with a view of the past that emphasizes the motives of the founding cohort of radicals, which are also the elite within the radical community.[11] Additionally, these were scholars who, after intense involvement in the organization of the radical community throughout the 1970s, abandoned active participation in URPE in the early 1980s. It is likely that this subjective distance leads these individuals to retrospectively consider URPE of lesser significance. A different perspective of this past arises when one records the life narratives of a younger cohort of radicals,[12] or of those who constituted the rank and file of URPE in the 1970s, who have to this day maintained their commitment to URPE.

In the remainder of this essay we focus on the life narrative of one radical economist, Laurie Nisonoff, as an entry point to some of the issues that affected URPE in the early 1970s.[13] Her life is not intended to be representative of a radical's life, and the subplots we selected from Nisonoff's narration should not be taken as a definitive account of the radical group's history. This life narrative is instructive when placed alongside evidence collected in other interviews or from URPE's publications. It is the corroboration (or contradiction) between these various bits of evidence that we wish to explore in detail.

11. *Elite* in this context is meant to denote an older cohort of scholars who were hired in the early 1970s by universities with graduate programs and research opportunities.

12. For the younger cohort the radical experience is not just one of conversion to radical ideas but also one of joining their older graduate colleagues and the young radical faculty. For instance, William H. Lazonick (2000, 414) recalls how he was surprised at Harvard University by the presence of a score of radicals who assisted him in developing his own critical ideas. For those entering graduate school in 1968–71, the story is no longer one of a solitary conversion to radicalism but of a collective undertaking. Consistent with our interpretation, research in political science has underlined the effect of generation and cohort in determining what events are recalled and how they are interpreted (see Schuman and Scott 1989).

13. Our approach echoes that of Mary Terrall (2006, 308–9), reflecting on how to consider issues of social identity in the context of a single life.

In 1968 Nisonoff decided to major in economics.[14] She had entered MIT the previous year to study mathematics. As was the case for many students of the late 1960s, the choice of economics was partly informed by leftist political convictions (Horowitz 1986). Nisonoff recalls:

> I discovered that not only was mathematics no longer very interesting, but mathematicians . . . had absolutely no social awareness, and absolutely no social skills and it was, it was incredibly lonely! Plus, you know, meanwhile back on the ranch, I had been doing all this political work for years. So I had all this political work over here, and then I have this beautiful pure mathematics over there, but there seemed to be no connection.

When she was asked about how she had joined URPE, Nisonoff did not produce a theoretical justification but remembered a collection of events that register her personal involvement with other radicals.[15] Nisonoff joined URPE after being introduced to the group by MIT leftists. What drew the MIT URPErs together were not merely shared intellectual concerns. What Nisonoff highlights in her narrative are the political convictions and activities they held in common, which distinguished them as a group:

> When URPE began, at MIT, . . . the undergrads, the graduate students and the young faculty just did things together. . . . In that fall, in early November, . . . soldiers that were trying to avoid being sent to Vietnam would go AWOL, and we protected them. This young man stayed with us at MIT and hundreds of people took turns staying with him. . . . I was [there] and . . . these various graduate students and undergraduates, . . . some of the faculty, including Duncan Foley and Matt Edel. . . . And we were talking about the war and imperialism, the left young faculty were actually teaching their classes there, my fellow majors had to come in to the occupation.[16]

14. Laurie Nisonoff was interviewed on 6 June 2003, at her office in Hampshire College, Amherst, Massachusetts.

15. The same was true of other interviews. For instance, both Michael Zweig (interviewed 18 June 2003, in New York) and John Weeks (interviewed 10 February 2006, in London) recalled the conflict between graduate students and teaching assistants and the Michigan faculty over the awarding of grades that would be the basis for the Selective Service System to draft half of the undergraduate students to fight in Vietnam (for further details, see Brazer 1982, 248–49).

16. This was a major event at MIT; see, for instance, Noam Chomsky's recollection of it in Chomsky et al. 1997.

In her narration about joining URPE, Nisonoff contrasted the identification she felt with the URPE group with estrangement from her conventional colleagues:

> 'Cause a lot of people had the social skills of furniture, and they did their homework, and they stayed in. . . . I got in a lot of trouble with the other women in my class. . . . it turned out that the room we were doing this in [protecting the AWOL soldier] was where our junior prom was supposed to be. At that point there were people in the women's dorm who never spoke to me again . . . to this day, because the junior prom was cancelled!

Trivial as these events may seem to our habitual historical discourse, they are the highlights in participants' life narratives, particularly as conveyed in interviews. In participants' perceptions, in their subjectivities, these events record the formation of bounds of identity (inevitably also of friendship) between fellow radicals in economics. Furthermore, it is also a testimony to the confrontational dynamics of this period: as the bounds between radicals strengthened, so did radicals' estrangement from their mainstream colleagues and teachers.

Our argument gives us cause to research which events took place in the formative years of URPE, roughly from 1968 to 1971; to provide their chronology; and to study their impact on the burgeoning URPE. For 1969 Nisonoff recalled the New England conference that she helped organize.[17] The conference was held in her last year at MIT prior to her departure to Yale University for graduate work. It appears the choice of Yale was made after she had befriended graduate students from that university, whom she had met at the New England conference and also, crucially, at the 1969 protest to the American Economic Association (for a report of the protests, see pages 487–89 of the *Papers and Proceedings* issue of the 1970 volume of the *American Economic Review*).[18] What is significant for our purpose is how the life story records the formation of a community. The example offered by Nisonoff's life story shows how conferences and the AEA protest were occasions to enlist new members for URPE and to strengthen ties of friendship and comradeship between URPE members.

17. For a report on the meeting, see URPE National Conference 1969 and New England Regional Conference 1969.

18. Nisonoff mentioned Heidi Hartmann, Peggy Howard, Fran Blau, and Rich Weisskopf from New Haven and Lourdes (Surkin) Beneria from New York.

In its early years URPE did not lack ambition. Radicals wanted their economics to be personal and political, and their organization to reflect that project by becoming more than a professional association (see Wachtel and Bluestone 1969). Outside the curricular calendar URPE organized an annual summer conference starting in 1969. The first one was held 24–31 August at Camp Sea Gull, in Charlevoix, Michigan.[19] The summer conferences had a diverse agenda. While nearly all sessions were concerned with economic topics, some were decidedly more oriented toward activism than others. This is evident with regard to sessions on imperialism (1969, 1970, 1971), teaching and curriculum (1969, 1970), radical paradigms (1971), political economy of health care (1970, 1971), capitalism's alternative (1969, 1971), women's liberation (1969, 1970, 1971), community action programs (1970, 1971), and ghetto and black liberation (1969, 1970, 1971).[20] The conferences were an occasion to debate organizational strategy for URPE, but they were also a place to celebrate and to play. The announcement for the first conference read: "All of the facilities of the camp including tennis courts, sail boats, canoes, power boats, swimming, archery, baseball, football, etc. are available to conference participants. We are planning to arrange the conference so that at least one-third of your time can be spent in recreation. Child care will be arranged. Participants should bring their own bedding and tennis balls. Pets are allowed" (URPE National Conference 1969). It is the element of play and passionate political debating that radicals recall best in interviews. For example, although today Herbert Gintis no longer sees promise in radical analysis and has dissociated himself from the community, he recalls with fondness the political work URPErs did together and the convivial character of their organization: "We got together to hand out, we sang, we made up songs, we, you know, we made love to each other."[21] And as another radical

19. The second conference was held at Camp Wakitatina, north of Pittsburgh, from 27 to 31 August. In this second year, there was not enough cabin space for all the expected participants, and URPErs were encouraged to bring tents (URPE Summer Conference 1970; Summer Conference Urges Action 1970).

20. The sessions were also standard fare at various national, regional, and local URPE-radical conferences held from 1969 to 1971, which also included sessions on critiques of mainstream economics, inflation, Marxist methodology, monopoly and monopoly capital, and the economics of housework; see the issues of the *Newsletter of the Union for Radical Political Economics* published between 1969 and 1971.

21. Herbert Gintis was interviewed on 6 June 2003, at his home in Northampton, Massachusetts. More generally, social activities, such as parties, lunches, dinners, and guerrilla theater, were built into most URPE-radical conferences; see the issues of the *Newsletter of the Union for Radical Political Economics* published between 1969 and 1971.

acknowledged with praise: "Those of us who attended left the [summer] Conference with a feeling of unity which could not have been attained in any other way" (Hinckley 1969).[22]

The point we are making here is one of community and identity. Participants' narratives of their lives register the formation of a radical economics identity, which sustains the community that is URPE. The life histories that radicals tell reveal that this identity was forged during protests within academia, where the radicals joined each other and where they became estranged from their conventional colleagues and faculty. The meetings organized under URPE's auspices further strengthened the identity: the regional conferences and the summer meeting. This identity was not strictly intellectual in content; it reflected a political and cultural overlap best illustrated in the activities of the summer conference. Play seems to have been as crucial to building a radical economics community as a conviction of the faults of mainstream economics.

2. Life Histories and Conflicts within the Radical Community

The argument of this essay is that life histories provide clues to the emergence of communities of scholars, revealing the making of bonds of identity that underpin their intellectual commitments. The same evidence can be instructive in understanding the emergence of difference within communities. Current historical scholarship has ignored a wealth of internal strife that reshaped the radical community in the 1970s. These controversies are salient in the primary literature, in the written record of URPE's *Newsletter*, most dramatically in its August 1975 issue.[23] Elsewhere in the secondary literature these debates are ignored, both in the intellectual histories (Gintis 1980, 1984) and in the more institutionally focused ones (Fleck 2003). Given the silence of the secondary literature and the relative paucity of the written primary record, we are drawn to life histories. It is through these life histories that we can best examine the transformation of URPE, from an ecumenical late-1960s genesis to its fracture in the mid-1970s into a plurality of groups that began to lead separate existences.

One of the major, if not the major, schism that placed stress on the radical economics community was the divide between men and women.

22. At the same time, it was lamented that the conferences were not intellectually productive (Hinckley 1969).

23. See Mata 2005 for a tentative history of this period.

In 1969 a women's group was created in URPE (Weisskoff 1970), meeting occasionally in its first couple of years with little effect. It appears that the group was too diverse to develop a common discourse and program for action: "Some were members of URPE, and were concerned with discrimination both in URPE and within the economics profession. Others of us resented any obligation to become involved in what was our husband's or boyfriend's organization, not ours" (Howard 1970, 4). In 1971 at URPE's summer conference, the women's caucus came to the fore, demanding representation at the editorial board of URPE's scholarly journal, the *Review of Radical Political Economics*, and at its steering committee. The proposal was initially resisted by the men, and only after some dramatic debating was it accepted (for a report of the events, see Horowitz et al. 1971). How are we to understand this passionate division of opinion, this bitter dispute in an otherwise harmonious community of self-identifying radical economists?

Once again, we draw on the Nisonoff interview for answers. From the start of her interview, Nisonoff proposed to tell "the story of how women's liberation came to URPE," adding jokingly that "it wasn't pretty." Already in this phrasing we have hints of the structure of her story. It is "women's liberation" and not "women's issues" or "women's studies"; for Nisonoff and for the other participants in these events the origins of the divide were political, coming from the emergent women's liberation movement (see Evans 1980 and Morgan 1970).

In her interview, Nisonoff offered a complete and articulate narrative of this period:

> There were two URPE chapters in the Boston area. . . . The two chapters are cooperating on running this conference in the fall of 1969 [the New England conference], and . . . the Harvard chapter decided, well Paddy [Patricia Quick] should work at the desk, and the MIT chapter decided that I should work at the desk. And this was a big mistake. . . . People should not just like assume these things, 'cause it's dangerous. So, in fact, at one point in that conference, Paddy and I just went to the ladies room and we didn't come back, during the business meeting, for like the better part of an hour.
>
> And then . . . there were usually one, or two, or three women in any given place, [but] when I got to New Haven . . . we had about, between the wives . . . and the . . . graduate students we had about . . . six or eight women, eventually ten or twelve women in URPE. In the spring of

> ’71, six of us, URPErs, . . . rented a house together, 700 Fountain Street, and . . . URPE began to have a lot of meetings there as well. . . . we began to decide that you know, something needed to be done. And there were other groups of women in Boston, . . . and in New York . . . , and in Washington, D.C.

In this first part of her story, Nisonoff gives us an example of the sexist behavior of male URPErs, who picked the two women in the group for the dull tasks of receptionists. She also offers an explanation of how the otherwise divided women’s caucus was able to organize for the 1971 protest, the explanation resting in the closely knit group of female graduate students at Yale University who began to share a house in 1970.

Nisonoff relates the events at the 1971 summer conference:

> When we were at the summer conference, a woman . . . , now known as Tucker Farley, . . . who is in comparative literature . . . and the Modern Language Association had allowed graduate students in, on to the board of the MLA, to incorporate all these new social movements and their impact on the disciplines, within the Modern Language Association. And Tucker said that what we needed in the AEA and in URPE . . . [was] our own official women’s caucus. And so we went off, into the woods, someplace, sat around on logs and talked about it, about twelve or fifteen of us, and we decided that we were going to propose three women, to join the editorial board, . . . and that . . . two would serve on the steering committee.
>
> We went to one of the business meetings, and we said that we had these proposals and everybody starts mumbling and grumbling and giving us a lot of trouble. . . . And at a certain point I had run out of the things we had decided. So I said, well, “Excuse me but I need to go outside, with the other women who are making this proposal,” but that isn’t what happened. Every woman in the room pretty much got up and left, so all their wives and girlfriends went with us! So it’s one thing when it’s ten or twelve annoying women graduate students—there was no woman faculty at URPE—but it’s quite another thing when every damn woman in the place goes out and stands outside and waits for us to say what we were gonna do!
>
> But out in the dark, we were trying to decide, we are not backing down and how we are going to organize ourselves, and we do in fact, get women’s caucus representation on to the steering committee, and that

> becomes sort of the model for every other group that has tried to be represented, people of color, gay and lesbians.

The climax of the Nisonoff story is the summer conference and the women's protest. Its message is one of solidarity. It is a noneconomist women's liberationist that gives women URPErs the idea for the protest and their demands. And it is thanks to the show of solidarity from the noneconomist women at the business meeting, by storming out with the economist women, that their demands were met.

The success of the 1971 protest signals in Nisonoff's narrative the beginning of the women's caucus as a functioning and vibrant group. In November 1971 the New Haven women ran a conference titled "Economic Perspectives on Women: Developing a Feminist Economics." Nisonoff recalls that three hundred people came to this conference, half of them academics and the other half activists: "People come from just all over the place and sleep on floors and, we have like thirty something panels, and . . . it's amazing!" She then adds:

> One thing that happens . . . at this conference . . . is that we decide that we also have to confront the AEA for its sexist policies. And, so . . . Marion Hill and I go to Tobin and Paddy goes to Galbraith and in December 1971 the keynote speaker for the AEA is Joan Robinson and we were actually introduced to her. We're also given some help by . . . Caroline Shawbell, who was an institutionalist, but a feminist. And, David Gordon's mother Margaret Gordon, who was tenured. . . . Through these powerful connections, we get on to the agenda of the business meeting, the foundation of CSWEP [Committee on the Status of Women in the Economics Profession].[24]

Two remarks ought to be made concerning Nisonoff's narrative. First, the structure of her story of the women's caucus mimics that of URPE's creation. Both are tales of shared political and personal commitments that culminate in the formation of a new organization. In both stories the new community announces itself by protesting the AEA: URPE in December 1969 and the women's caucus in 1971. Second, it is meaningful that in her interview Nisonoff was much more articulate in her narrative of these events than of others to which she had also been witness. It has been acknowledged that detailed recall in interview settings correlates with fre-

24. See "Minutes of the Annual Meeting" in issues 1–2 of the 1972 volume of the *American Economic Review.*

quent retelling or as a result of published memoirs (Lindee 1997, 43). This narrative is clearly an important one, one that has been retold to other women URPErs as the origin of their caucus.

Our focus in this section is on the fragmenting of the radical community in the 1970s. Nisonoff's narrative shows her experience of a new identity within URPE, that of the women URPErs. This new identity was a source of conflict, as the 1971 episode exemplifies. But the most important legacy of the events Nisonoff retells is that they led to the emergence of the women's caucus as an independent unit of action within URPE. Issues of the *Review of Radical Political Economics* soon appeared run by women's caucus collectives and dealing with women's issues (July 1972, Spring 1976, Fall 1977, Summer 1980, Spring 1984, Fall–Winter 1991, and Fall 2001). When URPE in 1972–73 turned to outreach work by promoting the writing of pamphlets for the public, a Women's Work Project was created to produce literature on women's issues (Keefe 1974). Women URPErs also began to build organizations that crossed over disciplinary boundaries with a shared commitment to women's liberation—one such organization was Marxism Feminist 1 (Petchesky 1979).

In the previous section we examined how in the late 1960s a community of radical economists was formed, mediated by the conflict that erupted on American campuses over the Vietnam War, by the URPE conferences and protests, and by the convivial atmosphere of the summer conference. In this section we have seen how new identities were being formed under the heading of radical economics. Women URPErs, increasingly conscious of the sexism of their male colleagues and increasingly closer to feminists in other disciplines, challenged the structures of URPE and carved out an institutional home for themselves within it.

3. What Is Hidden

The argument that we are advancing in this essay is that a *history* of heterodox economists and their communities is still to be written. We miss a story that makes sense of the academic lives and social activities of heterodox economists. We lack a narrative that successfully integrates agency and structure, the individual and the collective. Thus the kind of narrative we want is one that is chronological, has a plot that includes agency, and includes a historical ending that makes sense of the narrative (Elliott 2005). Hence from the perspective we are advancing here, the writing of heterodox economics' social history requires knowledge of the networks, interpersonal relationships, and subjective perspectives of the individuals who made up, for example, radical economics. Often these connections and subjectivity are hidden from view. Submerged by the more dominant narrative of mainstream economics, they may not be discerned from the standard sources of historians of economics, the published scholarly literature. Our strategy has been to uncover the hidden social dimensions through life narratives.

We explored life narratives to find the imprint of subjectivity. In interviews, radical economists recalled with intensity the collective experiences they shared in protesting the war in Vietnam, racism, and the political commitments of the economics profession, and in organizing events for URPE. They downplayed an identity constituted of shared subdisciplinary or research interests, ranked secondary to the emotional and convivial bounds. We interpret this discrimination as valuing a complex of political, affective, and intellectual experiences as the source of the radical community's identity.

Similarly, differences within URPE emerged from new solidarities and new experiences of conflict staged in the early 1970s. What is salient in our discussion of the divide between URPE men and women is not so much which aspects were selected for mention but the narrative's form. There is a seamless progression from women's grievances to their organizing and their ultimate self-determination in URPE. We are faced with a well-rehearsed narrative, one that suggests the inevitable outcome of the women's scission.

Through a life narrative, be it conveyed in an interview, autobiography, or oral history, we can study an individual's sense of self and location in society. The narrative selects and organizes the events and meanings that bound an individual to a community. We also unearth traces of change in the community, of solidarities broken and new ones established. How this social and cultural history fits with more standard historiographical practices in the history of economics is unclear. Our study was tentative and did not seek to establish a definite history of URPE. Further research is warranted in studying the gamut of radical subjectivities. Nor did we attempt to match in detail our narrative of shifting identities to existing intellectual histories. Indeed, how have changes to the radical community, for instance, with the emergence of the women's caucus, reshaped theoretical research? This is an empty canvas, but one that we can fill with the colors of enthusiasm, commitment, imagination, and a deep respect for the many different lives that inhabit the economics profession.

References

Arestis, P., and M. C. Sawyer, eds. [1992] 2000. *A Biographical Dictionary of Dissenting Economists*. Aldershot, U.K.: Elgar.

Backhouse, R., and R. Middleton. 2000. *Exemplary Economists*. Cheltenham, U.K.: Elgar.

Bluestone, Barry. 1969. Report of the Secretariat. *Newsletter of the Union for Radical Political Economics* 1.1:5–7.

Bowles, Samuel. [1992] 2000. Samuel Bowles. In Arestis and Sawyer [1992] 2000.

Brazer, Marjorie C. 1982. The Economics Department at the University of Michigan. In *Economics and the World around It*, edited by Saul Hymans. Ann Arbor: University of Michigan Press.

Chomsky, Noam, et al. 1997. *The Cold War and the University: Toward an Intellectual History of the Postwar Years*. New York: New Press.

Elliott, J. 2005. *Using Narrative in Social Research: Qualitative and Quantitative Approaches*. London: SAGE.

Evans, Sara. 1980. *Personal Politics: The Roots of Women's Liberation in the Civil Rights Movement and in the New Left*. New York: Vintage Books.

Fleck, Susan. 2003. The Union for Radical Economics: Its History and Nature. *Journal of Australian Political Economy*, n.s., 50:24–28.

Foley, Duncan K. [1992] 2000. Duncan K. Foley. In Arestis and Sawyer [1992] 2000.

Forget, Evelyn L. 2002. A Hunger for Narrative: Writing Lives in the History of Economic Thought. In *The Future of the History of Economics*, edited by E. Roy Weintraub. *HOPE* 34 (supplement): 226–44.

Gintis, Herbert. 1980. Radical Economics in the Decade of the 1970's. *National Forum* (December): 37–39.

———. 1984. The Reemergence of Marxian Economics in America. In *The Left Academy*, edited by Bertell Ollman and Edward Vernoff. Vol. 1. New York: McGraw-Hill.

Ginzburg, Carlo. 1992. Clues: Roots of an Evidential Paradigm. In *Clues, Myths, and the Historical Method*. Baltimore, Md.: Johns Hopkins University Press.

Gordon, David M. [1992] 2000. David M. Gordon. In Arestis and Sawyer [1992] 2000.

Harcourt, G. C. 1993. *Post-Keynesian Essays in Biography: Portraits of Twentieth-Century Political Economists*. Basingstoke, U.K.: Macmillan.

Hinckley, Bob. 1969. Personal Recollection of the URPE Conference. *Newsletter of the Union for Radical Political Economics* 1.3:14.

Historical Profile of URPE. 1976. *Newsletter of the Union for Radical Political Economics* 8.4–5:44–46.

Hodgson, G. 2004. *The Evolution of Institutional Economics*. London: Routledge.

Horowitz, Grace, et al. 1971. The Male Problem in URPE. *Newsletter of the Union for Radical Political Economics* 3.3:1–6.

Horowitz, Helen Lefkowitz. 1986. The 1960s and the Transformation of Campus Cultures. *History of Education Quarterly* 26.1:1–38.

Howard, M. C., and J. E. King. 1989. *A History of Marxian Economics*. Vol. 1, *1883–1929*. Princeton, N.J.: Princeton University Press.

———. 1992. *A History of Marxian Economics*. Vol. 2, *1929–1990*. London: Macmillan.

Howard, Peggy. 1970. Women's Liberation. *Newsletter of the Union for Radical Political Economics* 2.3:4.

Keefe, Jeff. 1974. PEA. *Newsletter of the Union for Radical Political Economics* 6.5:17–19.

King, J. E. 1995. *Conversations with Post Keynesians*. London: Macmillan.

———. 2002. *A History of Post Keynesian Economics since 1936*. Cheltenham, U.K.: Elgar.

Lazonick, William H. 2000. William H. Lazonick. In Backhouse and Middleton 2000.

Lee, F. S. 2000. The Organizational History of Post Keynesian Economics in America, 1971–1995. *Journal of Post Keynesian Economics* 23.1:141–62.

———. 2004a. History and Identity: The Case of Radical Economics and Radical Economists, 1945–1970. *Review of Radical Political Economics* 36.2:177–95.

———. 2004b. To Be a Heterodox Economist: The Contested Landscape of American Economics, 1960s and 70s. *Journal of Economic Issues* 38.3:747–63.

Lindee, Susan M. 1997. The Conversation: History and History as It Happens. In *The Historiography of Contemporary Science and Technology*, edited by Thomas Soderqvist. Amsterdam: Harwood Academic.

Mata, Tiago. 2005. Dissent in Economics: Making Radical Political Economics and Post Keynesian Economics, 1960–1980. PhD diss., London School of Economics and Political Science.

Moggridge, Donald. 2003. Biography and the History of Economics. In *Companion to the History of Economic Thought*, edited by W. J. Samuels, J. E. Biddle, and J. B. Davis. London: Routledge.

Morgan, Robin. 1970. *Sisterhood Is Powerful: An Anthology of Writings from the Women's Liberation Movement*. New York: Random House.

Morrissey, Charles T. 1998. On Oral History Interviewing. In Perks and Thomson 1998.

New England Regional Conference. 1969. *Newsletter of the Union for Radical Political Economics* 1.3:1, 3–7.

Peacock, James L., and Dorothy C. Holland. 1993. The Narrated Self: Life Stories in Process. *Ethos* 21.4:367–83.

Perks, Robert, and Alistair Thomson, eds. 1998. *The Oral History Reader*. New York: Routledge.

Petchesky, Rosalind. 1979. Dissolving the Hyphen: A Report on Marxist-Feminist Groups 1–5. In *Capitalist Patriarchy and the Case of Socialist Feminism*, edited by Zillah R. Eisenstein. New York: Monthly Review Press.

Portelli, Alessandro. 1991. The Death of Luigi Trastulli: Memory and the Event. In *The Death of Luigi Trastulli and Other Stories: Form and Meaning in Oral History*. Albany: State University of New York Press.

——. 1997. Philosophy and the Facts. In *The Battle of Valle Giulia: Oral History and the Art of Dialogue*. Madison: University of Wisconsin Press.

——. 1998. What Makes Oral History Different. In Perks and Thomson 1998.

Reich, Michael. [1992] 2000. Michael Reich. In Arestis and Sawyer [1992] 2000.

Schuman, Howard, and Jacqueline Scott. 1989. Generations and Collective Memories. *American Sociological Review* 54.3:359–81.

Seldon, Anthony, and Joanna Pappworth. 1983. *By Word of Mouth: Elite Oral History*. London: Methuen.

Sherman, Howard J. [1992] 2000. Howard J. Sherman. In Arestis and Sawyer [1992] 2000.

Summer Conference Urges Action. 1970. *Newsletter of the Union for Radical Political Economics* 2.3:1–8.

Terrall, Mary. 2006. Biography as Cultural History of Science. *Isis* 97:306–13.

Thirlwall, A. P. 1987. *Nicholas Kaldor*. Brighton, U.K.: Wheatsheaf.

Thompson, Paul. 1988. *The Voice of the Past: Oral History*. Oxford: Oxford University Press.

Tribe, Keith. 1997. *Economic Careers: Economics and Economists in Britain, 1930–1970*. London: Routledge.

URPE National Conference. 1969. *Newsletter of the Union for Radical Political Economics* 1.2:1–2.

URPE Summer Conference. 1970. *Newsletter of the Union for Radical Political Economics* 2.2:1–2.

Wachtel, H., and Barry Bluestone, eds. 1969. *The Conference Papers of the Union for Radical Political Economics: Philadelphia, December 1968*. Ann Arbor, Mich.: Union for Radical Political Economics.

Watson, Lawrence C. 1976. Understanding Life History as a Subjective Document. *Ethos* 4.1:95–131.

Weintraub, E. Roy. 2005. Autobiographical Memory and the Historiography of Economics. *Journal of the History of Economic Thought* 27.1:1–11.

Weisskoff, Fran. 1970. Report on Women's Caucus. *Newsletter of the Union for Radical Political Economics* 2.4:6.

Weisskopf, Thomas E. [1992] 2000. Thomas E. Weisskopf. In Arestis and Sawyer [1992] 2000.

Oral History and the Historical Reconstruction of Chicago Economics

Ross Emmett

George Stigler (1970, 426) once answered the question "what relevance have the details of a man's personal life to the nature of his scientific work?" by responding "I am tempted to answer: biography distorts rather than illuminates the understanding of scientific work." While he may be right about the relevance of biographical information to the rational reconstruction of economic theory (Emmett 2003), a historical reconstruction of the practice of economics necessarily requires biographical and institutional material that will assist the historian with interpreting what happened when and how economists went about creating the type of economics they practiced. Roy Weintraub has argued for some time that historians of economics need to expand their historical sources to include archival records such as correspondence, unpublished papers, and course materials

The participants in the Chicago Economics Oral History Project have been exceedingly generous with their time for interviews and in their patience waiting for transcripts. The author thanks Harold Demsetz, Sebastian Edwards, Al Harberger, Deirdre McCloskey, Richard Muth, and Wally Thurman for allowing material from their interviews to be included in this essay, and in some cases for correcting misleading information in a previous draft. The author also wishes to thank participants at the *HOPE* "Life Writing and the History of Economics" conference at Duke University (April 2006); the Summer Institute for the Preservation of the History of Economics in Economics at the Center for the Study of Public Choice, George Mason University, Fairfax, Virginia (June 2001); and the York University/University of Toronto Workshop on the History of Economic Thought (November 2003) for comments on earlier versions. All errors and misjudgments remain, of course, my own. Funding for the project was originally provided by the Earhart Foundation.

History of Political Economy 39 (annual suppl.) DOI 10.1215/00182702-2006-044

(Weintraub et al. 1998). The topic of this conference expands that list to incorporate various forms of life writings that economists may create: autobiographies, journals, diaries, testimonials, and personal correspondence. This essay examines the contribution that may be made to our understanding of the history of economics from a different category of expression about one's life: oral history interviews.

Oral history is generally understood as the recording of the memories of people's lives. In its simplest form, oral history has been practiced by everyone who has once asked a participant at some historical event "what was it like at . . . ?" In the more organized form discussed here, it involves the audio- or videotaping of arranged interviews, frequently extending to several interview sessions with the same individual or group. I have been engaged over the past six years in oral history interviews related to the history of Chicago economics. My purpose here is to draw upon this experience to relay the possibilities that oral history presents for historians of twentieth-century economics.

The Chicago Economics Oral History Project

The Chicago Economics Oral History Project (see Emmett n.d.) was created to expand the range and variety of historical material available to researchers on the history of economics at the University of Chicago by interviewing economists who were professors, graduate students, postdoctoral fellows, and academic staff at the University of Chicago between the 1930s and the 1980s. The interviewees need not have been members of the economics department; they may come from across the university, including the Graduate School of Business, the Law School, the Cowles Commission, and other schools, committees, or departments that incorporated economists. A variety of graduate student experiences are also sought: from graduates of the economics department, Graduate School of Business, or the Law School, to students who did not complete their degree at Chicago or those who took economics courses as part of their program in other schools, departments, or committees. To determine potential interviewees, I assembled a list of those who had completed dissertations at Chicago in the 1930s and 1940s, and I had student research assistants search the membership directory of the American Economic Association for members who identified their PhD institution as the University of Chicago. The Office of the Dean of Social Science at the University of Chicago has offered to assist with our completion of a list of all graduates. While one might think that such a list would be simple to construct, the number is actually quite large, considering the fact that the economics department alone routinely enrolled approximately one hundred new students per year in the graduate program during the postwar period. The Graduate School of Business and the Law School also had economists on the faculty, and many students went through their graduate programs.

Despite the large number of potential interviewees, an effort has been made from the start to interview people who could provide particular perspectives. For example, among the approximately twenty interviews carried out to date are included the views of a former department chair (Arnold Harberger), a former dean of the Graduate School of Business (George Shultz), a Chilean graduate student (Sebastian Edwards), female graduate students (Marianne Ferber, Rose Director Friedman, and Clare Friedland), faculty members who were graduate students and returned later as faculty (Gary Becker and Milton Friedman), faculty members who were not trained at Chicago (Harold Demsetz and Deirdre McCloskey), and a member of the academic staff (again, Clare Friedland). Recently, I was able to interview in the space of a week three individuals who represented three generations of graduate students, and hence three iterations of graduate study: P. J. Hill (late 1960s), Walter Thurman (late 1970s–early 1980s), and Andrew F. Hansen (mid-1990s). A complete list of the interviews conducted to date is found in appendix A.

In part, the project started because the standard stories of Chicago economics have been shaped by its success: we know the "Chicago" familiar to the Nobel laureates (Stigler 1988; Friedman and Friedman 1998; Kitch 1983; Reder 1982). I have taken the opportunity to interview the laureates where available, but letting them repeat stories and perspectives already told in their writings is not the purpose of the project. Instead, the primary objective is to interview those whose stories about Chicago are less well known. What of the Chicago economics known to the normal graduate student? The Chicago economics of those whose economics was not defined by the Knight-Friedman-Stigler-Coase-Becker-Lucas lineage? The Chicago economics program that failed many at the end of their first year in the core exams? The Chicago economics experienced by oh-so-few women in the 1940s, 1950s, and 1960s? The Chicago economics encountered by the freshly minted PhD from Harvard who has just landed a first job? And what of the reception that a recent Chicago graduate experienced in the 1960s or 1970s upon arrival in departments that viewed him (it *was* always a him) as an outsider? While the list of participants to date does not extend far in these directions, future interviews are being planned to do so.

In terms of my own research, the purpose of this project is to provide a larger foundation for writing a history of economics at the University of Chicago, focused especially on the period between the late 1920s and the 1980s. The history of Chicago economics during these years is most often told as the story of the rise to prominence of the so-called Chicago school of economics. Historiographical focus on a "school" of thought often leads to histories about great men and great ideas or, depending upon one's ideological leanings, histories that vilify the same men and ideas. The history of the Chicago school of economics is no exception to this trend (Miller 1962; Bronfenbrenner 1962; Coats 1963; Samuels 1976; Patinkin 1981a; Reder 1982; Schmidt and Rittaler 1989; Leeson 2000; Van Overtveldt 2006). But my purpose is somewhat different. Rather than tell the story of how a coherent set of ideas associated with a close-knit group of individuals came to dominate late-twentieth-century economics, I seek to reconstruct Chicago economics as it historically developed, recognizing that, in the context of its own time, the creation of a unique brand of economics with far-reaching influence could not be foreseen. For the purpose of historical reconstruction, I start with the notion that the economists at Chicago went about doing what they understood economics to be, engaging each other and the wider discipline (and sometimes the general public) in debates over theory, method, and policy. Simultaneously, they shaped an academic structure within which they could carry out their research and graduate students also could flourish and become competent economists. A host of historical questions about economics at the University of Chicago emerges from such a perspective—questions not only about economic theory but also about the internal and external debates, the structure of the research enterprise, the role of foundations and private monies in structuring academic research, how economics found its way into other departments and schools within the university, the role of social science (and social scientists) in American society and government service, and pedagogy (Emmett 1998). And, of course, we have to account for the school's success and, perhaps, eventual demise as a distinctive tradition in economics.

Oral History Objectives

Oral history provides individuals the opportunity to recount their memories of people and events they experienced. Because each person's memories are unique, oral histories often are used in the first instance to fill in the informational gaps in our historical knowledge. The Chicago Economics Oral

History Project started with this purpose, although as I show, other objectives have also come to play a role in the project. There are three ways in which an oral history project can complement the existing body of publications and manuscript-based archival materials (adapted from Cutler 1971). First, oral history can corroborate what we know from published and existing archival material or can fill in information gaps. Second, it can provide help with interpreting the intellectual context within which economic research and teaching was undertaken. And third, oral history can provide access to voices missing from the published record of economics, voices that are part of the story of economics but are absent entirely from the discipline's published record.

Corroboration and Extension of the Existing Record

The historical reconstruction of Chicago economics requires a different body of information than that provided by the research publications, critical literature, and professional correspondence of members of the faculty, research staff, and graduate students of the economics department, the Graduate School of Business, and the Law School. While archival material related to Chicago economics is available, to date the quantity of material is limited, relative to what is available for histories of economics at other institutions (e.g., Harvard University) and even for histories of other disciplines at the University of Chicago (e.g., sociology, physics, or philosophy). For example, while the papers of several notable Chicago economists are held in the University of Chicago Archives, most of the personal archival material of interest is scattered across several other archives, including the Economists' Papers Project at Duke University and the Hoover Institution Library and Archive, or is not publicly available yet. At Chicago, the University Archives did not have space until recently to collect systematically the papers of many Chicago economists: major collections of the papers of Frank H. Knight, Henry C. Simons, and George J. Stigler are joined by partial collections for a few others. Even when collections exist, catalogs of the material may be unavailable or not easily accessible,[1] or unable to guide researchers to the specific items that may assist their research agenda. Also, personal archival material is only part of the

1. For example, the finding guides to the archived collections of major Chicago economists (Knight, Stigler, and Simons) are not available online.

archival material of interest. The records of departments, schools, university groups, workshops, journals, and granting agencies and foundations will be of interest to the researcher. Some of the university, departmental school, and journal records are available, although most of their records are unavailable currently because of the University Archives' privacy restrictions.[2] Material that might shed light on other elements of the practices of economists at Chicago—especially the functioning of the workshops—is harder to find.

Furthermore, the publicly available records of a university may not always be complete or correct sources for personnel changes, faculty service, and student records. Official records often remain unavailable because of privacy rules, so interviews allow an opportunity to confirm basic faculty or student information such as years of service or attendance, titles held, interruptions for sabbaticals or government service, and any awards, fellowships, or scholarships held. Student records seldom provide names of those who attended but did not complete degrees; interviewees often provide the names of several individuals who can be interviewed later.

The interviews also allow individuals to affirm or reject information published about them in other sources. For example, when I contacted Al (as he was known familiarly) Harberger for an interview, he went to great lengths in rearranging his schedule to meet me. When we met, I discovered why he was so keen to meet: he wanted to "set the record straight" on his relationship with George Stigler. Stigler's lack of mention of Harberger in his memoirs and in his textbook has led some to speculate about whether there were any strains in the relationship between the two men (see, e.g., Banzhaf forthcoming, n. 9). Prior to the interview, Harberger asked me to provide him with an opportunity to comment on their relationship and the report that there were strains between them. When I asked the question, he sat up, crossed his arms with a satisfied look on his face, and said:

> I don't know where that kind of thing comes from. I always felt I had good relations with George. . . . I admired Stigler so much. He was one of the most innovative minds of the whole discipline in half a century or even a century.

2. The University Archives imposes a fifty-year rule on certain university records, stipulating that access to boxes containing those records is denied until the material is more than fifty years old and all individuals mentioned in the records have died.

Harberger then went on to identify accurately the difference between the two men:

> I had differences with him. . . . the thing I don't understand about George; he was a missionary—like I am, like Milton, like T. W., D. Gale, we're all missionaries. But George was much less of a missionary. He was more austere, above it all, and yet one of the earliest articles that bears his name was a little pamphlet—*Roofs and Ceilings*—there he was a missionary. . . . Somewhere in the interval he became [voice trails off]. I miss that element of fight in George.

As any academic knows, published debates do not always proceed in a linear fashion, with one protagonist responding directly to the points raised by the other. Tracing the lineage of a debate often leads to interruptions, dead ends, and strange turning points. Clues to the interpretation of those events can often be provided by interviews. Differing perspectives on Chicago economics can also be compared by interviews with individuals who were there at different points in time. Deirdre McCloskey (2001), when asked to characterize the "Chicago school," responded by saying, "We were embattled. . . . Everyone hated us." She arrived in the late 1960s, at the height of the controversies Chicagoans had with other members of the discipline. Sebastian Edwards, who was a graduate student in the late 1970s, identified Chicago economics as taking the data seriously and applying price theory to policy matters. When Edwards (2002) was asked why his definition lacked reference to the ideological context McCloskey had referred to, he said simply, "We won." The "embattled" atmosphere that McCloskey identified had largely disappeared. Wally Thurman, a contemporary of Edwards's in Chicago's program, made a similar point by suggesting that his class was probably the last to be trained in price theory the same way that classes had been trained since the 1930s. About 1980, the first-year course became more like first-year graduate classes in economics at any other university (Thurman 2005). McCloskey (2001) said it this way: "The curious thing about Gary [Becker] and Bob [Lucas] is that, while they spread Chicago economics far and wide, and to other disciplines, they made economics at Chicago into the same thing that it was everywhere else."

A final example of how the interviews may be able to expand the information available to the researcher on the history of Chicago economics regards the composition of the various workshops created in Chicago during the 1950s. These workshops were integral to Chicago economics, yet we know surprisingly little about their actual operation. Most critical histories of Chicago economics dwell on the papers and dissertations that emerged from these workshops, leaving us with little information about their week-to-week operation. My project will provide a documented history of the workshops, with descriptions of how particular workshops operated and the differences among them. The differences come through clearly in the discussions of the public finance, industrial organization, money, and economic history workshops that I had with interviewees.

Let me highlight the differences between the workshops as I have pieced it together from my own research (Emmett 1998) and from the interviews so far. The earliest workshop was in agricultural economics, run by T. W. Schultz and D. Gale Johnson, and set up immediately upon their arrival from Iowa State University. While Schultz and Johnson provided the start, their workshop operated differently from the ones that followed because theirs was created to provide a structure for domestic and foreign research. The first two formal workshops, with weekly meetings and external funding for graduate students and visitors, were the money workshop run by Milton Friedman and the public finance workshop run by Al Harberger. The two workshops could not be more different. Friedman's involved weekly discussion of papers by graduate students, faculty, and visitors, with Friedman running the show. Presenters were given little if any time to present formally, and Friedman stood at the front and went page by page through the paper, asking for comments from attendees. Harberger's workshop, on the other hand, was closed; only faculty and graduate students in the workshop participated. Students and faculty presented papers, with most of the presentations by students, who might present as many as three or four times per quarter. Presenters had fifteen minutes to talk about their successes, forty-five minutes to talk about their problems, and then the workshop group spent an additional hour trying to solve the problems. The other unique element of Harberger's model was the publication of two volumes based on the papers written by the students in the workshop (Harberger 1960; Harberger and Bailey 1969).

The Chicago workshops were unique because graduate students became an integral part of an ongoing research community. Today, most economics departments have at least one seminar or workshop, with professors and visitors presenting weekly, and graduate students presenting at least once during their studies. But today's standard workshop is not a Chicago workshop. What made (and still makes) Chicago unique are two things:

(1) the fact that all graduate students who have completed their preliminary field exams are incorporated into (at least one) workshop for the remainder of their graduate study; and (2) the sheer number of workshops in the department. When McCloskey (2001) inventoried the workshops in the department and the law and business schools around 1980, there were eighteen distinct workshops, each meeting at least once a week.

Of course, Chicago workshops are also known for the hard-nosed debate that characterized its most famous seminars: Friedman's money workshop, Stigler's industrial organization workshop, and Ronald Coase's law and economics workshop. These "classic" models of the Chicago workshop were dominated by the set of professors who regularly attended and controlled most of the debate. Graduate students generally remained quiet, although those who had earned their spurs in the workshop joined in the debate as well. Visitors presented at about two-thirds of the workshop meetings; the remainder were allocated to Chicago's own professors and graduate students. The organization of time within a workshop meeting was based on "Chicago rules": because papers were distributed ahead of time to allow participants to read beforehand, almost the entire seminar time was devoted to debate about the paper. Assuming the paper was good enough to engender debate, the speaker could expect to have the first question asked about five minutes into the presentation. Any aspect of a paper was fair game: data, methodology, or theory. McCloskey (2001) identified the point of the debate as "finding where the bodies were" in the paper; Harold Demsetz (2002) expressed it more succinctly: "Prove it." Although the presenter's job was to defend the paper, when a Chicago workshop worked well, the eventual paper became almost a joint product of the workshop participants.

But despite the classic model that the Friedman, Stigler, and Coase workshops present, the truth of the matter is that there was a wide variety of experiences for graduate students and faculty across the workshops, especially during the 1950s and 1960s, when Chicago rules were still under development. Oral history interviews complement the existing literature on Chicago economics by providing access to that breadth of experience.

Understanding Chicago Economics' Unique Intellectual Milieu

Oral history can help us understand the unique intellectual milieu of Chicago economics during this period. The University of Chicago's place at the forefront of American intellectual life, especially in the social sciences, had been established in the period prior to the 1930s. Surprisingly, perhaps, Chicago economics did not share the other social sciences' prominence in this earlier period. Yet the intellectual milieu within which other disciplines thrived was shared by economics, and students and faculty alike speak frequently of the intellectual quality of general academic life at the university. By the 1950s this milieu becomes translated into "taking economics seriously" or, as T. W. Shultz was wont to say: economists know economics, so when they speak, they should talk about economics (McCloskey 2001). I regularly ask interviewees to describe the Chicago they knew, and their replies largely corroborate the sense that the university, and the economics department, was unlike any other they have known. Al Harberger (2002) picked up this theme in the closing comments of my interview with him:

> There is no university like Chicago. You're not supposed to think *small* when you're at Chicago—it's just not right. You're not supposed to count the articles you've written and submitted to refereed journals and think you are going to get promoted just on that. You're supposed to *think.*

Richard Muth tells a story in his interview that captures this unique intellectual milieu that Chicago economics shared with the rest of the university. When I asked him if he thought there was an identifiable "Chicago school" of economics, he replied that there probably was when he was there in the 1950s, and he characterized it this way:

> The one thing that I remember about Chicago that was different from everywhere else I had been is that people were terribly serious about everything that they did. And, Chicago economics, this is probably because there was relatively little social life. I was invited to join faculty parties, and all they did was talk about economics. Whether this was typical of the university at the time, I don't know, but one of my fondest memories was on a bright day when I was walking down Fifty-seventh Street and saw a boy and a girl coming the other way walking hand in hand, and he whispered something in her ear. And as I passed, it was something like, now this was not what he really said, but it was like "Let *f* be a real-valued function defined in the positive." Well, obviously they were students of mathematics, and even though they were walking hand in hand on a beautiful spring day, they were talking mathematics. (Muth 2002)

Another aspect of the intellectual atmosphere of Chicago economics that is mentioned frequently in the interviews is the sense that, whatever is unique about Chicago economics, it separated Chicago from the rest of the discipline, at least during the 1950s–1970s. The sense of separateness from the mainstream of the economics discipline isolated Chicago economics and gave those economists at Chicago who associated with the Friedman-Stigler group the sense of being an embattled "remnant" of "right economics" (McCloskey 2001). As Frank Knight said, "You can be with the majority, or you can be right" (cited in Patinkin 1981b).

Continuity in the departmental administration and in the curriculum was a central part of what kept the Chicago milieu going. From the mid-1940s to the mid-1970s, Chicago's department was chaired by only three individuals: T. W. Schultz, Al Harberger, and D. Gale Johnson. During the same period, the first year of graduate price theory was primarily controlled by three individuals: Milton Friedman, Gary Becker, and Al Harberger, with Deirdre McCloskey as the primary instructor on ECON 300 (the first course for those without a background in price theory) from the late 1960s to 1980. In the twenty years prior to the mid-1940s, Chicago's price theory course was primarily taught by Jacob Viner and Frank Knight. Thus, in the fifty-year time span from 1930 to 1980, students at Chicago experienced a largely uniform approach to economics—the Marshallian price theory of Viner, Knight, Friedman, Becker, and Harberger. Part of "taking economics seriously" involved a serious commitment to teaching the first graduate courses in a way that ensured that students understood the kind of economics that they were to take seriously. Thurman (2005) made the same point about continuity in a different way, by remarking, when asked what students did to find a topic for their research, that they read over and over the price theory books by Stigler, Friedman, and Armen Alchian and tried to think of new ways to apply their insights to ordinary issues.

Similarly, interviews allow the researcher to obtain information about the personality and teaching style of Chicago economists that is not available elsewhere. Although there is a publication record related to the teaching of Chicago economists, the individuals discussed comprise a very small set of the economists teaching at Chicago—Knight, Viner, and Simons are the ones most often discussed. The interviews allow participants to talk about other professors who had a significant impact on their work, both in terms of their teaching and their thesis supervision. For Chicago economists such as Gregg Lewis, Allen Wallis, and Aaron Director, interviews may be the only way to obtain information about their central roles in the operation of Chicago economics.

Missing Voices

Finally, oral history projects provide the opportunity to document voices that are missing from the standard histories. Much is made of this function among oral historians today, and it would be inappropriate to compare the Chicago economics project with those projects that give voice to peoples with no documented history. But there are many missing voices in the story of Chicago economics: those who did not continue past the core exams, those who did not complete the requirements of the degree, women—both those who did complete degree requirements and those who did not (see Olson and Emami 2002)—those connected with the Cowles Commission while it was at Chicago, those who taught undergraduates in the college, and those who resisted the approach most frequently associated with Chicago economics.

To date, the closest my interviews come to a "missing voice" is in my interview with Marianne Ferber, one of the few women to complete a PhD in economics at Chicago in the postwar period and someone who does not identify herself with the Chicago school.[3] When she arrived for her dissertation defense, the room was packed. She had not expected this, but was told that she was the first woman to finish in such a long time that everyone had come to see! Earlier in the interview, she recounted poignantly the stories of Lloyd Mints telling her that he voted against her receipt of a major scholarship on the grounds that such monies should not be wasted on women who would not do anything with their studies, but instead marry and raise kids (she won the scholarship anyway), and of Simeon Leland telling her, with pride, that Jacob Viner has called her the "best girl he had ever taught." Because Viner was her favorite professor, she was more forgiving of his comment than Mints's—but the latter provided motivation to her in the years when she was raising kids and trying to finish her dissertation. She kept telling herself that he was not going to be right about her (Ferber 2002).

Ferber has also been helpful in providing names of other women who studied at Chicago but did not finish, either because they did not pass the

3. The two other women students I have interviewed, Claire Friedland and Rose Director Friedman, clearly self-identify with the Chicago school. Friedland was George Stigler's research assistant, and sometime coauthor, for thirty-three years.

core exams or because they discontinued their studies at Chicago for any number of reasons (not just family!). In her cohort of about one hundred entering students in 1944, there were a handful of women. According to her, about five or six women across two or three cohorts passed the core exams. That corresponds to the general failure rate of approximately 50 percent in Chicago's core exams.

Another voice that could be considered "close to missing" in the story of Chicago economics is that of Sebastian Edwards, one of the late-1970s-era Chilean students to come to Chicago. Edwards is a well-known commentator on international economic affairs, and earlier Chilean students at Chicago are well-known for the economic reforms they instituted under General Pinochet. Harberger (2002) told the story of setting up the fellowships that brought Chilean students to Chicago in the late 1950s; by the time Edwards arrived in the 1970s, Chicago had at least fifty Latin American students each year at different stages in the program. As Harberger pointed out in his interview, few of the Chilean students completed a dissertation, because there was little incentive in the Chilean academic or government environments to encourage completion. Edwards, then, was unusual among the Chilean students for finishing; in fact, he claimed that he was probably the first Chilean student to complete all the requirements for his doctorate in residence (Edwards 2002).

The Interview Process

Some additional detail about the interview process itself may help the reader understand the course of the project to date and the issues that face oral history interviewers (general treatments of these issues are in Odendahl and Shaw 2002; Ritchie 2003; Seldon and Pappworth 1983). The last section of the essay deals with issues specifically related to the audio- and videotaping of the interviews, so they will not be discussed here. The various issues involved in the review by university research ethics boards of oral history projects have also been left aside, because they could fill an entire paper.[4]

4. Oral histories present minimal risks under most research ethics board guidelines, but they do not fit the standard research model, because the interviewee's identity is usually known, and their responses can hardly be confidential. The guidelines for oral historians from the Oral History Association ([1989] 2002) provide a means for evaluating the issues involved. The Chicago Economics Oral History Project has undergone ethics review both at my former institution in Canada and now at Michigan State University. Participants have consented to use of their materials and names in publications arising from the project.

The interview process can be divided into three parts, of which the interview itself—the second part—is easily the briefest. The first part is preparation. While it is a truism to say that better preparation makes for a better interview, one should point out that for oral history the nature of the interview determines the type of preparation undertaken. Here the interests of the project differ sometimes from the interests of the interviewers; the historian's interests, for example, may differ from those of an interviewer interested in talking in detail about particular theoretical debates. Because my interest in the project is focused in the first instance on how Chicago economics built an institutional structure of graduate education and research that enabled it to succeed, and only secondarily on the specific debates that Chicago economists participated in both as theoreticians and as policy advocates, my preparation focuses on identifying what is already known about the interviewees' education and their linkages to the research infrastructure of Chicago economics, both during and after graduate school. Usually, not much is known about these issues, and the interview then focuses on asking for them. But I also read work by interviewees to see what their primary research interests have been and how they have evolved. In some cases, the evolution of their work provides the basis for questions about the impact of Chicago economics on their research in particular and the economics profession more generally. The greater the extent to which one can anticipate such connections beforehand, the better the follow-up questions during the interview are.

The interview itself occurs at a time and place of the interviewee's convenience. Once the interview begins, it follows an order of questions determined ahead of time—and communicated to the interviewees in advance so they are not completely surprised (see appendix B for the list of common questions). All of the interviews have begun with the question "what first attracted you to the study of economics?" Intended as an easy pitch that would put the interviewee at ease, this broad question has elicited responses ranging from quite specific references to a particular professor in college, to a synopsis of the individual's life story before graduate school. In most cases, questions about the individual's background prior to entrance in the Chicago graduate programs follow. Once the interview moves on to the interviewee's experience with Chicago economics, the questions divide into three groups. The first set focuses specifically on the interviewee's educational experience at Chicago. Follow-up questions often focus on particular professors, assigned readings, assignments, research topics, fellowships, and the structure of the workshop(s) the interviewee participated in or attended. The second set of questions addresses whether the interviewee thinks there is a unique Chicago approach to economics, how that approach would be characterized, and how the interviewee's own graduate and postgraduate work reflected it. Finally, questions are asked about the interviewee's reception as a Chicago economist in the profession. The final set of questions was originally aimed at individuals educated at Chicago between the 1930s and the early 1960s, to see if the reception of Chicago economists changed within the profession before the 1970s. I have found the question less conducive to discussion with more recent graduates.

The final stage of the interview process is the transcription of the interview and the authorization of the transcript for research use and archival deposition (Poland 2002). Transcription work is difficult, tedious, and therefore costly in terms of time and money. I have used undergraduate research assistants as transcribers, which requires a significant amount of time on my part to double-check the transcript. Verbatim transcriptions of the interview are sent to the participants, to provide them with the opportunity to clarify or add to what they have said. Eventually, under an agreement that all participants have signed, copies of the digital videotape of the interview and the transcription will be sent to the University of Chicago Archives, where they will be available to other researchers as part of the archives' permanent collection.

How Accurate Is the Information?

Economists share with many historians and other social scientists an inherent suspicion about the reliability of interview information. Oral history has been plagued with this question from its beginnings. Double-checking the information provided insofar as it is possible is important, and one must always pay attention to bias.

Roy Weintraub (2005) provides an intriguing new argument for the usefulness of the information gathered in the Chicago Economics Oral History Project. He turned to the psychological literature on autobiographically consequential memories (ACEs) and found that the accuracy of recalled memories from young adulthood (ages 25–34) was highest among recalled memories of all ages. One consequence of this study, which Weintraub (2005) points out, is that famous (and not-so-famous) economists are most likely to remember the economics of their early years best (the "ACE bump" associated with early adulthood) and to identify it as "the best" economics they knew. Interviews with Chicago economists certainly confirm this: Muth's reference to his graduate school years at Chicago as a visit to "Camelot" is the most memorable of several such comments! But Weintraub's argument also lends some support to the claim that we can utilize the information gathered in oral interviews with senior scholars about their days as graduate students and young faculty members.

But perhaps the key issue is not really the veracity of the information but the "meaning" given in an interview to information that is already known. Al Harberger's remarks on workshops are a good example. We can reconstruct how the various workshops worked, but his remarks provide meaning to the institutional detail, meaning reinforced by its repetition in Richard Muth's comments about Harberger's workshop.

Oral history is not just the extraction of useful knowledge from people's minds, in the absence of written commentary on a historical event or movement. It is a two-way gifting process: the interviewees gift the interviewer with information and meanings; the interviewer gifts the interviewee with the opportunity to remember (Thomson 1998). Muth's obvious joy in expressing what Chicago meant to him and Harberger's desire to "set the record straight" about his relationship with George Stigler are clear examples of something I have felt from almost all my participants: their appreciation for the opportunity to talk. The flip side of this, of course, was my interview with George Shultz, who appeared for most of the interview to be unwilling to move beyond the impartation of knowledge.

The Dual Product of Oral History Projects

One aspect of the oral history project that I did not expect when it started is the dual purpose that emerged as soon as I decided to videotape the interviews. One purpose is my own: what can I learn about Chicago economics from interviewing these people? The other purpose comes from the creation of a videotape. Once created, the videotape becomes a product independent of my own research purposes. What happens to the digital product?

The tension between these two purposes was brought home to me at the conclusion of my first videotaped interview, with James Buchanan. When I checked the videotape, I discovered that the microphones had not worked, and, while the video feed was good, there was no audio feed. Should I ask Professor Buchanan for another interview? While I chose not to, knowing that the conversation we had was a nonrepeatable event, the archived version of the project will always be one file short. A similar problem emerged during the Harold Demsetz interview. About halfway through the interview, he apparently knocked the microphone off his lapel. Suddenly, only my microphone picked up any sound. The result is a very limited transcription from the second half of the interview.

The tension between these two purposes is constantly present during interviews. Some interviewees are always aware of the camera eye trained on them, and I frequently check the view screen to ensure that the interview subject has not moved out of the camera's view. Although audiotaping the interviews to simplify the process can lessen the tension, it cannot be eliminated, as my interview with Martin Bronfenbrenner illustrated. On that audiotape, the transcriber had difficulty hearing my questions (sometimes a problem on my videotapes as well because of microphone inputs), and the flow of the interview was still interrupted by the change of tapes. And yet the benefits of videotaping the interviews still outweigh the costs, both for my own research and for future possibilities.

So what does one do with the videotape product after a transcript of the interview has been created? Although the interview may be designed for my own purposes and interests, the tapes may be of interest to future scholars of the history of economics at Chicago and others with an interest in oral history. With these future interests in mind, I discussed the project's archival possibilities with both the University of Chicago Archives and the Duke University Special Collections Library, which houses the Economists' Papers Project. While both sites were interested, we all agreed that Chicago would be the logical archival home, given that it now has the space to add this type of material. The university archivist at Chicago and I have been discussing the appropriate format for permanent digital recording of the material, and once transcription is finished and approved by participants, a transcript and permanent recording will be given to the University Archives.

There are also a number of nonresearch uses of the material on the interview tapes. Clips from the tapes may be used to develop a digital online Chicago economics project (Larson 2001). The University of Chicago may wish to make use of some of the material in its historical publications. And portions of the tapes may be used in a documentary on Chicago economics, although it is more likely that an additional set of interviews would be conducted specifically for that purpose.

Conclusion

The Chicago Economics Oral History Project has only just begun, but it promises to be a richly textured resource for the study of economics at the University of Chicago. Filling in gaps in the historical record of Chicago economics proves to be only the beginning of the uses for oral histories. Among the various possibilities for historical, archival, and documentary resources that may be pursued, the interviewer still finds the participants' appreciation for the opportunity to talk about the economist's "Camelot" (Muth 2002) the most gratifying.

Appendix A: Chicago Economics Oral History Project Interview Participants

Gary Becker
Martin Bronfenbrenner
James M. Buchanan
Harold Demsetz
Sebastian Edwards
Marianne A. Ferber
Claire Friedland
Milton Friedman and Rose Director Friedman
F. Andrew Hanssen
Arnold ("Al") Harberger
P. J. Hill
David M. Levy
Deirdre N. McCloskey
David J. Meiselman
Richard E. Muth
George P. Shultz
Walter N. Thurman
Gordon Tullock

Appendix B: Chicago Economics Oral History Project Common Interview Questions

1. What first attracted you to the study of economics?
2. What led you to study economics at the University of Chicago?
3. What led you to accept a position at the University of Chicago?
4. What do you think differentiates Chicago economics from economics at other institutions?

5. What were the requirements for graduate study (or tenure) in economics during your time at Chicago? Do you remember any of the questions from your comps?

6. Describe _________ (any of several students or faculty) as colleagues.

7. Describe _________ (any of several faculty at the university) as a teacher.

8. Do you think there is an identifiable "Chicago school" of economics? If so, what would you say are its central features?

9. How would you describe the reputation of the Chicago economics program among economists?

10. When you identify yourself as an economist (trained) at Chicago, what reactions do you receive from non-Chicago colleagues? From the media? From other academics? From others?

References

Banzhaf, H. Spencer. Forthcoming. The Chicago School of Applied Welfare Economics. In *The Elgar Companion to the Chicago School of Economics*, edited by R. B. Emmett. Cheltenham, U.K.: Elgar.

Bronfenbrenner, Martin. 1962. Observation on the "Chicago School(s)." *Journal of Political Economy* 70.1:72–75.

Coats, A. W. 1963. The Origins of the "Chicago School(s)"? *Journal of Political Economy* 71.5:487–93.

Cutler, William W., III. 1971. Oral History: Its Nature and Uses for Educational History. *History of Education Quarterly* 11.2:184–94.

Demsetz, Harold. 2002. Interview with Ross B. Emmett. Chicago Economics Oral History Project. University of California, Los Angeles, February.

Edwards, Sebastian. 2002. Interview with Ross B. Emmett. Chicago Economics Oral History Project. University of California, Los Angeles, February.

Emmett, Ross B. n.d. Chicago Economics Oral History Project. www.msu.edu/~emmettr/ceohp/ (accessed September 20, 2006).

———. 1998. Entrenching Disciplinary Competence: The Role of General Education and Graduate Study in Chicago Economics. In *From Interwar Pluralism to Postwar Neoclassicism*, edited by M. S. Morgan and M. Rutherford. *HOPE* 30 (supplement): 134–50.

———. 2003. Exegesis, Hermeneutics, and Interpretation. In *A Companion to the History of Economic Thought*, edited by W. J. Samuels, J. E. Biddle, and J. B. Davis. Oxford: Blackwell.

Ferber, Marianne. 2002. Interview with Ross B. Emmett. Chicago Economics Oral History Project. University of Illinois, Champaign, November.

Friedman, Milton, and Rose Director Friedman. 1998. *Two Lucky People: Memoirs*. Chicago: University of Chicago Press.
Harberger, Arnold C. 1960. *The Demand for Durable Goods*. Chicago: University of Chicago Press.
———. 2002. Interview with Ross B. Emmett. Chicago Economics Oral History Project. Los Angeles, February.
Harberger, Arnold C., and Martin J. Bailey, eds. 1969. *The Taxation of Income from Capital*. Washington, D.C.: Brookings Institution.
Kitch, Edmund W. 1983. The Fire of Truth: A Remembrance of Law and Economics at Chicago, 1932–1970. *Journal of Law and Economics* 26.1:163–234.
Larson, Mary A. 2001. Potential, Potential, Potential: The Marriage of Oral History and the World Wide Web. *Journal of American History* 88.2:596–603.
Leeson, Robert. 2000. *The Eclipse of Keynesianism: The Political Economy of the Chicago Counter-Revolution*. New York: Palgrave.
McCloskey, Deirdre N. 2001. Interview with Ross B. Emmett. Chicago Economics Oral History Project. Chicago, May.
Miller, H. Laurence, Jr. 1962. On the "Chicago School of Economics." *Journal of Political Economy* 70.1:64–69.
Muth, Richard. 2002. Interview with Ross B. Emmett. Chicago Economics Oral History Project. Atlanta, January.
Odendahl, Teresa, and Aileen M. Shaw. 2002. Interviewing Elites. In *Handbook of Interview Research*, edited by J. F. Gubrium and J. A. Holstein. Thousand Oaks, Calif.: Sage.
Olson, Paulette I., and Zohreh Emami. 2002. *Engendering Economics: Conversations with Women Economists in the United States*. London: Routledge.
Oral History Association. [1989] 2002. Oral History Evaluation Guidelines. http://alpha.dickinson.edu/oha/pub_eg.html#Oral%20History%20Evaluation%20Guidelines (accessed September 25, 2006).
Patinkin, Don. 1981a. *Essays on and in the Chicago Tradition*. Durham, N.C.: Duke University Press.
———. 1981b. Frank Knight as Teacher. In Patinkin 1981a.
Poland, Blake D. 2002. Transcription Quality. In *Handbook of Interview Research: Context and Method*, edited by J. F. Gubrium and J. A. Holstein. Thousand Oaks, Calif.: Sage.
Reder, Melvin W. 1982. Chicago Economics: Permanence and Change. *Journal of Economic Literature* 20.1:1–38.
Ritchie, Donald A. 2003. *Doing Oral History*. 2nd ed. New York: Twayne.
Samuels, Warren J., ed. 1976. *The Chicago School of Political Economy*. East Lansing: Association for Evolutionary Economics and Division of Research, Graduate School of Business Administration, Michigan State University.
Schmidt, Ingo L. O., and Jan B. Rittaler. 1989. *A Critical Evaluation of the Chicago School of Antitrust Analysis*. Dordrecht: Kluwer Academic.
Seldon, Anthony, and Joanna Pappworth. 1983. *By Word of Mouth: "Élite" Oral History*. London: Methuen.

Stigler, George J. 1970. Review of *The Evolution of Modern Economic Theory*, by Lord Robbins. *Economica*, n.s., 37.148:425–26.

———. 1988. *Memoirs of an Unregulated Economist*. New York: Basic Books.

Thomson, Alistair. 1998. Fifty Years On: An International Perspective on Oral History. *Journal of American History* 85.2:581–95.

Thurman, Walter N. 2005. Interview with Ross B. Emmett. Chicago Economics Oral History Project. Property and Environment Research Center, Bozeman, Mont., July.

Van Overtveldt, Johan. 2006. *The Chicago School: How the University of Chicago Assembled the Thinkers Who Revolutionized Economics and Business*. Chicago: Agate.

Weintraub, E. Roy. 2005. 2004 HES Presidential Address: Autobiographical Memory and the Historiography of Economics. *Journal of the History of Economic Thought* 27.1:1–11.

Weintraub, E. Roy, Stephen J. Meardon, Ted Gayer, and H. Spencer Banzhaf. 1998. Archiving the History of Economics. *Journal of Economic Literature* 36.3:1496–501.

Part 4
Studies in Biography

François Quesnay: A "Rural Socrates" in Versailles?

Christine Théré and Loïc Charles

Biographies, or lives, as a genre have lately experienced a remarkable resurgence (Nye 2006). This phenomenon has affected the way contemporary history of science is made. To many historians, "following individual scientist[s]" seems like "a fine strategy for demonstrating the wide scope of scientific activity" (Porter 2006, 314). The history of economics has not been immune to these changes (Forget 2002, 228–29). Yet the status of biographical writings as a form of intellectual history has been debated since at least the eighteenth century (Forget 2002). One trend is illustrated by the minisymposium on biography in the history of science published in a recent issue of *Isis*. The participants argued that scientific biography *is* history of science and that this category of writing affords an original and often irreplaceable perspective to approach their subject. Conversely, Evelyn Forget (2002, 231–33) documented three methodological positions that challenged the inclusion of the genre of biography in the history of economics: the first one is that of the history of economic analysis exemplified by Joseph Schumpeter, the second one is that of sociology of knowledge, and the third one takes its roots in the post-structuralist critique of the concept of author. However, the "hunger for narrative" has proven so permanent that despite all these reasons not

All translations are the authors' unless otherwise indicated. We thank the participants of the conference for their comments and suggestions. We are especially grateful to Evelyn Forget for her interventions on this text. Any remaining errors and omissions are our responsibility.

History of Political Economy 39 (annual suppl.) DOI 10.1215/00182702-2006-045

to take an interest in writing and reading lives of economists, more and more historians of economics are now doing both.

The first lives of economists were written in the context of the development of academies and scientific societies in eighteenth-century France. At that time, academic eulogy constituted the rhetorical model for almost all the biographies of men of science. Academic eulogy was at the service of a certain conception of what a man of science and his moral values should be. This conception had a significant influence on the type of biographical facts and narratives that academic eulogy contained. In the present essay, we investigate this influence through the case of François Quesnay, man of science and economic writer. Eulogies of Quesnay were written over a period of a few years following his death (1774). In these writings, Quesnay was introduced as a man profoundly marked by his rural origins and childhood. This theme was developed according to two narrative threads. On the one hand, his nostalgia for the country was invoked to explain why he created an economic theory where the land is the only true source of wealth. On the other hand, his rural origins were also used to argue that he was a stranger in the strange land of the king's court: the descriptions of his rustic manners as well as of his love of rural simplicity were used to present Quesnay as a true rural Socrates, foreign to the refined and artificial world of Versailles.

Lacking sufficient critical distance vis-à-vis the eulogies, the biographers of Quesnay believed the description of him as a kind of rural Socrates to be an accurate and objective reconstruction of his actual character. Hence this presentation of Quesnay's life has broadly nourished the main biographies of him (Daire 1846; Hecht [1958] 2005; Schelle 1907). From the portrait of Quesnay borrowed from the eulogists, the biographers constructed a narrative of his medical and economic careers that makes him the archetype of the ideal scientist, incapable of self-interested behavior and driven by a genuine desire to improve the common good. Moreover, his career progress and successes were said to derive exclusively from his intellectual capabilities and achievements. Some interpretations of Quesnay's economic thought have been explicitly based on this narrative (Foley 1973, 123–25). More generally, it has been widely used by historians of economic thought to explain why Quesnay was drawn to economics and wrote two articles on agricultural themes at the venerable age of sixty-three (see Groenewegen 2001, 98–99; [1983] 2002, 249–50; Meek 1962, 15–16). However, we show that the description of Quesnay's character found in the eulogies was heavily influenced by the rhetorical conventions of this academic genre. By analyzing the available biographical writings and putting the information they display in context, we are able to offer a new perspective on the links between the life of Quesnay and his intellectual activities, particularly those that gave rise to a scientific output.

1. The Biographical Genre in the French Enlightenment

The word *biographe* (biographer) existed in French at that time, but it was not widely used. According to the *Encyclopédie*, the biographer is an "author who wrote the particular life of one or of several famous characters" (An. 1752). *Biographie* (biography) was even less common. The *Dictionnaire de l'Académie* (1762) defined this word as "the history of the life of a group of individuals," not of a single individual. In the *Encyclopédie*, there is no entry for this word, and one has to go to *Vie* (life) to find an equivalent of the modern definition of biography. According to the chevalier of Jaucourt (1765), author of the article, this word meant a story that focused on the life of a single man and "in which one gives the details of his private behavior, as well as his handling of public affairs when he is a prince or a statesman." According to Jaucourt, the classics, most notably Plutarch, have excelled in this literary genre, which those "who want to know man" cherish. He also mentioned another tradition: the "lives of saints." Jaucourt was not interested in this type of life and simply pointed to the article *Légende* (legend) for further details. Still, the lives of saints was at that time a rhetorical canon that influenced many biographical writings.

In France, however, biographical texts dedicated to men of science followed another model, that of academic eulogy.[1] This latter genre was a rhetorical exercise practiced in specific institutions, the scientific and literary academies in which status was based on merit rather than birth. The canon of academic eulogy had been profoundly reshaped by Bernard de Fontenelle, secretary of the Royal Academy of Science, in the beginning of the eighteenth century.[2] Jean le Rond d'Alembert and the Marquis

1. In this paragraph and in the following, our analysis is based on Roche 1978, 1:166–81. See also Paul 1980.

2. There were three major royal academies in Paris at that time: the Académie royale des sciences (Academy of Science in the text), the Académie française, and the Académie royale des inscriptions et belles-lettres (Academy of Inscriptions in the text).

de Condorcet for the Academy of Science, and Charles Pinot Duclos, Voltaire, and Antoine-Léonard Thomas for the Académie française, followed Fontenelle's lead and transformed academic eulogy into a successful literary genre. Hence academic eulogies were largely disseminated and read during the Enlightenment. For example, the periodical press (e.g., *Mercure de France*, *Gazette de France*) announced and often published long abstracts of these texts.

Eulogy had three main functions: rhetorical, documentary, and hagiographic. The three roles were closely intermingled in the text's layout (Roche 1978, 1:167–68). D'Alembert, in the entry *Éloge* of the *Encyclopédie*, identified only two types of eulogy: the *éloges oratoires* from the Académie française and the *éloges historiques* from the Academy of Sciences and the Academy of Inscriptions.[3] In his opinion, the first ones, limited by strict stylistic rules, often descended into panegyric and had no pedagogic value. Conversely, *éloge historique* allowed the author to transform academic eulogy into the "philosophical eulogy" it should be (d'Alembert 1755, 527). The eulogies should be "memoirs for the history of letters," and "philosophical reflections should first and foremost constitute the soul of such writings" (527). For d'Alembert, academic eulogy had to show how the works made by the one whose memory was honored marked a progress in the history of letters and sciences. It should also underline the moral value of a life devoted to knowledge.

In the eulogy, the biographical materials had an essential function: to exhibit an exemplary life. Eulogy had to present to its reader the ideal academician in order to educate the readers and to encourage them to choose a scientific or a literary career (Roche 1978, 1:171). On the one hand, the author of a eulogy was concerned with historical truth and tried to gather definite facts to depict the life of the deceased (d'Alembert 1755, 527). Indeed, the panegyrist was usually furnished with biographical materials about the deceased academician by the latter's close friends or family; in Quesnay's case, Prudent Hévin, his son-in-law, provided them in a manuscript note, which circulated among the eulogists (Lorin 1900, 71). On the other hand, because of their educational role, "these *éloges historiques* are designed to tell the truth but not the whole truth, they are sprinkled with stylistic devices to emphasize certain truths at the expense of others" (Paul 1980, 14; see also d'Alembert 1755).

3. The distinction originated from Fontenelle, who created the genre of *éloges historiques* (Paul 1980, 13–19).

2. The Eulogies of François Quesnay

Quesnay died on 16 December 1774. Six eulogies were devoted to him in the years that followed his death. They emanated both from the learned societies to which he had belonged and from individual authors, some of whom had befriended Quesnay. In the Academy of Sciences, its secretary, Jean-Paul Grandjean de Fouchy ([1778] 1888), read the eulogy of Quesnay on 26 April 1775. Antoine Louis (1859), in the Academy of Surgery, read a second academic eulogy on 27 April 1775.

Two young noblemen who went to the Tuesday dinners of the Marquis de Mirabeau wrote other eulogies. The first one was the work of Count Claude-Camille-François d'Albon; it was published in the *Nouvelles éphémérides économiques*, the physiocratic journal, in May 1775 and reissued several times. This eulogy was presented to the Academy of Lyon, of which Quesnay had been a member (Jacquet 1736–85, 1:461–62).[4] The second one was written by Germain-Hyacinthe de Romance, the future Marquis of Mesmon, who belonged to a family of royal soldiers and lived in Versailles, where he was employed in the military house of the king.[5] These two eulogies followed the canon of the "philosophical eulogy" that d'Alembert cherished. They concentrated on Quesnay as a physiocrat rather than as a person, and a large amount of the text was concerned with his economic publications.

D'Alembert, who, like Quesnay, was a member of the Academy of Sciences, published a short eulogy in the *Mercure de France* on 15 November 1778, four years after Quesnay's death. Borrowing heavily from that of Grandjean de Fouchy, this eulogy distinguished itself by a few comments and ironic anecdotes, most notably on the doctor's mathematical writings. The funeral oration given by Mirabeau during a ceremony held in his Parisian hotel in memory of Quesnay a few days after his death is a bit different. Read on 20 December 1774 in front of an assembly of Quesnay's disciples, it was printed a month later in the *Nouvelles éphémérides économiques*. This homage was closer to the model of *éloges oratoires* criticized by d'Alembert. Mirabeau had practiced this genre in his youth as a member of the Marseilles Academy of Fine Letters. Consequently, although

4. Born of a military noble family, d'Albon served in the cavalry. In 1774 he published a pamphlet on taxes and an "Eloge de Chamousset" in the *Journal d'agriculture*, managed by a prominent physiocrat, the Abbé Roubaud. He was also a close acquaintance of Court de Gébelin, the well-known physiocrat and Freemason.

5. His *Eloge de François Quesnay* was printed anonymously in 1775 at the address of London; it was his first book.

he was Quesnay's most prominent disciple, Mirabeau's text contains almost no details on his mentor's life.

Eulogies of Quesnay had a moral and didactic dimension: their purpose was to reveal the deeper meaning of Quesnay's life as a man of science (the surgeon and physician as well as the economist). To meet this objective, the authors structured their texts according to three main themes: Quesnay and country; Quesnay and medicine; Quesnay as a kind of Socrates in Versailles. By doing this, the authors have reconstructed Quesnay's life so as to combine the different episodes of his life into a consistent and exemplary destiny, that is, to transform it into a "philosophical eulogy."

All the eulogies of Quesnay evoked his rural origins. Moreover, his rural childhood was presented as the founding element of his later involvement in *philosophie rurale*. The text of d'Albon (1775, 96–98) provided the most detailed narrative. While Quesnay's father, d'Albon said,

> took pleasure in forming his heart, and in instilling in him the principles of a healthy morality . . . [Quesnay] followed under the eyes of a very active mother the rural labor she liked so much. *It was there that he began studying* the operations of the benevolent nature and that he came to know the treasures and the variety of its productions. From then on, he felt growing in him a distinct taste, a decided tendency for agriculture, which he kept forever after. (97; emphasis added)

The idea that the innate qualities of the man of science manifested themselves at an early age constituted a common stereotype in academic eulogies (Roche 1978, 1:172, 175). Quesnay, as a would-be man of science, had the capacity to immediately go beyond the rudimentary lessons provided by his mother's activities: still in infancy, Quesnay already *studied* nature's operations. Likewise, in his eulogy, Grandjean de Fouchy ([1778] 1888, 17) mentioned that Quesnay was a child gifted with an "active and sharp mind," which allowed him to analyze what he saw and "to read from the great book of nature."

The description of how Quesnay learned to read, the second stage of his education, reinforced the stereotypes of his peasant background and of the early signs of his genius. Drawing on Hévin's note, all his panegyrists said that he learned to read with the *Maison rustique* of Liébaut, the first book he had.[6] Another significant (and mythical; see below) anecdote about the

6. Grandjean de Fouchy and d'Alembert followed Hévin in saying that Quesnay was helped by his mother's gardener (d'Alembert 1778, 147; Grandjean de Fouchy [1778] 1888, 17), while, for Romance de Mesmon ([1775] 1888, 77), Quesnay deciphered it almost without any assistance.

young Quesnay and books is interesting: Quesnay, then a teenager, had the habit of walking from Méré, where his parents lived, to Paris and back, to buy a book. The story goes that he usually read the book he just bought on the return trip (Grandjean de Fouchy [1778] 1888, 18; d'Albon 1775, 99; d'Alembert 1778, 147). In either case, the absence of proper schooling underlined the exceptional intellectual talents of the deceased.

Eulogies also established a causal link between the early period of Quesnay's life and the peculiar attention that he showed to agriculture in his economic writings some fifty years later. The Count of Albon (1775, 97–98) provided the most detailed view on this point:

> It is probably this study, this predominant love of the countryside, which subsequently turned his philosophy to matters of public utility; matters which drove him to the first principles of his political philosophy and to the demonstration he has made so clear: agriculture is the unique source of wealth, its progress is the true foundation of the prosperity of empires and of the success of all other economic activities. If Quesnay should have been raised in a city, perhaps we might never have had Quesnay.

Thus, although the doctor left the country for the city at the age of seventeen to spend the greater part of his professional life in Paris and, later, in the artificial world of Versailles, in the eyes of his biographers his rural childhood constituted his most notable life experience: Quesnay would not have been the same had he not spent his first years "in the fields" (Romance de Mesmon [1775] 1888, 77). It answers a literary convention of academic eulogies: the life of the scholar is framed into a destiny (Roche 1978, 1:172).

The second aspect of the life of Quesnay that attracted the panegyrists' attention was his career as surgeon and doctor. Here again, we find a number of academic stereotypes to underline the personal merit of the man of genius: Quesnay had to struggle against his family to realize his vocation (Grandjean de Fouchy [1778] 1888, 17; Romance de Mesmon [1775] 1888, 79); his vocation was born out of a wish to be useful to his compatriots (Grandjean de Fouchy [1778] 1888, 18; d'Albon 1775, 100–102). Quesnay's career was repositioned in this double perspective: utility and selflessness. When Quesnay left surgery to become a physician, he was not betraying his former company or giving in to social ambition; we are told that this move was justified by his health: the gout did not allow him to practice manual operations any more (Grandjean de Fouchy [1778] 1888, 31; Romance de Mesmon [1775] 1888, 84–85; d'Alembert 1778, 151). Also, the progressive social elevation of Quesnay, who put himself in the service of successively richer and more influential employers, is introduced as the unexpected consequence of a succession of strokes of good fortune, ultimately linked to his professional excellence (d'Albon 1775, 104; Grandjean de Fouchy [1778] 1888, 23, 25, 31; Louis 1859, 251, 255). The nature of the relation, patronage, which was then established between Quesnay and his employers, was evaded in the eulogies. Instead, their authors put forward the friendship that arose between Quesnay and his masters to explain either their choice of Quesnay as a physician or the kind of relations they had afterward.[7]

The story of his professional life was re-created as a succession of initiation rites through which Quesnay transcended his intellectual and moral qualities. Hence one anecdote had Quesnay, then a petty apprentice in surgery, the victim of an ignorant master who appropriated the product of his apprentice's research to obtain a medical degree (Grandjean de Fouchy [1778] 1888, 19; d'Alembert 1778, 148). Another one represented him as a young surgeon confronted by the jealousy of the surgeons of Mantes, who turned down his application to their corporate body. Nonetheless, Quesnay's medical reputation had grown rapidly and reached the attention of nearby lords (Grandjean de Fouchy [1778] 1888, 22; d'Alembert 1778, 148). Grandjean de Fouchy ([1778] 1888, 23–24) gave another typical anecdote: during the polemic with the physician Jean-Baptiste Silva on bleeding, when Quesnay offered to his adversary the possibility of acknowledging defeat while concealing it from the public to save his reputation, the latter refused. Quesnay's work was published and spread the scientific reputation of its author while Silva fell into disgrace.

The third feature of Quesnay's life underlined in the eulogies was his *esprit philosophique*. It is an aspect that they examined from several angles. First, they emphasized that "method was the distinctive character of his mind, the love of order was the predominant passion of his heart. Here is the origin of his discoveries; here is the source of his virtues" (Romance de Mesmon [1775] 1888, 109). Quesnay also showed a true philosophical detachment in the polemics in which he participated: "He debated only for the interest of truth, and never for his self-love" (109). Romance de Mesmon also reported an anecdote in which Quesnay, hav-

7. "The late marshall of Noailles had the opportunity to know him, and consequently, to esteem him and to love him"; "he entered into the Duke of Villeroy's service as his physician and his surgeon and, even more, as his friend" (Grandjean de Fouchy [1778] 1888, 23, 25; see also Louis 1859, 255).

ing learned that he indirectly had been the cause of a man's misfortune, offered his own money to compensate the man for his significant financial loss (109). The episode is all the more symbolic of the doctor's morality as it took place in Versailles, in a relation of patronage in which material and even monetary considerations are supposed to be preponderant. Hence the corrupted atmosphere of court life had no hold over the "Stoic" Quesnay. Indeed, eulogies drew an explicit parallel between Quesnay and the ancient philosophers. Quesnay practiced the art of conversation in much the same way as Socrates did in his own time: "By a succession of well-chosen questions, he led one to conclude for oneself what he might have given you for a principle; it was the way of Plato's dialogues. Opposed, like Socrates, to a crowd of sophists, he had his irony, and seemed, like the son of Sophronisque, to have made *the art of giving birth to people's minds* his specialty" (Romance de Mesmon [1775] 1888, 110; see also 109; emphasis in the original).[8] The parallel with Socrates (as well as with Confucius) was a commonplace among Quesnay's disciples long before the death of the master, and Mirabeau (1775, 203–6) used it in his funeral oration.

3. The Lives of Quesnay

Eulogies had been the main source for Quesnay's biographies. Hence the themes of his life and character found in the eulogies continued in the biographies. However, biographers also used new materials. On the one hand, they have drawn numerous anecdotes from the memoirs of Quesnay's contemporaries, which were published in the nineteenth century. On the other, they made use of several documents that they uncovered or borrowed from the works of local erudites. For the most part, these materials were employed to illustrate and to reinforce the portrait of Quesnay inherited from the eulogies.

Eugène Daire (1846, 9), in what can be called the first biography of Quesnay, took up almost without changes the narrative of Quesnay's rural childhood. Furthermore, he stressed Quesnay's reluctance to leave Mantes for Paris, where he lived, Daire said, like a philosopher devoid of any ambitions and enlivened by the public good. Conversely, Daire brought up

8. This sentence is particularly difficult to translate into English. The French reads as follows: "Opposé comme Socrate à la foule des sophistes, il avait son ironie, et semblait, comme le fils de Sophronisque, avoir fait son étude particulière de l'art d'*accoucher les esprits*." The pun is based on the use of a medical vocabulary ("son étude" means literally "his office," and "l'art d'accoucher" is the "art of giving birth") to describe the Socratic dialectics.

only in passing his presence at Versailles. The portrait of Quesnay as a Socrates of sorts, foreign to the sophisticated world of the court, was supported by an anecdote extracted from Jean-François Marmontel (Daire 1846, 16; Marmontel [1804] 1999, 173). Moreover, Daire (1846, 15) insisted on the parsimonious and unselfish use that Quesnay made of his credit at Versailles.

Daire's biographical note was a short piece for which he had not undertaken thorough research, but later biographies inserted much more new material. However, even when they called into question several details from the eulogies, they remained faithful to their overall presentation of Quesnay's life, at the price of some rhetorical contortions. Gustave Schelle's biography offers a telling example of this. He took a critical look on the content of the eulogies (Schelle 1907, 5). He also achieved an able synthesis of the erudite researches of the Société archéologique de Rambouillet and added several new elements from his own research on important aspects of Quesnay's life, such as his role in the debates between the surgeons and the physicians and the history of the *Tableau économique*. However, Schelle's study did not provide a new portrait of the economist. Schelle (1907, 21) emphasized, for instance, that the narrative of Quesnay's childhood found in the eulogies was highly unconvincing, but he nevertheless used the influence that country life had on Quesnay to interpret his career as a man of science and, in particular, an economist. His description of Quesnay's life at Versailles is also significant. Although Schelle (1907, 140, 162) added several new details drawn from new sources—du Hausset's and Marmontel's memoirs, Louis de Loménie's (1879) biography of Mirabeau, and the autobiography of Pierre-Samuel Du Pont de Nemours—his story simply recycles the narrative of the "rural Socrates" from the eulogies.

First, the link of Quesnay with the country was underlined to explain the oddity of Quesnay in the world of Versailles. Schelle (1907, 137) extracted appropriate anecdotes from du Hausset's *Mémoires*, for example: "He [Quesnay] liked to talk to me of the country; I had been brought up there, and he made me speak about the pastures, the wealth of the farmers, and of the methods of cultivation in Normandy and Poitou. Here was the best of ordinary men, aloof from the smallest intrigue. He was much more concerned at court with the best method of cultivating the land than with anything else that went on there" (du Hausset [1809] 1985, 85). Quesnay was living modestly in the palace of Versailles (Schelle 1907, 96–97). Moreover, while he was perfectly informed about all the plots that were designed in the apartments of Madame de Pompadour and was, "owing to his situation," associated with "unpleasant, or dangerous" affairs, the doctor remained nevertheless "inexperienced in the manners of high society," "timid in front of the king," whom he "however [distracts] by witticisms" (100, 103–12, 116–17).[9] Quesnay was described as a straightforward and guileless character, cautious, even timorous and very gentle. These traits explained his unselfish behavior, his dislike for intrigues, his limited ambition even though he had an important credit at court and was a prominent go-between to reach Madame de Pompadour (137, 134, 191).

Schelle wanted to play down the poor impression that Quesnay's servile, even ambiguous, attitude could leave with his reader, by pointing out that the doctor was able to secure a "real independence" for himself. This independence manifested itself by the fact that Quesnay received, in his *entresol*, people who belonged "to all parties." Schelle also stressed the freedom of speech that predominated in the doctor's apartments (123–26). As Socrates did, Quesnay often practised a caustic irony (143). Put in a wider perspective, it appears that the presence of Quesnay at court constituted a problematic aspect that the biographers felt compelled to legitimate. Hence, as in the case of the Abbé de Saint-Pierre, another philosopher and economist who had lived at court, Quesnay's biographers hypothesized that it was first and foremost "to get a better view of the principal actors on the stage of the world" that he went to Versailles and became a courtier (Higgs [1897] 2001, 16; Schelle 1907, 190–91).

Since 1958, Jacqueline Hecht's *La vie de François Quesnay* has constituted the main, and often the sole, reference for historians of economic thought with an interest in the physiocrat's biography. It is the most complete synthesis available. Nevertheless, like her predecessors, Hecht is not free from the clichés inherited from eulogies, in particular when describing Quesnay's life at court. She represented the doctor "as a wise man, distant from intrigues and from society turmoil." He had the character of a "peasant of Danube, unrefined and honest," and, when he undertook his research on agriculture, the fashionable subject of the moment, he has used the "memories of his childhood" (Hecht [1958] 2005, 1363, 1377). This last argument was taken up by historians of thought. For example, Vernon Foley (1973, 121–26), in a well-known article, explains that Quesnay,

9. These elements are based on passages from du Hausset [1809] 1985, 39–42, 85, 91–92 and Marmontel [1804] 1999, 173.

made uneasy by the life at court, developed "a nostalgia for rural life," which drove him to reflect upon the economics of agriculture.

More generally, the biographers' use of multiple sources has often ended in a juxtaposition of rival, and sometimes contradictory, facts and anecdotes without discriminating between them. Hecht's ([1958] 2005, 1334–35) description of Quesnay's first education is quite symptomatic in this respect. On the one hand, she called into question the plausibility of certain "extraordinary facts" recorded in the eulogies. For instance, the story of the young Quesnay who would often walk to Paris to buy a book and read it on the way home: Quesnay would have walked sixty miles in one day! On the other hand, she took up quite literally and without discussing them other stories that are as unlikely to have happened, such as the tale of the day gardener who helped Quesnay learn to read.[10]

The problem stems from the fact that biographers have used the eulogies as well as the other sources without enough critical distance. The sources of Quesnay's life, like other historical documents, have to be analyzed and contextualized to provide objective and trustworthy knowledge. In this respect, memoirs are not more dependable than eulogies, and even official documents, although generally easier to handle, may be incomplete or faulty.[11] Hence, to provide a scientific biography of Quesnay, it would be necessary to discuss critically the sources on which the narrative of Quesnay's life is constructed. This cannot be done here without exceeding the limits of this essay. It may, nonetheless, be worthwhile to furnish a few examples of the shortcomings that one has to overcome. Let us investigate the two main springs of anecdotes on Quesnay's life at Versailles: the *Mémoires* of Madame du Hausset, housemaid of the Marquise of Pompadour, and those of Marmontel (du Hausset [1809] 1985; Marmontel [1804] 1999). The origin of the text of the first is obscure, and one commentator has even questioned its authenticity (Gordon 2001). As for the second text, it is well-known that Marmontel often embellished facts and put forward his own role in the anecdotes he related. His modern editors have under-

10. This story is subject to two problems. First, there is no legal act mentioning a gardener in service of Quesnay's family. Moreover, their garden was so small that he probably never existed anywhere but in the imagination of Hévin, the source of this anecdote (Lorin 1900, 72). Second, day gardeners belonged to the lower classes of agricultural workers, among whom very few could read and write.

11. For instance, Quesnay's date of birth is not mentioned on his baptismal certificate. The ceremony took place on 20 June 1694, and it is only by the authority of Quesnay himself that his birthday was fixed on 4 June (Lorin 1900, 63).

lined how much Marmontel ([1804] 1999, 24) remained an "incorrigible dramatist" in writing his own life.

4. Quesnay: Portrait of a Client

We believe that Quesnay was a much more complex figure than the one found in the eulogies and, therefore, in the biographies. In particular, the narrative of the "rural Socrates" is clearly contradicted by Quesnay's social destiny. Quesnay, who was born to a humble rural family in 1694, began his career as a modest surgeon in the small town of Mantes in 1717. By the end of the 1730s, he was already at the service of an important court noble and power broker, the Duke of Villeroy, as well as a recognized medical theoretician and an eminent member of the academy of surgery. In the 1750s, as the private physician of Madame de Pompadour, the most powerful woman in the kingdom, Quesnay would get even closer to the summit of the social hierarchy of French society.

To climb the social ladder in ancien régime France, Quesnay made a cunning use of the system of patronage. Several facts and anecdotes recorded in the eulogies as well as in other sources point in that direction. However, the biographers passed them on without providing a proper perspective to interpret them. Consequently, this aspect has not raised much attention from the commentators of Quesnay's writings. While some alluded to the role of patronage in his career, no one linked it directly to his scientific practices and productions (Fox-Genovese 1976, 70–74; Groenewegen 2001, 94). However, Quesnay's life as a scientist could not be dissociated from the system of patronage.

First, the intervention of Quesnay's patrons was decisive in the launching of his medical career. In 1727 Silva, a reputed physician, published a treatise on bleeding. Quesnay, then a young surgeon from Mantes, prepared a refutation. He circulated his manuscript to draw some attention to his talents beyond the circle of his practice (Lorin 1900, 98). Informed about the existence of this text, Silva tried to discredit it and to ridicule its author. To counter this move, Quesnay called the Marshal of Noailles, a former minister and a close acquaintance of Louis XV, for help. A meeting was organized at Noailles's place to mediate the disagreement between the two men, but they held on to their positions. It is at this point that Quesnay brought the dispute to the judgment of the public. It was indeed the only means offered to a young and unknown surgeon to fight on an equal footing "M. Silva's reputation, which gave a very great weight to his work"

(Louis 1859, 252). Silva tried to stop the publication. Finally, permission to print was granted, thanks to the intervention of the chancellor d'Aguesseau, after a one-year delay (Grandjean de Fouchy [1778] 1888, 24; Lorin 1900, 98).

This episode shows that the publication of Quesnay's first medical writing was made possible by his network of protectors. Their intervention was decisive at two steps of the process. First, when Noailles intervened as mediator he counterbalanced the weight of Silva's reputation and protection: without his intervention the scientific opinion of Quesnay would not have had any social recognition whatsoever. Second, only the renewed intervention of Quesnay's patrons can explain why the minister himself (d'Aguesseau) bypassed his subordinate, the censor Pierre-Jean Burette (Silva's friend), to ensure that Quesnay's work was published. Quesnay alone could not have persuaded the chancellor: such favors were part of a whole system of gift and countergift between high courtiers. The favor was granted by d'Aguesseau to satisfy the power broker(s) who presented him the request and who was (were) then his *obligé*. In this instance, besides Noailles, we can think of other less-important figures who might also have played a role in this affair. The fact that Quesnay dedicated his book to Monseigneur d'Abos, a member of the Parlement of Paris and a prominent landowner in the Mantes area, clearly suggests that he also pleaded Quesnay's cause.[12] Quesnay would acknowledge publicly Noailles's role by dedicating his next work to him.

Another episode that happened a few years later, in 1735, confirms the decisive role played by patronage in Quesnay's career. Quesnay had just entered the service of the Duke of Villeroy, a distinguished court noble. Significantly, Quesnay had met the duke in the salons of his first patron, the Marshal of Noailles (Lorin 1900, 118–19). At that time, the institutional opposition between the surgeons "of Saint-Cosme" (whose cause Quesnay endorsed) and the physicians was taking a more dramatic turn.[13] The crea-

12. The d'Abos family had been in the Parlement for several generations (Bluche [1956] 2004, 55–56). It is also quite possible that it was d'Abos who introduced Quesnay to Noailles, who was, like d'Abos, an important landowner in the area of Mantes.

13. In a word, the surgeons were then assimilated into the corporation of barbers-surgeons and, as such, were categorized as manual workers. The surgeons of Saint-Cosme wanted to distance themselves from the barbers and enhance their social status by joining the liberal arts, alongside the physicians. It implied that the surgeons from Saint-Cosme showed that they matched the physicians as theoreticians. The surgeons ultimately obtained what they wanted, and the conflict ceased more or less in the 1750s. For a detailed presentation of the conflict between the two groups, see Gelfand 1980 and Brockliss and Jones 1997.

tion of chairs of surgery held by surgeons in 1724 and that of the academy of surgery in 1731 had manifested the rising power of the surgeons of Saint-Cosme, who claimed the recognition of surgery as a science on an equal footing with medicine. Quesnay, who had published nothing since his refutation of Silva, had prepared the joint publication of two important texts, *Essai phisique sur l'oeconomie animale* and *Art de guérir par la saignée*, that supported the surgeons' campaign.

It was therefore extremely important for Quesnay and the surgeons that the content of his works be validated by as much scientific opinion as possible and most particularly by the medical institutions. Hence Quesnay solicited the approbation of the Society of Arts, the Academy of Surgery, and the Academy of Lyon, three societies to which he belonged, as well as that of the Paris Faculty of Medicine, home of the physicians. The faculty was determined to uphold a strict separation between the physicians, who were allowed to theorize about the art of curing, and the surgeons, who were confined to practice medical operations under the guidance of physicians. The works of the surgeon Quesnay clearly called into question the difference in status defended by the physicians.[14] Besides, Quesnay had strong connections with prominent spokesmen of the surgeons such as La Peyronie, Garengeot, Malaval, Bassuel, Le Dran, and Petit.[15]

In this context, the faculty had obviously no interest in lending its public support to a work challenging its position. The Faculty of Medicine named two commissaires, the physicians Camille Falconet and Elie Col de Villars, to examine Quesnay's books. Falconet and Quesnay knew each other: at that time the former was curing the nephew of the Duke of Villeroy (INED 2005, 1159). This link between Falconet and Villeroy clarifies why Falconet agreed to be one of the censors of Quesnay's works as well as Falconet's laudatory report on them, which contradicted the interests of his corporation (INED 2005, 1160). Indeed, the faculty was surprised by the report's tone and decided to go against the opinion of its commissaires and refuse to give its approval to Quesnay's works. Meanwhile, the surgeons, who had anticipated the move, had already made a copy of the report. The copy was passed to La Peyronie, who "took it with the intention of having it printed, without even leaving any choice

14. In particular in the "Discours préliminaire sur la théorie de la médecine et de la chirurgie," a text that introduced the *Essai phisique*.

15. François Gigot de La Peyronie, René de Croissant de Garengeot, Jean Malaval, Pierre Bassuel, Henri-François Le Dran, and Jean-Louis Petit.

to me [Quesnay]" (INED 2005, 1157–58). However, this conduct threatened both Falconet and Quesnay. Falconet could not agree to the publication of a document that went against the Faculty's decision. Quesnay would also be in an uneasy position: the publication of the report without Falconet's agreement contradicted the patronage system's polite rules. Thus Quesnay tried to convince Falconet to accept this publication. Cunningly, he formulated his request as if the idea were coming from the Duke of Villeroy:

> He [Villeroy] answered me that I must not break away from my corporate body; especially with sir La Peyronie to whom I have much of obligation, to spare a corporation that has become my enemy . . . and that he was persuaded, that whatever ties that you have . . . with your corporation, you would not support its wrongdoings to the point of quarrelling with me in a circumstance where I am not free to make the sacrifice which might be required of me, while the faculty, on the contrary, is still free . . . to remedy its dishonest conduct. (1158)

But Falconet did not yield to Quesnay's pressure. Quesnay proposed a compromise, again under the aegis of their common patron, Villeroy. At a meeting with La Peyronie and in the presence of the duke, it was decided that the report would not be published, "since you ask it absolutely"; instead, there would be "only a small notice" (1159). The surgeons would be satisfied, since the text inserted in the first pages of the *Essai phisique sur l'oeconomie animale* revealed that the faculty had failed to approve the book, despite the favorable scientific opinion of its two representatives (1159). As the names of these two physicians did not appear in the printed note, Falconet's position vis-à-vis the faculty was also safeguarded. Hence he accepted Quesnay's proposal.

The way Quesnay became Madame de Pompadour's personal physician provides another illustration of the dominant role of patronage in his career. Quesnay met the Pompadour through the Countess of Estrades, her cousin and *dame d'atours* of Louis XV's daughters, to whom he was introduced by the Duke of Villeroy (Lorin 1900, 139–40; Hecht [1958] 2005, 1360). The countess had suffered an epileptic crisis in the company of Villeroy. The latter called for his physician, Quesnay, who decided to isolate immediately Estrades and to keep her disease secret. The countess had been extremely grateful for such a move, and, when her cousin, Madame de Pompadour, needed a private physician, she recommended Quesnay. What is interesting in this episode is that Quesnay's success was not due to a medical achievement (he did not cure Estrades) but to a social performance (he preserved her reputation).

Thanks to his mastery of the codes of the complex game of polite society, Quesnay was able to exceed rather early the limits imposed by his humble social and professional origin to obtain a comfortable and stable position. The strong link between his social progression and his network of patrons can also be attested by very different sources: the dedications of his medical works and his family records. Quesnay's social achievement can be grasped by comparing the conditions of the godparents of his children and his grandchildren. While the godparents of Quesnay's children, who saw the light of the day between 1717 and 1728, were bourgeois—traders from Paris and Mantes, petty ecclesiasts and law officials—those of his grandchildren born in Versailles were prominent courtiers and ministers.[16] His first grandson, Jean-Marie Quesnay, was baptized on 24 January 1750 in Versailles. His godfather was "Marc-Pierre de Voyer, Count of Argenson, minister [of war] and secretary of state" and his godmother was the "high and powerful lady Jeanne Poisson d'Etiolles, Marquise de Pompadour" (cited in Lorin 1900, 157). A few months later Quesnay's granddaughter, Charlotte-Louise Hévin, was born, to Nicole (Quesnay's daughter) and Hévin. The baptismal certificate indicated as godfather "the Count of Saint-Florentin, secretary of state" and for godmother the Countess of Estrades (cited in Lorin 1900, 159). The two documents conveyed the same signification: the joined patronage of Madame de Pompadour and her cousin Estrades.[17]

In the service of the king's favorite, Quesnay did remain indebted to his first patrons: the Duke of Villeroy and the Marshal of Noailles. To Noailles, he dedicated the second edition of the *Essai sur l'oeconomie animale* (1747); the *Traité de la gangrène* (1749) he dedicated to one of the marshal's sons, Louis of Noailles, Duke of Ayen. He paid tribute to Villeroy in the

16. We have gathered this information from several sources (Archives Départementales des Yvelines 1994, items 13–17; Hecht [1958] 2005, 1336–38; Lorin 1900, 85, 88).

17. In the first baptismal certificate, Estrades was indirectly represented by the Count of Argenson, her lover. In the second one and in a similar way, Saint-Florentin, who owed his position to the Pompadour, attested of her patronage of Quesnay. Interestingly, the baptismal certificate of the next child of Hévin, born on 1 June 1753, implicitly testified to the open conflict that had broken out between Estrades and the Pompadour in 1752 and Quesnay's allegiance to the latter: while Madame de Pompadour was still represented by her daughter "Jeanne-Alexandrine Le Normand d'Etioles" (godmother), the godfather was the minister of finances, "Lord Louis-Louis-Charles de Machault d'Arnouville," the archenemy of Estrades's lover, the Count of Argenson.

Traité des effets et de l'usage de la saignée (1750). Furthermore, the Duke of Ayen, son of Noailles, was the godfather of Jean-Louis Hévin (born 30 March 1761); the godmother was Madame de Pompadour (Lorin 1900, 160–61).

5. Conclusion

The social progression of François Quesnay owes a lot to the system of patronage. Furthermore, we were able to display the decisive role patronage played in his scientific career, particularly in his first steps as a medical writer. We believe that our interpretation of Quesnay's life as a scientist brings out a few important things about the relationship between biography and the history of science and economics. First, we have shown that the genre of lives or biographies of scientists has a history of its own and that the historian of thought who wants to use these materials for the purpose of doing intellectual history should be aware of this issue. Second, to produce a scientific biography—that is, to do history of science by other means (Nye 2006)—necessarily entails a reflection on the nature of the "act of science" (that is, the act or decision of trying to produce scientific knowledge) and how it interacted with the life of the author or scientist. Our article shows that the frontier between Quesnay's life in science and Quesnay's life *tout court* is both complex and quite peculiar to Enlightenment France. In this context, scientific activities, and Quesnay's in particular, were embedded in social practices and institutions that, like patronage, regulated the whole functioning of ancien régime French society.

Finally, the third point brings us back to the history of economics. While in the above we have focused on Quesnay's medical career, the system of patronage relationships is likewise a key to understanding Quesnay's scientific practices as an economist. As we have shown in another article (Charles and Théré forthcoming), the first economic collaborators of François Quesnay—Charles-Georges Le Roy, Charles de Butré, Etienne Marivetz, and Marmontel—were all clients from either the Noailles family, the Villeroy family, or Madame de Pompadour. Moreover, men of letters—like Mirabeau and Du Pont de Nemours, and officials like Pierre-Paul Le Mercier de la Rivière and, to a lesser extent, Turgot, who joined Quesnay between 1757 and 1763—were all aware of Quesnay's connections in Versailles and eager to benefit from them to boost their own social status and career. Quesnay replicated with them the patron-client relationship he had with Estrades, Noailles, the Pompadour, and Villeroy, only this time *he* was the patron.

References

Albon, Claude-Camille-François, comte d'. 1775. Éloge historique de M. Quesnay, contenant l'analyse de ses ouvrages. *Nouvelles éphémérides économiques ou Bibliothèque raisonnée de l'histoire, de la morale et de la politique* 5:93–175.

An. 1752. Biographe. In *Encyclopédie, ou dictionnaire raisonné des sciences, des arts et des métiers*, edited by Denis Diderot and Jean le Rond d'Alembert. 17 vols. Paris: Briasson.

Archives Départementales des Yvelines. 1994. "*Une vie, une oeuvre, un siècle*": *Exposition François Quesnay*. Versailles: Grande Ecurie du Roi.

Bluche, François. [1956] 2004. *L'origine des magistrats du Parlement de Paris au XVIIIe siècle (1715–1771): Dictionnaire généalogique*. 2nd ed. Paris: Patrice Dupuy.

Brockliss, Laurence, and Jones, Colin. 1997. *The Medical World of Early Modern France*. Oxford: Clarendon.

Charles, Loïc, and Théré, Christine. Forthcoming. The Writing Workshop of François Quesnay and the Making of Physiocracy. *HOPE*.

Daire, Eugéne. 1846. Notice sur la vie et les travaux de François Quesnay. In *Physiocrates*, edited by Eugéne Daire. Paris: Guillaumin.

D'Alembert, Jean le Rond. 1755. Eloge. In *Encyclopédie, ou dictionnaire raisonné des sciences, des arts et des métiers*, edited by Denis Diderot and Jean le Rond d'Alembert. 17 vols. Paris: Briasson.

———. 1778. Éloge de M. Quesnay. *Mercure de France*, November, 145–58.

Du Hausset, Nicole. [1809] 1985. *Mémoires de Madame Du Hausset sur Louis XV et Madame de Pompadour*. Edited by Jean-Pierre Guicciardi. Paris: Mercure de France.

Du Pont de Nemours, Pierre-Samuel. [1906] 1984. *The Autobiography of Du Pont de Nemours*. Translated by Elizabeth Fox-Genovese. Wilmington, Del.: Scholarly Resources.

Foley, Vernon. 1973. An Origin of the Tableau Economique. *HOPE* 5.1:121–50.

Forget, Evelyn L. 2002. A Hunger for Narrative: Writing Lives in the History of Economic Thought. In *The Future of the History of Economics*, edited by E. Roy Weintraub. *HOPE* 34 (supplement): 226–44.

Fox-Genovese, Elizabeth. 1976. *The Origins of Physiocracy*. Ithaca: Cornell University Press.

Gelfand, Toby. 1980. *Professionalizing Modern Medicine: Paris Surgeons and Medical Science and Institutions in the Eighteenth Century*. Westport, Conn.: Greenwood.

Gordon, Alden R. 2001. The Longest-Enduring Pompadour Hoax: Sénac de Meilhan and the Journal de Madame du Hausset. In *Art and Culture in the Eighteenth Century: New Dimensions and Multiple Perspectives*, edited by E. Goodman. Newark: University of Delaware Press.

Grandjean de Fouchy, Jean-Paul. [1778] 1888. Éloge de Quesnay. In Oncken 1888.

Groenewegen, Peter D. 2001. From Prominent Physicians to Major Economists: Some Reflections on Quesnay's Switch to Economics in the 1750s. In *Physicians and Political Economy: Six Studies of the Work of Doctor-Economists*, edited by P. D. Groenewegen. London: Routledge.

——. [1983] 2002. Quesnay's First Publication in Economics: The Article "Fermiers" for the *Encyclopédie*—an Introduction. In *Eighteenth Century Economics: Turgot, Beccaria, and Their Contemporaries*, by Peter D. Groenewegen. London: Routledge.

Hecht, Jacqueline. [1958] 2005. *La vie de François Quesnay.* In INED 2005.

Higgs, Henry. [1897] 2001. *The Physiocrats: Six Lectures on the French Economistes of the Eighteenth Century.* Reprint, Kitchener: Batoche Books.

INED. 2005. *Oeuvres économiques complètes de François Quesnay et autres textes*, edited by Ch. Théré, L. Charles, and J.-C. Perrot. 2 vols. Paris: INED.

Jacquet, Louis. 1736–85. Compte-rendus de l'éloge de François Quesnay par le comte d'Albon. In *Compte-rendus de l'académie de Lyon, 1736–1785.* Lyon: Bibliothèque de l'Académie de Lyon.

Jaucourt, Louis de. 1765. Vie. In *Encyclopédie, ou dictionnaire raisonné des sciences, des arts et des métiers*, edited by Denis Diderot and Jean le Rond d'Alembert. 17 vols. Paris: Briasson.

Loménie, Louis de. 1879. *Les Mirabeau. Nouvelles études sur la société française au XVIIIe siècle.* 4 vols. Paris: Dentu.

Lorin, Félix. 1900. François Quesnay. *Mémoires et documents publiés par la Société archéologique de Rambouillet* 14:61–237.

Louis, Antoine. 1859. Eloge de Quesnay, lu dans la séance publique du 27 avril 1775. In *Eloges lus dans les séances publiques de l'Académie royale de chirurgie de 1750 à 1792*, edited by E. F. Dubois. Paris: Baillière et fils.

Marmontel, Jean-François. [1804] 1999. *Mémoires.* Edited by J. P. Guicciardi and G. Thierrat. Paris: Mercure de France.

Meek, Ronald L. 1962. *The Economics of Physiocracy.* London: Allen and Unwin.

Mirabeau, Victor Riqueti, Marquis de. 1775. Éloge funèbre de M. François Quesnay. *Nouvelles éphémérides économiques ou Bibliothèque raisonnée de l'histoire, de la morale et de la politique* 1:197–216.

Nye, Mary Joe. 2006. Scientific Biography: History of Science by Another Means? *Isis* 97:322–29.

Oncken, August, ed. 1888. *Oeuvres économiques et philosophiques de F. Quesnay.* Paris: Peelman et Cie.

Paul, Charles B. 1980. *Science and Immortality: The Eloges of the Paris Academy of Sciences (1699–1791).* Berkeley: University of California Press.

Porter, Theodore M. 2006. Is the Life of a Scientist a Scientific Unit? *Isis* 97:314–21.

Roche, Daniel. 1978. *Le siècle des Lumières en province: Académies et académiciens provinciaux, 1680–1789.* 2 vols. Paris: EHESS.

Romance de Mesmon, Germain-Hyacinthe de. [1775] 1888. Éloge de François Quesnay. In Oncken 1888.

Schelle, Gustave. 1907. *Le docteur Quesnay.* Paris: Alcan.

Some Relationships between a Scholar's and an Entrepreneur's Life: The Biography of L. Albert Hahn

Jan-Otmar Hesse

"If Hahn is such an ardent anti-Keynesian, why is he so eager to publicize his pre-Keynesian Keynesianism?" This question was raised by Fritz Machlup in a volume in tribute to the German monetary theorist L. Albert Hahn on the occasion of Hahn's seventieth birthday. Machlup (1959, 50) saw the answers to this question to be "largely . . . psychological in character" and claimed: "The world lends a more sympathetic ear to repenting sinners, to converted believers, and to cured heretics." There certainly was a psychological element in Hahn's many articles and books, in which he cast the story of his life as a convert. But his success, in terms of maintaining a durable place in the discipline's memory, must remain doubtful: no entry under his name is found in the numerous recent national and international dictionaries of economists (Hesse 2003; Samuels 2003; Blaug and Vane 2003; Beaud and Dostaler 1995; Blaug 1985, 1989). The same is true for influential textbooks on the history of economics (such as Niehans 1990 and Backhouse 1985) as well as standard textbooks on international finance and monetary theory. Despite the obvious absence of Hahn's name in the general memory of the discipline, he is surprisingly alive in more specialized contexts. Donald Boudreaux and George Selgin (1990) described his role as a precursor of both Keynesianism and rational expectation theory. He was mentioned as one of the most important figures in the monetary discussion in Germany between the two world wars (Laidler and Stadler 1998) and among exiled economists (Hagemann and Krohn

History of Political Economy 39 (annual suppl.) DOI 10.1215/00182702-2006-046

1999). His 1920 book *Economic Theory of Bank Credit* was even considered valuable enough to translate into Italian (Hahn 1990) no less than seventy years after its first edition.[1]

This kind of interest in the life and work of L. Albert Hahn can be explained neither by Hahn's own aims nor by the motives of his audience. Rather, it refers to a special preoccupation of the architects of the discipline's memory, who apparently find in Hahn's life some essential features that are worthwhile to recollect. If we assume that economics selects its biographical memory for each time period not by accident but in a structurally determined way,[2] the question arises (and should serve as the key question in this article): for what reasons is Hahn remembered in every historical statement of the evolution of economics? The answer involves two different levels of analysis. The first is to examine whether the stories told about Hahn's life and the particular construction of these stories might be reasons for the discipline's particular recollection of Hahn while so many other economists are neglected. The second is at a more abstract level, and it is to consider the selection processes in economics: what institutional purpose could be served by references to the biography and the work of Hahn?[3] This second level of argument is in parts highly speculative and is touched upon in the conclusion.

Two related aspects of Hahn's life are examined in this article as explanations for the discipline's attention: first, his "conversion" from pre-Keynesianism to anti-Keynesianism; second, the fact that he earned his living as a professional banker, not as an academic. The latter aspect of his biography served increasingly to explain the theme of his "conversion." His "double life" was used to respond to the question of how he could remain neglected as a precursor of Keynesianism. This same double life, however, strengthens the value of Hahn's anti-Keynesian argu-

1. I thank Harald Hagemann for this source. Hahn's most accessible article for the English reader is his "Compensating Reactions to Compensatory Spending," published in 1945 in the *American Economic Review.*

2. At the *HOPE* conference in April 2006 it was suggested that there simply is a market demand for biographies. But since it seems probable that most of the recent dictionaries of biographies of economists are bought by economists, this argument refers to nothing else than to the demand of the discipline itself, which should be explained. Thus economists (or historians of economics) should not be limited to the role of the suppliers of biographical knowledge but have to be conceptualized as consumers as well.

3. This level of analysis is complicated by the fact that Hahn himself—insofar as he was part of the discipline—took part in the discipline's selection process.

ments, which were attributed to practical experience. Both aspects—his intellectual conversion and his practical experience—are highly mythologized, often by Hahn himself. The first part of this article examines how Hahn succeeded in introducing the story of his life into academic discussion, so much so that he has even been regarded as a precursor of rational expectation theory, which became influential long after his death. To do so, the present essay compares the common structures of academic and entrepreneurial self-description, recognizing that the latter dominated Hahn's self-description. In the second part, the analysis turns to Hahn's intellectual biography to show that the rhetoric of "precursorship" is more or less an intelligent strategy of self-marketing. Finally, in the third part, there is a discussion of the function of Hahn-type biographies in the evolution of economic discourse.

1. Hahn's Mixture of Academic and Entrepreneurial Self-Description

Hahn was never a regular university professor, either in Germany or abroad. His life revolved around his business as a private banker. He was—as he wrote later—"born with a golden spoon in [his] mouth" (Hahn 1964, 6; my translation). His grandfather was the owner of a private bank in Frankfurt, the Bankhaus L. Albert Hahn, founded in 1821. In 1872, the bank became a publicly traded company, although the family (Hahn's father and his uncle) remained majority shareholders (Deutsche Effecten- und Wechsel-Bank 1947, 17–20). After Hahn took his examination from the gymnasium in Frankfurt (where he met the three years' younger Edgar Salin, the well-known economist and founder of the Swiss journal *Kyklos*), he started working at the family's bank but was unsatisfied with the work. He decided to study law in Heidelberg and Marburg, where he finished his studies shortly before the First World War broke out. During the war he wrote an article on inflation that was accepted as a PhD thesis at the University of Marburg. In 1919 he became a member of the board of directors of the family's bank and replaced his father, who was ill and died in 1921 (Deutsche Effecten- und Wechsel-Bank 1947, 20). Until the Nazis took power in Germany, management of the bank, rather than academic work, was his main field of business. Nevertheless, in 1920 he wrote his *Economic Theory of Bank Credit*, which by 1930 had been released in two further editions. Because of the numerous articles he wrote on the questions of inflation and monetary reform, he received an honorary (unpaid) professorship from the University of Frankfurt, which carried no teaching duties.

His position as an outsider in economics continued when Hahn left Frankfurt some years after the Nazis came to power. He resigned from the board of trustees of the family's bank in 1936 and sold his assets to a consortium of big Berlin banks (Deutsche Effecten- und Wechsel-Bank 1947, 18). After living in Switzerland for three years, he moved to New York in 1939, where he had success as a banker and at the New York Stock Exchange. In 1949 he moved to Paris but returned periodically to Frankfurt, where his honorary professorship was revived. He gave several academic lectures in Frankfurt, but did not return to teach permanently.[4] He returned to the board of trustees of the family's bank, which still existed in Frankfurt in 1947, but never took over the management again. Instead he became a partly admired, partly hated adviser in the rebuilding of the German Central Bank (Muthesius 1959). Because of his experience as an international banker, his theoretical knowledge, and his knowledge of the German banking system (Hahn 1960), he was invited to participate in a meeting of international monetary experts in the villa Serbelloni in Italy, organized by Machlup in 1963 with the help of the Rockefeller Foundation.[5] This conference, which led to the Bellagio Group, was the last appearance of the seventy-five-year-old Hahn among economists. Hahn died in Zurich in 1968.

Hahn's biography, which is here defined as the different kinds of references to his life in autobiographical, biographical, and scholarly writing, was constructed from the worlds of both academia and business. But the patterns of life descriptions are very different in these worlds because such stories have different functions and goals in the two social systems. If we compare the semantic patterns of academic autobiographies, described by Jeremy Popkin (this volume), with biographies or autobiographies of entrepreneurs, we can find some striking differences. Popkin discerns in academic autobiographies such goals as reflecting social rules of a discipline, educating new scholars into a particular tradition, and surviving forever as part of the memory of a discipline. It

4. Oskar Morgenstern (1947) met Hahn in summer 1947 in Frankfurt during his (Morgenstern's) trip to Germany for the Rockefeller Foundation and noted Hahn's pessimistic attitude on any future academic work in economics.

5. Letter from Machlup to Hahn, 12 December 1963. Fritz Machlup Papers, box 42, Hoover Institution Archives, Stanford, California.

would be a breach of academic norms for a scholar to refer to his or her own ingeniousness or scientific accomplishments (Popkin, this volume). In contrast, biographies and autobiographies of entrepreneurs often appear while they are still running a business and are intended to strengthen a business leader and to demonstrate his or her particular ability to manage the corporation. Whereas academics are compelled to show how their scientific accomplishments grew out of a series of rational ideas and evolutionary improvement of a theory, entrepreneurs in contrast have to explain that a key decision could not be found by rational conclusion but by "intuition" or "instinct." The Bertelsmann manager Axel Ganz said in an interview that his business success is made of "80 percent work, 10 percent intuition for the market and 10 percent luck" (cited in Hansen 1992, 7; my translation). Such sources of success could hardly be described by a plausible and conclusive narration, but requires a strong metaphoric language. Autobiographies as well as biographies of entrepreneurs therefore use a stronger language than similar texts on academics.[6]

This difference is supported by the "market value" of stories about entrepreneurs and managers. There are many recent examples of how the resignation of key figures of an enterprise influenced its share value. That is mainly the result of a perceived capability of a person to run a corporation rather than a real capability, because the technical knowledge necessary to make the right decisions in every part of a large modern corporation is, in general, restricted. The public trust in a manager's capacity to govern a corporation successfully is therefore based more on a narrative story than on firm knowledge. As we know from historical research on entrepreneurs' biographies, such narrations are often built into the corporate cultures of large enterprises. Stories about the managers' lives in these corporations could actually be used to run the business, and therefore the enterprise itself sometimes takes part in the narrative construction to solve its particular governance problems (Plumpe 2003, 2005; Casson 1997; Raff and Temin 1991). The organizational theorist Alfred Kieser called the way in which General Electric's manager Jack Welch was narratively constructed a "hagiography" and described the structural compulsion in

6. These remarks on entrepreneurs' autobiographies are taken mostly from the detailed linguistic analysis of Sandra Markus (2002), who uses German examples, and Klaus Hansen (1992), who is concerned with autobiographies of American entrepreneurs such as Benjamin Franklin, Andrew Carnegie, Lee Iacocca, Donald Trump, and Thomas J. Watson.

the title of his article: "Control the construction of your legend, or everyone else will" (Hegele and Kieser 2001). In another example, the public construction of Ted Turner's life served as a tool to communicate his strategy of "corporate cross-dressing" (Guthey 2001). That is, the language of an entrepreneur's biography or autobiography differs from that of an academic because of its structural environment.

Most entrepreneurial autobiographies are written by businessmen involved in large manufacturing corporations. The problems of organization and strategic action, of personal leadership and competition, are much more prominent in these types of corporation than in the service industry, and most autobiographical self-construction refers primarily to these problems. Compared with such literature, autobiographical texts from the banking sector are less striking. Large parts of autobiographies from bankers are mostly concerned with family history, while organizing business plays a minor role. But in the case of Hahn things are different: neither his family nor his banking business appears much in his autobiographical texts. Although mostly concerned with his academic accomplishments, the semantic phrases and patterns in the self-descriptive texts of Hahn are much closer to what we would see in an entrepreneur's autobiography than in family histories or academic autobiographies. The rhetoric of the "two souls" is a typical metaphor used in entrepreneurs' biographies to describe their "ingeniousness," a trait that would be much harder to claim through rational argument.[7]

This semantic pattern was attached to Hahn's life not only by Hahn but also by most of the biographical texts on him. When he died in 1968, an obituary notice in the *Neue Züricher Zeitung* was sent to his academic friend Fritz Machlup. It contained this characteristic sentence: "He united the gift of an extraordinary scholar with the quality of an experienced banker in an ideal way."[8] This characterization was the dominant form used to sum up Hahn's biography as well as his economic thought from the mid-1950s. He himself used this discourse for the introduction of his autobiography: "Throughout my lifetime I never was what one would call a genuine practitioner and in a certain sense not a genuine theorist. I was, as a friend put it once, a theorizing practitioner or, as a less benevolent observer might, an odd in-between, and in Germany (as opposed to the

7. How the topic of the "two souls" works was broadly developed for a case study in Hesse 2002, which was based on linguistic theories taken from Parr 1992.

8. Obituary, probably from *Neue Züricher Zeitung*, 4 October 1968. Fritz Machlup Papers, box 42, folder 4, Hoover Institution Archives, Stanford, California. My translation.

Anglo-American countries) a rather rare, almost singular type. No wonder that all the genuine practitioners criticize me for being a theorist and all the genuine theorists said that my scientific-theoretical view of the world [*Weltbild*] was influenced too much by my practical experiences" (Hahn 1963, 1; my translation). The older he became, the more he repeated this discourse (Hahn 1964).

The discourse was not merely an instrument that Hahn used to historicize his own past: it showed up in other people's descriptions of him from the start. The very first review of his *Economic Theory of Bank Credit*, written by Ladislaus von Bortkiewicz, mentioned the fact that Hahn was an economist as well as a banker and decided the relationship between the two Hahns in favor of the latter. He would be a "practitioner with theoretical interests," Bortkiewicz (1921–22, 71; my translation) wrote, as if he would like to mitigate his own judgment. Similar descriptions can be found in Gottfried von Haberler's review (1930) and in Howard Ellis's (1934, 334). Even in nonpublic texts about Hahn, where discussion of his work was not necessary, his dual "capabilities" were mentioned. A confidential proposal of persons to be newly affiliated to the Mont Pèlerin Society claims: "Although Hahn lost almost all his fortune when he left Germany, he has operated so intelligently at the U.S. Stock Exchange that he has now a nice fortune of several millions of dollars. At the same time Hahn is a very good economist and a fervent opponent of Keynesianism."[9] Since many businessmen became members of the Mont Pèlerin Society, in this case the discourse did not mark Hahn as an outsider. Rather, the attribute of being a good economist as well as a businessman could lend his statements a special authority.

The entrepreneurial discourses attached to Hahn's life are especially striking when compared with the semantic and narrative patterns in academic autobiographies. For the history of economics this fact only appears important because these patterns violate the rules established by the discipline and therefore lead to "irritation" (to use Niklas Luhmann's term) in the discipline's memory. Since the irritation caused by flouting rules is an important impulse for scientific progress or change in economics, it is worthwhile to examine to which results the story of Hahn's life led. When academic discourses referred to Hahn's biography, the question of precursorship of Keynesianism and the relationship between theory and practice were particularly stressed.

9. "Proposal for New Members," 11 April 1950. Mont Pèlerin Society Papers, box 6, folder 7, Hoover Institution Archives, Stanford, California.

2. From Pre-Keynesianism to Anti-Keynesianism: Hahn's Intellectual Biography

Hahn's contributions to the theory of economics consist of a small book and a bundle of articles in economic journals and in newspapers. Hahn later bound the articles together and published them in a couple of anthologies, reproducing his own works several times (e.g., Hahn 1924, 1949a, 1960). *The Economic Theory of Bank Credit*, which was first published in 1920, was without doubt his most important work. In this book he demonstrated the banking system's ability to create money. Because of the reciprocal granting of credit by banks, the money supply could rise without increasing the amount of cash or central bank money. The commercial banks granted credits that could exceed the sums available to them from savings. Hahn described the process of money creation through commercial banks in detail and opposed the basic assumptions in German literature of this time.[10] However, he criticized Anglo-Saxon monetary theory as well. This fact is remarkable enough, since this type of economic theory was not well-known in Germany during the 1920s. Hahn did not reject Anglo-Saxon monetary theory but showed that the quantity theory of money, as the classics had formulated it, did not fit the economy of the 1920s. The quantity theory would have been valid for an economy based on the circulation of specie. But for the modern economy as it appeared after the First World War, where only a small percentage of the money supply consisted of cash, the quantity theory of money was no longer valid, nor was the "neo-quantity theory" as described by Irving Fisher, who included deposit money in the money supply. According to Hahn, Fisher still saw most of the money supply in the form of cash, claiming that the largest part of money supply consisted of money deposits created by the commercial banking system.

The controversial aspects of Hahn's *Economic Theory of Bank Credit* could be found in the book's second part, where he was concerned with the effects of credit expansion on production. Hahn (1920, 141) was convinced that the expansion of credit could stimulate production: "Credit produces goods out of nothing, in that, without it, they would not have been produced" (as translated in Ellis 1934, 328). Hence he abandoned the idea of the neutrality of money because of the fact that the monetary sys-

10. Georg Halm (1963, 384) draws our attention to Chester A. Phillips's *Bank Credit* from the same year on exactly the same topic. The book was a PhD thesis with Irving Fisher at Yale.

tem in modern economies had changed. To explain this connection he went back to an analogy used by Joseph Schumpeter in his *Theory of Economic Development* when he talked of "roundabout production," a term taken from Eugen von Böhm-Bawerk's theory of capital: the granting of credits strengthened capital-intensive production and led to goods remaining longer in the production process so that they would be available for consumption only later. At the same time the demand for labor would grow, and thus wages would increase. People who preferred not to work before the credit expansion would now decide to supply labor (Hahn 1920, 134–39). In short, Hahn claimed that credit expansion could increase employment by the expansion of production. As early as the 1920 edition of *The Economic Theory of Bank Credit*, we find the claim that the extension of state demand could trigger these effects through expanding credit (Hahn 1920, 151).

Hahn's book was intensively discussed in German monetary theory during the 1920s. Especially during the German hyperinflation in 1922–23 and after the stabilization of the German currency, Hahn's rather optimistic view of inflation was an object of agreement as well as considerable critique. Since most of the monetary literature in Germany was written from the perspective of state theory of money, Hahn's work was considered an original and new contribution (Laidler and Stadler 1998, 819–21). That was more the case as he challenged the quantity theory as well. In his well-known and oft-quoted review of Hahn's book, Haberler talked of a real "Hahn-literature" (see Ellis 1934). But during the years of monetary discussion, Hahn changed his attitude as well. As early as his article "Credit" for the influential *Handbook of Political Economy* (*Handwörterbuch der Staatswissenschaften*), he had restricted the range of his arguments insofar as he now viewed only a part of the credits as influential for economic growth, that part which was not produced out of the savings of an economy. Only this "inflationary credit"—as he called it—could lead to an extension of production and only to the extent to which the government would be willing to accept the lowering of the exchange rate of the national currency or until the newly produced goods could not be sold any longer (Hahn 1922). Since the second edition of his book (Hahn 1924) remained unrevised (which Hahn later attributed to his banking job), the new concept did not enter *The Economic Theory of Bank Credit* before the third edition of 1930. With this third edition Hahn completed a step-by-step move away from his rather bold theory of the early twenties. Although he adhered in principle to the possibility of a credit spending policy financed by inflation, he no longer regarded the consequent economic growth as durable because he believed low interest rates would not persist within the banking sector, as the central bank would increase interest rates to stabilize the currency. He now labeled himself a supporter of the monetary theory of business cycles as it could be found in Wilhelm Röpke's and Ludwig von Mises's writings at the same time (Hahn 1930, 141–51).

Even though Hahn never quoted Keynes's works in the several editions of *The Economic Theory of Bank Credit*, the similarities between that work and Keynes's *General Theory* are striking: the inequality of savings and investment, the rejection of the neutrality of money, and the conviction that money demand depends not just on the interest rate. Furthermore, he anticipated a central piece of Keynesian economics, the possibility of employment extension by credit expansion and the connection of the money market and production. But the differences are no less striking: Hahn had no all-embracing economic theory. The priority of demand over production in Hahn's work was applied only to the banking sector (the demand for credit that should be logically superior to saving). The same was true for his idea of a "liquidity preference," which Hahn (1949a, 217) applied only to the bank sector and not to the consumer. Hahn had no idea of a marginal propensity to consume or the multiplier effect, nor did he have the idea of a stable equilibrium with underemployment.[11] He had not developed a systematic macroeconomic theory; rather, he just summed up some selective considerations (see also Schneider 1952, 1953). Nevertheless, he took credit for anticipating the *General Theory* soon after it appeared in 1936 (Hahn 1936), and he did so much louder than all the other German "pre-Keynesians" (Garvy 1975).

Hahn's first reaction to Keynes's *General Theory* appeared as an extensive book review in the *Neue Züricher Zeitung*, the most influential Swiss daily newspaper, in November 1936. While he still held the opinion that during a depression the expansion of inflationary credit could indeed raise employment, he opposed Keynes's claim that money wages would lag behind the increase of consumer prices so that inflation could be an instrument to lower wages and return to durable full employment (Hahn 1936).

11. The argument of Halm (1963, 382) that Hahn meant only voluntary unemployment, which became part of the production process in the case of higher real wages (through credit expansion), whereas Keynes explicitly excluded this kind of unemployment, is not correct, since Hahn (1920) thought of all kinds of unemployment and used voluntary unemployment only as an example.

The "money illusion"—only later did he use Fisher's term—of the workers would persist for just a short period so that, in fact, it would be the Keynesian theorists who had been subjected to an "illusion." For his 1949 anthology he coined the phrase "economics of illusion" for Keynesian economics (Hahn 1949a, 173; 1949b; 1954, 217). After the Second World War he extended his criticism to the assumption of a general liquidity preference and the priority of demand (Hahn 1949b). His own position from the 1920s he now called a "sin of my youth" (Hahn 1949a, 6). His proposal to make money cheap during the boom and to compensate demand in the beginning of a depression he regretted most, he wrote in 1949 (225). In an introductory textbook, published in 1954, he restricted the range of his earlier assumption about the extension of production through inflationary credit a step further. It should now be considered relevant only for cases in which the wages could not fall below a certain level because of the influence of political regulation. Only then, Hahn (1954, 97) said, could inflationary credit expansion lead to an expansion of employment. Whereas Keynes attacked the classics for describing only situations of equilibrium, which are very rare in reality, Hahn was convinced that the Keynesians themselves made their analysis out of exceptional situations, which they tend to conserve with their policy recommendations (223).

If we sum up his intellectual biography, we could maintain that Hahn's pre-Keynesianism was not really Keynesianism, nor was his later anti-Keynesianism absolute. It was a step-by-step retreat that resulted directly from his discussion of Keynesianism. There are good reasons to include Hahn in the "German quantity-theorist" group of the 1920s, as Laidler and Stadler (1998) as well as Ellis (1934) did, for he tried to improve the quantity theory of money by describing the money supply more precisely. On the other hand, he never stepped back from his conviction that there is a relationship between money and production levels of the economy. Certainly, questions of precursorship and opposition are hard to decide, especially if a paradigm itself is as fluid as Keynesianism. But in the case of Hahn there is evidence that he himself largely took part in the story to construct his own work in the game of similar questions. For example, he tried to play down the difference between his and Keynes's work as a matter of "language" because he did not express his results mathematically. When he got a manuscript for the *American Economic Review* back from Machlup, the review editor, he commented on the latter's proposals for a revision as follows: "You are right that the Keynesian jargon has to be used. Where the whole world is speaking Keynesian Carl alone could not stay away. . . . It's a pity that I am not familiar with the mathematical instruments. It then would be easier to impress the Keynesian fortress, even though most of the equations say no more than if p is 'Pepsi' and c is 'Cola' than p + c has to be Pepsi-Cola."[12]

In his *Economics of Illusion*, Hahn (1949a, 226) asked the question directly that he "ha[d] never been able to understand, why Keynes did not quote my works in his *General Theory* although there is no doubt he knew it, for he quotes me in the German translation of his *Treatise on Money*." But Hahn certainly knew that Keynes's reference to Hahn's 1922 article appeared as a reference to Mises and seemed to be taken from the latter's book *Geldwertstabilisierung und Konjunkturpolitik* (Keynes 1932, 140). That is, it was Hahn himself who brought his own work into the discussion about the roots and the critics of Keynesianism. It was part of his self-construction and his self-marketing. And he even invented a "slogan" for this "campaign" with the sentence: "All that is wrong and exaggerated in Keynes I said much earlier and more clearly." The quote was first used by Henry Hazlitt in his introduction to the 1949 collection of Hahn's articles. Hazlitt claimed that he took the sentence out of Hahn's review of Keynes's work in 1936, although it cannot actually be found there. Hahn (1963, 6) himself later offered the same source.

It can be concluded that the question of Hahn's precursorship was strongly woven into the particular self-construction of his biography. He "promoted" his intellectual contributions with the professional perspective of an entrepreneur, and he focused on his own theory in terms of its "success" compared with "competing" paradigms. That should not lower the value of his economic reasoning by any means, but is only a possible, more complex answer to Machlup's question that opened this essay. Whereas for the discipline Hahn's originality would have been of interest, Hahn himself stressed his former similarity to Keynes and his analysis of the reasons why there had been a case of "market failure" in the development of economic theory.

3. Conclusion: A Vehicle for the Bias between Theory and Practice

As shown in the previous two sections, the self-construction of Hahn's life played a large part in his academic contributions. His books, as well as his

12. Letter from Hahn to Machlup, 1 June 1944. Machlup Papers, box 42, folder 4, Hoover Institution Archives, Stanford, California. My translation.

original and reflective articles, have always been related to his profession as a banker. Even in the semantics we see the relationship between his academic and his professional life. And even the question of to what extent he should be considered a pre-Keynesian was in some ways influenced by his "entrepreneurial" behavior in telling the story of his own life. But another level of the question has been excluded from my analysis up to this point: the question of why Hahn's life is apparently interesting for some special subfields of current economic thought. This question refers to the selection processes in the discipline's memory. Within these processes, Hahn's particular biography and the more or less accidental mixture of academic and entrepreneurial discourses apparently show advantages. Therefore a few more examples of the relationship between Hahn's academic and his professional life should be examined.

When Hahn gave a talk at the Institute for Foreign Commerce in Zurich in 1953, the head of this institute, Albert Hunold, who was at the same time the secretary-general of the Mont Pèlerin Society, wrote a short introduction. Not very surprisingly, Hunold started with the famous quotation from Goethe's *Faust I* that Hahn had "two souls in his breast." "When one asked an economist from Germany in the 1920s about Prof. Hahn," Hunold continues, "he would answer, 'Hahn is an ingenious banker but a poor economist.' If one asked a banker instead, then Hahn would be an 'ingenious economist but a poor banker.' That was the German judgment. That this is not the Swiss judgment, however, the speaker is able to recognize from the fact that we invited him for a second time in two years."[13] From this quotation it could be shown that the discourse of the two Hahns, that is, the "two souls in his breast," was much more than a literal translation of his interesting biography. It served as a vehicle to reflect the theory-practice bias in economics in general. Hunold differentiated a "Swiss judgment" from a "German judgment" in this example and implied that in Swiss economics it need not be a contradiction to be both a good economist and a good banker. One can see from Hunold's introduction that Hahn's biography not only recounted the story of his life but also served a particular function as a vehicle for the criticism of the scope of economics.

Another example is similar: a newspaper article from 1959 summing up some recommendations on international monetary policy given by Hahn in an article for *Kyklos* from the same year emphasized the value

13. Introductory note of A. Hunold, 1953. Mont Pèlerin Society Papers, Correspondence, box 33, folder 8, Hoover Institution Archives, Stanford, California.

of his recommendations. For the journalist the value results from Hahn's position as an outsider in economics: "Hahn was a loner from the very beginning, who stripped the currency questions from all the myths with his keen mind" (my translation).[14] Of course, such themes should not be overstressed—especially since it is very probable that they themselves are a product of Hahn's self-marketing. But they would not even have been worth mentioning if they were not part of Hahn's economics as well. They are relevant for my theme, because they bring a new aspect into the analysis of Hahn's role in the discussion of Keynesianism: the aspect of contesting a theory with practical experiences.

In a 1944 letter to Machlup, Hahn asked the question: "Of course it is doubtful if I, a common banker from the ordinary ranks of society, could win against the whole Keynesian fiddling regime, isn't it?"[15] In a first superficial reading, Hahn seemed to suggest the impossibility of intervening in economic discourse for "ordinary people" (although this attribute can only have been meant ironically in connection with Hahn). But from his own economic reasoning Hahn must have been convinced that an important chance to fight economic paradigms lay in the intervention of practitioners. This topic had already appeared in his *Economic Theory of Bank Credit*, in which Hahn did not judge the quantity theory wrong but only inconsistent with the current shape of the modern economy. That the interest rate would not be a price for the transfer of capital and therefore a price for the renunciation of consumption of the creditor but a price in the capital market, which results out of supply and demand for credits, would have been "well known to practitioners for a long period of time" (Hahn 1920, 116; my translation).

This was the same book in which he developed a general model for the connection between theory and practice. According to Hahn, scientific progress would be possible only with the help of external heretics, who would be able to compare theory and reality: "The more closed and logical a scientific theory is, the more disastrous it is, because it produces an incentive to keep this theory alive even if the real preconditions changed." Therefore one had to differentiate between further economic theories: "If they are correct, that means logically confirmable, and if they are true, that means matching with the real preconditions" (15; my translation). The

14. "Baue das Haus so, daß es für sich allein stehen kann." *Die Tat*, 30 August 1960, 27. Mont Pèlerin Society Papers, box 41, folder 11, Hoover Institution Archives, Stanford, California.

15. Letter from Hahn to Machlup, 1 June 1944. Fritz Machlup Papers, box 42, folder 4, Hoover Institution Archives, Stanford, California. My translation.

whole book, as he later wrote (Hahn 1963, 5), evolved from his experience in his family's bank, in which nobody could explain to him exactly what kinds of goods were traded in the credit division. The connection between theory and practice remained the subject of his analysis throughout all of his writings and was scarcely changed by Hahn's turn from pre-Keynesianism to anti-Keynesianism. In 1949 he compared, for example, the behavior of (Keynesian) economists with businessmen: "Economists make the same mistake as businessmen and stock exchange traders who during a boom see only the bullish argument and during a depression only the bearish argument" (Hahn 1949a, 7).

Hahn's preoccupation with theory and practice, as applied to the problem of economic forecasting in the 1950s, led Boudreaux and Selgin (1990) as well as Robert Leeson (1997) to consider him a precursor of "rational expectation theory" as it was developed in the late 1960s. In fact, as early as 1952 Hahn compared the capacity of economists to foresee the future with that of entrepreneurs. He wrote the key passage in terms that foreshadowed rational expectation theory: "There is not a single reason to assume that in the high game of forecasting the future needs, the theorists on average are more successful than the business people. On the contrary, one can assume that business people on average will be the better prophets, since they will be more responsible. The business people will suffer from losses if they are wrong, whereas the theorists predict without any risk—not even for their reputation. Hence the world cannot be divided into the theorists who have the monopoly to account future investment and consumption and business people, for whom the future remains uncertain and therefore speculative" (Hahn 1954, 260; my translation).[16] If we therefore would like to discover something rather modern and "protomonetarist" in these sentences, it becomes possible because Hahn made himself part of his own theory.

As demonstrated in the previous two sections, it is the large amount of self-marketing that differentiates Hahn's biography from the bulk of other life descriptions in the history of economics, a semantic pattern that marched into the description of Hahn's life alongside his entrepreneurial attitude. For the problem of life writing in economics, the case of Hahn is

16. The quotation is taken from the 1954 reprint of Hahn's article "Propheten des Unprophezeibaren," which appeared in 1952 in the *Zeitschrift für die gesamte Kreditwirtschaft* as well as under the title "Predicting the Unpredictable" in the same year in the *Freeman*. See also Boudreaux and Selgin 1990, 271–72, which quotes similarly from the *Freeman*, which apparently was not exactly the same as the German article.

therefore helpful not only to differentiate the self-construction of a biography from other sources of description but also to show how different sources of (auto)biographical writing can be distinguished with the knowledge of particular semantic patterns and metaphors. However, the fact that Hahn is still remembered by the discipline cannot be explained by his successful strategy of self-marketing alone. The particular construction of Hahn's life was introduced as an example of how each biography of an economist satisfies a special demand of the discipline. Hence this article makes a plea for the integration of that metalevel of analysis into the consideration of each economist's life.

In the case of Hahn, the discipline's demands seem to rest in the relationship between theory and practice. In the systems approach of Luhmann, the social systems "science" and "economy" are strictly separated from each other. Whereas the economy follows the basic code "payment/nonpayment," science has to follow the code "true/false." Both systems cannot communicate but only "irritate" one another, for they are "structurally connected" (Luhmann 1998, 95–118). Biographies serve as such "structural connections": they are able to bring the reality of business into economics, in the same way that data and legislation do—but nevertheless, according to the systems approach, these things always remain only a simulation of reality. In this context Hahn's biography was used to continuously reflect the relationship between theory and practice in economics. According to the systems approach, such continuous consideration is essential for the evolution of a social system (i.e., the discipline of economics in our case). Furthermore, from this perspective, biographies could serve as extraordinary explanations, fundamental for the efficiency of economics. Since from the basic code of science an economic paradigm always comes into existence because it is true and would disappear if it were false, economics needs a special explanation if a "true" paradigm is available but neglected for a considerable period of time. Biographies (in the above-mentioned broad sense) could explain this contradiction, as Hahn did with his own story. The biography of an outsider in economics might be an explanation of why a "true" theory comes late. The story of Hahn's life can be used to explain the detours of Keynesian arguments. Reference to biographies in this context is a way in which economics solves its basic paradox: to explain why the whole world works by economic laws, whereas within its own discipline "true" theories, rather than those that are merely economically successful, come into existence. Wherever economic paradigms change, there will be a strong demand for life writing in the history of economics. We do not remember Hahn's contributions to economic theory because he was successful in promoting the story of his own life and his theory. We remember him because his career is an example of the unavoidable structural deficit of a discipline that triggers a demand for biographical explanations for detours and occasions to discuss the relationships between theory and practice.

References

Backhouse, Roger E. 1985. *A History of Modern Economic Analysis*. Oxford: Blackwell.

Beaud, Michel, and Gilles Dostaler. 1995. *Economic Thought since Keynes: A History and Dictionary of Major Economists*. Translated by Valérie Cauchemez with Eric Litwack. Aldershot, U.K.: Elgar.

Blaug, Mark. 1985. *Great Economists since Keynes*. Brighton: Wheatsheaf Books.

———. 1989. *Great Economists before Keynes*. Brighton: Wheatsheaf Books.

Blaug, Mark, and H. Vane. 2003. *Who's Who in Economics*. 5th ed. Cheltenham, U.K.: Elgar.

Bortkiewicz, Ladislaus von. 1921–22. Das Wesen, die Grenzen, und die Wirkungen des Bankkredits. *Weltwirtschaftliches Archiv* 17:70–89.

Boudreaux, Donald J., and George A. Selgin. 1990. L. Albert Hahn: A Precursor of Keynesianism and the Monetarist Counterrevolution. *HOPE* 22.2:261–79.

Casson, Mark C., ed. 1997. *Information and Organization: A New Perspective on the Theory of the Firm*. Oxford: Clarendon Press.

Deutsche Effecten- und Wechsel-Bank vormals L. A. Hahn. 1947. *75 Jahre*. Frankfurt am Main.

Ellis, Howard S. 1934. *German Monetary Theory, 1905–1933*. Cambridge, Mass.: Harvard University Press.

Garvy, George. 1975. Keynes and the Economic Activists of Pre-Hitler Germany. *Journal of Political Economy* 83:391–405.

Guthey, Eric. 2001. Ted Turner's Corporate Cross-Dressing and the Shifting Images of American Business Leadership. *Enterprise & Society* 2:111–42.

Haberler, Gottfried von. 1930. Review of third edition of *Bankkredit*, by L. Albert Hahn. *Zeitschrift für Nationalökonomie* 1:771.

Hagemann, Harald, and Claus-D. Krohn. 1999. *Biographisches Handbuch der deutschsprachigen wirtschaftswissenschaftlichen Emigration nach 1933*. Munich: Saur.

Hahn, L. Albert. 1920. *Volkswirtschaftliche Theorie des Bankkredits*. Tübingen: Mohr.

———. 1922. Kredit. In vol. 3 of *Handwörterbuch der Staatswissenschaften*, edited by Ludwig Elster, Alfred Weber, and Friedrich Wieser. 4th rev. ed. Jena: G. Fischer.

———. 1924. *Geld und Kredit: Gesammelte Aufsätze*. Tübingen: Mohr.

———. 1930. Volkswirtschaftliche Theorie des Bankkredits. 3rd rev. ed. Tübingen: J. C. B. Mohr.

——. 1936. Die neue Konjunkturtheorie von Keynes. *Neue Züricher Zeitung*, 19 and 20 November.

——. 1945. Compensating Reactions to Compensatory Spending. *American Economic Review* 35.1:28–39.

——. 1949a. *Economics of Illusion: A Critical Analysis of Contemporary Economic Theory and Policy*. New York: New York Institute of Finance.

——. 1949b. Die Grundirrtümer in Lord Keynes' General Theory of Employment, Interest and Money. *Ordo, Jahrbuch für die Ordnung von Wirtschaft und Gesellschaft* 2:170–92.

——. 1954. *Wirtschaftswissenschaft des gesunden Menschenverstandes*. Frankfurt am Main: Knapp.

——. 1960. *Geld und Kredit: Währungspolitische und konjunkturtheoretische Betrachtungen*. Frankfurt am Main: Knapp.

——. 1963. *Fünfzig Jahre zwischen Inflation und Deflation*. Tübingen: J. C. B. Mohr.

——. 1964. *Rückblick und Ausblick: Vortrag, gehalten anläßlich seines 75. Geburtstages am 12. Oktober 1964 in Frankfurt am Main*. Tübingen: Mohr.

——. 1990. *Teoria economica del credito, a cura di Lapo Berti*. Naples: Edizioni Scientifiche Italiane.

Halm, Georg. 1963. L. Albert Hahn und John Maynard Keynes. *Zeitschrift für Nationalökonomie* 23:381–88.

Hansen, Klaus P. 1992. *Die Mentalität des Erwerbs: Erfolgsphilosophien amerikanischer Unternehmer*. Frankfurt am Main: Campus.

Hazlitt, Henry. 1949. Introduction to *The Economics of Illusion*, by L. Albert Hahn. New York: New York Institute of Finance.

Hegele, Cornelia, and Alfred Kieser. 2001. Control the Construction of Your Legend or Someone Else Will: An Analysis of Texts on Jack Welch. *Journal of Management Inquiry* 10.4:298–309.

Hesse, Helge. 2003. *Ökonomen-Lexikon: Unternehmer, Politiker, und Denker der Wirtschaftsgeschichte in 600 Porträts*. Darmstadt: Wissenschaftliche Buchgesellschaft.

Hesse, Jan-Otmar. 2002. Der "Postbismarck" und seine "Stephansjünger": Heinrich von Stephan in der Unternehmenskultur der Reichspost- und Telegraphenverwaltung 1876–1897. In *Kulturalismus, Neue Institutionenökonomik oder Theorievielfalt: Eine Zwischenbilanz der Unternehmensgeschichte*, edited by Jan-Otmar Hesse, Christian Kleinschmidt, and Karl Lauschke. Essen: Klartext-Verlag.

Keynes, John M. 1932. *Vom Gelde* (*A Treatise on Money*). Translated by Carl Krämer and Louise Crämer. Munich: Duncker & Humblot.

Laidler, David, and George Stadler. 1998. Monetary Explanations of the Weimar Republic's Hyperinflation: Some Neglected Contributions in Contemporary German Literature. *Journal of Money, Credit, and Banking* 30:816–31.

Leeson, Robert. 1997. Influence (or the Lack of It) in the Economics Profession: The Case of Lucien Albert Hahn. *HOPE* 29.4:635–38.

Luhmann, Niklas. 1998. *Die Gesellschaft der Gesellschaft*. 2 vols. Frankfurt am Main: Suhrkamp.

Machlup, Fritz. 1959. Why Not Hahnism? In *Eine Freundesgabe für Albert Hahn zum 12. Oktober 1959*, edited by Volkmar Muthesius. Frankfurt am Main: Knapp.
Markus, Sandra. 2002. *Bilanzieren und Sinn stiften: Erinnerungen von Unternehmern im 20. Jahrhundert*. Stuttgart: Franz Steiner Verlag.
Morgenstern, Oskar. 1947. Oskar Morgenstern Papers and Diaries, box 14, fol. 4, 30 June. Special Collections Library, Duke University, Durham, N.C.
Muthesius, Volkmar, ed. 1959. *Eine Freundesgabe für Albert Hahn zum 12. Oktober 1959*. Frankfurt am Main: Knapp.
Niehans, Jürg. 1990. *A History of Economic Theory: Classical Contributions, 1720–1980*. Baltimore, Md.: Johns Hopkins University Press.
Parr, Rolf. 1992. *"Zwei Seelen wohnen, ach! in meiner Brust": Strukturen und Funktionen der Mythisierung Bismarcks (1860–1918)*. Munich: Fink.
Plumpe, Werner. 2003. Die Unwahrscheinlichkeit des Jubiläums—oder: warum Unternehmen nur historisch erklärt werden können. *Jahrbuch für Wirtschaftsgeschichte* 1:143–56.
——. 2005. Das Ende des deutschen Kapitalismus. *Westend: Neue Zeitschrift für Sozialforschung* 2.1:3–25.
Raff, Daniel M. G., and Peter Temin. 1991. Business History and Recent Economic Theory: Imperfect Information, Incentives, and the Internal Organization of Firms. In *Inside the Business Enterprise: Historical Perspectives on the Use of Information*, edited by Peter Temin. Chicago: University of Chicago Press.
Samuels, Warren J. 2003. *European Economists of the Early Twentieth Century: Studies of Neglected Continental Thinkers of Germany and Italy*. Cheltenham, U.K.: Elgar.
Schneider, Erich. 1952. Hahn contra Keynes. *Schweizerische Zeitschrift für Volkswirtschaft und Statistik* 88:395–404.
——. 1953. Der Streit um Keynes: Dichtung und Wahrheit in der neueren Keynes-Diskussion. *Jahrbücher für Nationalökonomie und Statistik* 165:89–122.

"Between Worlds," or an Imagined Reminiscence by Oskar Morgenstern about Equilibrium and Mathematics in the 1920s

Robert Leonard

"*I was born in 1902 in Görlitz, a small provincial town in Germany, and raised in Vienna, the great city of the multinational Austro-Hungarian empire. On my father's side, my family goes back to about 1530 in Saxony, my Lutheran forebears having been farmers, church wardens, judges, and businessmen. My mother was a natural daughter of Frederick III of Germany . . .*"

Yet another account of myself, for yet another encyclopedia. Italian, this time. Once again, I put pen to paper and collapse the events of fifty years ago to a few familiar milestones. Now what shall I tell these Italians?

"*I finished the Gymnasium and took my Dr. Rer. Pol. at the University of Vienna in 1925. Awarded a Rockefeller Memorial Fellowship, I spent the next three years in England, the United States, France, and Italy. Returning to Vienna, I soon became Docent, later Professor, at the University, and Director of the Austrian Institute for Business Cycle Research . . .*"

And then there will be the doctoral thesis, *Wirtschaftsprognose*, the other institute, Princeton, and so on. It is remarkable really, the rehearsed inevitability of it all. . . . So often have I gone through exercises of this kind that there are times when I even begin to believe them myself.

This article was originally published in the September 2004 issue of the *Journal of the History of Economic Thought*. It has been republished here with the kind permission of the History of Economics Society and has been edited for house style.

History of Political Economy 39 (annual suppl.) DOI 10.1215/00182702-2006-047

"I never accepted the standard economic theory, mathematical or not, seeing the difficulties of accounting for foresight and anticipation, for the effect of predictions on the course of events, as already examined in my first book, Wirtschaftsprognose *(1928). These concerns brought me together, in 1938, with John von"*

Then, that other voice returns again, reminding me of the complexity of matters—a voice rooted no doubt in Dilthey, Rickert, and other early readings. Make room for ambiguity, it urges. For once, acknowledge the richness of things.

1. The Crucible

Of the years leading up to entry at the University of Vienna, my recollections remain fragmented. My father had originally come to Austria from Görlitz, in Silesia, having lost the family fortune on poor business ventures. In Vienna, he worked for Julius Meinl and Co., the coffee and tea importer, and we were modestly comfortable.

My fellow gymnasium students, too, came from the families of small businessmen and minor professionals, all of whom had suffered the hardship of the postwar years. We had seen, firsthand, the effects of famine and desolation. Academically, I was strong in German, less so in Latin and mathematics. It was around this time that I became aware that some of the blood flowing in my veins was that of Frederick III of Saxony, something I have always been happy to make known. Like many of my fellow eighteen-year-olds then, I entertained strong German nationalist feelings, writing strident polemics that I now find it amusing to reread: "What would Europe be, what would the world be without the German people and its achievements! Germany can be satisfied with itself, there is no need to borrow from foreign peoples, who force it to further intellectual enslavement, but from its simply inexhaustible resources it is able to give to all those who want to receive. And yet, Germany does borrow: theater and poetry are signs of a depressed mind. This has to be fought. All the foreign dirt that will wipe out healthy ideas, has to be removed with violence." This narrowness notwithstanding, I soon developed a taste for things foreign. As tuberculosis in the postwar years ravaged the young of Vienna, those families who could afford it shipped their children off to breathe better air in the country and abroad. Thus I spent the summers of 1921 and 1922 in the company of relatives in Sweden, where I gained a passing knowledge of the language. I entered the University of Vienna in

the autumn of 1922, at twenty years of age, to pursue a *Dr. Rer. Pol.* Though nominally a degree in political science, it allowed one to pursue political economy.

As a beginning student in Vienna of the 1920s, I was most struck not by anything learned in the lecture halls but by those matters of social order and civil society—the "crowds and power" that would soon haunt the imaginations of Canetti, Broch, and others. Anti-Semitism in Vienna was not new, going back to the Middle Ages, but it took on new forms with the end of the war.

The undoing of the Austro-Hungarian empire had seen an inflow of Jewish population from the eastern provinces, the return of veterans to higher education, and the onset of acute economic hardship. I remember the over-

crowding at the university and the anxiety about the future beyond it. An anti-Semitic wave found support among students of both German and Austrian nationalist inclination. When I arrived there in 1922, the student fraternity organizations such as the *Deutsche Burschenbund* and the *Deutsche Studentenschaft* were popular, both having been founded after the war with the express aim of diminishing the "racially alien" presence. I even recall one day, several months after entering the university, sympathetically watching a group gathered in the front square, shouting in support of a *Numerus clausus*, or restriction on the Jewish presence at the university. They also had the support of a great many professors and teachers, many of whom were openly German nationalist, and the tacit approval of sections of the university authorities who provided them with facilities. With the dissipation of the empire, Vienna had shrunk in stature. The sense of loss, the hardship, and the sight of the numerous orthodox Polish, Romanian, and Hungarian Jews who had flooded the city after the war: these were the things to which I would point were I to explain our attitudes then. Hayek would later put it aptly when he said that Vienna of the 1920s and 1930s was unintelligible without the Jewish problem, that it was not simply a problem of Christians and Jews but the mixed group in between, or baptized Jews and Jew-friendly Christians. Indeed, he himself was then too close to the Jews for my liking. The issue thoroughly pervaded social life, and relations among my teachers were not spared.

2. The Prima Donnas

As was traditionally the case in the German-speaking universities, political economy at the University of Vienna was taught under the auspices of the law faculty, a fact that colored our training. While we were exposed to a good deal of idealistic philosophy, political and economic history, and economic theory, we received no instruction in mathematics or the sciences, and some time would pass before I came into contact with these fields. During my time, the three professorships in economics in the Faculty of Law were held by Count Ferdinand Degenfeld-Schönburg, Othmar Spann, and Hans Mayer. When I arrived, Degenfeld-Schönburg had been there for a short while, having replaced the Marxist economic historian Carl Grünberg, who had gone to Germany in the early 1920s to head the Institute for Social Research, or Frankfurt school, as it later became known. Spann had been there longer, having replaced Böhm-Bawerk, who had died in 1914. Mayer was a recent arrival, having succeeded in 1922 to the chair vacated by his protector, von Wieser, who was still at the university. While I would not join in the claim later made of Degenfeld-Schönburg that he had not "the slightest notion of the problems of economics," I cannot say that I gained much from him. Of the university professors, the most important to me were Spann and Mayer. The other figure in Viennese economics to whom I owe a debt of influence—Degenfeld-Schönburg's critic, in fact—was Ludwig von Mises. Although without a university chair, he was an engaging figure, as important to our intellectual lives as any of the others. Spann, Mayer, and von Mises, in time, dubbed the "Prima Donnas" by my friends in the Rockefeller Foundation, formed a tense triangle.

The Prophet

Like so many others, I was first greatly taken by Spann, the social philosopher. Although he had studied under Carl Menger a generation previously, by the time I encountered him, his teachings bore absolutely no resemblance to what I would later recognize as Austrian economics. After several years in Frankfurt, he received his *Habilitation* in 1908 and spent the following decade as professor of political economy at Brünn (Brno). Having been wounded, and decorated, in the war, he returned to Vienna. I should mention that when Spann was appointed to a chair on the death of Böhm-Bawerk, the person "passed over" was none other than Joseph Schumpeter, who was put aside because of his involvements as finance minister in the first coalition government of the Austrian Republic. In that position, for several months in 1919, amid growing postwar inflation, Schumpeter had refused to compensate holders of government bonds, something that left him with a tarnished reputation in Vienna. By the time I was a student, he had already left Austria and was well established at Harvard.

The main influence on Spann was the German Romantic Adam Müller, author of the 1809 magnum opus *Die Elemente der Staatskunst*. This neofeudal tome portrayed as society's natural form the corporatist state, or *Ständestaat*, a hierarchical arrangement in which harmony would stem from individuals' adopting the role for which they were destined by nature. These ideas had been well received by the Hapsburg court, and a certain tradition had been maintained by various Austrian Catholic writers, such as von Vogelsang, who continued to target democracy and individualism. For example, von Vogelsang had responded to the Viennese stock market crash of 1873 with a sustained critique of the capitalist competitive ethic, arguing for the role of the state as a countervailing force against the anonymous forces of the market and proposing that the territorial system of representation be replaced by an occupational one in which parliamentary deputies would represent particular trades or professions. Then there was Karl Lueger, the dominant force in Austrian conservative Catholic, anti-Semitic politics at the turn of the century. Spann, who was active in the *Verein fur Sozialpolitik*, was also influenced by the Tübingen sociologist and well-known corporatist opponent of Marxism, Albert Schäffle.

By the mid-1920s, Spann had given up all pretense of being an objective scholar and had enrolled students and others in spreading the neo-Romanticist utopian doctrine. Abandoning liberal rationalist ideas, and

with that any trace of Mengerian economics, he moved over to that long-standing Romantic and idealistic tradition. This resistance to rationalist thought had taken on renewed importance after the war, when democracy and mass society were interpreted as synonymous, not with coordinated social interaction but with degeneration and drift. In the chaos and uncertainty of postwar Austria, which had seen the poor scour the woods of Vienna, and furniture chopped up for fuel, it was easy to be swept along on this irrational tide.

Spann's lectures, which had us spellbound, were a war against individualism, atomism, psychologism, Marxism, and all the "other dead sciences," as he called them. There were two ways of understanding social behavior, he said: the genetic, or causal, interpretation, which was methodologically individualistic, and the functional one, which considered the individual as subordinate to the social group. Spann rejected individualist accounts, which he said were premised on a mistaken belief in individual freedom, a refusal to recognize the centrality of society, and the *Geist*. Only functional explanations, he said, could portray social phenomena as parts of a larger totality. This individualist-universalist distinction had already been explored by Karl Pribram, a prominent social thinker at the university, but Spann made it pertinent in a way that was like no other. The effect of Pribram, the Jewish pessimist, was very different from that of this charismatic preacher.

Spann championed "Universalism," an organic view with roots in German Romanticism. Only when the telos governing the evolution of society was known, he said, could the behavior of the individual be understood. The social whole was the final cause that gave purpose to its subtotalities. Although Spann was clearer about what he was against than what he was for, I do remember his strange emphasis on certain elementary social pairings, which he regarded as fundamental to social life, such as man and woman, youth and age, Man and God. In any of these relations, he said, neither part played a role without the other, and the whole was greater than the sum of the parts.

Not only did methodologically individualistic social science ignore the fact that individuals functioned in society, said Spann, but the effect of our *adopting* such theories was to further reinforce contemporary feelings of malaise and dislocation. Decrying individualism as the enemy of the German nation, and Marxism as a distortion of idealist thought, he immersed us in the philosophy of Fichte, Hegel, and Schelling. His later writings celebrated the mysticism of Novalis and Augustine. "Looking at my papers, work and reading," I wrote in my diary, "one would think I were a student of philosophy and not of economics. But that is no disgrace. . . . my philosophical knowledge is very fragmentary in comparison to my knowledge of economics." Almost twenty years later, when I had fallen in with von Neumann, I would regard time spent on philosophy as time wasted. I remember struggling with Fichte back then and convincing myself, or almost, that I understood Spann's proclamations about God willing Himself and the world willing God, and that this was the mystical core of all history and all social pairing. It was quite unknown to me then that the century's most significant philosophical assault on language of this kind was being quietly prepared just a short distance away in the same university. There, at meetings at the physics building on Boltzmanngasse, in the name of clarity and democracy, Hans Hahn, Rudolf Carnap, Moritz Schlick, and others of the *Schlick Kreis*, or *Wiener Kreis* as it would later be known, were attempting to purge philosophy of all such metaphysics. Within a few years, their writings would become important to me, but, for the moment, for my fellow students and me, there was nothing "meaningless" about Spann.

Unlike most professors in Vienna, who rarely deigned to leave their pedestals, Spann showed genuine interest in his students. We often discussed my studies as we walked through the university, and I even recall him broaching the possibility that I should eventually become *Privatdozent*—and this during my first year at university! Politically astute, he saw his disciples, the "Spannianer," occupy influential positions in government, industry, and the youth movements. His views were used by rightist forces in Germany and Austria, and his network of influence embraced the Pan-Germans, Christian Socials, and the Nazi front-organization, the *Kampfbund für deutsche Kultur.* Although he did not join the Nazi movement, I do remember Spann, in November 1923, praising Hitler's recently attempted putsch. In 1929, on the centenary of his hero Müller's death, respects were paid by both the Nazi students and the Catholic newspaper, the *Reichspost.*

Nonetheless, although it did not end abruptly, my interlude with Spann was short-lived. It was around early 1923, I remember, at the same time as I was reading and criticizing Marx for Spann's Sunday morning seminar, that I encountered Böhm-Bawerk's work. I also became aware of the towering presence of Carl Menger, who had died only in 1921, but whose passing had added to the aura surrounding him. For reasons that were themselves not without a hint of intrigue, Menger had retired much earlier from university life and, although increasingly plagued by difficulties with hearing and eyesight, had continued to work away quietly at home. I began reading his *Grundsätze* and that year also got hold of the revised edition, the one with the detailed introduction by his son Karl, a student in mathematics at the university, whom I didn't know then but who had been pointed out to me. Later that year, I took a class in sociology, broadly, with one of Menger's disciples, von Wieser. Resolutely opposed to Spann, he repeatedly emphasized the methodological individualism of Austrian theory and dismissed as dangerous metaphysics all approaches that smacked of German idealism. As is usual for such changes, my intellectual transition at this time was not a straightforward one. Although my admiration for von Wieser was to grow rapidly, I recall smarting initially at his criticisms of Spann and being somewhat suspicious of him: "Might he be Jew, or half Jew, or liberal?" I asked in my journal. However, by degrees, I became aware of the existence of a different perspective on economics, a tradition based at the university itself, stretching back some fifty years, and the organic view gradually lost its hold on me. Critical in this process, and stepping in to fill the void created by my break with Spann and his circle, was that man's enemy, and von Wieser's chosen successor, Hans Mayer.

The Critic

In the history of the interwar Austrian economics community, Mayer is a neglected and maligned figure. Although I seldom later acknowledged it in public, this difficult, and ultimately disgraced, man played a critical role in shaping my theoretical interests. A native of Vienna, born in 1879, he lectured at Freiburg in Switzerland and was then decorated in the war. He went on to teach at Prague and Graz, before returning to Vienna, where Wieser stepped aside for him in 1923. Like Spann, toward whom he bore great antipathy, Mayer assembled a group around him and ran a seminar, both of which involved his assistants Paul Rosenstein-Rodan, Alexander Gerschenkron, and me. He was the first editor of the *Zeitschrift für Nationalökonomie* and was made president of the *Nationalökonomische Gesellschaft*, or National Economic Society, when it was resurrected in 1928.

A theorist in the tradition of Menger and von Wieser, Mayer devoted much time to the imputation problem (*Zurechnung*), that of identifying the proportions of the value of the final product attributable to the factors of production used in its creation. In his analysis of the distinction between economic and technical rationality, he was also a source of inspiration to an occasional visitor to Vienna, Lionel Robbins, in his famous *Essay*. However, in Mayer's seminar with us in the mid-1920s, it was the nature and significance of the "time factor" in equilibrium theory that was most important. It was an intellectually gripping issue, going to the core of what economics was all about, raising questions concerning the psychological bases of marginalist analysis and the use of mathematical formalisms. If Spann had spoken to my youthful romanticism, it was Mayer who cultivated the critic in me. His writings were stimulating and, as I thumb back through these yellowing pages, I am reminded of just how much I owe him.

As early as 1911, in a review of Schumpeter's *Das Wesen und der Hauptinhalt der theoretischen Nationalökonomie*, Mayer had criticized the use of the differential calculus in economics. While useful in the measurement

of time and space, he said, infinitesimal change was inapplicable in the consideration of economic quantities. What sense did it make to speak of the satisfaction yielded by an infinitesimal portion of, say, a shoe? In the realm of economics, said Mayer, the adoption of mathematical methods that had proven themselves in the natural sciences marked a surrender to pure "form." This view became a constant in his work.

With a fine-tooth comb, he took us critically through the early work of Cournot, the Walrasian theory of general equilibrium, the marginalist value theory of Jevons, and other such writings. Mayer said the problem with mathematical equilibrium theories—the "disguised fiction" that lay at their heart—was that they bound together, in simultaneous equations, magnitudes that were not simultaneous but emerged in genetic-causal sequence in time. Subjective action in time, he said, could not be reduced to a static, mathematical description. By treating in synchronic fashion, as a state of rest, something that was fundamentally generative, you eliminated precisely that which was essential to economic action and life.

It is curious how terms are malleable, their rhetorical power contextual. The labels used by Spann, "genetic-causal" and "functional," were now being appropriated by Mayer, but interpreted differently. The functional theory promoted by Spann was one that underlined the primacy of society, the operating whole of which the individual was but a subordinate element. On the other hand, when Mayer spoke against functional theories, he had in mind not the holistic theories of Spann but the mathematical economics of Jevons and Walras, which he found to neglect the Mengerian concerns of time, emergence, "genesis." And to complete the circle, Spann had rejected Austrian theory so as to better address genesis, not in the sense intended by Menger and Mayer but in that of a social teleology.

Mayer brought together his thinking of this period in a rather hefty epistemological critique of equilibrium price theory, which appeared sometime in the early 1930s. Its thrust I remember clearly. The formal systems of Jevons, Walras, Cournot, and others were of limited application to economic processes, because their underlying ideal-typical assumptions deviated from the normal preconditions of reality. Although Jevons appeared to have set out with a causal-genetic type of inquiry in mind, hoping to explain the process of price formation, he had succumbed to representation using a mechanical concept of equilibrium and, in particular, the law of equal marginal utility. With that, said Mayer, Jevons had fallen short of a dynamic, causal theory.

Everything up to the law of the equalization of marginal utility coincided with what the Austrians sought in a causal theory. But the Austrians did not put forward the law of equimarginal utility; they expressly rejected it. This law, said Mayer, mistakenly assumed that the individual's utility functions for each good were not only continuous but already in existence at the *outset* of the choice problem, so that a change in income could be distributed among all possible wants. On the contrary, experience tended to show that changes in income gave rise to the disappearance of certain kinds of consumption and the appearance of new ones. New wants emerged in time, depending on the degree to which existing wants had been satisfied. It was invalid to assume that all wants were present at the beginning of the "problem," to which equilibrium was the "solution." The law of equal marginal utility is impossible, said Mayer, "in the real world of the psyche." And if this was the law on which the theory of general equilibrium depended, then the whole theoretical system of equilibrium prices was without foundation. As a music lover, I remember him saying that to assume general equilibrium was akin to listening to all the notes of a melody played together at once, rather than hear them unfold in time.

He took us through Jevons's equations of exchange, in which the marginal utility of the last of the infinitely small partial quantities of commodities exchanged was in inverse proportion to that of the magnitudes of the increments exchanged. Mayer said that Jevons's assumption that the price ratio was *constant* during the exchange process leading to equilibrium was invalid. The English economist realized fully that the assumed succession of minor exchanges by which equilibrium was reached, coming one after the other, would alter the determinants of utility and thus the exchange relations. However, he deliberately elided this problem of dynamics by resorting to the static law of indifference, according to which any two units of the same good coming onto the market at the same time must fetch the same price. One could not assume, Mayer said, that in the case where two individuals formed the entire market, the marginal exchange ratio would be the same as the previous partial exchange ratios. Instead of inquiring into the process by which price ratios emerged genetically from the sequence of exchanges, Jevons had resorted to a static picture in which were given not only the utility scales but indeed that which it was the theory's task to explain, the price ratio. He had jumped to the conclusion, Mayer said, to the representation of an already attained equilibrium, forsaking time and emergence. The exchange totals in the final price ratio could be known only after the successive, partial exchanges were made, just as, at the beginning of a game of chess, the result was neither known to the players nor objectively settled.

Although it was not a game for which I ever had any particular affinity, chess was enormously popular in Vienna and Budapest at this time. Many of the cafés had their own chess clubs, and night after night familiar faces could be seen gathered around the tables. The chessmasters were heroes to many, with the *Neue Wiener Schachzeitung* enjoying great circulation and posters appearing often to advertise big tournaments. Yet the game also carried with it a suggestion of opprobrium. Many of the best players were strange, and this obsessive playing in smoke-filled cafés somehow lacked bourgeois respectability. Nabokov's *Luzhin* captured all that so well. And, then, so many of them were Jewish. . . . Nonetheless, when Mayer said that collapsing the process of price determination to a predetermined equilibrium was akin to collapsing the game of chess without actually passing through the moves of a game, it was a resonant analogy. You could no more evacuate time from price determination than you could predict the result of a game of chess. Time was essential to the resolution of both.

At Mayer's hands, Walras suffered a similar fate. If I have always taken a certain pride in being able to reproduce, *ex tempo*, the equations from the eleventh lesson of his 1874 *Elements of Pure Political Economy*, it should be said that my mastery dates not from those early days but from several years later when I studied Walras in the company of a research assistant and mathematics tutor, Abraham Wald, whose interest in the equations was quite different. Nonetheless, Mayer did take us through the Walrasian system: those three sets of simultaneous equations for an exchange economy of *m* goods, the roots of which were the prices and quantities whose equilibrium values cleared all markets. As with Jevons, albeit on a grander scale, said Mayer, this closed, simultaneous system excluded time and causality. It took as simultaneously given the structural elements that determined and maintained equilibrium. It was a theory of stasis, a failure as a genetic-causal account of price formation. In short, whether in Jevons or Walras, or even in Marshall with his image of balls coming to rest in the bottom of the bowl, Mayer taught us that the mechanical metaphor of equilibrium was inadequate to dealing with subjectivity and time, both of which were fundamental to the Austrian heritage.

Coming to all of this from the speculative heights of Spann's dreamworld, it took me a while to adjust to the fine—impossibly fine, some would say conceptual distinctions being drawn by Mayer. Within a short period, I had moved from a vast critique of the social order and contemporary alienation to the minute examination of mathematical systems that purported to say something about choice and value. For a young mind, the descent was a jarring one. Yet, if the former clearly spoke to the material and social difficulties of Vienna of the twenties, so too did the latter—in a way that is more difficult to explain but was nonetheless real—speak to the psychological uncertainty of the time. As I look back on it now, there was something culturally appropriate to this strange realm into which Mayer led us, this floating world where individual desire confronted algebra, so to speak, without the reassuring linchpin of equilibrium. Although his critical analysis scarcely provided a foundation for constructive work, it did suggest the inevitability of having to choose in economics between mathematical tractability and a reasonable degree of psychological complexity. Even after I finally broke with Mayer, these issues would remain central to my work.

Though less hesitant than Mayer in his speculations, my third mentor dealt with similar matters. I cannot recall exactly when I became involved in the *Mises Kreis*; it was probably in 1924–25, the last year of my studies, for most students drew closer to Ludwig von Mises when they were fairly well advanced. I was likely introduced by Haberler, he being a year ahead of me. As with Mayer, my recollections of Mises have been colored by the turns subsequently taken in our relationship. Yet, with some effort, I can try to speak of him fairly.

The Ideologue

Mises occupied a curious position in Viennese economics. He had studied at the University of Vienna in the first decade of the century, completing several historical studies under Carl Grünberg. Following stints at various independent academies and institutes, he was appointed *Privatdozent* at the university in 1913.

Several years later, he became professor *Extraordinarius*, or associate, but did not go any further in academia. If Schumpeter had been the person passed over in favor of Spann, then Mises was the "unlucky one" in 1923 when von Wieser moved aside for Mayer. Why Mises had failed to be appointed was, even in Vienna of the 1920s, the subject of some speculation, but Hayek was probably right when he suggested that it was because Mises was Jewish and, politically, an outspoken liberal. A Jew required the support of the Jewish faculty, most of whom were social democratic, Left-leaning progressives: a liberal Jew had nobody to turn to. To this may be added a certain brusqueness of manner in Mises that didn't help him. All in all, he never had the academic career he sought and for which he was in many respects so superbly suited. It was a source of bitter disappointment. He was resentful of Mayer's success, and their mutual acrimony pervaded our lives as students. Much later, after the *Anschluss*, when Mayer collaborated in the expulsion of Jewish members of the Economic Society, it was Mises's scathing account of him that colored the view of Mayer held abroad, both then and thereafter.

Mises had made his early reputation as a monetary expert, writing several essays on Austro-Hungarian monetary policy and emerging as an independent thinker, unafraid to oppose powerful interests. In his 1912 book *The Theory of Money and Credit*, he broke with the implicit Austrian view that money was neutral, standing apart from *real* economic activity, the exchange of goods and services. Mises wanted to cover ground that Menger and Böhm-Bawerk had neglected, and he placed new limitations, beyond anything occurring in Menger's *Grundsätze*, on what could be said about "value." There were acts of valuation of individual objects, Mises claimed, but it was not possible to calculate or measure value, and any imputation of the value of a total supply from that of a part, or vice

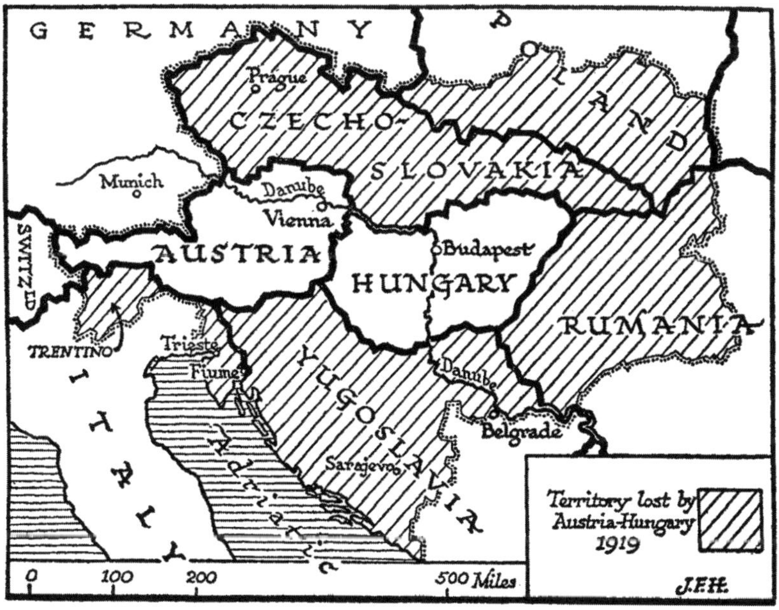

versa, was illegitimate. This sharply disaggregative view left no place for the equations of exchange of Irving Fisher or Gustav Cassel, for it made no sense to speak of a constant relationship between the quantity of money and *the* price level. To consider the effects of changes in the quantity of money, one had to do a step-by-step analysis, explicitly allowing for time and the effects, with varying lags, on different economic quantities.

As an official at the Vienna Chamber of Commerce, Mises was involved only part-time with the university, yet his occasional class or seminar was consistently popular. In the early 1920s, he had also begun conducting an evening *Privaatseminar* at his Chamber office, twice a month, parallel to the Mayer group, with which the clientele overlapped. It was above all here, among Haberler, Hayek, Felix Kaufmann, Fritz Machlup, Rosenstein-Rodan, Karl Schlesinger, Alfred Schütz, and others, that I learned how to discuss and debate.

In terms of the Austrian economic lineage, just as Mayer had looked to von Wieser, so Mises was closer to Böhm-Bawerk. The latter had been finance minister throughout Mises's involvement in the prewar monetary debates and had acted as confidante. In the first decade of the century, when Böhm-Bawerk took a special chair on retirement from the ministry,

Mises was a brilliant participant in his seminar. By the time I was a student, this seminar had achieved legendary proportions as the site of intense political debate, with Böhm-Bawerk and Mises aligned against Bauer and Neurath, the socialists who ran Vienna until 1934. Just after the war, with socialism gaining ground in Hungary, Germany, and Austria, and the climate of popular opinion tending toward planning, the arguments of Engels, Kautsky, Neurath, and others dominated discussion. Mises had responded with a famous 1920 paper, "Economic Calculation in the Socialist Commonwealth," launching a vigorous attack against the argument for state ownership of the means of production. This he followed with a 1922 book, *Socialism*. At one point or another, all students in Vienna read these works.

As I reread his 1920 paper, I am struck by the power and simplicity of Mises's arguments against planning. Exchange, he said, was central to value-determination, and it relied on both private ownership of the goods to be traded and the freedom to enter exchanges. The socialization of the means of production, by removing them from the nexus of exchange, would sever the causal link running from valuation of consumption goods to valuation of factors, or goods of higher order. The value of the latter would have to be ascribed by fiat, by the arbitrary design of a committee. With money prices denied their role as signals of social value, the process of production through time, the perpetual allocation and reallocation of scarce factors to different uses, would become mere "gropings in the dark." Without price signals, there would be no way of making rational decisions. The degree of chaos emerging would be directly linked to the size and sophistication of the exchange economy being annihilated. As Mises liked to say, human rationality was an outcome of economic life.

The importance of price signals was related to the limited capacities of the human intelligence when faced with the complexity of the economy. While one individual, Mises said, could conceivably plan the activities of a *household* through time without the benefit of monetary exchange, it quickly became impossible with an economy of any size. With Mises, the existence of limitations on human knowledge became an argument in defense of the market system. He insisted on the limited intelligence of single individuals in comparison with the complex organization achieved by the economy, the latter being made possible through a division of intellectual labor among decision makers.

For Mises, the use of mathematical formalism was, at best, a concise way of portraying ideas already formed prior to the use of formal notation: it could never add anything by way of theoretical insight. At worst, the inappropriate use of mathematics could induce one to "see" economic activity in a mechanical matter, to search for "equilibrium" when, in reality, there was no equilibrium to be found, when overcoming "frictions" was what economic action was all about. I remember Mises repeatedly saying that the concept of static equilibrium was quite alien to economic life and action, that it was merely a mental picture, an image of a state of nonaction used in order to comprehend human action. We never studied equilibrium, he said, but motion. Similarity with Mayer's views notwithstanding, the personal conflict between the two men ensured that any form of reconciliation was quite out of the question.

If Mises's brand of Austrian economics was linked in the public eye with a pronounced liberal politics, prior to him, it was not so easy to equate the two. Menger was a liberal but had been muted in his political utterances. Of the next generation, Böhm-Bawerk was the most liberal, but he was also quite comfortable with his involvements in the prewar bureaucracy that intervened to regulate the financial markets and control economic development. Von Wieser, for his part, stood firmly behind the interventionist Austro-Hungarian state and stressed governmental responsibility in the matter of social welfare. Von Wieser's protégé, Mayer, in turn, rejected Mises's fusion of Austrian economics and liberal politics. He was always keen to insist on the distance separating Wieser and himself from Mises. My attitude toward Mises was thus intricately tied up with the fact that I shared the authoritarian politics and vague anti-Semitism, it must be said, of von Wieser and Mayer. I had a visceral resistance to this liberal Jew who wanted to equate rational economics with the politics of *laisser-faire*.

These questions concerning the knowledge and rationality of the economic actor, this Misesian heritage, would be foundational for both Hayek and me in the years that followed. With hindsight, I can see that the parting of our paths in the 1930s lay in the different ways in which we handled these matters. Sharing Mises's blind faith in the liberal order, Hayek ensured that, in his analysis of "economics and knowledge," the coordinating powers of the market remained intact. Lacking any such faith, I was more prepared to give weight to doubts concerning the *logical* interaction of beliefs and expectations of actors. This became all the more important the more my power in Vienna relied on my associations with local mathematicians. But this is to carry us ahead of ourselves.

If all this seems somewhat labyrinthine, then so be it. It was not easy being a student of battling teachers. Many of us were participants in both groups, so we had to tread carefully. It was at Mayer's recommendation that von Wieser recommended me for a postdoctoral fellowship to Karl Pribram, the Rockefeller Foundation's liaison at the university. Dispatching an essay on marginal utility, I had now completed my first degree, my "doctorate" under Mayer, and, in June 1925, I took off to see the world.

3. Time Abroad

I have always enjoyed being close to the powerful. When I entered the university, the latest Rockefeller philanthropy, the Laura Spelman Rockefeller Memorial, had been in existence for several years. Named after John D. Rockefeller's widow, it had an endowment that ran to over seventy million dollars and had quickly become the main source of Rockefeller support for the social sciences. In 1929, it was absorbed into the Rockefeller Foundation. If the Memorial was well-disposed toward social science research during the 1920s, it was due largely to its director, Beardsley Ruml, who had come to Rockefeller with a PhD in experimental psychology from the University of Chicago. Interested in the construction of a less abstract social science, one that would be of immediate use to the "social engineer," Ruml created a system of grants, placing emphasis on empirical research.

In the United States, money went to universities such as Chicago, Harvard, Columbia, and Iowa State, and research institutions such as the National Bureau of Economic Research. In England, it was the London School of Economics (LSE) and, later, Oxford. The Cambridge of Keynes and Robinson, on the other hand, showed little interest in shifting focus in response to Rockefeller, and was passed over. In continental Europe, Rockefeller tended not to support universities directly, in the well-founded belief that European social science was still highly speculative, that the universities were often torn by internecine strife, and that the risks of wasting money through bureaucracy were high. Consequently, it put money into the funding of independent institutions and into a program of fellowships intended to broaden the minds of future teachers and ensure they weren't too tied to their own mentors. The choice of Rockefeller Fellows depended on the favor of local advisers, such as Pribram in Vienna and Gösta Bagge in Sweden, and every year, around forty graduate students visited various institutions in Europe and the United States, very often those centers already receiving Rockefeller research support. I left Vienna in September 1925 and over the next three years visited England, the United States, France, and Italy.

England allowed me to put some distance between me and my Austrian mentors. I spent most of my time in London, where I was registered at the LSE. Apart from improving my English, I made efforts to become familiar with recent work in economics in that country. At the LSE, I met Professors Bowley and Gregory, and in frequent meetings at the Political Economy Club and the Athenaeum, Professor Edgeworth, from Oxford. The latter impressed me greatly. His work embodied that quality of *Wertfreiheit* so stressed by Weber, and there was a modesty in his theoretical aims that appealed to me. Two years later, after his death, I would write that Edgeworth "came closer to the ideal of the 'pure scientist' than hardly (sic) any other in the social sciences . . . His theories are generally free from value judgments, to a higher degree . . . than those of many of his contemporaries, and he was fully aware of this need in regard to logical properties and necessities." With good reason, I went on to say that Edgeworth "helped to protect economics in England from those extravagances which are so typical to the development of economics in Germany [where] every beginner believes . . . that he should create entirely 'new' foundations and a completely new methodology. In England, however, the use of mathematics is more common than elsewhere, a further circumstance to frighten away dilettantes who are only half interested in economics."

As the tone of the above suggests, by the late 1920s I was beginning to find my feet. The Rockefeller fellowship was having the desired effect. My exposure to Edgeworth, and increased reading in mathematics and logic, brought about a subtle, but important, shift in my attitude. It was not so much that I came to reject Mayer's criticisms of contemporary theory as to tailor my ambitions. Edgeworth agreed with our Austrian complaint that the temporal dimension of economic theory was its most unsatisfactory and difficult aspect, and he repeated often that the mathematical difficulties here were very great, yet he did not share Mayer's nihilism in the matter. For Edgeworth, the most helpful applications of mathematics to economics were those that were short and simple and employed few symbols. They aimed at throwing a bright light on some small part of the big picture rather than on its endless complexities. Without feeling compelled to jettison my Austrian concerns, I began to appreciate this kind of argument.

From there, it was onward to the United States, just before Christmas 1925, in time for the annual meetings of the American Economic Association. This was followed by six months in New York, at Columbia University, where my closest contacts were with Wesley Mitchell and Henry Moore. I also frequently saw Professor Fetter from Princeton. After that came several months at Harvard, where I had contact with Charles Bullock, Warren Persons, and others involved in the analysis of business cycles.

My choice of business cycles as a topic of study was rooted in my days as a student in Vienna. Mises had been particularly interested in this work for some time. To him, Mitchell's "purely empirical" examination of business cycles, unhindered by theoretical preconceptions, smacked of historicism. Even if no satisfactory theory of the business cycle yet existed, Mises said, it was not going to emerge inductively from the consideration of masses of statistical data. He saw Mitchell's form of institutionalism as an American reincarnation of the German historical method—and both, of course, as species of statist apologetics. Then there was the aim of the Harvard group to use certain statistical barometers to help predict the future, and Bullock's group was already selling its services to private companies. To Mises, the idea that the future path of the economy could somehow be predicted using statistical measurement was anathema. What statistics could say about the economic order was very limited and was purely historical in that it referred to the past. The functioning of the economy could be grasped, in the sense of being understood, when one reflected on the motivations governing individual economic action. This was bound up with the evolution of beliefs, motivations, and expectations, all of which were in perpetual flux. The economy, while it could be "understood," could be only inadequately represented by statistics, and it could never be predicted. More dangerous to Mises was the short step that lay between believing that one could "capture" the economy through statistical representation and advocating state intervention to effect economic control.

In preparation for my American sojourn, I had read widely in the business cycle literature of the time: the attempts by Henry Ludwell Moore, like Jevons before him, to show the existence of a periodic economic cycle generated by noneconomic forces and the empirical work by Mitchell, Persons, and Bullock. With Hayek, who in 1924 returned from a year as a research assistant at New York University, I had discussed the barometer work at Harvard.

By 1927, when I visited him at Columbia, Mitchell was the preeminent figure in international business cycle research. In *Business Cycles and Their Causes*, he had stated that theories of the business cycle were to be tested not by further examining their logic but by studying the facts they purported to explain. Thus his book gave a massive range of statistics for four countries, the United States, England, France, and Germany, for the period 1890–1911, covering prices and quantities, and other phenomena such as migration patterns. His analysis of these statistics, the central part of the book, was limited to the presentation of averages and to comparison by means of graphs. Looking at his data, Mitchell concluded that no theory could ever be perfectly adequate because of the process of cumulative change of the real economic world. Cycles were not regular but varied in duration and intensity. Every point in every cycle was unique, the outcome of a unique set of circumstances. Extraneous factors such as the weather, war, and policy changes also mattered in giving each cycle its unique character. He pointed to the Harvard business barometers, suggesting that their improvement might help in making predictions and thus in perfecting our control over the economy. In his second book, *Business Cycles: The Problem and Its Setting* (1927), which was a survey of the field, Mitchell was more hesitant than ever about attempting to define the term "business cycle" and wondered how useful the term was at all.

The person most responsible for the decomposition of time series, and the construction of indicators of business activity with a view to improving forecasts, was Warren Persons. He had joined the faculty at Harvard in 1919, having been brought there by Charles Bullock's Committee for Economic Research, newly established in 1917. In 1919, the committee launched the *Review of Economic Statistics* to provide an outlet for work in the collection and interpretation of same. Persons was still at Harvard in 1927 when I visited, although he left the following year to go into the more lucrative consultancy business.

Persons's approach to the business cycle was resolutely empirical. For example, a 1919 paper combined the derived cyclical data of twenty time series to construct composite indicators of economic activity. In order to combine the various series into well-matched groups, Persons superimposed them on transparent sheets and asked "observers" to compare them by eye. It was clearly hazardous, as the extent to which any two series seemed to match each other depended on how the superimposition was done, that is, the length of the lag allowed. Opinions differed as to the degree of correlation observed. Persons settled on three groupings that he used to construct three indices of the business situation, the Harvard A-B-C curves, representing speculation, physical productivity, and the financial markets. The result was a representation of economic activity, constructed with minimal recourse to a priori theory and intended to improve forecasting. The whole was very dependent on simple visual techniques; statistically, nothing more than two-variable correlation techniques were used so that the interdependence between three and more variables remained unanalyzed; the question of the theoretical mechanism linking the observed patterns remained open.

4. Reading

If I can give a workmanlike synthesis of Mitchell and Persons, it must be said that I didn't find the subject particularly captivating. I was more likely to stay up late struggling not with business cycles but with new readings in logic and the philosophy of science. In the previous years in Vienna, Spann, naturally, had no interest in scientific philosophy, regarding it as a sign of the century's spiritual impoverishment. Neither with Mayer were these issues discussed in any detail. In the Mises group, we had touched on recent developments in the philosophy of science, and I was beginning to become aware of discussions among the mathematicians and physicists of the *Schlick Kreis*, which included another of Mises's enemies, his brother Richard, but in the economist's circle, more attention was paid to the phenomenological writings of Husserl and Alfred Schütz. In England, however, things began to change. I had just left Vienna, where questions of method were not only foremost but linked, in my mind, to deep personal hostilities. In the course of three short years, I had been buffeted between Spann, who offered a way of seeing the world that had little to do with economic inquiry; Mayer, who was more concentrated on theory but inevitably drew one into his political-academic intrigues; and Mises, who had even stronger views and managed to politicize so much of our discussions. The Weberian counsel of *Wertfreiheit*, that social theory should be "value-free," had been much touted in debate in Vienna, but in a setting riddled with political intrigue. Coming after this, Edgeworth's calm and simplicity was like a breath of fresh air.

The qualities I encountered in Edgeworth I found again in Allyn Young, whom I met at Harvard early in 1927, the year he was honored with the call to succeed Edwin Cannan at the University of London. Like Edgeworth, whom he admired greatly, Young was as much mathematician

Persons' "Index of General Business Conditions."
Bi-monthly Averages, 1903 to June, 1914.
From *Review of Economic Statistics*, April, 1919, Preliminary vol. i, pp. 112-113.

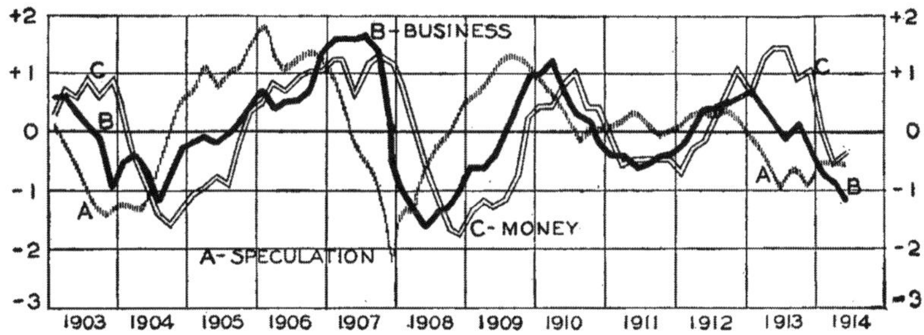

and statistician as economist, and he was enormously stimulating for the younger set surrounding him in evening discussions at his home in Cambridge throughout the best part of 1927. Looking to Vienna as the only source of hope in the German literature, he emphasized the need for a reconciliation of the Austrian and Lausanne schools.

My reading expanded, taking me to an earlier little book on mathematical philosophy by Russell, whose work on paradoxes in set theory I would, in time, try to incorporate into my discussion of the logic of economics. The bulk of Wittgenstein's *Tractatus* left me mystified. I also tackled Herman Weyl's book of the late 1920s on the philosophy of mathematics and science, and during my time in Cambridge, Massachusetts, I was lucky enough to meet Alfred North Whitehead. He had an open house on Sunday evenings, where we talked long and extensively about everything: one evening it was Kant and Husserl; the next Dewey, Mumford, and Emerson. At his invitation, I attended his Friday private seminar, where we discussed Russell, Wittgenstein, Mill, and others. At yet another, it was Keynes's ideas on probability. I also read Whitehead's own Lowell Lectures of two years earlier, "Science and the Modern World."

In that book, Whitehead wrote of the dissolution of the scientific cosmology that had obtained, for the last three centuries, a scientific materialism that presupposed the ultimate fact of an irreducible brute matter. With the development of relativity and quantum theories, he said, this worldview had now become obsolete. Science had reached a turning point. The old foundations of scientific thought were becoming unintelligible, he said. Time, space, matter, material, ether, electricity, mechanism, organism, configuration, structure, pattern, function: all required reinterpretation.

What, he asked—and I distinctly remember the phrase—is the sense of talking about a mechanical explanation when you do not know what you mean by mechanics? Emboldened, I imagined confronting my Viennese teachers with such questions.

In "Mathematics in the History of Thought," Whitehead emphasized the human achievement represented by abstract mathematics and the astonishing capacity the latter had shown in applications to various parts of empirical science. Mathematics in the seventeenth century provided the imaginative background with which the early men of science approached the observation of nature. Galileo, Descartes, Huyghens, and Newton: they all produced formulas. Their analyses of periodicity, which gave birth to modern physics, were made possible only because mathematicians had already worked out the abstract notions surrounding periodicity. It was paradoxical, but true, said Whitehead, that it was only by means of utmost abstractions that we were able to approach concrete facts. He drew the parallel between the two periods in which mathematics had had its greatest influence on general thought, that from Pythagoras in the sixth century BC to Plato, and then in the seventeenth and eighteenth centuries, saying that in both of these times the general categories of thought fell apart. There were waves of religious enthusiasm, he said, a turning inward to the self to find enlightenment, and a movement toward the reconstruction of traditional ways. And now, he said, we had reached such a point again. He also said that the pursuit of mathematics was a sort of divine madness of the human spirit, a refuge from the goading urgency of contingent happenings, beside which paragraph, in the margin, I jotted "Vienna!" Although no mathematician, I was struck by this idea that mathematics was a kind of refuge from the contingency of the everyday.

Vividly, I remember being moved by such reading. Folding my book, leaving the Widener, and crossing Harvard Yard, I wrestled with how to reconcile Whitehead, who pressed for the mathematical analysis of ultimate abstractions, with the discussions in Viennese circles. Was it that, in disregarding the time element, Jevons and Walras, or for that matter Edgeworth or Bowley, had not achieved the correct degree of abstraction before analyzing the interconnections? Was it a question of conceptually grasping the time factor properly and *then* proceeding with the mathematics? And how could one reconcile the concept of equilibrium, which had proved so useful in providing a formal mathematical apparatus, with the insistence of my Austrian teachers on the centrality to economics of motion and change? Then, as if in escape, I would remind myself that I had a *Habilitation* thesis to write—and that Whitehead was not the one it had to satisfy.

5. A "Truly Superfluous Austerity"

I would subsequently refer to *Wirtschaftsprognose* ("Economic Prediction") as the place I first addressed the theoretical complications arising from the fact that beliefs about others, and thus beliefs about beliefs, can affect economic actions. And it is true: it was here that I became interested in this problem, sufficiently enough to take it up again in the early 1930s, in a changed context. However, *Wirtschaftsprognose* was much more than the "prelude" to game theory that my repeated reference to Sherlock Holmes after 1944 might lead one to believe. It was a treatise on the methodology of economic forecasting, in which I determined to prove the futility of all attempts at prediction, such as that being done by the Harvard, Babson, and Moody's agencies. And, at this point, ambiguity of later accounts notwithstanding, I was not appealing to the mathematicians. I was explicitly pessimistic about any possibility of treating these questions in a formal manner. The monograph was not without its limitations—Arthur Marget would dissect it brilliantly in his 1929 review—but it had the energy of an ambitious twenty-five-year-old.

I set out to show the impossibility of making any complete forecast of the state of the economy, given the complexity of the (unknown) mechanisms that shape economic events. Prediction could be shown to be useless as a tool of rational economic stabilization. It was "in principle" impossible, I said, to use economic theory and statistics to make economic forecasts. The lack of homogeneity and the small size of samples made data wholly inadequate for statistical induction. Attempts to understand the business cycle based on statistical considerations alone could never facilitate economic forecasting. For that, one needed to look to the underlying processes, of which prices were the surface phenomena. These mechanisms, however, lacked the regularity necessary to make them useful for any kind of prediction: only loose and inexact laws could be discovered. And even when predictions were made, their effect was to create anticipations on the part of consumers, whose reactions would only serve to undermine the original forecast. For unlike astronomy or medicine, the social sciences had the peculiarity of being able to affect their object of study.

Echoing Mises, I wrote that static theory assumed a rationality of economic acts so perfect that there was no reasoning involved: "In the static economy, nobody acts economically any more, and that means that they no longer ascribe value, and that no more acts of choice are made, and no decisions are made, because everything stands still." However, given that Mayer was my protector, the thesis contained no direct reference to Mises. As the latter wrote later, those who sought to qualify for a university lectureship had to be careful not to be known as his students.

In the real economy, individuals had a system of orientation points (*Orientierungspunkte*), which included not only their knowledge of the laws of nature but also their knowledge and beliefs about other economic subjects: every action influences the other actions, and each is reflected in the other. This element of interdependence defeated any attempt at economic prediction. I considered a thought experiment involving a comprehensive forecast by the public authority, indicating, say, certain increases in price level, interest rates, rate of stock accumulation, and industry orders, over a certain future period. Because economic agents would incorporate such a forecast into their plans, the prediction could *never* be realized. They would buy tomorrow, if possible, what they would have bought over a longer time, given constant prices, and so forth. Should the forecasting agency and the public try to outguess each other, they would end up in an infinite regress of prediction, reaction, and revised prediction, from which there was no escape. I introduced the celebrated Holmes and Moriarty anecdote to illustrate it:

> Sherlock Holmes, chased by his enemy Moriarty, leaves from London to Dover with a train that stops at an intermediate station; he gets off the train instead of going on to Dover. He saw Moriarty at the train station and, considering him very intelligent, expected that Moriarty would take the faster train, to await him in Dover. This anticipation of Holmes turned out to be right. But what if Moriarty had been even more intelligent and had considered Holmes's capacities even greater, and therefore had predicted Holmes's action? Then he [Moriarty] would obviously only have gone to the intermediate station. Again Holmes would have calculated that, and therefore would have chosen Dover. Thus Moriarty would have acted differently. And from so much thinking, there would have come no action, or the less intelligent one would have handed himself to the other at Victoria Station because all the fleeing would have been unnecessary. Examples of that kind could be taken from everywhere. Chess, strategy, etc., but there one needs to have special knowledge, which simply makes the examples more difficult.

Once again, the metaphor of chess helped to highlight the *intractability* of sequential interaction, the difficulty of dealing with process. Although the context had changed—with Mayer, it was the problem of price formation; here, it was that of stabilizing a prediction—chess still served as an exemplar of the complex, the unforeseeable.

In reviews of *Wirtschaftprognose*, Arthur Marget and my friend Eve Burns dealt deftly with my nihilism. Marget rebuffed me in my own words, saying that, despite my declared intention, I had written a satire—and he proceeded to strip my thesis bare. The Harvard methods did *not* rely on the use of probability techniques, he said, and even if they had, this in itself was not an argument against prediction per se; there was no a priori reason why anticipations should respond to predictions in such a way as to contradict the forecast; my claim that a prediction, to be useful, must be *exactly* right, was an unrealistic demand; and my argument against prediction based on the operation of noneconomic factors was, if interpreted logically, he said, an argument against economic science itself. Burns, likewise, suggested that my emphasis on complexity was tantamount to abandoning all hope of creating a usable economic science.

Lionel Robbins later read the work, and while he admitted that the disastrous experiences of the Depression had revealed forecasting to be a fiasco, he too felt that I was going too far. But he was polite about it. "I do not believe . . . that it is necessary to arrive at a skepticism like that which my friend Dr. Oskar Morgenstern has shown in *Wirtschaftsprognose*. If I had to choose between Dr. Morgenstern and Harvard, I would be very embarrassed. But in order not to suppress all hope of the future of economic science, I would maintain Harvard in being." In disowning prediction *tout court*, he said, I had shown "a truly superfluous austerity." Privately, Haberler, my closest friend in Vienna, wrote long letters taking me to task: "You say 'I wanted to write a formal methodological work. And there I can't mix in empirical research.' To respond to that concretely: I suggest that, for you, the knowledge goal (the impossibility of prediction) is more important than the method, and that's why you say that the knowledge goal cannot be reached with empirical methods. If you want to concentrate on formal methodological methods . . . you have to choose another topic, one that can be handled that way."

Thus, negative reaction, yes, but to be met with harsh criticism is so much better than being met with silence. With this monograph, I had taken an important first stepping stone in a university career and creation of a professional self. Writing it, I also sensed the possibility of a rhetorical style in which stridency might play as important a role as that of careful argument. As I wrote to an American friend at the time, affairs of the heart were simple, but the empire of the mind was reserved for those who were competent to rule there. I had entered the realm of the intellect, and books were power.

6. Return

From the United States, I returned temporarily to Vienna, where my future was taking form. Mayer indicated that he wanted me to assist with the editorship of the *Zeitschrift für Nationalökonomie* when my fellowship ended. That same year, with the support of Rockefeller funding for research on economic stabilization and "social engineering," Mises had set up a small Institute for Trade Cycle Research. Appointing Hayek as director, he intimated that there would probably be some work for me when I returned to Vienna. The following year, I spent a few months in Paris and Rome, where I met the French and Italian economists and completed the revisions to my thesis, all the while reading further in mathematics and philosophy. I even got to see Hilbert and Weyl speak in Rome.

Once finally back in Austria, I reintegrated myself into familiar circles. Every fortnight or so, the Mises group would meet at seven in the evening for several hours, before dispersing or retiring to the café. There were frequent visitors from abroad, including Robbins from the LSE, Howard Ellis from the United States, and John Van Sickle from Rockefeller. In my absence, the tension between Spann and Mayer had risen, with the former actually succeeding in blocking Mayer's plan for my *Habilitation*, arguing that Mayer constantly supported Jews (sic!) such as me. It was thus delayed for a year. I found that Mayer had lapsed into a reverie, wasting hours in the café decrying Spann. His slothfulness delayed my publications, and I became increasingly impatient with him. His conflict with Mises continued unabated.

As I slipped back into familiar surroundings after three years of travel, I felt as though in some respects I had grown, though, in others, it was as though I had never been away. In a bid to bridge the gap between Mayer and Mises in 1928, the *Nationalökonomische Gesellschaft*, or National Economics Society, was reconstituted, largely through Hayek's efforts. Mayer was made president, and the meetings were intended to draw on the common pool of participants. We met in rather formal meetings at the offices of the National Bankers Association, and we continued the discussion into the early hours at the Café Künstler. It was at that point also that I became involved in the *Geist Kreis*, which in 1921 had grown up around Hayek and Herbert Fürth, who preceded me in their defection from the Spann circle. An eclectic group of students of economics, history, law, and psychoanalysis, among them Machlup, Schütz, Kaufmann, and Mintz, they discussed widely in economic and political philosophy, literature, art, and music. As interesting as the discussions were, I felt uncomfortable among this largely Jewish group, confiding to my diary that I was the only pure Aryan among them, Hayek included.

No less than before, Mises managed to give matters a political slant, and all of his deliberations, whether on the difficulty of dealing with time in economic theory or on the naturalness of "frictions" in human action, invariably issued in the endorsement of a nonmathematical economics based on the rationality of individual action, with all public intervention or attempts at collective action being deemed irrational. It was around this time that my discomfort with him began to grow. It was not a matter of fundamental disagreement over a single issue but rather a range of simmering tensions and differences. It must be remembered that we were not peers: I was not even thirty years old, and Mises was almost twenty years my senior. However, I never warmed to him as a person, and I retained an instinctive dislike of those who gathered around him. Nor, as I have already said, did I share his rather liberal outlook, identifying more with the political worldview of von Wieser and Mayer. Now with my *Habilitation* completed, and feeling more independent than before, I found myself resisting Mises's fusion of economics and liberalism and searching for a way to respond to it.

At the same time, on the foot of Edgeworth, Whitehead, and other readings, I found myself questioning his dismissal of the use of mathematical formalism. He made rhetorical appeals to logic and science in defense of his liberal economics, yet he lacked the exactness I was growing to appreciate in Hilbert, Weyl, and now Carnap. I wrote to Haberler about moving away from Kantian philosophy, Husserl, and idealism to embrace Carnap's *Logical Structure of the World*. Mathematical logic and epistemology were essential, I claimed. Mises, while he dismissed Spann and the romantic revolt against "science and logic," showed little interest in what was actually occurring in the most recent writings on science and logic. I began to perceive his opposition as a crudely conceived one, based on a vague understanding of the role of mathematics in science. It was a creeping change of opinion, yet the resistance had set in.

Thus stood matters at the close of the 1920s. Although such entanglements and tensions are not the comfortable stuff of encyclopedia entries, they do bring us closer to the truth of the matter. Although I had no unified view of the world, no clear plan for theoretical achievement, I began the 1930s looking toward mathematics and symbolic logic, and this turn would shape my writings of the following decade. In Karl Menger, whom I had met when back on a visit to Vienna in 1927, I found someone who was a mathematician, knew social science intimately, and, sharing my doubts about Mises, Neurath, and all ideologues, was utterly committed to evicting personal values from scientific work. Through him, I drew closer to Schlesinger, Wald, and others, all of whom became important allies as I evolved throughout the 1930s. By the same token, I drew away from my mentors, so that within a few years of my taking over the institute, Mises and Mayer were no longer welcome there. It was also a way of safeguarding my power in the world of economics in Vienna—but more of that on another occasion.

Thus, for the moment, my theoretical concerns were still quite "Austrian"—the difficulties of accounting for time, uncertainty, expectations; the inadequacy of mechanical structures to the description of social processes—but I was becoming a reluctant Austrian, trying to reconcile my mentors' interests with a style of scientific argument they had rejected. I also glimpsed the attractions of occupying a third position, between the world of my teachers and that of the mathematicians and philosophers I was beginning to read. There, I sensed, completely immersed in neither community, and therefore fully responsible to neither, I would find new possibilities for the affirmation of an independent self. This proximity to things foreign to my mentors would somehow set me apart and that, as the reader will have long since gathered, was one of my deepest personal needs.

Author's postscript

The reader who has been good enough to read through to the end deserves at least a few words of explanation. Although my success in doing so will be judged by others, I can say that the choice of the first-person singular to describe this phase of Morgenstern's life came completely naturally. As was intimated at the beginning of the essay, it seemed the most fitting way to capture certain nuances of perception and impression that could be only imperfectly conveyed through the historian's usual narrative-plus-footnotes. This is not to say that the above is unconstrained by archival sources of the usual kind: quite the contrary. It did, however, require forsaking the usual rigorous documentation of sources marshalled. Perhaps, as one referee pointed out, it demands a greater degree of trust on the part of the reader than would a normal article, although I am not quite convinced of that. Beyond my own exploration of the Morgenstern diaries and papers, I found valuable the work of Earlene Craver, Hansjörg Klausinger, Mary Morgan, and Urs Rellstab. The sources for the images used were as follows: Morgenstern family, Oskar Morgenstern Papers, Duke University; Austria-Hungary map, Horrabin 1934; Spann, Räber 1937; Mayer, Grass 1952; Mises, Mises 1976; Persons' Index of Business Conditions, Mitchell 1927. For comments on an earlier draft, I am grateful to Bruce Caldwell, Philippe Fontaine, Frédéric Hanin, Fabrice Thierry, and two anonymous referees.

References

Berkley, George E. 1988. *Vienna and Its Jews: The Tragedy of Success, 1880s-1980s*. Cambridge, Mass.: Abt Books.

Böhm-Bawerk, Eugen von. 1961. Unresolved Contradiction in the Marxian Economic System. In vol. 1 of *Shorter Classics of Eugen von Böhm-Bawerk*. South Holland, Ill.: Libertarian.

Bulmer, Martin, and Joan Bulmer. 1981. Philanthropy and Social Science in the 1920s: Beardsley Ruml and the Laura Spelman Rockefeller Memorial, 1922–29. *Minerva* 19 (Autumn): 347–407.

Burns, Eve. 1929. Statistics and Economic Forecasting. *Journal of the American Statistical Association* 24.166:152–63.

Carnap, Rudolf. [1928] 1967. *The Logical Structure of the World and Pseudoproblems of Philosophy*. Translated by Rolf A. George. London: Routledge & Kegan Paul.

Craver, Earlene. 1986a. The Emigration of the Austrian Economists. *HOPE* 18.1:1–32.

———. 1986b. Patronage and the Directions of Research in Economics: The Rockefeller Foundation in Europe, 1924–1938. *Minerva* 24.2–3:205–22.

Fosdick, Raymond B. 1952. *The Story of the Rockefeller Foundation*. New York: Harper.

Fossati, Eraldo. 1957. *The Theory of General Static Equilibrium*. Edited by G. L. S. Shackle. Oxford: Blackwell.

Gerschenkron, Alexander. 1977. *An Economic Spurt That Failed*. Princeton, N.J.: Princeton University Press.

Grass, Nikolaus, ed. 1952. *Österreichische Rechts- und Staatswissenschaften in Selbstdarstellungen*. Innsbruck: Wagner.

Haag, J. 1976–77. Othmar Spann and the Quest for a "True State." *Annual Austrian History Yearbook* 12–13 (pt. 1): 227–50.

Hayek, Friedrich. 1991. *The Trend of Economic Thinking: Essays on Political Economists and Economic History.* Vol. 3 of *The Collected Works of F. A. Hayek.* Chicago: University of Chicago Press.

———. 1994. *Hayek on Hayek: An Autobiographical Dialogue.* Edited by Stephen Kresge and Leif Wenar. London: Routledge.

Horrabin, J. F. 1934. *An Atlas of Current Affairs.* New York: Knopf.

Johnston, William M. [1972] 1983. *The Austrian Mind: An Intellectual and Social History, 1848–1938.* Berkeley: University of California Press.

Mahr, Alexander. 1956. Hans Mayer-Leben und Werk. *Zeitschrift für Nationalökonomie* 16.1–2 (March): 3–16.

Marget, A. W. 1929. Morgenstern on the Methodology of Economic Forecasting. *Journal of Political Economy* 37 (June): 312–39.

Mayer, Hans. 1911. Eine neue Grundlegung der theoretischen Nationökonomie. *Zeitschrift für Volkswirtschaft, Sozialpolitik, und Verwaltung* 20.

———. [1932] 1994. Der Erkenntniswert der funktionellen Preistheorien. In vol. 2 of *Die Wirtschaftstheorie der Gegenwart,* edited by Hans Mayer. Vienna: Springer. Reprinted as The Cognitive Value of Functional Theories of Price: Critical and Positive Investigations concerning the Price Problem. In *Classics in Austrian Economics: A Sampling in the History of a Tradition,* edited by Israel Kirzner. London: Pickering.

Menger, Carl. [1871] 1981. *Principles of Economics.* Translated by J. Dingwall and B. Hoselitz. New York: New York University Press.

Mises, Ludwig von. [1922] 1936. *Socialism.* Translated by J. Kahane. London: Cape.

———. [1933] 1960. *Epistemological Problems in Economics.* Princeton, N.J.: Van Nostrand.

———. 1978. *Notes and Recollections.* South Holland, Ill.: Libertarian.

———. 1996. *Planning for Freedom.* 4th ed. Grove City, Penn.: Libertarian.

Mises, Margit von. 1976. *My Years with Ludwig von Mises.* New Rochelle, N.Y.: Arlington House.

Mitchell, W. C. 1913. *Business Cycles and Their Causes.* Vol. 3. Berkeley: California University Memoirs.

———. 1927. *The Problem and Its Setting.* Vol. 1 of *Business Cycles.* New York: National Bureau of Economic Research.

Moore, H. L. 1914. *Economic Cycles: Their Law and Cause.* New York: Macmillan.

———. 1923. *Generating Economic Cycles.* New York: Macmillan.

Morgan, M. 1990. *The History of Econometric Ideas.* Cambridge: Cambridge University Press.

Morgenstern, Oskar. 1928. *Wirtschaftprognose: Eine Untersuchung ihrer Voraussetzungen und Möglichkeiten.* Vienna: Julius Springer.

———. 1931. Mathematical Economics. In *Encyclopaedia of the Social Sciences,* edited by E. R. A. Seligman. New York: Macmillan.

———. [1927] 1976a. Francis Y. Edgeworth. *Zeitschrift für Volkswirtschaft und Sozialpolitik* 5 (10–12): 646–52. Reprinted in Schotter 1976.

———. [1927] 1976b. Friedrich von Wieser, 1851–1925. *American Economic Review* 17 (December): 669–74. Reprinted in Schotter 1976.

———. [1929] 1976. Allyn Abbot Young. *Zeitschrift für Nationalökonomie* 1 (May): 143–45. Reprinted in Schotter 1976.

———. [1951] 1976. Joseph A. Schumpeter, 1883–1950. *Economic Journal* 61.241:197–202. Reprinted in Schotter 1976.

———. n.d. Autobiographical note, box 1, folder: Info. Series Autobiographical Material. Oskar Morgenstern Papers, Special Collections Library, Duke University, Durham, N.C.

Muller, Adam. 1809. *Die Elemente der Staatskunst*. Berlin: Genudg.

O'Brien, D. P. 1988. *Lionel Robbins*. New York: St. Martin's.

Oxaal, Ivar, Michael Pollak, and Gerhard Botz, eds. 1987. *Jews, Antisemitism, and Culture in Vienna*. London: Routledge & Kegan Paul.

Pauley, Bruce F. 1992. *From Prejudice to Perdition: A History of Austrian Anti-Semitism*. Chapel Hill: University of North Carolina Press.

Persons, Warren M. 1919a. Indices of Business Conditions. *Review of Economic Statistics* 1.1:5–110.

———. 1919b. An Index of General Business Conditions. *Review of Economic Statistics* 1.1:111–205.

Räber, Hans. [1937] 1961. *Othmar Spanns Philosophie des Universalismus: Darstellung und Kritik*. Hildesheim: Georg Olms.

Rellstab, Urs. 1991. From German Romanticism to Game Theory: I. Oskar Morgenstern's Vienna in the 1920s. Mimeo, Department of Economics, Duke University, Durham, N.C.

———. 1992. *Ökonomie und Spiele: Die Entstehungsgeschichte der Spieltheorie aus dem Blickwinkel des Ökonomen Oskar Morgenstern*. Zürich: Verlag Rüegger.

Robbins, L. [1932] 1935. *An Essay on the Nature and Significance of Economic Science*. London: Macmillan.

———. [1938] 1988. The Methods of Economic Observation and the Problems of Prediction in Economics. In *Lionel Robbins*, edited by D. P. O'Brien. New York: St. Martin's.

Russell, Bertrand. 1919. *Introduction to Mathematical Philosophy*. London: Allen and Unwin.

Schotter, Andrew, ed. 1976. *Selected Economic Writings of Oskar Morgenstern*. New York: New York University Press.

Silk, Leonard. 1977. The Game Theorist. *New York Times*, 13 February.

Spann, Othmar. 1911. *Die Haupttheorien der Volkswirtschaftslehre*. Leipzig: Quelle & Meyer.

———. 1924. *Kategorienlehre*. In vol. 1 of *Ergänzungsbände zur Sammlung Herdflamme*. Jena: Gustav Fischer.

Walras, Léon. 1874. *Éléments d'économie politique pure, ou théorie de la richesse sociale*. Lausanne: Paris.

Weber, Wilhelm. 1961. Hans Mayer. In vol. 7 of *Handwörterbuch der Sozialwissenschaft*. Stuttgart: Gustav Fischer.

Weyl, Hermann. 1927. *Philosophie der Mathematik und Naturwissenschaften*. Munich: R. Oldenbourg.

Whitehead, Alfred N. [1925] 1967. *Science and the Modern World*. New York: Free Press.

Wiggershaus, Rolf. 1995. *The Frankfurt School*. Translated by Michael Robertson. Cambridge, Mass.: MIT Press.

Wistrich, Robert S., ed. 1992. *Austrians and Jews in the Twentieth Century: From Franz Joseph to Waldheim*. New York: St. Martin's.

Wittgenstein, Ludwig. [1921] 1993. *Tractatus Logico-Philosophicus*. Translated by D. F. Pears and B. F. McGuinness. London: Routledge.

Maynard and Virginia: A Personal and Professional Friendship

Craufurd D. Goodwin

> Maynard—very truculent, I felt, very formidable, like a portrait of Tolstoy as a young man to look at, able to rend any argument that came his way with a blow of his paw, yet concealing, as the novelists say, a kind and even simple heart under that immensely impressive armour of intellect.
>
> Virginia Woolf, memory of John Maynard Keynes before World War I

Many historians of economics tend to be uncomfortable with historical reconstructions of progress in the science, especially with those that attribute causality to selected variables. Are casual friendships, family ties, or religion relevant to the formation of an economist's ideas? Who can be sure? History has so many variables, and most of them unquantifiable, that one should draw connections among them only with great caution. These historians tend to be more satisfied with *rational* reconstructions in which the progress of science is postulated from internal challenges and responses in the published literature. Rational reconstructions are more like the economist's models in which the messiness of reality is avoided by the use of assumptions. Nonprofessional activities may be assumed away. Sometimes historians of economics will venture into limited historical reconstructions, taking into account, for example, an economist's education, interactions with professional colleagues and students, and exchanges with policymakers. But they are uncomfortable with an account that goes much

I am grateful to Donald Winch, an anonymous referee, and the contributors to this supplemental issue for helpful suggestions.

History of Political Economy 39 (annual suppl.) DOI 10.1215/00182702-2006-048

deeper into personal life or events that seem remote from economics. As George Stigler once famously asked of William Jaffé at a meeting of the History of Economics Society, where would such biographical speculation end? Would it be suggested that the toilet training of Léon Walras was relevant to his fascination with general equilibrium?

Yet we all know from personal experience that human life is not neatly divided into "professional" and "personal" compartments. What influences professional life may, in fact, be only dimly understood. Biographers of political, cultural, or business figures are typically much less squeamish than historians of economics about suggesting complex explanatory relationships in the lives of their subjects. This may be because they see their craft as at least as much an art as applied social science. If their intuition suggests that a causal relationship exists between the behavior of their subject and certain factors in the environment, they follow this lead to see what they can turn up.

This essay is a case study in the exploration of what might be thought of as an improbable connection in the history of economic thought, between John Maynard Keynes and the distinguished novelist Virginia Woolf. The construction of Keynes's celebrated macroeconomics has been explored over many decades by a host of economists and historians of economics. Yet there are aspects of his economic thinking that remain a puzzle: for example, his concern for how people should live their lives in advanced market economies, a subject that most economists since the marginal utility revolution have been inclined to argue lies beyond the economist's legitimate area of inquiry, and not anyone's business but the economic actors. Keynes did not agree with this judgment. He was anxious to comprehend why humans acted as they did in their personal lives in the consumption of goods and services, how they should behave to achieve the "good life," and what role leaders in society might have in perfecting the process. Undoubtedly, many factors help explain why Keynes chose to address these questions, but one certainly was time spent among his collection of friends called the Bloomsbury Group. In the preface to the *General Theory*, Keynes (1936, vii) explained that in arriving at his revolutionary ideas he was "dependent on criticism and conversation." This statement has been understood to refer primarily to his relationships with such prominent senior economists as Dennis Robertson and Ralph Hawtrey, and with his younger colleagues in the "Cambridge Circus" and elsewhere. But it should be taken also to include the Bloomsburys, his friends in the humanities and the arts.

Elsewhere I have discussed the impact of Bloomsbury overall on Keynes (Goodwin 2006). This essay focuses on Keynes's relationship with a single member of the group, Virginia Woolf, a close friend who had an impact on twentieth-century fiction comparable in some ways to Keynes's impact on economics. The hypothesis of this essay is not so strong as to suggest that Woolf directly and demonstrably influenced Keynes's economic thought. It is something less than this: it is that a case can be made that Woolf's influence overall may well have been significant in forming Keynes's worldview and is worth the attention of historians of economics. I begin with an account of the Keynes-Woolf friendship, which lasted more than thirty years. Then I examine that part of Keynes's thought that may have been subject to Woolf's influence. I conclude with a review of the evidence that such influence existed.

The Friendship of Maynard with Virginia

> Maynard, besides being our greatest living economist, has a dancer for a mistress. . . . we have all mastered the art of life, and very fascinating it is.
> —Virginia Woolf, diary entry (6 September 1922)

Virginia seems to have met Maynard for the first time in 1907, three years after she and her sister Vanessa escaped the stifling atmosphere of their parents' home at 22 Hyde Park Gate, Kensington, and moved to the liberated world of 46 Gordon Square, Bloomsbury (Woolf 1975–80, 1:396). Maynard lived in nearby Fitzroy Square, having recently come down from Cambridge to a position at the India Office. The two sisters found much in common with Maynard; they grew up in the same British intellectual aristocracy and they too had deep Cambridge roots. They dined together often, and Maynard took part in the exciting evening gatherings where conversation was thrilling and rules of decorum were forgotten. In 1907 Virginia gave up Gordon Square upon Vanessa's marriage to Clive Bell, and she set up house nearby in Fitzroy Square. In 1911 she moved again to 38 Brunswick Square with several other "inmates," including her brother Adrian; the painter Duncan Grant, her future husband, Leonard; and Maynard (1:467). Virginia assumed some of the organizational responsibilities for the establishment, and one of her last acts before leaving on her own honeymoon was to send Maynard his monthly bill (1:508). When Virginia leased Asheham House in Sussex as a country retreat, Maynard became a regular guest, and he even rented the house for a reading party of the Cambridge secret society the Apostles in April 1914 (2:47). During the war when Maynard served in the Treasury he acted as listening post for Bloomsbury within government (2:133, 155). Notwithstanding this useful subversive role, like the other Bloomsburys Virginia tried to persuade Maynard to resign from government in protest, lest he be "lost to humanity" (2:206). When he declined to do so, she was comforted that at least Lytton Strachey's critical spoofs of Winston Churchill and other "big wigs" might compensate in the scheme of things "for all Maynard's crimes in the matter of worldliness" (2:360, 385). When Maynard did finally resign in 1919, he moved as Vanessa's guest to the Charleston farmhouse near Firle and close to Rodmell where Virginia and Leonard had settled. There he wrote *The Economic Consequences of the Peace*. After Maynard married Lydia Lopokova in 1925, they leased Tilton, a house within sight of Charleston, and until Virginia's death in 1941, the two couples met regularly for meals and informal visits.

When one reads Virginia's diary and letters over the years of close friendship with Maynard, one gets the sense that she came to see him almost as a brother. She never hesitated to ask him for help with current projects, for example, to save conscientious objectors during World War I (2:247) or to find suitable employment for T. S. Eliot (3:10–11, 14–15, 20). Yet Maynard as a human being remained a puzzle to Virginia, and her diary and letters are filled with thumbnail sketches and attempts at interpretation. They vary from the deeply affectionate and playful to the suspicious and harshly caustic. She was puzzled that despite his eminence Maynard was inclined to boast and seek praise (Woolf 1977–84, 2:121). She had particular difficulty in determining whether Maynard's notorious generosity was genuine or just manipulative. As the years went on, she became more comfortable with her subject and confident in her characterizations. Here are some representative comments over time. "I talked to Frankie [Francis Birrell] and Keynes most of the time. But it was desperate work" (letter of 25 December 1909 [1975–80, 1:415]). "I heard of you [Katherine Cox] last riding along with Maynard. No: being in Spain does not make me love him better" (letter of 4 September 1912 [1975–80, 2:7]). "He is like quicksilver on a sloping board—a little inhuman, but very kindly, as inhuman people are" (diary entry, 20 January 1915 [1977–84, 1:24]). "The dominion that 'Bloomsbury' exercises over the sane and the insane alike seems to be sufficient to turn the brains of the most robust. . . . Oddly, though, Maynard seems to be the chief fount of the magic spirit" (diary entry, 14 January 1918 [1977–84, 1:106]). “Maynard . . . has the generosity and something of the manner now of an oriental prince” (diary entry, 12 October 1918 [1977–84, 1:201]). “Maynard seems much the same as ever only more and more genial, and superficially kind!” (letter of 14 September 1919 [1975–80, 2:390]). “Went to Charleston for the night; and had a vivid sight of Maynard by lamplight—like a gorged seal, double chin, ledge of red lip, little eyes, sensual, brutal unimaginative: one of those visions that come from a chance attitude, lost so soon as he turned his head. I suppose though it illustrates something I feel about him. Then he’s read neither of my books—In spite of this I enjoyed myself” (diary entry, 26 September 1920 [1977–84, 2:69]). Four years later not much had changed. “And Maynard is grown very thick and opulent; but I like him for his innocency” (diary entry, 15 August 1924 [1977–84, 2:311]).

At times Virginia’s relationship to Maynard seemed like that of a very close sister, free to interfere with his private affairs, as in her short-lived efforts to derail the love affair with, and ultimately marriage to, Lydia Lopokova (Woolf 1975–80, 2:594). In this instance her efforts seem a mixture of selfishness and earnest concern. As she wrote Jacques Raverat in 1924: “Maynard is very heavy and rather portentous; Maynard is passionately and pathetically in love, because he sees very well that he’s dished if he marries her, and she has him by the snout. You can’t argue solidly when Lydia’s there, and as we set now to the decline, and prefer reason to any amount of high spirits, Lydia’s pranks put us all on edge; and Bloomsbury steals off to its dens, leaving Maynard with Lydia on his knee, a sublime but heartrending spectacle” (3:115). Virginia softened toward Lydia rather quickly when she came to know her better. Within less than a year she could write in her diary: “Little Lydia I liked: how does her mind work? Like a lark soaring; a sort of glorified instinct inspires her: I suppose a very nice nature, and direction at Maynard’s hands” (1977–84, 3:18; similar sentiments are on p. 43). The two couples celebrated holidays and took trips together to Studland Beach, Bindon Abbey (1977–84, 2:199; 1975–80, 3:70), and other places. Maynard kept Virginia informed of his various schemes such as one to build a residential hotel in Sussex and, perhaps, to seek the provostship of King’s College (1977–84, 2:199; 1975–80, 3:265).

Virginia shared fully in the teasing and good-natured banter in Bloomsbury about Maynard’s consumption habits. She approved of the purchase of a Cézanne for what they would call his imaginative life (Woolf 1975–80, 2:230), but not of a secondhand Rolls Royce for emulative purposes. Fine

Persian rugs fell somewhere in between. "Nessa has children, Maynard carpets" (Woolf 1977–84, 3:107). She found fault with Maynard's stinting of their collective biological life at the dinner table with a wine decanter that was "not entirely full" and sometimes filled with "cheap cherry brandy" (Woolf 1975–80, 4:50).

In 1927 Virginia contributed to the *Charleston Bulletin*, a paper brought out by Vanessa Bell's children, a whimsical and affectionate pseudobiography of Maynard titled "Tiltoniad: The Life and Adventures of Mr. and Mrs. Keynes." This was part of a series by Virginia and the children on "Eminent Charlestonians" (pace Lytton Strachey) with text by Virginia and illustrations by the precocious Quentin Bell. "Tiltoniad" is mentioned in a letter to Vanessa (Woolf 1975–80, 3:415), but the manuscript was only discovered a few years ago and purchased by the British Library. It is not yet processed and available for public use. The biography has eighteen short chapters revolving around significant moments in Maynard's life, most treated very briefly. His service during the war is assessed as follows:

> Mr. Keynes
> Because of his brains
> During the war
> Became richer than before

Chapter 7 contains an illustration showing Maynard dictating "to Lloyd George precisely how the world should be ruled for the next million years." It was reported that when Maynard purchased the *Nation* magazine, the capitalization and italics of the word *nation* were ignored and there was much excitement in all quarters about this supposed coup d'état. Eventually the crisis was averted by King George. Finally, an account is given by Virginia of Maynard's supposed valedictory address.

> Having married Madame Lopakova and stabilised the peseta, having acquired undying glory and uncounted Abyssinean pots, Maynard issued at last upon that ultimate peak of empire—vide licet the Rock of Gibralter—, where, wrapped in the Union Jack, grasping the Trident, and crowned with Thor's Belt (or the Great Bear) he addressed the assembled parties of the world in their conglomerated Blue Jackets upon Glands, Gold, and Birth Control: thus consummating a career, and putting climax to a work, which assuredly has no counterpart elsewhere on the habitable globe.

By the end of the 1920s Virginia had settled into a warm affection for both Lydia and Maynard that lasted until the end. She reported to her diary on 21 April 1928: "Dined with Lydia and Maynard: two couples, elderly, childless distinguished. He and she both urbane and admirable. Grey comes at Maynard's temples. He is finer looking now: not with us pompous or great: simple, with his mind working always, on Russian, Bolshevists, glands, genealogies; always the proof of a remarkable mind when it overflows thus vigorously into byepaths. . . . Lydia is composed and controlled. She says very sensible things" (Woolf 1977–84, 3:181). The following diary entry from 2 October 1938, as war loomed, reflects the relationship in the final years. "M. and Lydia very congenial—dear old M. so sanguine, so powerful, somehow lovable too, and Lord how brilliant. I kissed him. Hope all is forgotten and forgiven. A life time—what remains—of peace now" (5:179).

Virginia Woolf, Economist

Maynard recumbent, but with a stock of ideas. Bentham the origin of evil.
—Virginia Woolf, diary entry (10 March 1938)

Virginia had no formal training in economics, or in any other academic subject, for that matter. But she was exceptionally widely read and a quick study, and she was interested in a broad range of economic topics, even if they might not be recognized as "economic" by the modern economist. There is abundant evidence that she read Maynard's work as it came out, starting with *The Economic Consequences of the Peace*, which she described as "a book that influences the world without being in the least a work of art: a work of morality" (Woolf 1977–84, 2:33). She also knew and interacted with other prominent economists over her lifetime. Gerald Shove, the Cambridge economist and Maynard's close friend, was for a while on the fringes of the Bloomsbury Group. She met from time to time with Ralph Hawtrey. Her early recollections of Cambridge May Week included "gallopading round the room with Hawtrey" (Woolf 1976, 151). When Hawtrey, together with Saxon Sidney-Turner, came to visit the Stephen sisters on vacation in 1905, they were a "great trial." "They sit silent, absolutely silent, all the time; occasionally they escape to a corner and chuckle over a Latin joke. Perhaps they are falling in love with Nessa; who knows?" (Woolf 1975–80, 1:208). After the move to Gordon Square the relationship with Hawtrey thawed somewhat. Virginia recalls trying to persuade him "that there is such a thing as atmosphere in literature" (Woolf 1976, 168).

And there were other economists. Hubert Henderson, not a great favorite, was editor of the *Nation* while Leonard was literary editor. "Maynard is his standby. Bloomsbury his pest" (Woolf 1977–84, 2:268). She knew but did not much like Sidney and Beatrice Webb, and she regretted that "the great Keynes" was "completely under their sway" (Woolf 1975–80, 3:289). After dining with Frank Ramsey at the Keynes', she described him as "something like a Darwin, broad, thick, powerful, and a great mathematician, and clumsy to boot. Honest I should say, a true Apostle" (Woolf 1977–84, 2:231). When depression struck and Britain went off the gold standard, Virginia sat "talking economics and politics" for a long time with Richard Kahn (4:45). We must conclude when we read in Virginia's diary that, after a dinner party with economists, she complained to them she did not "know how to invest her emotional capital," that she was influenced to some degree by their way of thinking and vocabulary (2:231).

The public policy question that puzzled Virginia most was why women had not had more impact on society, politics, culture, and the economy. She recoiled at the suggestion, often made at the time, that the explanation was biological—that women were physically unable to perform in these spheres as well as men. She turned this question over in her essays, fiction, and correspondence with friends. She found it especially puzzling that even after the Industrial Revolution women had not performed as one might have expected. "There they remain, even in the early part of the nineteenth century, a vast body, living, marrying, bearing children in dull obscurity until at last we begin to wonder whether there was something in their condition itself—in the age at which they married, the number of children they bore, the privacy they lacked, the incomes they had not, the conventions which stifled them, and the education they never received which so affected them that though the middle class is the great reservoir from which we draw our distinguished men it has thrown up singularly few women to set beside them" (Woolf 1986–94, 4:419). In her first novel, *The Voyage Out* (1915), a male character, Hirst, is aghast that the heroine Rachel had reached the age of twenty-four without having read Gibbon (Woolf [1915] 1990, 158). But then he wondered, as the economist Laurence Summers would wonder nearly a century later, whether, as a woman, she could ever do so with complete understanding and whether her problems of comprehension arose from nature or nurture. "'It's awfully difficult to tell about women,' Hirst mused, 'how much, I mean, is due to lack of training, and how much is native incapacity. I don't see myself why you shouldn't understand—only I suppose you've had an absurd life until now—you've just walked in a crocodile [a line of school girls], I suppose with your hair down your back'" (159). Rachel found herself unable to respond. "When Rachel tried to explain, she found it very difficult. She could not say that she found the vision of herself walking in a crocodile with her hair down her back peculiarly unjust and horrible, nor could she explain why Hirst's assumption of the superiority of his nature and experience had seemed to her not only galling but terrible—as if a gate had clanged in her face" (160).

The explanation for why women had not performed better through history, Virginia concluded, lay in a kind of economic determinism. The answer was not primarily with biology, the restricted suffrage, the institution of marriage, or religious values, but in the distribution of income and wealth. Because they did not have income or wealth they did not have education, privacy, or leisure time. And the process was self-regenerative. Another character, Hewet, remarks: "The daughters have to give way to the sons; the sons have to be educated; they have to bully and shove for their wives and families, and so it all comes over again. And meanwhile there are the women in the background. . . . Do you really think the vote will do you any good?" (221). This economic determinism is the theme of two lectures to Cambridge women's colleges that became Virginia's powerful essay *A Room of One's Own* (1929). There she argued that women had contributed relatively little because they did not have command over capital (real estate) or free time with which to make contributions outside the home. In her second essay on this theme, *Three Guineas* (1938), she developed a more complex argument, based evidently in part on the ideas of Thorstein Veblen, that men driven by the instinct of emulation had taken control of the organs of power such as government, education, the military, the church, and the professions, and they wasted resources on competitive conspicuous consumption. Even though these men had established a strong patrimony that allowed them to pursue their emulative games on a grand scale, leading often to exploitation of women and to violence and warfare, if women with their different private experiences and more benevolent behavioral drives could be integrated more effectively into society, the world would be a better place. She enraged her critics, including Maynard, by illustrating *Three Guineas* with photographs showing the absurd regalia worn by a general, heralds, a university procession, a judge, and an archbishop, all presumably under the influence of Veblen's need for conspicuous consumption. Maynard might have sensed that this touch was aimed directly at him. Two years before in an article for the *Listener* titled "Art and the State," he had called for more "public shows and ceremonies" like the late King's Jubilee for which he believed there was a public craving. "Are we convinced that this emotion is barbaric, childish, or bad? I see no reason to suppose so. At any rate the provision of proper opportunities for the satisfaction of this almost universal human need should rank high in the arts of government; and a system of society which unduly neglects them may prove to have done so to its peril" (Keynes 1982, 346).

Virginia was clear about reforms in *A Room of One's Own*. Redistribution of income and wealth would rectify other inequalities in society. She was more tentative in *Three Guineas* because now she saw that the problem had deeper roots in the powerful human instinct of emulation. She was particularly concerned that if just a few women were invited as tokens into the patriarchy, they would be assimilated to prevailing male values, and there would be no significant change overall. The only long-run solutions to the problems identified in *Three Guineas*, Virginia implied, must be through reform of higher education. Her recommendations to the universities come straight from Bloomsbury. "Now since history and biography—the only evidence available to an outsider—seem to prove that the old education of the old colleges breeds neither a particular respect for liberty nor a particular hatred of war it is clear you must rebuild your college differently. . . . Do not have chapels. Do not have museums and libraries with chained books and first editions under glass. Let the pictures and the books be new and always changing. . . . The poor college must teach only the arts that can be taught cheaply and practised by poor people; such as medicine, mathematics, music, painting, and literature. It should teach the arts of human intercourse; the arts of understanding other people's lives and minds, and the little arts of talk, of dress, of cookery that are allied with them. . . . The teachers should be drawn from the good livers as well as from the good thinkers" (Woolf 1938, 49–50).

Maynard did not offer an opinion publicly on *Three Guineas*, but Quentin Bell (1972, 2:205), Virginia's nephew and biographer, reports confidently that Keynes thought it contained a "silly" argument and certainly was not timely as the war clouds darkened over Europe.

Economic Progress or Civilization?

> I draw the conclusion that, assuming no important wars and no important increase in population, the *economic problem* may be solved, or be at least within sight of solution, within a hundred years. This means that the economic problem is not—if we look into the future—*the permanent problem of the human race*. . . . Will this be a benefit? If one believes at all in the real values of life, the prospect at least opens up the possibility of benefit.
> —John Maynard Keynes, "Economic Possibilities for Our Grandchildren" (1930)

> "And what d'you feel about immortality, Maynard?" I asked. "I am an idealist," said Maynard, "and therefore on the whole I suppose I think that something may continue. Clearly the brain is the only exciting thing—matter does not exist."
> —Virginia Woolf, diary entry (27 December 1931)

There is ample evidence that Virginia read a good deal of Maynard's economic work as it was in process or recently published. She was also acquainted in a general way with the policy implications of his evolving macroeconomic theory, and she was not very comfortable with them. She commented to Francis Birrell in September 1933, while Maynard was still working out the proposals that would flow from the *General Theory*, about the political implications of macroeconomic intervention by the state: "We are going over to Tilton, to be converted by Maynard to what I suspect of being a form of Fascism" (Woolf 1975–80, 5:222). It is clear also that Maynard read and commented on much of Virginia's work, too, both her fiction and her essays. She was annoyed that he seemed unenthusiastic about her second novel *Night and Day*, but she was pleased that he liked *The Common Reader* (Woolf 1977–84, 3:15). He expressed a preference for her relatively conventional novel *The Years* over the more abstract *The Waves* (Woolf 1977–84, 5:80), and he was especially fond of her reminiscences for the Memoir Club. He found her essay on Gibbon—a Bloomsbury hero—one of the best pieces he knew on that subject. Maynard acknowledged that Virginia, "who reads all of them," was his guide through "memoirs and biographies" (Keynes 1982, 330, 331), even though she was certainly not his guide through important questions in economics.

So if Maynard found little of interest in what Virginia considered to be her most original economic ideas contained in *A Room of One's Own* and

Three Guineas, and if Virginia expressed doubts about Maynard's plea for government attention to aggregate demand, what could they have had in common in economic discussion? The answer may lie in a body of doctrine that the modern economist might not consider "economic," but the Bloomsburys definitely did. One of the unifying elements in Bloomsbury thought was a social philosophy developed mainly by Roger Fry with inputs from G. E. Moore, propagated especially by Clive Bell, and explored by all the others in various ways. The central hypothesis was that progress by the human race involved much more than economic growth. Progress, they insisted, must be to some preferred state of being that they called "civilization." To explore this idea further they postulated that human life is divided roughly into three spheres of activity that are more or less self-explanatory from their titles. First there is the "active," or "biological life," wherein people provide for their conventional needs for food, drink, shelter, procreation, and so forth. Then there is an emulative life that humans may control but probably cannot eliminate altogether from their existence; it is essentially wasteful because emulative competition is endless and empty. Finally, there is the imaginative life—the life of the mind—that includes all the arts, literature, and pure science. This last category contains the distinctly human elements of existence and yields results to humans essentially different from the other two forms of life. A truly "civilized" society, Clive Bell insisted, was one in which the imaginative life of citizens was as rich as it could possibly be.

Although the Bloomsburys were quite certain that the imaginative life was most important to humans, they were never agreed on precisely what it should contain or how much it would be possible to achieve. Maynard assured them that the economic means required to support a full imaginative life would be available quite soon, thanks to capital accumulation and technological change, but as he explained in the quotation at the head of this section, he was uneasy about whether humans would be able to respond satisfactorily to the opportunity. The challenge was, as far as he could see, psychological rather than economic. The distinctive contribution Virginia made to Maynard's musing on this subject was to reflect in her writings, sometimes obliquely, on several things: first, what the imaginative life looked like. Would you recognize it when you saw it? Second, what conditions would have to be met and devices employed to promote the imaginative life in a civilization? Third, what were the most serious obstacles likely to be faced in achieving this objective? And finally, what policies should be in place to meet the goal?

In his reflections on how to make a "civilization" in his book by that name, Bell (1928, 149) argued that the main challenge to achieving a civilization was to nurture a small cadre of aesthetes with "a sense of values" and "reason enthroned" who would patronize, and in some sense lead, those who practiced the arts and literature. The aesthetes would act like yeast, in time leavening the whole bread of society with their values. In Bell's imagined society, the shortage of resources would mean that many would for a time have to act like "slaves" of the aesthetes. Conditions would eventually get better, but for a while the wants of the masses would have to be suppressed for the greater good of society in the long run.

With these views of Maynard and Clive Bell, Virginia profoundly disagreed. For starters she was dubious about Maynard's optimistic forecast of the results of saving and technological change; human failings, she feared, would get in the way. For example, she criticized a study that prophesied enormous bounty from the development of electricity. "It is a fascinating little model, but as tends to be the case with all forecasts of this kind, too much stress seems to be laid upon the development of electricity and too little upon the development of humanity" (Woolf 1986–94, 2:285). She introduced into the discussion of civilization the theme of income and wealth distribution that dominated her reflections on other economic topics; because she could not see the Elysium of unlimited income and wealth coming any time soon, she was confident that a satisfactory distribution of income and wealth was as critical to achieving the imaginative life gradually as it was to improving the status of women and to destroying the roots of conflict. She thought that it was a dangerous mistake to ignore pockets of poverty when celebrating the growth of total output. Some of her most poignant comments on this issue are contained in her first novel *The Voyage Out*, written when the early discussions about civilization within Bloomsbury were most intense. During the war years the Bloomsburys felt compelled to explore the meaning of civilization because the British propaganda machine kept announcing that this was a war to preserve "civilization." Clive Bell's book was started then but was not published until 1928. One of the characters in *The Voyage Out*, about to embark on an ocean voyage, drives through London and is impressed by the products of this manufacturing hub. But then she is reminded that this apparent prosperity is at the expense of the poor. "For some reason it appeared to her as a small golden tassel on the edge of a vast cloak. . . . Mrs. Ambrose understood that after all it is the ordinary thing to be poor, and that London is the city of innumerable poor people" (Woolf [1915] 1990, 4, 5). During the voyage Richard Dalloway, who would have a more prominent role in a later novel, advises the heroine Rachel Vinrace always to keep a vision before her as an organizing principle: "A human being is not a set of compartments, but an organism. Imagination, Miss Vinrace; use your imagination; that's where you young Liberals fail. Conceive the world as a whole" (63). But, Dalloway admits, an obstacle to achieving vision and imagination may be "the misery of the poor" (65). Another character reports that one of his three favorite authors is Henry George, whose scheme for wealth redistribution in *Progress and Poverty* (1879) was a favorite of the British Fabians, with whom Virginia's husband, Leonard, was closely involved (Woolf [1915] 1990, 50). Virginia often denounced the doctrine that happiness for everyone resulted from accumulation of goods and services and therefore a serious reduction in social utility would result from taxing even the very rich. On the contrary, she observed, since the very rich often did not seem to be very happy, it followed that they could be taxed without great social cost. The distribution of some of their wealth among the poor would help lay the foundation for civilization. She rejoiced in telling the story of Thomas Coutts, whom she described as the richest man in Britain in the nineteenth century, but whose life nevertheless was filled with misery. Indeed, Coutts wrote to a friend "my spirit's gone, and my mind worn and harras'd," and "I am now rather an object of pity than resentment" (Woolf 1986–94, 3:187). It seemed clear to Virginia that the likes of Mr. Coutts would barely miss a little of their income and wealth if it were extracted from them to alleviate poverty.

In addition to a reduction in poverty and a reasonable distribution of income, Virginia, like Maynard, suggested that civilization required the right set of attitudes toward life and style, and in particular it required that limits be placed on the Benthamite attitude that the production of goods and services mattered most to society. On driving through London, a character in *The Voyage Out* observes: "It appeared that this was a great manufacturing place, where the people were engaged in making things, as though the West End, with its electric lamps, its vast plate-glass windows all shining yellow, its carefully-finished houses, and tiny live figures trotting on the pavement, or bowled along on wheels in the road, was the finished work" (Woolf [1915] 1990, 4). But, if the right attitude was not to be found in manufacturing, then where? Perhaps in the arts, or in politics! Richard Dalloway, himself a politician, makes a case for the latter over the former: "A gross commonplace set of people; but we see both sides; we may be clumsy, but we do our best to get a grasp of things. Now your artists find things in a mess, shrug their shoulders, turn aside to their visions—which I grant may be very beautiful—and leave things in a mess" (39). Nor did academics seem to be the answer. Mrs. Dalloway comments on several fellow voyagers: "The worst of it is, these people—a man and his wife and a niece—might have been, one feels, just like everybody else, if they hadn't got swallowed up by Oxford or Cambridge or some such place, and been made cranks of. The man's really delightful (if he'd cut his nails), and the woman has a fine face, only she dresses, of course, in a potato sack, and wears her hair like a Liberty's shopgirl's" (44). And another passenger wondered "whether it was necessary that thought and scholarship should thus maltreat their bodies, and should thus elevate their minds to a very high tower from which the human race appeared to them like rats and mice squirming on the flat" (213). But with this all said, Mr. Dalloway acknowledged that the academics did have a special role. "'It's the philosophers, it's the scholars,' he continued, 'they're the people who pass the torch, who keep the light burning by which we live. Being a politician doesn't necessarily blind one to that'" (72).

In contrast to Clive Bell's recommendation that to achieve civilization it was necessary only to increase the number of aesthetically sensitive patrons of the arts, Virginia thought it would be necessary to attend to a balance of attitudes and behavioral drives within individuals and within society overall. She was particularly uneasy about the degree of "worldliness" demonstrated by some, including Maynard, meaning presumably attention to the biological and emulative needs above imaginative ones. But she appreciated that worldliness made the world go round, and the challenge was to moderate rather than eliminate it: "These were the people with money, and to them rather than to others was given the management of the world. Put among them some one more vital, who cared for life or for beauty, and what an agony, what a waste would they inflict on him if he tried to share with them and not to scourge!" (Woolf [1915] 1990, 137). Virginia's position, like that of the other Bloomsburys, was that all segments of society could contribute to the imaginative life. One character in *The Voyage Out* says of the landed gentry: "They have never heard of Gibbon. They only care for their pheasants and their peasants. They are great big men who look so fine on horseback, as people must have done, I think, in the days of the great wars. Say what you like against them—they are animal, they are unintellectual; they don't read themselves, and they don't want others to read, but they are some of the finest and the kindest human beings on the face of the earth! You would be surprised at some of the stories I could tell. You have never guessed, perhaps, at all the romances that go on in the heart of the country. There are the people, I feel among whom Shakespeare will be born if he is ever born again. In those old houses, up among the Downs" (209–10).

The Imaginative Life: What Is It?

> Within the last ten years the authorities of the National Galleries have refused to purchase works by Cezanne, and more lately even to accept on loan important examples of the master. . . . Even if it is inevitable that the official world should move with a slower velocity, and that the voice of Mr. [Roger] Fry, swiftly voyaging into undiscovered lands amidst new flowers and untasted fruits, should seem to come from the wilderness rather than from the Promised Land of the future, one cannot but sigh a little that this should be so.
> —John Maynard Keynes, *Social, Political, and Literary Writings* (1982)

As both Maynard and Virginia appreciated, before progress could be made in achieving civilization and strengthening the imaginative life, it was necessary to understand precisely what the imaginative life was. Roger Fry, following Tolstoy and G. E. Moore, suggested that it was mainly about communication of aesthetic emotion through the arts. The most successful communicator in the visual arts, Fry believed, was Paul Cézanne. Virginia tested this hypothesis about communication sometimes through the careers of those she considered especially effective communicators in literature. Michel Montaigne, that "great master of the art of life," was one of her favorites. Of his essays she wrote, noting in particular his emphasis on the Moorean values of love and candor: "These essays are an attempt to communicate a soul. On this point at least he is explicit. It is not fame that he wants; it is not that men shall quote him in years to come; he is setting up no statue in the market-place; he wishes only to communicate his soul. Communication is health; communication is truth; communication is happiness. To share is our duty; to go down boldly and bring to light those hidden thoughts which are the most diseased; to conceal nothing; to pretend nothing; if we are ignorant to say so; if we love our friends to let them know it" (Woolf 1986–94, 4:76, 78). To the question of why aesthetic communication was crucial to the imaginative life Virginia did not attempt an answer. "Why this overmastering desire to communicate with others? Is the beauty of the world enough, or is there, elsewhere, some explanation of the mystery? To this what answer can there be? There is none" (4:79).

James Joyce was another writer for whom Virginia had great respect as a communicator of aesthetic emotion. Yet for her his gift still remained elusive. "In contrast with those whom we have called materialists, Mr. Joyce is spiritual; he is concerned at all costs to reveal the flickerings of that innermost flame which flashes its messages through the brain, and in order to preserve it he disregards with complete courage whatever seems to him adventitious, whether it be probability, or coherence, or any other of those signposts which for generations have served to support the imagination of a reader called upon to imagine what he can neither touch nor see" (4:161). Virginia believed that effective communication by an artist required just the right mix of involvement in society and solitude. "His state then is a precarious one. He must expose himself to life; he must risk the danger of being led away and tricked by her deceitfulness; he must seize her treasure from her and let her trash run to waste. But at a certain moment he must leave the company and withdraw, alone, to that mysterious room where his booty is hardened and fashioned into permanence by processes which, if they elude the critic, hold for him so profound a fascination" (4:405).

But the artists were not the only dwellers in the imaginative life. There were also the aesthetes, the patrons of the arts who were celebrated in Clive Bell's book *Civilization*. Virginia saw them as collaborators with the artists in a seamless process. "To read a book well, one should read it as if one were writing it. Begin not by sitting on the bench among the judges, but by standing in the dock with the criminal. Be his fellow worker, become his accomplice. Even, if you wish merely to read books, begin by writing them" (4:390).

When exploring the nature of aesthetic communication, Virginia developed a point made by Roger Fry in his "Essay in Aesthetics" that must have resonated with Maynard. She agreed with Fry against Tolstoy that any attempt to incorporate a moral or a message in a work of art interrupted the communication of aesthetic emotion. In a review of fellow Bloomsbury novelist E. M. Forster's writings, she complains that social theory intrudes too much in *Howards End*. "So, exerting ourselves to find out the meaning, we step from the enchanted world of imagination, where our faculties work freely, to the twilight world of theory, where only our intellect functions dutifully" (4:499). As one way of understanding the successful imaginative life, Virginia reflected on the aesthetes who would benefit therefrom. They are "by nature or by circumstances in a position where they can use their faculties to the full upon things that are of importance. They are not necessarily happy or successful, but there is a zest in their presence, and interest in their doings. They seem alive all over" (4:431).

All the arts had had a place in the imaginative life, Virginia insisted, "music, letters, sculpture, and architecture" (4:243). In Britain, however, there had been a singular neglect of music, and the society would ultimately pay for it. "To be civilised is to have taken the measure of our own capabilities and to hold them in a perfect state of discipline; but one of our gifts has, as we conceive, so slight a power of beneficence, so unmeasured a power of harm, that far from cultivating it we have done our best to cripple and stifle it. We look upon those who have given up their lives to the service of this god as Christians regard the fanatic worshippers of some eastern idol. This arises perhaps from an uneasy foreknowledge that when the pagan gods come back the god we have never worshipped will have his revenge upon us. It will be the god of music who will breathe madness into our brains, crack the walls of our temples, and drive us in loathing of our rhythmless lives to dance and circle for ever in obedience to his voice" (1:29–30).

Since Virginia was convinced that works of art play a central role in the imaginative life, she made heroic efforts to specify them. For example: "There is one peculiarity which real works of art possess in common. At each fresh reading one notices some change in them, as if the sap of life ran in their leaves, and with skies and plants they had the power to alter their shape and colour from season to season." And "a book in order to live, must have the power of changing as we change, and we have to ask ourselves whether it is possible that Charlotte Bronte can have kept pace with us" (2:27).

But if works of art were central to the imaginative life so also was wild nature. Nature took on a new significance for the Bloomsburys during World War I when virtually all of them left central London, for part of their time at least, to take up country living in Sussex, Wiltshire, Surrey, and elsewhere. They also spent more time in rural settings in countries around the Mediterranean. Maynard moved into the Charleston farmhouse to write *The Economic Consequences of the Peace* and then took a lease on Tilton, the property next door. There was considerable discussion, especially among the critics of Bloomsbury, about the meaning of this out-migration. Was it retreat from reality or avoidance of social responsibilities? Virginia argued that it was neither and that closeness to nature was a complement and stimulus to the imaginative life. Wordsworth was an inspiration in this regard: "It is no mere curiosity or a taste for the picturesque that drives him to walk out among the hills, and to know all that can be known about the things that grow there. Rather he is trying to read the signs which, whatever their meaning, are to him rather made in vain. And, conscious as he is of a beautifully adjusted symmetry in all natural things, his condemnation is most severe of those whose arrogance leads them in any way, by their buildings or plantations to violate the order" (1:107–8). Samuel Taylor Coleridge, she thought, was a rare aesthete capable of enjoying all the arts and nature, too. "If Coleridge heard music he wanted hours and hours of Mozart and Purcell; if he liked a picture he fell into a trance in front of it; if he saw a sunset he almost lost consciousness in the rapture of gazing at it" (2:224).

Like Roger Fry, Virginia observed that appreciation of nature in the imaginative life was more intense outside Britain than within. In a review of the autobiography of a colonial civil servant stationed in Burma, she wrote: "He determined that he would set himself to learn the clearly visible faith which makes the Eastern life so different from the Western, and decided that the fundamental difference was to be found in the consciousness, which the Burmese at least still cherish, of the live presence, the message, of nature. Inspired with this belief he lived on in the midst of the people and put to them the questions that no European asks of another: 'What is it you think of life? What is man's soul?' The state of civilisation in which these questions are naked and urgent provides also an atmosphere of such clarity that very broad answers are possible" (1:172). She admired the American Transcendentalists, and Henry David Thoreau in particular. "From nature he had learnt both silence and stoicism. He had never spoken of the things that had moved him most in his private fortunes. But from nature, too, he had learnt to be content, not thoughtless or selfishly content, and certainly not with resignation, but with a healthy trust in the wisdom of nature, and in nature, as he says, there is no sadness" (2:138). Of Walt Whitman she remarked: "The capacity for pleasure seemed never to diminish, and the power to include grew greater and greater" (2:207). She was disgusted that the slaughter of wild animals became an obsession with Teddy Roosevelt, but she noted with some satisfaction that "Nature, outraged, sent him back with a fever in his bones from which he died years before his time. So difficult is it at this late stage of civilisation for one and the same person to have both body and brain" (3:226).

The Imaginative Life: How to Get There?

> Why should not we begin to reap spiritual fruits from our material conquests? If so, whence is to come the motive power of desirable change?
> —John Maynard Keynes, "Clissold" (1928)

> I think with dread of the readjustment of the habits and instincts of the ordinary man, bred into him for countless generations, which he may be asked to discard within a few decades.
> —John Maynard Keynes, "Economic Possibilities for Our Grandchildren" (1930)

A vital question for Virginia, addressed often in Bloomsbury gatherings, was whether the social and behavioral sciences could successfully lay out the path to the imaginative life. She was skeptical. A wise old character in *The Voyage Out* favored a theory that "made chaos triumphant, things happening for no reason at all, and every one groping about in illusion and ignorance" (Woolf [1915] 1990, 235). One of the social theories, perhaps picked up from Maynard or his economist friends, that she sought to test was that civilization would occur naturally as people got richer with the gradual replacement of work, and time devoted to the biological life, with leisure: time available for the imaginative life. As the economists might have put it to her, civilization was an income-elastic good. In her second novel, *Night and Day* (1919), the two main male figures, William Rodney and Ralph Denham, dream of escaping the workplace into the imaginative life, in the first case to write poetry and in the second to write a new history of England. They both are quite certain that with sufficient income these goals are attainable. Yet they appreciate that unless the imaginative life is grasped early, it may be lost forever: "The old conclusion to which Ralph had come when he left college still held sway in his mind, and tinged his views with the melancholy belief that life for most people compels the exercise of the lower gifts and wastes the precious ones, until it forces us to agree that there is little virtue, as well as little profit, in what once seemed to us the noblest part of our inheritance" (Woolf [1919] 1992, 104).

While writing *Night and Day*, Virginia had relatively few close male acquaintances; they included most prominently her brother's Cambridge friends, and this may be why Ralph Denham in *Night and Day* bears a striking resemblance to Maynard. Ralph's attraction to a pretty young woman had little to do with the opposite sex, reflecting Maynard's predilections at the time, and was based solely "upon common interests in impersonal topics, such as the housing of the poor, or the taxation of land values" (66). The description of Ralph by his sister Joan could hardly have been anyone else among Virginia's friends but Maynard.

> Ralph had saved, perhaps, three or four hundred pounds. Considering the sacrifices he had made in order to put by this sum it always amazed Joan to find that he used it to gamble with, buying shares and selling them again, increasing it sometimes, sometimes diminishing it, and always running the risk of losing every penny of it in a day's disaster. But although she wondered, she could not help loving him the better for his odd combination of Spartan self-control and what appeared to her romantic and childish folly. Ralph interested her more than any one else in the world, and she often broke off in the middle of one of these economic discussions, in spite of their gravity, to consider some fresh aspect of his character. (22)

Despite his adventures in the stock market Ralph seems to derive most satisfaction from groping for the imaginative life and never knowing whether he has found it. Joan asks: "Aren't you happy, Ralph?" and he replies, "No, are you? Perhaps I'm as happy as most people, though. God knows whether I'm happy or not. What is happiness?" (23). The question raised here seems to be, if Ralph (Maynard), the ultimate man of reason, cannot see clearly how to attain true happiness in the imaginative life and know it when he finds it, who can? The answer Virginia seems to suggest is that the imaginative life may be gained along many routes. It might even come during a scholar's delightful dinner party. "The lamps were lit; their lustre reflected itself in the polished wood; good wine was passed round the dinner table; before the meal was far advanced civilization had triumphed" (427). Exploring an idea proposed by Roger Fry, Virginia explains that Katherine Hilbury, with whom Ralph is finally falling in love, secretly pursues pure mathematics which, in the same way as pure science, could bring the voyager to the imaginative life without the intervention of literature, music, or the visual arts: "Upstairs alone in her room, she rose early in the morning or sat up late at night to . . . work at mathematics. No force on earth could make her confess that. Her actions when thus engaged were furtive and secretive, like those of some nocturnal animal" (34).

Conclusion

> Maynard Keynes is Bloomsbury. He wrote the [Economic] Consequences of the Peace.
> —Virginia Woolf, letter to Benedict Nicholson (24 August 1940)

Like Daniel Defoe, Henry Fielding, Charles Dickens, Tom Wolfe, and many other celebrated novelists who have engaged with economic ideas, institutions, and policies, Virginia Woolf seldom addressed her subjects head-on or advocated alternatives to them. Her posture was mainly reactive, and she preferred to be elusive rather than direct. In her many writings she had much to say about the distribution of income and wealth, the alleviation of poverty, the nature of artistic patronage in the art markets, the role of the critic in adult education, the varied audiences for poetry and prose, and other matters that she believed were essential to the attainment of civilization through the imaginative life. Her special gift might have been interpreted by the social scientist as the capacity to test social theory with an unusual data set and the laboratory of fiction. But Virginia's assertions after conducting her tests were typically tentative and modulated, and her writings were likely to be dismissed by most impatient and hard-nosed social scientists as mere light entertainment. Economists by the time she wrote were constrained by an accepted methodology that privileged models constructed with highly simplified assumptions—the antithesis of fiction—and they regarded "storytelling" as a serious breach of methodological orthodoxy. A distinctive feature of the account given in this essay is that Maynard Keynes, the most celebrated economist of his day, came to know well, to understand, and to appreciate these writings by one of the most innovative novelists of the twentieth century. He paid close attention to her essays and fiction, as she did to his economics. Biographical study of this unlikely relationship may help us appreciate some features of this economist's and this novelist's achievements that would not emerge from more conventional study of each one alone. It may also offer insights into what might be hoped for from a more intimate association of these two rather isolated cultures—economics and creative writing—in our own time.

References

Bell, Clive. 1928. *Civilization*. London: Chatto and Windus.

Bell, Quentin. 1972. *Virginia Woolf: A Biography*. London: Hogarth.

Forster, Edward Morgan. 1910. *Howards End*. London: Arnold.

Fry, Roger. [1909] 1998. An Essay in Aesthetics. In *Art and the Market: Roger Fry on Commerce in Art*, edited by Craufurd D. Goodwin. Ann Arbor: University of Michigan Press.

Goodwin, Craufurd D. 2006. The Art of an Ethical Life: Keynes and Bloomsbury. In *The Cambridge Companion to Keynes*. London: Cambridge University Press.

Keynes, John Maynard. 1920. *The Economic Consequences of the Peace*. New York: Harcourt Brace and Howe.

———. 1936. *The General Theory of Employment, Interest, and Money*. London: Macmillan.

———. 1982. *Social, Political, and Literary Writings*. Vol. 28 of *The Collected Writings of John Maynard Keynes*. London: Macmillan.

Woolf, Virginia. 1927. Tiltoniad: The Life and Adventures of Mr. and Mrs. Keynes. Supplement to the *Charleston Bulletin*, uncataloged holdings of the British Library.

———. 1929. *A Room of One's Own*. New York: Harcourt Brace.

———. 1938. *Three Guineas*. New York: Harcourt Brace.

———. 1975–80. *The Letters of Virginia Woolf*. 6 vols. Edited by Nigel Nicolson and Joanne Trautmann. London: Hogarth.

———. 1976. *Moments of Being: Unpublished Autobiographical Writings*. Edited by Jeanne Schulkind. London: Sussex University Press.

———. 1977–84. *The Diary of Virginia Woolf*. 5 vols. Edited by Anne Olivier Bell and Andrew McNeillie. New York: Harcourt Brace Jovanovich.

———. 1986–94. *The Essays of Virginia Woolf*. 4 vols. Edited by Andrew McNeillie. New York: Harcourt Brace Jovanovich.

———. [1915] 1990. *The Voyage Out*. London: Hogarth.

———. [1919] 1992. *Night and Day*. London: Penguin.

The Intimate Spaces of Community: John Maynard Keynes and the Arts

Patricia Laurence

John Maynard Keynes's early interest in the arts was nourished by a group of artistic friends who eventually became known as the Bloomsbury Group. As one of the most influential cultural and intellectual circles in England, the Bloomsbury Group did much to mold the direction of taste and accomplishments in literature and art in the early twentieth century. Keynes, a part of it, was also one of the most important figures in the history of economics. He made his reputation early, establishing himself in 1911 with his work on Indian monetary policy when he was only twenty-eight years old. He possessed power and access to leaders in the British government as one of the most important policymakers in England and the author of *The General Theory of Employment, Interest, and Money* (1936). Unlike many of the Bloomsberries, he was "worldly."

Given this background, how are we to situate him in the company of artists and writers in Bloomsbury? How am I as a literary critic without expert knowledge of Keynesian economics to enter this conversation? I mull over different biographical approaches. What are the advantages of presenting a figure not as an isolated anomaly but as part of a cultural constellation? I move to the community of Bloomsbury to focus on friendship and emotion, and the importance of the "intimate" in Keynes's career, a trend in biographical writing. This essay argues that Keynes's interest in structuring national arts policies in the last decade of his life grew out of his early sympathy and feeling for his artistic friends in Bloomsbury: the influence of the intimate on the national.

History of Political Economy 39 (annual suppl.) DOI 10.1215/00182702-2006-049

A Post-Structuralist Perspective

Evidence of Keynes's growing interest in the arts can be captured through the conversation of his early years. His web of friendship and its intellectual and emotional traces are limned in his essays, memoirs, and reviews as well as the letters to friends cited throughout this essay. This essay examines his early correspondence with one of his closest friends, Vanessa Bell, beginning in 1907; with Lydia Lopokova, who joined with Diaghilev's ballet company in London in 1922; and with Kingsley Martin, his longtime friend and editor of the *Nation*. Private letters are sometimes an undervalued source in the biographical writing of economists. Letters illustrate, as Partha Chatterjee (1993, 147) notes, "the inner spaces of community . . . the sphere of the intimate." They reveal the life of feeling, the affective life, and gossip that is often denied importance in relation to the intellectual. In this study, the voice in the letters and reviews of Keynes are read to illuminate the inner spaces of feeling and community.

In addition, letters, as Edward Said (1982, 22) has suggested, as well as memoirs and reviews, restore the "non-sequential energy of lived historical memory and subjectivity." This subjectivity then tells other stories "than the official sequential or ideological ones produced by institutional power." Keynes's letters and memoirs to his friends present hidden parts of his consciousness, expression, and changing views of the role of the arts in the British nation. This can be observed not only early in his career—a concentration in economists' life writings that D. E. Moggridge (1992) notes—but also in the later years.

The art Keynes collected and the places he lived also constitute a part of this narrative. For what is valuable in the study of literature—as a life—is the interanimation of conversations, emotions, relationships, stories, and ideas among a group of people as well as where and how they lived. This essay demonstrates, along with Craufurd Goodwin's in this volume, that an economist's community—both personal and informal institutional relationships—can be "a stimulus for reflection" in narrating his or her life. This essay emerges, then, from a post-structuralist perspective and joins a trend at the 2006 *HOPE* conference: a new attention to discourse analysis and "voice" that can be linked to the thinkers Michel Foucault and Jürgen Habermas. "Voice" and "face" in the studies of post-structuralists, as noted by Rei Terada (2001, 13), "can be seen as part of the study of emotion." This essay, emerging from a literary perspective, offers a more inclusive model of the mind and biography that indulges emotion, personal relationships, and the subjective in a way that might be antithetical to certain models of the mind and the presentation of a life in the biographies of economists. Discourse analysis broadens the notion of "text" and gives attention to speech, writing, and jargon as well as institutions, communities, architecture, and moral and social dispositions. The life of the subject, then, is a "construction" of multiple discourses embodied in the subject. It is the biographer's job to discover these discourses. Paul John Eakin, for example, in focusing on the concept of "narrative identity" in this volume, advances that "the labor" of a little girl selling watercress in the East End of London in the mid-nineteenth century "is a function and a description of herself."

In presenting different kinds of discourse here—the personal and emotional as well as the professional writings and relationships, and the community and art that surrounded him—I offer a fuller, more inclusive portrait of Keynes. Bruce Caldwell, Paul John Eakin, and Jeremy Popkin also discuss in this volume different kinds of discourse and the role of narrative in shaping identity in the biographies of economists. "Thick description," as advanced by the anthropologist Clifford Geertz, becomes a value; "polyphony" and the multiple voices and discourses in a life, as advanced by the formalist critic Michel Foucault (1977), is acknowledged. This inclusion of the personal, the social, the architectural, and the moral life questions the so-called objective perspective and voice that motivates some biographies. Such biographies can falsify, flatten, and deaden the voice of the subject and the reader's experience of it. Tiago Mata, Frederic S. Lee, and Ross Emmett (this volume) also search for this rich voice in "stories" in the oral histories of economists in various social and institutional settings. They gather information about the "community" of economists that is often absent from the public record and that, they assert, should be a part of the sociohistorical narrative of an economist's life and the discipline. And in a surprising turn, Robert Leonard (this volume), dramatizes the personal voice of an economist in his groundbreaking portrait of the inner life of Oskar Morgenstern: a "factual" re-creation.

The Early Years

Given his worldliness and global interests, how did Keynes connect with the sometimes detached artistic and intellectual community of Bloomsbury? Metaphors are often an organizing principle for those who work in the humanities, and Vanessa Bell's metaphor for Keynes's early role in Bloomsbury is apt: "You are rather like a Chinese Buddha. You sit

Vanessa Bell, *The Memoir Club* (ca. 1943). From left to right: Duncan Grant, Leonard Woolf, David Garnett, Vanessa and Clive Bell (on sofa), Maynard and Lydia Keynes (center, back), Desmond and Mary MacCarthy, Quentin Bell, E. M. Forster; portraits on wall of Virginia Woolf, Lytton Strachey, and Roger Fry (all deceased at time of painting). National Portrait Gallery. With the kind permission of Angelica Garnett.

silent . . . and manage to create an atmosphere in which all is possible." But, Bell (1907–36) added wryly, in her April 1914 letter, "Perhaps you talk more than a Buddha would." She would represent Keynes and the Bloomsbury circle in her painting *The Memoir Club*, a group of thirteen close friends who gathered beginning in 1920 to read intimate memoirs to one another that were dedicated to complete "truth." Keynes, who some said was an improbable member of this antiestablishment group, nevertheless sits in the center of the painting and this essay—Buddha-like—established in the profession of economics and in a high position in official government circles.

After 1919, and the publication of *The Economic Consequences of the Peace*, Keynes would become a public celebrity, leaving less time for his Bloomsbury friends and their artistic interests. Nevertheless, his pattern of friendships was set. The character Neville in Virginia Woolf's 1931 novel *The Waves* was, according to her husband, Leonard, modeled on Keynes. Can qualities in a fictional character enlighten us about a "life"? We learn of Neville—Keynes's father's middle name—that he is "scissors-cutting, exact" (117) and that he likes "order." We also learn from Neville of the "law" of his being:

> "But by some inscrutable law of my being sovereignty and the possession of power will not be enough. I shall always push through curtains to privacy, and want some whispered words alone." (60)

Often on the public stage, Keynes would develop a need to retreat from the stress of public life. Virginia Woolf (1985, 206) would say of Keynes in "Old Bloomsbury": "Pigs, plays, pictures—he will talk of them all. But never of Prime Ministers and peerages. Alas and alas—Maynard is not a snob." Frances Partridge reports in *Memories* that Keynes was not always the dignified economist and danced the can-can with his wife, Lydia Lopokova, the Diaghilev ballerina, at a Bloomsbury party at Tilton in 1926, parodied in Vanessa Bell's painting *The Keynes-Keynes.*

Keynes observed the experience of his artist friends, particularly the painter Duncan Grant, whom he first met in 1908 when he, Keynes, was twenty-five. Keynes "took little interest in painting" (Scrase and Croft 1983, 19) at this time, according to Dadie Rylands, a Cambridge friend. D. E. Moggridge (1992) has also documented that Keynes's friends in Bloomsbury viewed him early on as having "provincial" aesthetic tastes. His friendship with Grant and his relationship with Lydia Lopokova, beginning in 1922—both creative artists—would inspire his further understanding, admiration, and later patronage of the arts.

Vanessa Bell and Roger Fry would further sensitize Keynes to the financial plight of artists, particularly when Fry founded the Omega Workshop, in 1913–16, a commercial venture that encouraged the decorative arts. Through the workshop, artists were able to create and sell their crafts a few days a week, reserving the rest of the time for their art. Artists like Vanessa Bell, Duncan Grant, and Roger Fry made art that was adapted to "use." Some of these objects can still be seen in the Victoria and Albert Museum. And in an exhibit, Art Made Modern: Roger Fry's Vision of Art, at the Courtauld Institute in January 2000, many of the home furnishings, carpets, pottery, dresses, printed books and woodcuts, and crafts were on display. Keynes's art catalogs with his annotations (in the Modern Archives, King's College) also document the continued development of his tastes in these early years.

Vanessa Bell, *The Keynes-Keynes* (1927?). Copyright Estate of Vanessa Bell. Courtesy of Henrietta Garnett.

Keynes, as has been noted by others, is distinguished from other economists in his own attention to voice and language in his writing. He not only won math prizes at Eton but also came in first in the English essay. Robert Skidelsky (1992, 317) describes his writing style as "full of fancy, sparkle and paradox." Keynes wrote about economics and history, as G. B. Shaw said, with "interest" and "inextinguishable sparks of culture." These "sparks of culture" would fly from the world of literature, painting, and theater into his graceful and cultured writing about the arts as well as economics, and many a literary critic has commented on the readability of *The Economic Consequences of the Peace*. Always sensitive to language, Keynes (1982, 42) would criticize Karl Marx and Friedrich Engels in a January 1935 letter to Shaw not only for their economic principles but also for "their vile manner of writing." Savoring language, he would communicate to his friend Kingsley Martin, the editor of the *Nation*, "Words ought to be a little wild, for they are the assaults of thought upon the unthinking" (Keynes 1982, 28:154).

Keynes often went to the ballet and theater, and wrote short puff pieces for the *Nation* and *Athenaeum* beginning in 1923. His public voice in the arts—though grounded in his own longtime personal commitment—developed in tandem with his relationship with Lydia Lopokova. He was an amateur but sensitive critic.

After the War

Lydia was persuaded to live at Gordon Square while Keynes lived most of the week at Webb's Court, Cambridge, working on the King's College Council, writing and riding with Sebastian Sprott (a homosexual who represented Keynes's "old way of life"). He would marry Lydia in 1925, though Bloomsbury friends would look on in dismay. Virginia Woolf (1977, 76) expressed the ambivalent attitude toward Lydia in a November 1923 letter to Jacques Raverat: "Poor little wretch, trapped in Bloomsbury . . . nobody can take her seriously." And then in 1925 before Keynes's marriage, a concession: "Little Lydia, I like: how does her mind work? Like a lark soaring, a sort of glorified instinct inspires her: I suppose a very nice nature, and direction at Maynard's hand" (181). Bloomsbury ambivalence remained, but Lydia brought charm and lively conversation to her relationship with Keynes and was painted by Bloomsbury artists and often sketched by Pablo Picasso.

Despite Bloomsbury's view, Keynes would be drawn affectionately to the Russian ballerina because of her charm, talent, and humorous infelicities with the English language. He described her not only as "a poet" but also as having "more literature" in her letters than well-known novelists. He never tired of her myriad charming ways of expressing affection (with the assistance of her ever-present dictionary) in her letters: "Miely miely Maynorachka . . . Milenky . . . with caresses large as sea I stretch out to you . . . I send you a chirp from under the left breast . . . I place melodious strokes all over you . . . I send you my pulsations." He would respond with more reserve but affectionately, "My dearest pupsik, My mother came in this morning to bring me an anti-baldness mixture which she says is very good (you will have to rub it on) and to tell me that you were dancing at the Coliseum last night" (Hill and Keynes 1989, 337).

Their letters reveal not only Keynes's growing affection for Lydia—they wrote almost every day—but Keynes's daily involvement with the arts, dance, and theater in the years following World War I.

In 1922 when Keynes first renewed his relationship with Lydia, he would write to her about becoming a ballet "producer" in order to survive economically and to find opportunities to perform. His sympathy with the plight of artists like Lydia is evident in his letters as she borrows money from Vanessa Bell to pay for lunch and ballet skirts (letter, 14 October 1922, in Hill and Keynes 1989, 58). He suggested creative new economic relationships, urging Lydia to pay Leonid Massine, the great Russian dancer and choreographer, 50 pounds a week as the producer and choreographer of her ballet "Togo: Or the Noble Savage."

Keynes also introduced her to Duncan Grant, "a real scene painter," she said, for producing the decor and costumes, and Duncan looked forward to involvement in "Togo" (letter, 22 September 1923, in Bell 1907–36). Believing always in the value of the artistic production, Keynes advised Lydia that "noble failure is preferable to cheap success, that financial ruin was not so desperately important"—though her hiring of Duncan Grant put her in conflict with her friend the choreographer Vera Bowen (letter, 31 October 1922, in Hill and Keynes 1989, 64). Bowen would refer to Lydia's new ideas for economic arrangements as "Keynes's plans." Mary Glasgow (1975, 262), the secretary of the Committee for the Encouragement of the Arts (CEMA), also noted that in discussions with Keynes in 1940, "it was standards that mattered, and the preservation of serious professional enterprise."

Keynes—sitting in the center of the Bloomsbury circle—helped make things possible for other artist friends also, many of whom would manage their financial lives "with a mixture of family wealth and such money as they could pick up on the edges of literary and artistic London" (Moggridge 1992, 218). Vanessa Bell and Keynes were close, and their extensive correspondence—arguably more intimate than his with Virginia Woolf—intertwines gossip and personal economic matters. Vanessa shored up her modest income like Lydia, and these letters reveal her frequent consultation about personal and professional financing; investments; better exchange rates when staying in Cassis, France; managing income for a mentally disabled sister, Laura; helping arrange for Duncan Grant's and David Garnett's conscientious objector status during World War I; intervening with David Leach to settle a broken Queen Mary decoration contract that she had made in 1935; renting the Gordon Square apartment; consulting about artists' organizations that marketed her paintings; and obtaining a guaranteed income each year. And then there were the times when she would write, "I am absolutely penniless" (letter, 15 March 1919, in Bell 1907–36), to which Keynes would respond with his usual generosity.

A History of Feeling: The Shift from "I" to "We"

In addition to these letters, there were the conversations, relationships, and the philosophy of the group engaged as they were in talk and appreciation of the aesthetic advanced in the philosophy of G. E. Moore and the aesthetic discussions of Roger Fry. This philosophy can be gleaned from Keynes's early essays. Moore, an influential teacher at Cambridge University, in his well-known chapter "The Ideal," espoused a philosophy toward life and art that sustained Keynes throughout his life: the value and pleasures of conversation and the enjoyment of beautiful objects.

In September 1938, with the war approaching, Keynes wrote a memoir, "My Early Beliefs," in which he looked back with skepticism on his youthful intellectual circle, the Bloomsbury Group. In this essay, originally delivered to the Memoir Club, he praised its "merits—our charm, our intelligence, our unworldliness, our affection," but targeted its "naiveté" before World War I. "I can see us as water-spiders," writes Keynes (1972, 450), "gracefully skimming, as light and reasonable as air, the surface of the stream without any contact at all with the eddies and currents underneath." A sober 1930s economist had since come into contact with those "currents underneath": the terrible loss of lives in World War I; the incompetence of the Versailles Treaty; the 1930s depression and unemployment problem; the Spanish Civil War and the growing fascist movements in Europe. Keynes (1972, 446–47) is here in dialogue with his youthful self, acknowledging in hindsight the "luxury" of Bloomsbury "individualism" and its repudiation of a "personal liability . . . to obey general rules." Keynes would describe himself as an "immoralist" during this period, behavior that led D. H. Lawrence to describe some in the set, including Keynes, as dark, morally menacing "beetles" in British society, given to what he labeled the cult of homosexuality.

However, in 1938, Keynes (1972, 244) repudiated his early stance, asserting that one can no longer live "secure in the undisturbed individualism which was the extraordinary achievement of the early Edwardian days." Keynes was not alone in this belief. Even in 1911 when he lived among the Bloomsberries at Brunswick Square, the intellectuals and writers in his circle—though naturally cultivating their own individualism and talents—were beginning to write about the kind of "civilization" they lived in and to act on behalf of others in the nation. This stance was strengthened after the devastations of World War I. The extension of knowledge through education and the arts to people in other classes and provinces in England was a trend among Cambridge intellectuals. Generally, critics will demonstrate Keynes's commitment to the national arts by citing his projects at the end of his life, but the notion of the "enlargement of knowledge" was in the air in Bloomsbury and among Cambridge friends from the beginning of his career.

Examples of the trend to extend education and the arts—to give up the coveted "individualism"—are Bertrand Russell's turn from philosophy to pragmatism in 1912 and Virginia Woolf's experiment in teaching literature and history to working-class women. In the early part of the century the Home University Library of Modern Knowledge flourished, publishing inexpensive books written by scholars and philosophers for a popular audience. One of the earliest books it commissioned in 1911 was Russell's *Problems of Philosophy*, in which Russell thanks Keynes for his contributions to the study of induction. In this work, Russell turns from a study of logic to a theory of knowledge, concentrating his philosophical attention on the notion of a "table." Philosophically troubled by the fact that "a table is not strictly known to us at all," but only by sense data, memory, and induction, Russell ([1911] 1959, 161) labels this our "experience" of the world. As a result, Russell was led to distinguish between two kinds of knowledge: of "truth" and of "things." Out of this he developed an appreciation of experience and the importance of the "impulse to share knowledge." Though attacked for his shift of interest—he had recently completed *Principia Mathematica*—and becoming a "popularizer," Russell was increasingly concerned with connecting "knowledge" to the "real" world.

He was not alone. Virginia Woolf taught evening classes in British history, literature, and composition to working-class women from 1905 to 1907 at Morley College on Waterloo Road, a college founded in 1880 by a textile magnate and temperance worker. Even G. E. Moore gave classes at Morley in metaphysics in 1908. Woolf's sympathies for the working class increased after her marriage to Leonard Woolf, who supported Margaret Llewellyn Davies in her work with the Women's Cooperative Guild. In 1913 Leonard and Virginia Woolf traveled the north of England, observing the working conditions in Manchester, Leicester, Leeds, and Glasgow where they "saw every kind of horror and miracle" (letter, 11 April, in Woolf 1913).

The same sympathy is discernible in Keynes after the war. He, like Bertrand Russell, and Leonard and Virginia Woolf, viewed his economic expertise and knowledge as part of a broad cultural vision. Economics became for him "a handmaiden to civilization." Viewing the Paris peace talks as "an ancient tragedy," Keynes ([1919] 2003, 4–5) wrote *The Economic Consequences of the Peace*, "fearful of the convulsions of a dying civilization, as one whom though an Englishman, feels himself a European." Keynes believed from early in his career that England's economic and cultural lives were linked. He would predict that "the day is not far off when the Economics Problem will take the back seat where it belongs, and the arena of the head and heart will be occupied . . . [with] the problems of life, and of human relations, of creation and behaviour and religion" (Glasgow 1975, 269).

The Collector

As an Eton College King's scholar in 1901, at the age of eighteen, Keynes won the top math prize and spent the 32 pounds on a number of books, among them *The Faerie Queene* in six moroccan-bound volumes that later became a part of his Edmund Spenser collection. Few would associate Keynes with Spenser, and yet Keynes's attraction to and love of books and the arts were a part of the private man. He was particularly drawn to painting—guided in his purchases by Duncan Grant, Vanessa Bell, and Roger Fry, who would advise him, at various times, on what to purchase as he built up both his personal collection after success in investing and, also, the collection of the National Portrait Gallery. And he loved English literature, particularly poetry and drama (coming from a family that loved the theater). Mary Glasgow notes that in the letters Keynes wrote to her in the early 1940s, his attention to and pleasure in theater and players occupies most of the space. Later—under the tutelage of Lydia—he would develop professional support for the ballet.

Keynes began collecting paintings early in 1918 after Duncan Grant picked up a sale catalog at Roger Fry's studio. He persuaded Keynes to get a loan from the Treasury to purchase paintings from a sale of Degas's picture collection in Paris for the National Gallery. In March 1918 Keynes and a representative of the gallery, C. J. Holmes, would travel to Paris, then under bombardment, to purchase paintings. Bell (1907–36, letter, 15 March 1918) would write, "We have great hopes of you and consider that your existence at the Treasury is at last justified." On 27 March, she would telegraph:

> Do buy Ingres portrait of self Cezanne Elly Corot Even at Cost of Losing Others. (Bell 1907–36)

They did purchase paintings by Eugène Delacroix, Jean-Auguste-Dominique Ingres, Camille Corot, and Edouard Manet; Holmes was, unfortunately, not taken with the Cézannes, and none were purchased for the gallery, to the dismay of Vanessa Bell. At the same time, Keynes bought for himself an Ingres drawing, two small paintings by Delacroix, a drawing from the Palais Bourbon decoration that he gave to Duncan Grant, and a still life of Cézanne's. The purchase of this painting, *Six Apples by Cezanne*, reverberated through the house of artists. Vanessa Bell raved: "The Cezanne is really amazing and it's more exciting to have it in the house. Its so extraordinarily solid and alive" (Shone 1996, 175). Virginia Woolf (1977–84, diary, 13 April 1918) ruminated,

> what can the 6 apples not be? I began to wonder. There's their relationship to each other, their color, their solidity. To Roger and Nessa, moreover, it was a far more intricate question than this. It was a question of pure paint or mixed; if pure which colour: emerald or viridian; and then the laying on of the paint; and the time he'd spent, and how he'd altered it, and why, and when he'd painted it—We carried it into the next room, and Lord! How it showed up the pictures there, as if you put a real stone among sham ones.

In 1919 Keynes, with the proceeds from *The Economic Consequences of the Peace*, would make another wonderful purchase, of Georges Seurat's *Study for La Grande Jatte*, from a German refugee. He was motivated not only by its beauty but its value as an investment. In 1920 Bell (1907–36, letter, 15 May 1920) would write, "I want to talk to you about some important pictures you've got to buy by Picasso and Braque." Keynes would continue to collect contemporary British art with money gained from economic speculation, joining the Contemporary Art Society. And Duncan Grant and Vanessa Bell would urge him in 1921 to begin a collection of "cheap modern works"—particularly landscapes by a young penniless French painter, Landau. They would advise him of a scheme to buy paintings, exhibit them in Cambridge, and eventually house them in the Fitzwilliam Museum. Also, Keynes would himself become the subject of Bloomsbury art. Vanessa Bell would often plead from Charleston—"please come back soon . . . you could sit all day and be painted. We're badly in need of a model"—making him one of the best-represented economists in the world of art. Keynes not only owned the portraits painted by Bell and Grant but commissioned them to decorate his rooms in Webbs Court, Cambridge, where he served as bursar among other roles in his lifelong connection with King's College. Keynes was then working on *A Treatise*

Paul Cézanne, *Still Life with Apples*, sometimes referred to as *Six Apples*. The Fitzwilliam Museum. © The Provost and Fellows of King's College, Cambridge, U.K. (Keynes Collection).

on Money (1930) while surrounded by decorated panels painted by Vanessa Bell and Duncan Grant of saints derived from the fifteenth-century paintings of Bono de Ferrara. Italianate in feeling, these saint-caryatids represented law, science, and history, though Vanessa Bell would comment, "You mightn't think it—in fact we're always changing the arts and sciences. They're about 5 ft. high and 2 1/2 ft wide and so it's rather an undertaking" (Shone 1996, 222). Keynes's rooms—his style of living—reflect the Bloomsbury mixture of art, intimacy, and domesticity, a style he adopted, observing Vanessa Bell and Duncan Grant's lifestyle and decoration of their home, Charleston.

A Review of the Literature: In the Company of Artists

In placing Keynes in a circle of friendship and the context of British culture—instead of the company of economists—I join Jennifer Wicke in "Mrs. Dalloway Goes to Market" (1994), Craufurd D. Goodwin in *Art and the Market: Roger Fry on Commerce in Art* (1998), Jed Esty in *A Shrinking Island: Modernism and National Culture in England* (2004), and D. E. Moggridge in his impressive *Maynard Keynes: An Economist's*

Biography (1992). All have demonstrated a new cultural understanding of Keynes and his economic principles and policies by placing him in new and broader cultural contexts. Wicke (1994, 11), a literary critic, rereads Keynes in relation to Virginia Woolf, noting that "the nature of the order created by the economist was provisional, momentary, and intertwiningly intricate, a cast of mind overlaid in the blooming buzzing confusion of the market." She observes that Woolf's trope of consciousness and modernist strategy is of a piece with Keynes's stance toward the market: in my interpretation, Woolf, in her fiction, attempts to record the "chaos" or "the atoms of the mind" on the page; Keynes reorders a "chaotic" market through his theories of present consumption and future investment. Though the comparison may, at times, be a stretch, Wicke initiated a new direction for Keynes studies. Similarly, Goodwin (1998, this volume), an economist with broad aesthetic interests, places Keynes alongside the art critic Roger Fry and alongside Virginia Woolf. Goodwin illustrates how Keynes's friendship with Fry, and his writings about "cultural economics," stimulated Keynes's reflection and actions about the place and support of the arts in society. In addition, Goodwin's work, in general, shows the rearrangement of economic models and ideas in the 1930s in tandem with other changes in literature and culture. Recently, Jed Esty has extended these ideas in reading Keynes's economic theories alongside his English literary contemporaries in the late thirties. He finds in their "shared context . . . and textual impulses" that Keynes's *General Theory*, Virginia Woolf's *Between the Acts*, and T. S. Eliot's *Four Quartets* take their place among the attempts "by modernist writers in the 1930s, to come to terms with the obsolescence of that most successful intellectual habit of the 1920s, and to recover a usable core of English national culture from the derelict body of British imperialism" (Esty 2004, 166–67). Finally, Moggridge in his rich biography of Keynes and the 2005 article "Keynes, the Arts, and the State" describes and explains Keynes's stance toward, and economic ideas for, state support of the arts. Keynes's emphasis on and recovery of the national arts in the 1940s—like these modernists, argues Esty—mark the cultural moment when the ethic and aesthetic of "we" replaced "I" in England during the war.

The Later Years: Public Support of the Arts

From this early private foundation, Keynes's transition to public involvement in the arts was natural. He became a member of the Contemporary Art Society and, about ten years later, was one of the founders and guarantors of the London Artists Association that operated from 1925 to 1933. Keynes (1982, 289) met with a group of artists who had found themselves in the difficult situation of not having an organization for selling their pictures because of the "precariousness and irregularity of their incomes . . . [with] no regular prospects on which they could rely." He found an inexpensive room in Hanover Square and, with the help of Samuel Courtauld (who later developed the beautiful Courtauld Galleries in London), created an organization based on cooperative principles that would act as the agent for the artists and exhibit and market their works. Member artists included Vanessa Bell, Duncan Grant, and Roger Fry, among others, and the association guaranteed an annual income of 150 pounds if they failed to generate that income through the sale of paintings. Vanessa Bell (1907–36, letter, 13 February 1927) would write to him from Cassis about the organization, stating that the guarantors should be willing to run more risk and "be willing to support only artists that we think good . . . even if they aren't a paying proposition at first." She would report her personal disapproval of the acceptance of the work of Paul Nash and Alan Walton.

Keynes observed the crossing of Continental civilization to England with Serge Diaghilev's troupe in 1919. But beginning in 1911, he reported on the activities of Diaghilev to friends, attending the performances of his Russian troupe in London with refugees from Europe—Anna Pavlova, Vaslav Nijinsky, and Maria Tallchief. He would also observe its eventual collapse when it was divided into the Ballet Russe of Monte Carlo under the direction of Massine, and another group, Original Ballet Russe, that toured Australia beginning in 1932 under the direction of Wassily de Basil, who was sometimes described as Lydia Lopokova's "platonic lover" (Hill and Keynes 1989). The groups were in tension, and after the ballet wars in London, these troupes would go their separate ways in 1938: Massine to America and de Basil to Australia.

Keynes saw Lydia's career through the demise of Serge Diaghilev (1872–1929), the remarkable impresario who assembled avant-garde artists, ballet dancers, and choreographers to produce some of the most splendid spectacles of early modernism: the best in ballet and painting united. Always struggling to finance his productions, Diaghilev, though initially scornful of English audiences, eventually came to appreciate them. Interested in Diaghilev's sets, Keynes would observe the artistry of Juan Gris for the decor of the ballet "Colombe," and, later, in some productions encouraged by Lydia, Duncan Grant would become involved in set design. Some of the most talented artists of the day would design, including Henri Matisse, Picasso, Andre Derain, Georges Braque, Max Ernst, and Juan Gris. Keynes encouraged this development and, indirectly, through ballet, participated in modernism.

Keynes was always seeking venues for Lydia's ballet talents, and in 1928 he reviewed a performance at the Cambridge University Amateur Dramatic Club where Lydia acted and danced to Igor Stravinsky's *Soldier's Tale* and Shakespeare's *Lover's Complaint*. In 1930 he founded the Camargo Ballet Society for the promotion of ballet in London after the deaths of Diaghilev and Pavlova, and this eventually led to the development of the Vic-Wells ballet company. At the demise of Camargo in 1935, he conceived of and funded another institution, the Cambridge Arts Theater, which has performances to this day. It opened in 1936 with Lydia, then thirty-seven years old, in a major dramatic role in Henrik Ibsen's *Doll's House* and *Master Builder* (Ibsen was one of Keynes's favorite playwrights). Keynes, a progressive member of Bloomsbury, accorded égalité to women at a time when England did not. He was always attuned to Ibsen and "the emergence of the modern woman." Sensitive to theatrical subtleties and the "poetry" in productions, he once observed in Eleanora Duse's return to acting in Ibsen's *Lady from the Sea* how she emphasized "realism at the expense of poetry" (Keynes 1982, 313). And after viewing W. H. Auden and Christopher Isherwood's play, *On the Frontier*, he blasted its "infantilism and amateurism" in a letter to Kingsley Martin (128). Mary Glasgow, a close friend in his later years, would report that Keynes's greatest love remained the theater.

With England's entrance into the war came Keynes's expanded consciousness and belief that expression in the arts was linked to the health and culture of the nation. W. J. Turner wrote an article in the *Nation* calling for a national theater, and Keynes (1982, 357) responded with a supportive letter: "We are apt pupils of the Dictators in the arts of war. Let us, for once, imitate them on a modest scale in the arts of peace." In 1939 Keynes would write to Raymond Mortimer about a performance of the Joos Dance Company—in flight from Hitler because of its avant-garde productions—and would reveal his interest in the intertwining of art and politics. Though Mary Glasgow reports that there were those who were critical of his support of this company, he asserted that their production of *Chronica* about the "rise and fall of a dictator" was "the only example we yet have, where the emotion of an artist has successfully handled the contemporary scene with bitterness and political purpose washed away" (129).

Keynes would urge that the arts be transported out of London to the provinces, "to provide hundreds of factory concerts, to carry the drama to mining villages and war hostels where many of the audience see the living stage for the first time, to assist holidays at home and the provision of entertainment in parks and public places" (360). He worked for the British Institute of Adult Education to encourage this expansion. This was a new turn for Keynes, as most of Bloomsbury knew nothing of the provinces, the Midlands and Lancashire. He worked to disperse art to the northern industrial towns. And though he had been attacked in 1926 by Beatrice Webb, the Fabian, for being "contemptuous of the common man" (Webb and Webb 1992, 102), when writing to Lydia while he campaigned for some Liberal candidates near Blackburn in 1924, he expressed his sympathy for—at least—the industrial working class: "I feel very democratic. I like the people here. They are serious and intelligent—quite a different type from London working classes" (Hill and Keynes 1989, 134).

In "The Function of British Institute of Adult Education: The Rebuilding of Britain," Keynes (1982, 360) described a ballet company: the company "working in association with us (I pay a tribute to Mme Rambert) played to the wild delight of 3000 workers within the walls of a Midland factory." Keynes encouraged ballet in the provinces, allowing "every merry Englishman to be merry in his own way." After the war, in 1945, Keynes would praise the BBC for its role in creating audiences for art among the working class, for "forming new tastes and habits and thus enlarging the desires of the listener and his capacity for enjoyment." It was Keynes's wish at that time that "in every blitzed town in this country one hopes that the local authority will make provision for a central group of buildings for drama and music and art. . . . Death to Hollywood" (271).

In 1936 Keynes received a letter from J. R. Ackerly, who was trying to organize a series of articles on art and the state for the *Listener* (336). Keynes wrote in his essay that the artist was not easy to help, alternating as many did from "economic imprudence . . . to an excessive greediness." Keynes concluded that the state could help the artist best by "promoting an atmosphere of open handedness, of liberality, of candor, of toleration, of experiment, of optimism" (345). Roger Fry, expertly described by Craufurd Goodwin in *Art and the Market*, had written an essay with the same title twelve years earlier, as well as the influential "Art and Commerce" for the Hogarth Press. In this 1926 pamphlet, Goodwin notes that Fry would develop a notion of "cultural economics" that undoubtedly influenced Keynes's later views about the place of arts in society and the supportive role of government.

He also worked to recover Covent Garden for ballet and opera of a national character, as he was as concerned with making London "a great artistic metropolis, a place to visit and wonder at" (Glasgow 1975, 264) as he was to distribute art to the provinces. As part of this effort, he championed and helped fund CEMA. In Mary Glasgow's warm portrait of Keynes, she evokes, in a way, Vanessa Bell's metaphor of the Buddha:

> Keynes lay on a sofa, propped up by white pillows against a background of heavy red velvet curtains. (His doctors insisted that he spend as much time as possible lying down.) He began at once asking awkward questions with alarming courtesy. He wanted to know why the council was spending so much money on amateur effort. (262)

She describes him as "formidable." CEMA evolved into the British Arts Council four years after Keynes's death, and this important council was, as Noel Annan (1990, 429) has observed in *Our Age,* more than just a way for the state to distribute funds to the arts. Keynes, in following the European tradition of patronage for the arts, "made Britain part of the Continent. . . . each year the queues at the National Theatre, the Royal Shakespeare Company, the Royal Opera House and the Coliseum, the museums and galleries grew longer." It was, as Anna Upchurch (2004, 203) argues, a precedent not only for the British Arts Council but also for the National Endowment for the Arts in the United States and similar arts organizations in Canada, New Zealand, and Australia.

Politics and Language

But while Keynes and Fry focused on guiding artists through the market system, Virginia Woolf was concerned about another aspect of the state. She also wrote an essay, "The Artist and Politics," at this time and observed that "art is the first luxury to be discarded in a time of stress" (Woolf 1948, 227). Artists feared that the "loudspeaker" voice of the radio, the newspapers, and the government—leading up to and during World War II would eclipse the personal and individual voice. She, like other British artists, questioned the abuses of public language during this time, that is, the propaganda to build the war mind and to address the national distress. But Keynes was not part of this trend. He proved to be sensitive to the individual poetic voice and the importance of intimate relations even in his writing about foreign policy. In July 1937 he wrote an essay on British foreign policy and England's stance toward the Spanish Civil War in the *New Statesman and Nation*. He began with a discussion of Auden's poem "Spain":

> W. H. Auden's poem "Spain," is fit to stand beside great predecessors in its moving, yet serene expression of contemporary feeling towards the heart-rending events of the political world. (Keynes 1982, 61)

Nevertheless, Keynes viewed "with revulsion" the struggle between the two ideologies in Spain and rejected Auden's expression, "the necessary murder," his belief that the conflict could be settled "by a force of arms." Though Auden, he said, "teaches us, as a poet should, how we should feel, the object of this article is to question whether he rightly directs how, at this moment at least, we should act" (61). Just after Keynes wrote this essay, Julian Bell, Vanessa Bell's son, died in the Spanish Civil War while driving an ambulance near the brutal battle of Bilbao on 18 July 1937. Julian, like many young European and American men, had made the "romantic" choice that Auden lauds in the poem. Keynes then wrote to Kingsley Martin: "Julian's death last week led me to spend even more time than usual thinking about these things, and trying to disentangle one thing from another" (73). He then wrote "Further Thoughts on British Foreign Policy," sixteen days after his first essay, distinguishing between "the rights of personal protest and the criteria of national policy," defending Julian's or anyone's right "to make his protest with his life" (77). Nevertheless, the position for those in the government is entirely different, Keynes asserted: "They have no similar right of representative protest merely on the ground of their own individual feelings, but only if they are convinced that these feelings are also representative of the great majority" (77). Keynes believed in government by discussion and that dissenters should not be alienated.

In his essay "The Arts in Wartime," Keynes would praise CEMA for rescuing the Theater Royal in Bristol, the oldest theatrical building in England with continuous performances. The theater was preserved, according to Keynes (1982, 360), by "extraordinary chance from bombs and fire amidst surrounding desolation." This scene connects with an earlier one in wartime Paris, 1918, when Keynes traveled there to purchase impressionist paintings—by Cézanne and by Ingres—for the National Gallery with a grant from the Treasury. These two images—rescuing paintings in war-torn Paris and supporting CEMA, which saved the Bristol theater amid bombed streets in 1942—form a progression that might well stand for Keynes's stance toward the arts, developed in the intimate spaces of Bloomsbury. He worked to preserve a civilized cultural haven in the midst of moral, cultural, and physical desolation and to create a "material shed" for the future development of the national arts in England.

This essay demonstrates why personal lives and documents like memoirs, letters, and diaries of well-known economists and friends in their circle—though traditionally ignored in the "rational reconstruction" of a life—are important. Keynes's early relationships in Bloomsbury with Duncan Grant, Vanessa Bell, and Roger Fry nurtured his aesthetic tastes, his early habit of collecting art, and established the attitude of the importance of the arts in civilized daily life. Importantly, his democratic feelings about the expansion of ballet—encouraged by his relationship with Lydia Lopokova—and the theater to the Midlands during the war led to the development of economic schemes to make such experiences more widely available. In his later years, he found new ways of economically structuring national policies and support of the arts that led to the exemplary model, the British Arts Council, now emulated in many countries.

References

Annan, Noel. 1990. *Our Age*. New York: Random House.

Bell, Vanessa. 1907–36. Letters to J. M. Keynes (83 ALS + 3 postcards + 1 telegram). Morgan Library, New York.

Chatterjee, Partha. 1993. *The Nation and Its Fragments*. Princeton, N.J.: Princeton University Press.

Esty, Jed. 2004. *A Shrinking Island: Modernism and National Culture in England*. Princeton, N.J.: Princeton University Press.

Foucault, Michel. 1977. *Discipline and Punish: The Birth of the Prison*. New York: Vintage.

Glasgow, Mary. 1975. The Concept of the Arts Council. In *Essays on John Maynard Keynes*, edited by Milo Keynes. Cambridge: Cambridge University Press.

Goodwin, Craufurd D. 1998. *Art and the Market: Roger Fry on Commerce in Art*. Ann Arbor: University of Michigan Press.

Hill, Polly, and Richard Keynes. 1989. *Lydia and Maynard: The Letters of John Maynard Keynes and Lydia Lopokova*. New York: Scribner's.

Keynes, J. M. 1972. *Essays in Biography*. Vol. 10 of *The Collected Writings of John Maynard Keynes*. London: Macmillan.

———. 1982. *Social, Political, and Literary Writings*. Vol. 28 of *The Collected Writings of John Maynard Keynes*. London: Macmillan.

———. [1919] 2003. *The Economic Consequences of the Peace*. New Brunswick, N.J.: Transaction.

Moggridge, D. E. 1992. *Maynard Keynes: An Economist's Biography.* London: Routledge.

——. 2005. Keynes, the Arts, and the State. *HOPE* 37.3:535–55.

Russell, Bertrand. [1911] 1959. *The Problems of Philosophy.* Oxford: Oxford University Press.

Said, Edward. 1982. Opponents, Audiences, Constituencies, and Community. *Critical Inquiry* 9.1:1–26.

Scrase, David, and Peter Croft. 1983. *Maynard Keynes: Collector of Pictures, Books, and Manuscripts.* Exhibition catalog, Fitzwilliam Museum, Cambridge.

Shone, Richard. 1996. *Bloomsbury Portraits: Vanessa Bell, Duncan Grant, and Their Circle.* London: Phaidon.

Skidelsky, Robert. 1992. *John Maynard Keynes: The Economist as Saviour (1920–37).* New York: Penguin.

Terada, Rei. 2001. *Feeling in Theory: Emotion after the "Death of the Subject."* Cambridge, Mass.: Harvard University Press.

Upchurch, Anna. 2004. John Maynard Keynes, the Bloomsbury Group, and the Origins of the Arts Council Movement. *International Journal of Cultural Policy* 10.2:203–17.

Webb, Beatrice, and Sidney Webb. 1992. *The Webbs in Asia: 1911–1912 Travel Diary.* Hampshire: Macmillan.

Wicke, Jennifer. 1994. Mrs. Dalloway Goes to Market: Woolf, Keynes, and Modern Markets. *Novel* 28.1:5–23.

Woolf, Virginia. 1913. Woolf to Dickinson. King's College Modern Archives, Cambridge, U.K.

——. 1931. *The Waves.* New York: Harcourt Brace Jovanovich.

——. 1948. The Artist and Politics. In *The Moment and Other Essays.* New York: Harcourt Brace Jovanovich.

——. 1977. *Letters of Virginia Woolf.* Vol. 3. Edited by Nigel Nicholson and Joanne Trautmann. New York: Harcourt, Brace, Jovanovich.

——. 1977–84. *The Diary of Virginia Woolf.* 5 vols. Edited by Ann Olivier Bell. New York: Harcourt, Brace, Jovanovich.

——. 1985. Old Bloomsbury. In *Moments of Being*, edited by Jeanne Schulkind. New York: Harcourt, Brace, Jovanovich.

Part 5
The Biographer's Craft

Biography and Autobiography: Harry Johnson

D. E. Moggridge

Economists are producing a lot of autobiographical material these days. Judging from its spread across journals and collected volumes, there appears to be a substantial demand for it, and the supply has grown rapidly. This material has also been the object of some discussion in the literature, but the emphasis thus far has largely been on the article-length memoir such as those commissioned for the *Banca Nazionale del Lavoro Quarterly Review* by Jan Kregel (1988–89) and interviews. In 2003, I noted 198 of these—an underestimate of the total stock, as it ignored certain journals such as *Econometric Theory* and *Macroeconomic Dynamics*. The memoirs have certain characteristics that have been captured by Roy Weintraub (2005), most notably that, as with all sorts of autobiographical memories, they concentrate on the years of late youth and early adulthood. The interviews may differ from the memoirs, if the interviewer is doing his or her job, because the interview itself can be structured to cover a longer period. However, one still has to cope with the nature of the autobiographical memory and its evolution, as Bruce Caldwell (1998) clearly and carefully demonstrated in the case of Friedrich Hayek.

For permission to quote from unpublished papers I am grateful to Elizabeth Simpson (Johnson Papers); the provost and scholars of King's College, Cambridge (Kahn Papers); Milton Friedman (Friedman Papers); Christopher Johnson (Robbins Papers); and the University of Chicago (University of Chicago Archives). I am grateful to Susan Howson, an anonymous referee, and participants at the 2006 *HOPE* conference for comments on earlier drafts. All references to Johnson's own papers, which are in the Regenstein Library at the University of Chicago, refer to the item, the box number, and the file title.

History of Political Economy 39 (annual suppl.) DOI 10.1215/00182702-2006-050

Caldwell's paper also raises the problem of the serial autobiographer or interviewee, of which Hayek was a good example. An even more substantial example is John Kenneth Galbraith, the object of a recent biography (Parker 2005). In his lifetime Galbraith, who died in 2006 at age 97, published a lengthy autobiography (1981), a childhood-family memoir (1964), and several fragments of memoirs (1971, 1979), as well as a journal from his period as ambassador to India (1969) and accounts of visits to Eastern Europe (1958) and China (1973). And he was quite freely available for interview, not only for the latest biography but for predecessors, most notably Peggy Lamson's (1991), and for other purposes (Stanfield and Stanfield 2004). Such a mass of material may or may not be consistent. Even if it is, it still leaves a biographer with problems in using it.

Then there are the fragmentary histories with strongly autobiographical elements, exemplified by the late writings of Richard Kahn (1974, 1976, 1984, 1989), Joan Robinson (1978), and Paul Samuelson (1998).

There are also episodic memoirs. Perhaps the best known are those associated with the Memoir Club of Old Bloomsbury, to which Keynes gave his *Two Memoirs* (1949), "Melchior: A Defeated Enemy" (2 February 1921) and "My Early Beliefs" (11 September 1938), the second of which has been grist not only for Keynes's biographers but also for those interested in his philosophical development (Runde and Mizuhara 2003).

Finally, there are the full-scale autobiographies. In economics these are relatively few in number, but they include one classic, John Stuart Mill's *Autobiography* ([1873] 1989). To this one can add those by James Buchanan (1992), Alec Cairncross (1998), Eleanor Lansing Dulles (1980), S. Herbert Frankel (1992), Milton and Rose Friedman (1998), John Kenneth Galbraith (1981), Benjamin Higgins (1992), John Atkinson Hobson (1938), Calvin Bryce Hoover (1965), Charles P. Kindleberger (1991), Donald MacDougall (1987), Raymond F. Mikesell (2000), Franco Modigliani (2001), Lionel Robbins (1971), Eric Roll (1985), and George Stigler (1988).

In my own experience as a biographer, I have had to deal with two individuals with autobiographical material. The first, of course, is Keynes. The second is my current biographical subject, Harry Johnson.

Johnson's case is interesting in that he left his successors nine published and unpublished autobiographical pieces, seven of which date from after the beginning of the breakdown of his health in 1972. The published ones, "Cambridge in the 1950s: Memoirs of an Economist" ([1974] 1978) and "Cambridge as an Academic Environment in the Early 1930s: A Reconstruction from the Late 1940s" (1978), were collected together with other pieces on Cambridge and Keynes in *The Shadow of Keynes* (Johnson and Johnson 1978). To these one can add "Analysis of Rooming House Group" (1945–46);[1] "Autobiographical Notes" (1969); "Harry Johnson's Contributions to Economics: An Analysis by Himself" (1 February 1974; hereafter called "Self-Evaluation"); and a series of memoirs written in August–September 1974 covering his life to 1943, which concentrates on his undergraduate education at the University of Toronto (1974 Memoir I); his year (1943–44) as the economics department at St. Francis Xavier University in Antigonish, Nova Scotia (1974 Memoir II); and his years (1966–74) at the London School of Economics (LSE) (1974 Memoirs III, IV, and V).[2]

In dealing with this Johnson material, if I looked at my economist predecessors, I would not have much guidance. Only Mill's *Autobiography* has generated a substantial literature—but not by economists. In the case of Galbraith, in both *The Scotch* and *A Life in Our Times*, he explicitly referred to problems of accuracy and memory.

> This is the kind of story where memory plays one tricks. I have checked names, places and events. But records are sketchy and it was forty years ago. I can only hope that I have been spared. (Galbraith 1964, viii)

> I have relied . . . on recollection (though with some support from notes, records and published writing), I have done so with similar confidence. My memory proved very good on the larger shape of events and also on the more salient conversations, actions, pronouncements, speeches, scenes and absurdities. However, it was sadly defective on dates, middle initials, minor geography and the other trivia so necessary, nonetheless, for verisimilitude. For help in getting things right or nearly so . . . (Galbraith 1981, viii)

Galbraith's latest biographer does not see any possible problems in using this material—or at least he does not explicitly address them. In the course of the book, however, he does correct the autobiographical account with new evidence (Parker 2005, 573 n. 12; 709 n. 17; 737 n. 99), but he also prefers, without saying why, the autobiography to a more contemporary account by Galbraith (690 nn. 30, 32).

1. This was a paper submitted to a course on human relations in industry that Johnson took as an MA student at the University of Toronto during 1946–47. Its autobiographical nature comes from its narrator, Harry, who is stationed at Canadian Military Headquarters, and its close-grained detail, which makes the writing rather different from anything else Harry wrote.

2. These memoirs are in the possession of Elizabeth Simpson, to whom I am grateful for copies.

In the case of Mill's *Autobiography* we know a lot about its composition and the treatment of the manuscript after Mill's death (Stillinger 1983; Robson and Stillinger 1981). There have also been substantial discussions of the accuracy of his account, the importance of events and influences glossed over, and the links between his personal history and his ideas. Naturally, opinions have varied. There is a strong element of "Hogarthian or Dickensian caricature" in Mill's account of his education (Stillinger 1991, 34). Mill's chronology of his "mental crisis" is, as Robert Cumming pointed out in 1964, internally inconsistent, but there is the difficulty that there is very little evidence about Mill's state during this period (Thomas 1971, 342; 1985, 33; Ryan 1974, 11). Opinion has also varied on Mill's account of Harriet Taylor's influence on his ideas. In the 1950s, Hayek (1951) accepted Mill's account, and Michael St. John Packe (1954), his first modern biographer, went even further in his emphasis of Harriet's importance, but then in the 1960s a reaction set in. By 1968 John Robson could remark that "one is overwhelmed by the manifest exaggeration" (56) and, after reviewing the evidence, conclude,

> This mighty labour, then, only brings into view the mouse with which it began. The conclusion in Pappé's words [1960] (vii) is that "Harriet assisted Mill in his work and took an understanding and active interest in it." . . . Without her, one may guess, he might not have written *On Liberty* and the *Autobiography*, but she was not their author. Also, it is likely that without her, *Utilitarianism*, the *Principles of Political Economy*, and the essays on Nature and the Utility of Religion would not have been quite the way they are. . . . she was in and of his intellectual and emotional life on an unusual degree, but not in an unexampled way, and she was not, in any meaningful sense, the "joint author" of his works. (68)

Subsequently, there have been examples of both Harriet philia (Capaldi 2004) and Harriet phobia (Carlisle 1991), but the recent conclusion of José Harris (2004, 162) rings true:

> These rather conflicting accounts (of Harriet as faithful research assistant but also as intellectual master) suggest that her challenge to Mill's mental outlook was perhaps more fundamental than he cared to admit or was even aware of; that it might have amounted not just to a radicalization of specific opinions, or the contributions of a useful helpmate, but to a wider change of underlying sentiment and social philosophy.

However, as Robson (1989, 21) noted, "There will be no final judgement, the evidence being what it is and new juries being empanelled in each generation."

The literature on Mill's *Autobiography* suggests very clearly that one must test the text against the available evidence. It also suggests that authorial intention plays an important part in the discussion, for Mill ([1873] 1989, 25–26) made his motives explicit at the outset and carefully shaped and reshaped the text in their light—not always successfully (Ryan 1991).

With Harry Johnson the author's reasons for writing the memoirs were various. The earliest provided raw material for a graduate term paper. The 1969 "Autobiographical Notes," which unlike the 1974 "Self-Evaluation" he listed in his bibliography (Longawa 1984, 703), accompanied the creation of a depository for his published works at Lakehead University in Thunder Bay, Ontario. The first of the published sketches was prepared for a pair of talks given by Johnson and his wife, Elizabeth, at Amherst College on 19 February 1973 and then revised for publication; the second was an attempt, as he put it, to answer the question "what, then, was Cambridge like as an environment for economic discussion and research in the period of the writing of *The General Theory*?" (Johnson 1978, 84) as a contribution to a 1975 conference devoted to those years of creation. Part of the origin of the 1974 "Self-Evaluation" was a remark by Gerard Curzon on telling Johnson that his name had been suggested for the Nobel Prize: the only person who could do justice to the range of his interests was Johnson himself. The result was a thirty-two-page evaluation written in the third person, to which he attached a brief CV and a bibliography classed by type of publication. There were probably other influences. His 1973 stroke and 1974 resignation from the LSE shook Johnson deeply and forced him to reevaluate his past. His stroke also presented a problem: before the event an important outlet for his immense restless energy had been wood carving. Although he was ambidextrous, he carved with his dominant left hand. The stroke affected his left side and forced him to find substitutes for carving. He tried working with a vise attached to his desk and using his right hand. For a time he tried animal silhouettes made with an electric saw and Elmer's glue. He also tried modeling small figures in plasticine. Memoir writing became a form of therapy for a time in the late summer of 1974 as he was clearing up his affairs in London, but in the end travel became the best therapy. But autobiography kept intruding, as in his last published paper, "Networks of Economists and Their Role in International Monetary

Reform" (1982), which was a reflection on two such networks (Bellagio and the problem-oriented meetings of younger economists that began with a conference organized by Robert Mundell and Johnson in 1966), and his tribute and reminiscence "Ruth Cohen: A Neglected Contributor to Contemporary Capital Theory," which appeared in *The Shadow of Keynes*.

The surviving autobiographical material is heavily weighted toward the years of late youth and early adulthood. The "Autobiographical Notes" match the typical memoir discussed by Weintraub—the first seven pages concerned with Johnson's family and his education, the next two with Cambridge between 1949 and 1956, and the last seven with his subsequent career. His "Self-Evaluation" is naturally more unusual in devoting only three pages to his student days, three to his years in Cambridge, three to Manchester, and then eleven each to Chicago from 1959–66 and the LSE and Chicago years. The balance of the 1974 fragmentary memoirs is heavily weighted toward his early adulthood, as are the published Cambridge memoirs.

The internal consistency of the memoirs is quite high. However, there are some contradictions. He claims in 1974 Memoir I that summer work on his parents' farm outside Toronto prevented the summer cottage socializing his contemporaries enjoyed, but informs the reader of his 1974 Memoir II that he had been to summer camp one year with a two-week canoe trip in the Gatineau. The Gatineau trip also contradicts his statement in 1974 Memoir I that he had not been out of Ontario until his fourth-year university experience as an emergency wartime wheat harvester at Ernfold, Saskatchewan. In his "Autobiographical Notes," he claims that when he went to Chicago in 1959 he had "not intended to take any interest in Canadian economic problems" (Johnson 1969, 13); in his "Self-Evaluation" he repeats this claim but admits that "he had written an extensive critical review article on the preliminary report of the Royal Commission on Canada's Economic Prospects" (Johnson 1974, 10; Johnson 1958a).

Inevitably, there are discrepancies between the memoirs and other available sources. For example, in his 1974 Memoir I, he is often unclear as to the subject matter of particular undergraduate courses that he took between 1939 and 1943, particularly in political science. In his "Autobiographical Notes" Johnson cannot remember why he started teaching in Cambridge in January 1949, when that date was chosen to accommodate his November 1948 "generals" examination at Harvard where he had been a doctoral student since September 1947 (Johnson 1947).

The published Cambridge memoirs are also not always accurate in detail. Johnson (1978, 128) related that when he went to Jesus College, Cambridge, in 1945 he "had not been forthoughted enough to stipulate King's College which shows my lack of understanding of economics at the time," an odd statement from one who had read and taught Keynes's *General Theory*, where the author's college affiliation is on the title page. Similarly, his attempt to make the reader sympathetic to Dennis Robertson's position in Cambridge causes problems.

> He had been prevented from receiving what he (and many others) considered was the final reward of a serious academic career, namely the professorship at Cambridge; for that reason he had gone to the London School of Economics as a professor. Fortunately for him, the war broke out—and the London School of Economics moved to Cambridge. So he could be a professor at the London School and still live in his old rooms. At the end of the war, when it was clear that Keynes was never going to return to academic life these people persuaded Robertson to take the chair on the basis of promises that they would "stop the persecution," would "live and let live" and so forth. (139)

The problem with the first part of the story is that the Cambridge chair was not vacant in 1938 when Robertson went to the LSE: A. C. Pigou, the incumbent, was some years from retirement. The reasons for Robertson's move to London were much more complex. They had something to do with disputes in Cambridge, but they also reflected Robertson's own fragile psychological state at the time. The second problem is that when war did break out, Robertson went into the Treasury, so he could not follow the LSE back to Cambridge, much less reclaim the rooms he had given up when he resigned his Trinity fellowship at the end of December 1938. Third, when it came to filling Pigou's chair, Keynes was offered it in January 1944. He declined it because he could hold it for long before retirement, and he did not need it for influence in Cambridge. Moreover, he did this knowing that Robertson would be asked next, as he was (Moggridge 1992, 603). Finally, there is no indication in the surviving correspondence surrounding Robertson's appointment that anyone made any promises as to future good behavior.[3]

3. Robertson (1944) acknowledged a "helpful" letter from Richard Kahn while he was still dithering over accepting, but we know nothing of its contents. Robertson finally made up his mind on the position on 19 February.

One could go on to smaller details in the Cambridge memoirs. One could also point out similar problems in his memoirs of his London years.

But other discrepancies in the various memoirs are more substantial. For the purposes of this discussion I shall take five, in chronological order. These concern the Cambridge wrangles over liquidity preference in the 1940s and 1950s; Johnson's choice of his fields of academic specialization; his work on his Harvard dissertation; his decision to leave Manchester for Chicago in 1958; and his relations with his senior colleagues in monetary economics at Chicago.

The Cambridge wrangles over liquidity preference versus loanable funds figure substantially in Johnson's published Cambridge memoirs. They were definitely in progress when Johnson returned to Cambridge as an assistant lecturer in January 1949, where the evidence in the papers and the published record is consistent with the memoirs. However, the records from Johnson's first postwar year in Cambridge suggest the story differed from his memoir (1978, 128–29, 152).

From his lecture and reading notes for 1945–46 one can trace his exposure to monetary economics. As far as formal lectures were concerned, two sets are relevant: Joan Robinson's "Money" in the Michaelmas term of 1945 and Dennis Robertson's "Theory of Money and Economic Fluctuations" in the Easter term of 1946 (Johnson's notes on both are at Cambridge University, box 44). The Robinson lectures had a minimal discussion of the determination of the rate of interest: to judge from Johnson's notes, loanable funds was touched on only in passing in a lecture on 9 November. The lectures were not really about monetary theory but about employment theory and employment policy. The Robertson lectures, the first set of which he gave in 1946, were eventually published as volume 3 of his *Lectures on Economic Principles* (1959). In these Robertson criticized Keynes's theory of the rate of interest. But the real dispute between Keynes's disciples and Robertson in undergraduate instruction did not break out until the end of the 1945–46 academic year, when, knowing the content of Robertson's lectures, the Cambridge Keynesians believed that they had to "inoculate" students against Robertson's Easter term lectures (see, e.g., Robertson 1946).

Confirmation of this comes from Johnson's surviving supervision essays for Maurice Dobb—where the issue, as Johnson had reported (1978, 128–29), was not discussed (Johnson 1975c)—and from the tripos examination papers themselves: there was no place, even in the "money" paper, for a student to demonstrate his skill or position on the liquidity preference versus loanable funds issue. Confirmation also comes from the memory of Aubrey Silberston, another undergraduate economist at Jesus who had returned to college after learning economics as a prisoner of war and who, incidentally, was being supervised by Robinson.

> I soon discovered that Harry already knew a lot of economics. . . . He hadn't, however, done much Keynesian economics, which was very much a Cambridge specialty. . . . I vividly remember walking around the College playing fields with Harry for an hour or more, trying to sort out the Keynesian theory of liquidity preference. There was little attempt at critical appraisal. We were simply trying to understand what was then a novel and difficult theory. . . . We did not become fully aware of Dennis Robertson's criticisms of Keynes' theory until later in the year because Robertson discussed these issues only in the final term. (Silberston 1978, 2)

The level of Johnson's interest in 1946 is best indicated by the fact that he did not buy Robertson's *Essays in Monetary Theory* until he was back in Cambridge in 1947, after his year in Toronto.[4]

Johnson is unclear as to why or how he chose the fields of specialization he did. In his "Autobiographical Notes" he related that in Cambridge he "was required to teach money and banking and allowed to give a short course in the theory of international trade" (Johnson 1969, 8). In his "Self Evaluation," written in the third person, he related the following:

> His early interests at Harvard, under the influence of his Toronto teachers Harold Innis, Vincent Bladen and Karl Helleiner and Harvard's Joseph Schumpeter, were in economic history and especially the history of economic thought. . . . However, it was clear to him that economic history and the history of thought were likely to become backwaters of research, given most notably the exciting developments in economic theory following the "Keynesian Revolution" and less obviously the application of the geometrical and mathematical methods of general equilibrium analysis, and his interests turned rapidly to the version of Keynesian economics being taught by Alvin Hansen and to international trade theory as taught by Gottfried Haberler. (Johnson 1974, 2–3)

4. This copy is in the author's possession.

Yet when it came to discussing his possible Cambridge teaching with Dennis Robertson in February 1948, he wrote,

> Concerning possible lecture subjects, I am at present most interested in the history of economic thought, and in particular in examining the development of economic theory in order to elucidate the nature of economic problems, and the application of economic concepts in solving them. I am hesitant about suggesting this subject, however, since I am fully aware that a proper presentation of it requires many more years of research and experience than I should be able to bring to it; and I should appreciate any alternative suggestions you might care to make. For my "generals" I am preparing to present money and banking, international trade, economic theory and economic history, which will serve as some indication of the fields in which I shall be best qualified on my arrival in Cambridge. (Johnson 1948)

Robertson replied on 4 March that the faculty's needs would probably lie in the areas of money and banking and international trade. The die was cast.

Johnson's discussion of his Harvard dissertation differed between 1969 and 1974: in 1969 he stated that he had "no chance to get started on a thesis at Harvard" and "never did write one" (Johnson 1969, 7); in 1974 he reported that "his plans for doing a thesis on the Dalton cheap money experiment under Hansen were . . . changed by the reception and acceptance of an Assistant Lectureship at Cambridge" (Johnson [1974] 1978, 3). The actual story is more complicated.

When he applied for the Ramsey-Berry Fellowship at King's in 1949, after ten months in Cambridge, he told the electors,

> The applicant is at present engaged in research into postwar British monetary policy, with special reference to the "cheaper money" policy of Chancellor [of the Exchequer, Hugh] Dalton [in 1946–47]. It is intended to complete this study within the next eighteen months. (Johnson 1949)

He had gone some way in collecting statistics and background material, when at his first meeting of the Association of University Teachers of Economics in December 1949 he found that "three others were already engaged in studies of cheap money, one of whom was in the process of submitting a completed thesis to a Midlands university." But as he told Alvin Hansen,

> I have become interested in British joint-stock banking, a subject on which very little research has been done since the beginning of the war. . . . and I feel that a study of changes in British banking in the period 1930 to 1950 would offer more scope for original work, and at the same time be of more general usefulness. (Johnson 1951b)

Accordingly, he asked permission to change his topic. He also enclosed the first fruits of his work on the new topic, an article that had been accepted for publication in the *Economic Journal* (Johnson 1951c). Hansen (1951) agreed to the change in subject. But beyond another article (Johnson 1951a), Johnson did not proceed much further with this research. Instead, when he heard from Carl Kaysen in July 1956 that Harvard had changed its degree requirements to allow the submission of previously published work, he submitted the revised papers published in *International Trade and Economic Growth* (1958f) and was examined by James Duesenberry, Paul Samuelson, and Franco Modigliani in August 1957.

The various memoirs are also misleading on Johnson's departure from Manchester to Chicago in September 1959. The move was agreed on in May 1958, just under a year after the Chicago department had unanimously agreed to try to hire him. In his "Autobiographical Notes," Johnson (1969, 10–11) stated that

> I decided to go to Chicago for two reasons. The first was that it was increasingly clear that English economics was stuck in a groove, largely because of its conquest by Keynesian economics and its politicization in favour of the Labour party socialism, and that the only progress in the subject that was being made was occurring in the United States. . . . The second was that it was already apparent that fiscal and balance-of-payments pressures on the government were forcing it into policies it has increasingly pursued since, of starving the university system of funds and forcing it to emphasize teaching and administration rather than research.[5]

5. "A subsidiary consideration was that, as a result of never earning more than the equivalent of U.S. $7000 a year, heavily taxed and with a family to support, I had been unable to accumulate any capital whatsoever, and my children were approaching an age at which money would become useful to improve their educational opportunities" (Johnson 1969, 11). In "Cambridge in the 1950s" he also referred to "the material poverty that English academic life in the provinces imposed" (Johnson 1978, 150).

He mentioned in the previous paragraph the fact that a chair at the LSE was open after James Meade's move to Cambridge. He reported that

> had I been offered it I would have felt obliged to take it out of loyalty to my friends at L.S.E., and my concern over the state of economics in Britain, but it went instead to [Ely] Devons, which pleased me because I felt he deserved a larger sphere of operations. (10)

In his "Self-Evaluation," the notion of Britain becoming an academic backwater was also mentioned, as was the observation "that the British academic system offered little stimulus and time for scientific work as compared with the American" (Johnson 1974, 9). The actual story, again, is more complicated.

Johnson had first come to Chicago's attention during Milton Friedman's 1953–54 sabbatical year in Cambridge. Friedman introduced Johnson's name to his colleagues in the context of Chicago's longer-term staffing plans in a letter to T. W. Schultz on 28 October 1953. Friedman repeated the suggestion in March 1954, and in April, when Northwestern consulted him about possible senior and junior visitors, he said that Johnson was the ideal candidate for a visit, which Friedman thought might be coupled with a quarter at Chicago. The proposed Chicago quarter did not work out, and Johnson's second appointment in 1955 after Northwestern was at Stanford.

Chicago maintained an interest in Johnson. The department was rebuilding after weathering a crisis, but after the loss of Tjalling Koopmans, Jacob Marschak, and Frederick Harbison, along with the retirement of Frank Knight and the illness of Lloyd Metzler, it needed to hire outside at a senior level (Schultz 1956). The response was encouraging, and during the next year the department began to consider candidates. On 9 April 1957 the department met to discuss a major appointment for Johnson's Manchester colleague W. Arthur Lewis. The minutes noted, "In general there was a consensus of a kind that can best be described by saying that no one amongst those present expressed an objection to his appointment." They also noted that the "chief alternative" to Lewis was Johnson. A vote on the relative ranking or priority of approach to the two found that 6 of the 13 present favored Johnson, 5 favored Lewis (Minutes 1957).

On 28 May the department met again to discuss the possible appointment of Lewis and Johnson. At the end, "a motion was passed unanimously authorizing the chairman to proceed to negotiate the appointment of Harry Johnson to a major tenure post in the Department" (Minutes 1957).

While Johnson was at the Merrill Centre on Long Island in July 1957, working up *International Trade and Economic Growth* as his Harvard PhD thesis, D. Gale Johnson visited and sounded him out as to the possibility of moving to Chicago. Johnson responded favorably, although he said that he would not be able to come immediately if he accepted. Thereafter, Arnold Harberger appears to have been his main contact in the department, although others played supporting roles. Harberger's presence in England in 1958 at the LSE and Cambridge expedited matters.

Johnson received other inquiries. Toronto tried in summer 1957, when Johnson's mother congratulated him on discouraging them—the offer was "*too small*" (Johnson 1957a). But Johnson (1957b) promised Vincent Bladen, the chair of the Toronto department, "not to close with any American university without giving you a chance to see what you can do," and Bladen (1958) wrote about possible terms on 17 February. Johns Hopkins also inquired about an appointment in March 1958.

Johnson was interested in Chicago, but he did not rush into negotiations. He had discussions with Carl Shoup about a Ford Foundation visiting professorship at Columbia and, after talking with the vice-chancellor and his colleagues at Manchester, told Shoup on 15 January 1958 that he was prepared to come in 1960–61. Columbia replied on 22 January that they would be willing to have him then, but when Johnson wrote again on 10 March, he declined the Columbia offer.

> The reason for the delay and the change of heart . . . is that I have pretty well decided to move to the U.S.A., and in that event I should have to break off my commitment to you in fairness to my new university. (Johnson 1958b)

In the interval, Harberger had been in Manchester on 29 and 30 January.

Chicago still did not have Johnson completely in the bag. In February Stanford and Princeton both approached him with very attractive offers. Chicago responded with an improved offer. He was also still getting letters from possible Chicago colleagues. To one, from Lloyd Metzler, he replied:

> Thank you for your two letters. The first was both generous and helpful in giving me an idea of what life is like in Chicago for the minority opinion; I would like you to know that your presence there is an important attraction—I have been a fan of yours since I read your work and heard you speak at the AEA in 1947.[6] (Johnson 1958c)

6. At the meeting in Atlantic City in January 1947, when Metzler discussed in a session on domestic and international equilibrium on 24 January.

The second letter, the only one that survives, pursued a loose end from a 1955 discussion over Johnson's article "The Transfer Problem and Exchange Stability" (1956).

But there was that other factor in the background to the negotiations. Robertson retired from the Cambridge professorship of political economy in 1957. Meade was elected to succeed him, thus opening the LSE chair in commerce with special reference to international trade. With Robbins at the helm, the LSE's wheels turned slowly—deliberately so. There were no immediate teaching needs in international economics that could not be covered by Alan Day and Helen Makower, and graduate supervision was not a problem. To Robbins it was more important to fill Hayek's former chair, the Tooke professorship in economics and statistics, so that the LSE could retain A. W. H. Phillips. This appointment had the advantage of being uncontroversial. Replacing Meade presented major problems. Some members of the staff might be considered to have claims. And there were outsiders to consider, including Johnson. In a mid-September 1957 paper setting out the whole position, Robbins provided his view of Johnson.

> *Johnson*. I mention him because I know some members of our profession think him to be eligible. I have indeed heard his name mentioned as a desirable choice by one of the juniors at the School. I have no doubt that he is a clever fellow and I can conceive that in years to come we may want to have him. But I definitely do not want him now. His articles, though showing obvious power, seem to me to lack a sense of direction and his practical judgment to be definitely poor, and it is a relevant circumstance that, when he deputised for Alan Day while the latter was at the Treasury, he was certainly not a success as a teacher. I know that Meade, who was responsible for inviting him, was worried about this.[7] In any case, I cannot think that he is as good as at least four of our Readers and I should be very sorry indeed to appoint such a man over their heads. (Robbins 1957)

Lurking behind this was also Johnson's (1951d) highly critical review of James Meade's *Balance of Payments*, which had caused a storm at the LSE.[8] Robbins's preferred strategy was to leave the chair vacant for

7. Meade (1954) had communicated his worries to Johnson at the time.

8. At the time Alan Peacock (1951) reported to Johnson: "Robbins announced in stentorian tones at lunch the other day that he thought you must have some personal antipathy to J. E. M. Ralph [Turvey] and I rose to your defence but of course Lionel is uncrushable." Robbins did not speak to Johnson between 1951 and Arnold Harberger's wedding in London on 15 March 1958, after he had successfully prevented Johnson's getting Meade's chair.

eighteen months to two years in the hope that his favored internal candidate, Day, could grow up to it, but Robbins was prepared to consider an outsider senior to Johnson, initially Cairncross.

Robbins was correct that the junior members of staff might hold different views. It was indicative of the gap between the professors and the young that Robbins had only heard Johnson's name from one, for he had probably not talked to any others about the issue. Yet Johnson was by this time the undisputed leader of the younger generation of serious economists outside Cambridge. Moreover, his possible LSE appointment was associated with expectations that he would become an advocate for all the changes the younger people desired—more mathematics in the curriculum, more attention to graduate work, and so forth. According to Richard Lipsey (1978, S41 n. 14), "The LSE junior staff whom I knew had a short list containing only one name, H. G. Johnson."

On 3 February 1958 Robbins wrote a personal letter to Ely Devons, like Cairncross a friend from wartime Whitehall, sounding him out as to his availability for the chair. At the time Devons (1951, 1952, 1954) had published three articles on international trade. Yet Robbins (1958) thought that the domain of the chair could be defined to make it "a field in which . . . [Devons's] special qualifications [in statistics] would be deployed with quite peculiar advantage." Devons was interested, arrangements for an election proceeded, and Devons was formally offered the chair on 18 April. He formally accepted the offer on 23 April and had told the vice-chancellor of Manchester that he would go to the LSE from 1 April 1959 (Devons 1958). Robbins was delighted: "The flags are definitely out in Houghton Street" (Robbins 1958). On the announcement, according to Lipsey (1978, S43 n. 14), "many of the full professors were surprised that the less-senior staff thought it a scandal that Harry was not appointed."

Johnson may have been "pleased" for his Manchester colleague, but, given Devons's lack of expertise, he was outraged "that the British academic establishment could apparently decide appointments on what seemed to him irrelevant grounds" rather than on competence in the field (Lipsey 1978, S43 n. 14). Lipsey (2001, 616) remembered Harberger's visit to the LSE and that

> Johnson happened to be in London when (or very soon after) he found out that he had been passed over. The three of us went out for one of the famous Harberger-Johnson drinking bouts with which I was just barely able to keep up. One of my memories of that evening is of a cab refusing to pick us up at 4 a.m. on some London street corner—I guess

> we seemed too disreputable for the cabby. My more important memory is of Al working on Harry, relentlessly saying that, as Harry was not appreciated in England, it was time for him to move to Chicago.

By 10 May, Johnson (1958d) was writing Friedman, thanking him for an earlier letter (unfortunately lost),

> which played its part in my decision to accept Chicago's offer. I don't agree with your view that the British intellectual climate has been inhibiting me—rather the reverse—but we can argue about that some other time.

He also told Richard Kahn on 12 May of his impending move to Chicago (Johnson 1958e). Later in the month, letters of congratulation started to arrive.

Thus although the 1969 and 1974 memoirs tell part of the story of Johnson's decision to move to America, its timing seems to have had a lot to do with developments at the LSE. Indeed, one might go even further, for if, as is likely, Devons had consulted Johnson during what the latter later reported as "his considerable heart-searchings over abandoning what he had created in social science at Manchester" between Robbins's approach in February and his decision to let the formal proceedings begin (1968), Johnson's announcement to Shoup on 10 March of his own decision to move fits very well into the tale. Later comments about the British intellectual climate do not mesh with the statement to Friedman. Johnson (1978, 150) later said that "my days in Manchester were probably the happiest in my life, professionally speaking." He also told Jack Johnston on 2 December 1959 that

> if Chicago had come after me in my third year at Manchester instead of the second, I should have stayed there; by that time I had things going the way I wanted to, had worked out relations with Ely, Bill [Mackenzie] and Max [Gluckman], and had participated in enough appointments to feel that it was my Department. (Johnson 1959b)

But, of course, he could not tell his former Manchester colleague the story I have outlined above.

In his "Self-Evaluation," Johnson (1974, 16) states that in Chicago he "followed his Cambridge policy of avoiding conflict with senior economists—specifically Milton Friedman." This stretches the truth. He arrived in Chicago in September 1959 and spent his first year without any teaching responsibilities. On two occasions in his early days in the department Johnson deliberately created difficulties. Things did not improve thereafter.

Johnson and Jagdish Bhagwati published a joint paper, "Notes on Some Controversies in the Theory of International Trade," in the *Economic Journal* for March 1960. The last section of the paper, according to Bhagwati (1977, 224), "was almost wholly Harry's contribution" and dealt with Marshall's theorem concerning the stability of international equilibrium. At the end of the section Johnson added a footnote almost a page long that dealt with Friedman's assertion and Egon Sohmen's alleged proof that in an unstable foreign-exchange market, equilibrium is necessarily enclosed by stable equilibrium points. Referring to Sohmen's contribution, Johnson continued,

> These sentences illustrate the extent to which *non sequitur* and *ignoratio elenchi* can be accepted as valid argument if the conclusion purportedly reached is of sufficient propaganda value. (Johnson and Bhagwati 1960, 93)

Bhagwati (1977, 224) later recollected that

> what astonished Harry and me was that, at Chicago, Milton Friedman was up in arms. Oddly, Friedman considered the footnote to be an unprofessional piece of writing, and also to constitute unwarranted bullying by Harry of a lesser economist. Unfortunately, he would not keep these notions to himself and to Harry. This style of skirmishing was entirely novel to both of us and left Harry acutely embarrassed and uncomfortable.

Bhagwati may have been more astonished than Harry. Johnson (1959a) had written to Roy Harrod, the editor of the *Economic Journal*, with regard to publication dates:

> I should be sorry to see it delayed as late as June 1960 for one particular reason which is that Bhagwati and I will both be at the University of Chicago this coming year and the last part of the article is a pretty hard-hitting criticism of some strongly-held Chicago views. I should like the article to appear before he has left Chicago.

Friedman's grievance over the reference to Sohmen ended up in the files of the *Economic Journal*.

> Until I received your letter with its enclosed comment, I had not looked at the Bhagwati and Johnson piece. Your letter led me to do so and I

> was profoundly shocked by what I found. I have told Johnson so, that he ought to be ashamed of himself and that he owes you a public apology. (cited in Sohmen 1960)

When the controversy between Sohmen on the one side and Johnson and Bhagwati on the other finally concluded in the *Economic Journal* for June 1961, the latter allowed in a footnote that "we should not perhaps have used the word 'propaganda' in this connection, however, since to some casual readers of our footnote it seems to have conveyed an implication of deliberate deceit which was in no way intended" (Johnson and Bhagwati 1961, 427). This was hardly "a public apology," nor would Friedman have been pleased at being thought of as a "casual reader."

Some of his grounds for unhappiness with the department surfaced in a speech Johnson gave to the Chicago graduate student Political Economy Club at a cocktail party on 28 October 1960, "A Keynesian's Impressions of Chicago." He reported that "at least in some quarters in Chicago" a Keynesian meant something different from what he had always taken it to mean. In Chicago,

> a Keynesian . . . is a weak and spineless creature, who blindly follows the master along the path of error, refusing to modify or develop the system of thought Keynes started, or to test it in any way, or to consider the allegedly conclusive evidence thrust before his nose by Chicago economists. (Johnson 1960a)

He noted that this was not his first contact with Chicago. He had met Chicago theory in the work of Veblen and Knight, whom he had read in Toronto in 1946–47 under the guidance of Harold Innis, a Chicago graduate. He had met Chicago again at Harvard in 1947–48 where he had read the work of Oskar Lange and Lloyd Metzler as they developed Keynesian theory and integrated it with general equilibrium theory.[9] At the time he was also aware

> that there existed in Chicago a lonely group of theorists so devoted in principle to free enterprise that they wanted to reconstruct the world in the image of perfect competition, with government reduced to the single function of exchanging cash for consols or consols for cash as the needs of price stability might dictate. (1960a)

9. He had actually first read both in Toronto in 1946–47.

Finally, before he left Manchester he had come to know a Chicago where the careful, imaginative statistical testing of hypotheses seemed promising. He had observed it in the spring of 1955 from the safety of suburban Evanston, where he was struck by "the missionary zeal of the place and the theological character of its discussions" (1960a).

Johnson continued,

> I have referred to three main themes or motifs of Chicago economics as it appeared to me from outside Chicago—speculation about the nature and quality of capitalism as a human society, together with a sceptical questioning of the relevance of formal economic theory to this problem; the theological interpretation of the theory of static equilibrium; and the insistence of testing theory by statistical means. So far as the first of these is concerned, it is abundantly clear to me that this manifestation of Chicago's originality in economics is now totally dead—whether by suicide or murder I cannot say, though I have my suspicions. . . . I think this indifference, or even hostility towards, social speculation is a great pity. . . .
>
> In contrast . . . the second motif . . . is very much in evidence. Chicago is probably the only department in the country, with the possible exception of some Southern universities, where the principle of marginal productivity is still regarded as a manifestation of divine justice. . . . I have heard it said that Chicago is the only department in the country where a Ph.D. is a joint degree in economics and theology, but this is an unfair exaggeration. . . . A high degree of unanimity [of opinion] there certainly is. . . . But one senses a certain pressure to conformity underlying the unanimity, a certain self-searching to make sure the principles of free enterprise are being properly applied at all times, and a certain anxiety to be the first to attack a new idea and root out any possible heresy. One senses this especially in the products of the system, the Chicago Ph.D.s who can usually be distinguished from other universities . . . by a certain grim and joyless earnestness of expression and an inability to laugh at intellectual jokes.
>
> Thirdly, there is the empirical work on hypothesis-testing. It is on this last that Chicago's claims to professional prestige mainly, and quite justifiably, rest. . . . the work tends to be restricted to a rather narrow range of problems, and to be dominated by the objective of proving either that the price system is efficient or that the government is not . . . and it is not altogether obvious that the only possible way to

find out how the economy works is to sit for two years in a cellar behind a calculating machine.

Such blunt speaking caused a stir. As David Laidler once communicated to me, some bewildered graduate students shuffled up to Friedman and asked if they should have been amused. Members of the minority approved. Anthony Downs (1960) congratulated Johnson on "outstanding . . . wit, candour and trenchancy." Jacob Mincer called it "a fair hit—and that includes fair in the sense of even-handed and generous." But Mincer (1960) mentioned that his colleagues were piqued, although he could not decide if it was in response to Johnson's reference to Chicago's statistical testing or to joylessness. The next spring, Joan Robinson (1961a), visiting Chicago, reported to Richard Kahn that Johnson had "caused such grave offense that he was more or less sent to Coventry." She reported him "subdued and hopeless" (Robinson 1961b). According to Alvin Marty, who was visiting Chicago at the time, Johnson was concerned that he might have to leave Chicago because life in the department had become so unpleasant (Moggridge 2004).

But he did not cease to be critical of Friedman: one need only think of Johnson's (1965) review of *A Monetary History of the United States* and his "Keynesian Revolution and the Monetarist Counterrevolution," with its references to "scholarly chicanery" (Johnson [1971] 1978, 198).

I have talked about the factual accuracy of Johnson's memoirs. However, they have other common characteristics that reflect Johnson's definition of himself. First of all, he tended to see himself as an outsider. This probably made sense for a sixteen-year-old, socially unsophisticated, and insecure undergraduate at the University of Toronto in 1939. It certainly made sense at St. Francis Xavier where he found himself, a twenty-year-old protestant and "one of 'the drinking Scots' with a strong admixture of Irish fecklessness" from a Toronto still dominated by the Orange Order, teaching in a Catholic university run by "'the sober Scots' . . . [whose] cautiousness [was] irritating beyond civil endurance" (1974 Memoir II, 4). It also made sense when he arrived in Cambridge in October 1945 or in Chicago in 1959. But the pose looked odder the longer he stayed in Cambridge after 1949, particularly when he became a Fellow of King's in 1950 and, soon after, an Apostle, although he may have been less comfortable than some in the rather fey atmosphere depicted by Christopher Foster (2001) in his memoir of Noel Annan. It looked even odder when he returned to England in 1966 as Robbins's successor at the LSE. Perhaps because the Chicago connection gave him a sense of distance, he was still to behave as if he were a social anthropologist examining the behavior of a newly discovered tribe in whose most intimate ceremonies he was a reluctant, disapproving participant. Interestingly enough, he dropped the outsider pose in Chicago soon after his 1960 speech.

A second characteristic of Johnson's memoir persona is his continued emphasis on how he progressed without the support of colleagues or with obstruction from them or from the administration. This was a theme at Toronto in 1946–47 (Johnson 1978, 86), Cambridge between 1949 and 1956 (89–90), and the LSE particularly in the early 1970s when he was developing the monetary approach to the balance of payments (1974 Memoir IV, 38–39). For all Johnson's emphasis on Robertson in his Cambridge memoirs, and his tendency in correspondence to attribute to Robertson's example his tendency to understate his own originality,[10] he did not remember Robertson's regular responses to his drafts and his encouragement. Johnson was in an odd position in Cambridge: although running with the Cambridge Keynesians, with his Harvard training he was not completely one of them, and he was, unlike any of them, willing to collaborate with Robertson. Manchester and Chicago were more professional, more stimulating, and more supportive.

So much for a selection of confrontations between Johnson's autobiographical writings and the evidence. Some of the discrepancies were probably inevitable. For example, he could not have told the full story about his move from Manchester in 1969, even if he had known some of the details set out above, because Lionel Robbins was still very much alive, and Ely Devons, for whom he had great respect, had died in December 1967. In private in 1974 he was not so constrained, except by his previous rehearsal of the events that would have become part of his autobiographical memory. Nor was he at all constrained by potential readers in his 1974 "Self-Evaluation" to say what he said about avoiding controversy with Milton Friedman. Moreover, in that case, there was public evidence of their disagreements in documents such as his 1970 Ely Lecture, "The Keynesian Revolution and the Monetarist Counter-revolution." However, given his views about the professionalism of his Chicago colleagues and the "them

10. "I do in all probability overdo the no-originality, recognition of other people's work, but it is likely that I learned it from Dennis Robertson" (Johnson 1972).

versus us" view of the department in many circles, when writing without documents at hand he probably suppressed his memory of the 1960 speech. Moreover, that suppression is consistent with his behavior in Britain, where he went to great lengths to avoid emphasizing any differences with Friedman in the interests of furthering interest in monetary economics. In other cases, he probably just trusted his memory, which failed him in dealing with Robertson's position in Cambridge before 1945: in cases where he did not, for example in connection with the Mill Lane lecture rooms mentioned in "Cambridge in the 1930s," he actually consulted Phyllis Deane (Johnson 1975a).

But perhaps Craig R. Barclay (1986, 97) caught the nature of the autobiographical enterprise when he wrote:

> It appears that most autobiographical memories are true but inaccurate. What is remembered in particular does not reflect the way some event really happened. These errors . . . may be mediated by an accurate "self-portrait" because not just any "memory" is as acceptable as one's own. The sense of familiarity created by an event is associated with a judgment that the event is true to what most likely occurred and consistent with what should have happened.

References

Barclay, Craig R. 1986. Schematization of Autobiographical Memoirs. In *Autobiographical Memory*, edited by D. C. Rubin. Cambridge: Cambridge University Press.

Bhagwati, Jagdish N. 1977. Harry G. Johnson. *Journal of International Economics* 7 (September): 221–29.

Bladen, Vincent. 1958. Letter to H. G. Johnson, 17 February. Box 31, Correspondence to 1963, unsorted.

Buchanan, James M. 1992. *Better Than Ploughing and Other Personal Essays*. Chicago: University of Chicago Press.

Cairncross, Alec. 1998. *Living with the Century*. Fife: Iynx.

Caldwell, Bruce. 1998. Why Didn't Hayek Review Keynes's *General Theory*? *HOPE* 30.4:545–69.

Capaldi, Nicholas. 2004. *John Stuart Mill: A Biography*. Cambridge: Cambridge University Press.

Carlisle, Janice. 1991. *John Stuart Mill and the Writing of Character*. Athens: University of Georgia Press.

Cumming, Robert D. 1964. Mill's History of His Ideas. *Journal of the History of Ideas* 24:235–66.

Devons, Ely. 1951. Some Features of International Trade in 1950. *Three Banks Review* 10 (June): 3–24.

——. 1952. Some Aspects of United Kingdom Exports. *Lloyds Bank Review* 25 (July): 28–45.
——. 1954. Statistics of the United Kingdom Terms of Trade. *Manchester School* 22 (September): 258–75.
——. 1958. Letter from D. W. Logan to E. Devons, 18 April; letter from S. Caine to E. Devons, 25 April; letter from E. Devons to S. Caine, 29 April. Devons Papers, British Library of Political and Economic Science.
Downs, Anthony. 1960. Letter to Harry Johnson, 3 November. Johnson Papers, box 25, Writing 1960.
Dulles, Eleanor Lansing. 1980. *Chances of a Lifetime: A Memoir.* Englewood Cliffs, N.J.: Prentice Hall.
Foster, Christopher. 2001. *Lord Noel Gilroy Annan, 1916–2000: Fellow, Provost—a Memoir.* Cambridge: King's College.
Frankel, S. Herbert. 1992. *An Economist's Testimony: The Autobiography of S. Herbert Frankel.* Oxford: Centre for Postgraduate Hebrew Studies.
Friedman, Milton. 1953. Letter to T. W. Schultz, 28 October. Department of Economics, Records, box 42, folder 10, Prospective Appointments. Regenstein Library, University of Chicago.
Friedman, Milton, and Rose Friedman. 1998. *Two Lucky People: Memoirs.* Chicago: University of Chicago Press.
Galbraith, John Kenneth. 1958. *Journey to Poland and Yugoslavia.* Cambridge, Mass.: Harvard University Press.
——. 1964. *The Scotch.* Boston: Houghton Mifflin.
——. 1969. *Ambassador's Journal: A Personal Account of the Kennedy Years.* Boston: Houghton Mifflin.
——. 1971. *A Contemporary Guide to Economics, Peace, and Laughter.* Boston: Houghton Mifflin.
——. 1973. *A China Passage.* Boston: Houghton Mifflin.
——. 1979. *Annals of an Abiding Liberal.* Boston: Houghton Mifflin.
——. 1981. *A Life in Our Times: Memoirs.* Boston: Houghton Mifflin.
Hansen, A. H. 1951. Letter to H. G. Johnson, 29 May. Johnson Papers, box 54, Toronto Correspondence 1952.
Harris, José. 2004. Mill, John Stuart, 1806–1873. *Oxford Dictionary of National Biography* 38:155–75.
Hayek, F. A. 1951. *John Stuart Mill and Harriet Taylor: Their Correspondence and Subsequent Marriage.* London: Macmillan.
Higgins, Benjamin Howard. 1992. *All the Difference: A Development Economist's Quest.* Montreal: McGill-Queen's University Press.
Hobson, John Atkinson. 1938. *Confessions of an Economic Heretic.* London: Allen and Unwin.
Hoover, Calvin Bryce. 1965. *Memoirs of Capitalism, Communism, and Nazism.* Durham, N.C.: Duke University Press.
Johnson, Elizabeth S., and Harry G. Johnson. 1978. *The Shadow of Keynes: Understanding Keynes, Cambridge, and Keynesian Economics.* Oxford: Blackwell.

Johnson, Harry G. 1945–46. Analysis of Rooming House Group. Johnson Papers, box 54, Toombs, Human Relations in Industry.
——. 1947. Letter to D. H. Robertson, 3 December. Johnson Papers, box 44, Cambridge University.
——. 1948. Letter to D. H. Robertson, 21 February. Johnson Papers, box 44, Cambridge University.
——. 1949. Letter to the provost of King's College, 29 October. Johnson Papers, box 44, Cambridge University.
——. 1951a. Clearing Bank Holdings of Public Debt, 1930–1950. *London and Cambridge Economic Service Bulletin* 29 (November): 102–9.
——. 1951b. Letter to A. H. Hansen, 24 May. HUG(FP) 3.11 A.H., Hansen Correspondence 1926–1959, file 1951. Houghton Library, Harvard University, Cambridge, Mass.
——. 1951c. Some Implications of Secular Changes in Bank Assets and Liabilities in Great Britain. *Economic Journal* 61 (September): 544–61.
——. 1951d. The Taxonomic Approach to Economic Policy. *Economic Journal* 61 (December): 812–32.
——. 1956. The Transfer Problem and Exchange Stability. *Journal of Political Economy* 64 (June): 212–25.
——. 1957a. Letter from mother, 15 October. Johnson Papers, box 31, Correspondence to 1962, unsorted.
——. 1957b. Letter to Vincent Bladen, 17 February. Department of Political Economy Papers, A65-0005/0001, 16 October. University of Toronto Archives.
——. 1958a. Canada's Economic Prospects. *Canadian Journal of Economics and Political Science* 24 (February): 104–10.
——. 1958b. Letter, 10 March. Johnson Papers, box 33, Correspondence to 1963, unsorted.
——. 1958c. Letter to L. Metzler, 11 April. Johnson Papers, box 43, Miscellaneous Correspondence.
——. 1958d. Letter to M. Friedman, 10 May. Friedman Papers, box 28, folder 33. Hoover Institution Archives, Stanford University, Stanford, Calif.
——. 1958e. Letter to R. Kahn, 12 May. RFK 13/48A. King's College, Cambridge.
——. 1958f. *International Trade and Economic Growth: Essays in Pure Theory.* London: Allen and Unwin.
——. 1959a. Letter to R. F. Harrod, 26 June. Royal Economic Society Archives, RES 6/2/111. British Library of Political and Economic Science.
——. 1959b. Letter to J. Johnston, 2 December. Johnson Papers, box 31, Correspondence to 1963, unsorted.
——. 1960a. Writing 1960, Johnson Papers, box 25.
——. 1960b. Writing 1960, 3 November, Johnson Papers, box 35.
——. 1965. A Quantity Theorist's Monetary History of the United States. *Economic Journal* 75 (June): 388–96.
——. 1968. Ely Devons: Obituary. *LSE Magazine* 35 (June): 13.

——. 1969. Autobiographical Notes. 28 June.
——. 1972. Letter to M. Corden, 30 July. Johnson Papers, box 51, Correspondence 1971–77.
——. 1974. Harry Johnson's Contributions to Economics: An Analysis by Himself. Johnson Papers, box 31, Manuscripts 1974.
——. 1975a. Letter from Phyllis Deane, 12 August. Johnson Papers, box 35, Writings 1975 I.
——. 1975b. *On Economics and Society.* Chicago: University of Chicago Press.
——. 1975c. Writings, part 3, Johnson Papers, box 34. Cited in Johnson 1975b.
——. [1971] 1978. The Keynesian Revolution and the Monetarist Counterrevolution. In *The Shadow of Keynes: Understanding Keynes, Cambridge, and Keynesian Economics*, by Elizabeth S. Johnson and Harry G. Johnson. Oxford: Blackwell.
——. [1974] 1978. Cambridge in the 1950s: Memoirs of an Economist. In *The Shadow of Keynes: Understanding Keynes, Cambridge, and Keynesian Economics*, by Elizabeth S. Johnson and Harry G. Johnson. Oxford: Blackwell.
——. 1978. Cambridge as an Academic Environment in the Early 1930s: A Reconstruction from the Late 1940s. In *The Shadow of Keynes: Understanding Keynes, Cambridge, and Keynesian Economics*, by Elizabeth S. Johnson and Harry G. Johnson. Oxford: Blackwell.
——. 1982. Networks of Economists and Their Role in International Monetary Reform. In *Knowledge and Power in a Global Society*, edited by W. M. Evan. Beverly Hills, Calif.: Sage.
Johnson, Harry G., and Jagdish N. Bhagwati. 1960. Notes on Some Controversies in the Theory of International Trade. *Economic Journal* 70 (March): 74–93.
——. 1961. Notes on Some Controversies in the Theory of International Trade: A Rejoinder. *Economic Journal* 71 (March): 427–30.
Kahn, Richard. 1974. *On Re-reading Keynes.* Oxford: Oxford University Press for the British Academy.
——. 1976. Historical Origins of the International Monetary Fund. In *Keynes and International Monetary Relations*, edited by A. P. Thirlwall. Basingstoke, U.K.: Macmillan.
——. 1984. *The Making of Keynes' General Theory.* Cambridge: Cambridge University Press.
——. 1989. *The Economics of the Short Period.* London: Macmillan.
Keynes, John Maynard. 1949. *Two Memoirs.* London: Rupert Hart-Davis.
Kindleberger, Charles P. 1991. *The Life of an Economist: An Autobiography.* Oxford: Blackwell.
Kregel, Jan. 1988–89. *Recollections of Eminent Economists.* 2 vols. Basingstoke, U.K.: Macmillan.
Laine, Michael, ed. 1991. *A Cultivated Mind: Essays on J. S. Mill Presented to John M. Robson.* Toronto: University of Toronto Press.
Lamson, Peggy. 1991. *Speaking of Galbraith.* New York: Ticknor & Fields.
Lipsey, R. G. 1978. Harry Johnson's Contributions to the Pure Theory of International Trade. *Canadian Journal of Economics* 11 (November, supplement): S34–54.

——. 2001. Harry as Mentor of Young Economists. *American Journal of Economics and Sociology* 60 (July): 611–18.

Longawa, Vicky M. 1984. Harry G. Johnson: A Bibliography. *Journal of Political Economy* 92 (August): 659–711.

MacDougall, G. D. A. 1987. *Don and Mandarin: Memoirs of an Economist.* London: Murray.

Meade, James. 1954. Letter to H. G. Johnson, 14 December. Johnson Papers, box 43.

Mikesell, Raymond F. 2000. *Foreign Adventures of an Economist.* Eugene: University of Oregon Press.

Mill, John Stuart. [1873] 1989. *Autobiography.* Edited by John Robson. London: Penguin Classics.

Mincer, Jacob. 1960. Letter to Harry Johnson, undated. Johnson Papers, box 25, Writings 1960.

Minutes. 1957. Department meeting, 9 April and 28 May. Department of Economics Records, box 41, folder 2. Regenstein Library, University of Chicago.

Modigliani, Franco. 2001. *Adventures of an Economist.* New York: Texere.

Moggridge, D. E. 1992. *Maynard Keynes: An Economist's Biography.* London: Routledge.

——. 2003. Biography and the History of Economics. In *A Companion to the History of Economic Thought*, edited by Warren J. Samuels, Jeff E. Biddle, and John B. Davis. Oxford: Blackwell.

——. 2004. Interview with Alvin Marty, 10 October, New York City.

Packe, Michael St. John. 1954. *The Life of John Stuart Mill.* London: Secker and Warburg.

Parker, Richard. 2005. *John Kenneth Galbraith: His Life, His Politics, His Economics.* New York: Farrar, Straus and Giroux.

Peacock, Alan. 1951. Letter to H. G. Johnson, 8 November. Johnson Papers, box 44, Correspondence 1949–56.

Robbins, Lionel. 1957. Notes on the Vacant Chairs in Economics, 17 September. Robbins Papers, LSE Staff File II (1950–57).

——. 1958. Letter to E. Devons, 3 February; letter to E. Devons, 1 May. Robbins Papers, LSE Staff File III (1958–61).

——. 1971. *Autobiography of an Economist.* London: Macmillan.

Robertson, Dennis. 1944. Letter to Kahn, 11 February. Kahn Papers, 13/88, King's College, Cambridge.

——. 1946. Letters to J. Robinson, 20 May and 3 November. Robertson Papers C8/1, Trinity College, Cambridge.

——. 1959. *Lectures on Economic Principles.* London: Staples.

Robinson, Joan. 1961a. Letter to Richard Kahn, 21 April. RFK 13/90/6/219, King's College, Cambridge.

——. 1961b. Letter to Richard Kahn, 27 April. RFK 13/90/6/215, King's College, Cambridge.

——. 1978. Reminiscences. In *Contributions to Modern Economics.* Oxford: Blackwell.

Robson, John M. 1968. *The Improvement of Mankind: The Social and Political Thought of John Stuart Mill*. Toronto: University of Toronto Press.

———. 1989. Introduction to Mill's *Autobiography*. London: Penguin.

Robson, John M., and Jack Stillinger, eds. 1981. *Autobiography and Literary Essays*. Vol. 1 of *The Collected Works of John Stuart Mill*. London: Routledge.

Roll, Eric. 1985. *Crowded Hours*. London: Faber.

Runde, Jochen, and Sohei Mizuhara. 2003. *The Philosophy of Keynes's Economics: Probability, Uncertainty, and Convention*. London: Routledge.

Ryan, Alan. 1974. *J. S. Mill*. London: Routledge.

———. 1991. Sense and Sensibility in Mill's Political Thought. In Laine 1991.

Samuelson, Paul A. 1998. How *Foundations* Came to Be. *Journal of Economic Literature* 36 (September): 1375–86.

Schultz, T. W. 1956. A Program to Rebuild the Department of Economics. Box 74, President's Papers 1952–60, folder 2, Economics Department 1955–58. Regenstein Library, University of Chicago.

Silberston, Z. A. 1978. *Harry Johnson as a Young Man*. London: Imperial College.

Sohmen, Egon. 1960. Letter to R. F. Harrod, 4 June. Royal Economic Society Archives, RES 6/1/451. British Library of Political and Economic Science.

Stanfield, James Ronald, and Jacqueline Bloom Stanfield, eds. 2004. *Interviews with John Kenneth Galbraith*. Jackson: University of Mississippi Press.

Stigler, George. 1988. *Memoirs of an Unregulated Economist*. New York: Basic Books.

Stillinger, Jack. 1983. Who Wrote J. S. Mill's Autobiography? *Victorian Studies* 27 (Autumn): 7–23.

———. 1991. John Mill's Education: Fact, Fiction, and Myth. In Laine 1991.

Thomas, William. 1971. John Stuart Mill and the Uses of Autobiography. *History* 56.188:341 59.

———. 1985. *Mill*. Oxford: Oxford University Press.

Weintraub, E. Roy. 2005. Autobiographical Memory and the History of Economics. *Journal of the History of Economic Thought* 27 (March): 1–11.

Life Writings: On-the-Job Training with F. A. Hayek

Bruce Caldwell

Don't believe a word of what you read in this essay on the childhood influences that led me to become a scientist. Don't believe a word of what you read in the other essays, either.
—Steven Pinker, "How We May Have Become What We Are" (2004)

I notice this very much nowadays, how selective my memory is increasingly becoming. . . . Another phenomenon of which I have recently become aware—I sometimes wish I could return to psychology, I have so many ideas in that field—how much memory depends on having remembered the thing before. And if you have never remembered the thing before, usually it is gone.
—F. A. Hayek, interview with W. W. Bartley III, Freiburg (10 February 1983)

New Yorker cartoon, picture of a shocked Ronald Reagan sitting in a movie theater: Ronald Reagan suddenly realizes that a cherished childhood memory was actually a scene from a movie.

Like many here, I am a historian of economic thought. This means, first, that I am concerned mainly with only one branch of life writings, namely, intellectual history, and second, that I was trained as an economist, not as a historian. I had to learn my craft on the job, as it were. My mentor, or some might say guinea pig, in learning on the job was the economist

I gratefully acknowledge helpful comments from Roy Weintraub, an anonymous referee, and the participants at the *HOPE* conference "Life Writing and the History of Economics" held at Duke University on 7–9 April 2006. I thank Stephen Kresge and the Hayek estate for granting permission to quote from the Bartley-Hayek interview.

History of Political Economy 39 (annual suppl.) DOI 10.1215/00182702-2006-051

Friedrich A. Hayek, on whom I chose to write. It turns out that he was of great help to me, though as I show (and he would much appreciate this), his assistance was often an unintended consequence of his own purposeful human action.

In approaching Hayek as a subject, I took my task to be the standard one of explicating the context in which his ideas were formed and the process by which they developed. I suppose that different people pose different challenges for those who try to play Boswell to their ideas. In Hayek's case, one problem that I faced was to try to offer a plausible account of the many twists and turns in his intellectual development. A thumbnail sketch of his intellectual journey should indicate why this was a problem.

As a youth Hayek had a strong interest in the natural sciences, with an emphasis on biology and especially botany. At the University of Vienna, where he enrolled directly following World War I, he sat in on many different sorts of classes, but concentrated on psychology and economics. When he finally embarked on a career in economics, his first contributions were in monetary theory and the theory of the trade cycle. Though he continued work in that area throughout the interwar period, he also began writing about the economics of socialism and about what would come to be called "the knowledge problem." In World War II he switched again, penning a popular book on the political implications of planning, *The Road to Serfdom*, that would gain him worldwide fame and, in some quarters, notoriety. He immediately switched yet again, beginning work in summer 1945 on a book on the foundations of psychology, *The Sensory Order*. The book, published in 1952, drew on his early student work on psychology. In the 1950s and 1960s Hayek wrote on political philosophy and the methodology of the social sciences, in the process developing theories of cultural evolution and of spontaneously forming complex orders. Few twentieth-century social theorists have contributed in so many different areas.

Trained as an economist, I had no special expertise in any of the other fields to which he contributed. So I knew at the outset that trying to understand, much less make sense of, his peripatetic intellectual journey was going to be a major undertaking. I took some comfort from the realization that, in this age of academic specialization, virtually anyone trying to deal with a figure like Hayek would (or should) encounter similar feelings of inadequacy.

I was heartened, though, when I stumbled upon a five-hundred-odd-page transcript of interviews that Hayek had done after having won the Nobel Prize. Undertaken under the auspices of the UCLA Oral History

Project, the interviews were done in October and November 1978. They were exceedingly rich: Hayek talked in clear prose both about the development and content of his ideas and about the many people he had encountered during his long life. These interviews clearly would be of great assistance in helping me reconstruct his path. I had also learned a great deal of background information about the Austrian school from the very first of the *HOPE* conferences, organized in April 1989 to commemorate the acquisition by Duke of the Carl Menger papers. I had already read a lot of what Hayek had written, and in the early 1990s I was invited by Stephen Kresge, then the second general editor of *The Collected Works of F. A. Hayek*, to edit two of the volumes in the series. The editing job would further deepen my knowledge of Hayek's work. What I had learned at the Menger conference would allow me in my book to set the stage for Hayek's entrance, and the interviews would allow me to block out his various moves on the stage. It seemed like a perfect plan. Ah, the sweet naïveté of youth (or actually, in my case, early middle age).

On-the-Job Lesson No. 1: Hayek Reminds Me of the Unreliability of Memory

Autobiographical accounts based on memory are unreliable, period. Steven Pinker, an experimental psychologist, tells us some of the reasons why. Certain important determining factors of our experience, genes and chance, are invisible to us. But we like to tell stories, so we make up causal sequences in order to form a coherent narrative. We also may want to spare our audience: "Accurate renderings of life are famously boring—just think of home movies." And last but not least, "We all want to look good" (Pinker 2004, 84).

Hayek apparently appreciated this, too, and like Pinker, he heightened the irony by telling us so in the midst of an interview in which he was reminiscing about his past.[1] Karl Popper's biographer Malachi Hacohen discovered it when, in comparing Popper's own autobiographical writings against evidence in the Popper archives, he found multiple discrepancies. Hacohen's (2000, 14) reaction is worth repeating:

1. Hayek's own research in psychology focused in part on the role of memory. See Hayek 1952 and chapter 12 of Caldwell 2004. I recognize that the approach taken in this essay, where I recall various experiences I have had in writing about Hayek, is similarly suspect.

> [Popper] produced an anachronistic account of his intellectual development, reading his later philosophy back into the interwar years. While writing my dissertation, I suspected either amnesia or willful distortion, but neither seems necessary to explain his account (and neither is likely). Autobiographical anachronism is common, and Popper's memory failure may not even be as surprising as I still occasionally find it.

There seem to be a number of things going on here. First, what we recall is always selected from the vast amount of sensory input we receive, and different people select different things. Ironically, given what his biographer experienced, Popper himself used to illustrate this point (in trying to show that science was not based on induction but was a hypothetico-deductive system), when he would ask his students to observe what they saw in his classroom and to write it down. Obviously, without further instruction, each would select different things to write down. Furthermore, in autobiographical accounts, whatever gets selected is then integrated into a larger narrative—we construct stories about our lives, just as Popper constructed a narrative of the process of his intellectual development. Finally, with repetition our construction becomes what we remember, or at least the constructions are what we return to when others ask about us. This last point was highlighted by Donald Moggridge (2003, 597) who, quoting from a book on memory (by F. C. Bartlett), noted the following of the author's conclusions: "Accuracy of reproduction, in a literal sense, is the rare exception"; "with frequent reproduction the form and items of remembered detail very quickly become strengthened and thereafter suffer little change"; "in long-distance remembering, elaboration becomes more common in some cases; and there may be increasing importation, or invention"; and "detail is outstanding when it fits in with a subject's pre-formed interests and tendencies. It is then remembered, though often transformed."

Here is how Hayek helped me understand all this. I experienced the same combination of perplexity and suspicion that Hacohen did while I was editing the *Collected Works* volume titled *Contra Keynes and Cambridge*. Hayek and John Maynard Keynes had a rather famous public spat when Hayek arrived from Vienna to teach at the London School of Economics (LSE). Hayek precipitated the tiff by publishing a heavily critical two-part review of Keynes's *Treatise on Money* (1930), and Keynes did his share by replying before the second half of Hayek's review had come out and by quickly turning from defense of his own work to a blistering critique of Hayek's own book on the same topic, *Prices and Production* (1932). Half a decade later Keynes published *The General Theory*, the book that would both establish his own reputation and give rise to "Keynesian policies" worldwide, policies that Hayek thought wrongheaded for reasons both theoretical and political. Hayek was never one to back down from a challenge. So the question arises: given their previous history, why did Hayek not review Keynes's *General Theory*? I found this to be a particularly interesting question historiographically, because it involved explaining why something *did not happen* rather than why something did.[2] This involves the author in a double burden: first, to establish why it is reasonable to expect something to happen, then to show why it did not. I thought it was a question that still could be answered, because, luckily, it was an episode that Hayek had talked about frequently. Indeed, I had a number of sources where he discussed it: a previously unpublished lecture that he had given in October 1963; an article published in 1966; the 1978 interviews, where he had talked about the episode more than once; an article published in 1983; and an interview with Bill Bartley that took place sometime in the mid-1980s.

This audience will anticipate what is coming next. As I documented in my *HOPE* piece on the riddle of the review (Caldwell 1998), there were two main problems with Hayek's accounts. First, over the years he had offered at least six different reasons for why he did not do the review. (In brief: he was tired of controversy; he thought Keynes would change his mind again; he thought *The General Theory* was a tract for the times and as such not worth a review; he would have to challenge Keynes's whole macroeconomic approach, and that was too large an undertaking; he was in the midst of preparing his own alternative model in *The Pure Theory of Capital* but by the time he had it ready they were on same side, fighting against inflationary wartime policies; he was anticipating that Keynes would soon come out against his own "Keynesian" followers, but then Keynes suddenly died.) Some of Hayek's reasons made more sense than others, so I thought I could still tell a plausible story.[3] But

2. This problem of figuring out why something *did not* happen might be referred to, following Weintraub 1991, 54, as a "dog that did not bark" problem, after the Sherlock Holmes story "Silver Blaze."

3. I argued in my paper for a combination of "tired of controversy" and "in the midst of preparing his own model." Based on her examination of letters that Hayek had sent to Fritz Machlup and Gottfried Haberler in 1936, Susan Howson (2001) added another reason. A. C. Pigou published a sharply critical review in the May 1936 issue of *Economica*, the journal that would have been the logical outlet for Hayek's own review. Hayek apparently did not want to

there was another problem: whenever Hayek recounted a particular reason, he would use almost exactly the same language, word for word, even in sources that were separated by as much as twenty years in time! Quite clearly, Hayek was vividly remembering the story that he had told before, rather than the episode itself.

Like Hacohen had been with Popper, I was initially shocked, but now realize I should not have been. Indeed, now that I am conscious of the point, I realize that I have also been "guilty" of the practice. I am frequently asked to talk about Hayek, and when I do so (apparently "off the cuff"), I am now aware that I return to the same tried-and-true stories, and to ways of phrasing things, that allow me to make whatever point I am making most effectively. People do not like to sound like idiots in interviews; repeating passages that have worked before is a good way to try to avoid the problem.

A Partial Solution:
Make Friends with the Archival Record

An obvious check on the reconstructions we call memory is the contemporaneous archival record. Of course, for this to be possible, an archive must exist. In Hayek's case, this is not a problem—it currently weighs in at 130 boxes, and more will soon be added. Archives, though, are often only a partial solution. They *can* help one to sort out dates and a sequence of events, and this can help one to see whether a subject's account makes sense chronologically. I think that Malachi Hacohen has very effectively demonstrated the use of archives for this purpose in his reconstruction of what Popper thought when.

The Hayek archives have yielded similar tidbits. For example, in an interview Hayek reported that he began work on *The Sensory Order* in 1946, but we know from his letters that he actually began the summer before. One can trace out rather exactly the painful progress (or, maybe better, the false starts and lack of progress) that Hayek encountered in writing *The Pure Theory of Capital* from his letters in the 1930s to Fritz Machlup, who provided detailed editing advice. Hayek's letters to Machlup during the war also allow us to reconstruct his steps in shifting from

appear to be "piling on," so he told Haberler that if he was going to submit anything it would be a note to the *Economic Journal*. But he never did. At the conference Craufurd Goodwin offered his own solution to the mystery: maybe no one asked Hayek to write a review! But, of course, had he really wanted to, Hayek could still have submitted that note to the *Economic Journal*.

the Abuse of Reason project to *The Road to Serfdom*. Perhaps the best example, though, has to do with the Beveridge memo.

In an interview Hayek (1994, 102) recounted that *The Road to Serfdom* started out as a memo to William Beveridge, the director of the LSE:

> A very special situation arose in England, already in 1939, that people were seriously believing that National Socialism was a capitalist reaction against socialism. It's difficult to believe now, but the main exponent whom I came across was Lord Beveridge. He was actually convinced that these National Socialists and capitalists were reacting against socialism. So I wrote a memorandum for Beveridge on this subject, then turned it into a journal article.

From the interview it appears that Hayek wrote the memo, or gave it to Beveridge, in the late 1930s. This was my presumption when I searched for the memo in the Hayek archives. I never found it, so I figured it had long been lost, a victim of one of Hayek's moves.[4]

At a conference in Cambridge in June 2004 I mentioned the missing memo, and another conference participant, Sue Howson, said brightly: "I've seen that memo in the Beveridge papers." Being Sue, she had a photocopy of the memo squirreled away in her attic in Cambridge, and she was kind enough to get it out and make a copy of it for me that very evening.

I knew I had seen the memo before, in the Hayek archives. Once I got home and compared the two, it was clear they were identical as far as the text was concerned. One difference was that the Hayek archives copy was dated "Spring 1933"; according to the memo's content, Hayek was referring to events taking place in May of that year. As a result of Sue's sleuthing, we had found the memo and could date its composition to May or June 1933. The memo is reproduced in the *Collected Works* edition of *The Road to Serfdom* (2007).

The reason I had not realized that the memo was hiding in plain sight all this time is that I had taken at his word Hayek's reminiscence that he had written it in 1939.[5] There are two lessons here: to take reminiscences

4. In a 1975 letter Hayek once explained that his moves "have been the occasion of recurrent ruthless destructions of accumulated letters."

5. Hayek turned his memo into a magazine article published in 1938, which then became a longer public policy pamphlet published in 1939; both of these are reproduced in Hayek 1997. Hayek may have confused the date of the memo with that of the later work that grew from it.

with a grain of salt and, whenever possible, to consult *multiple* archival sources.[6]

There are some questions, though, for which archives will not be of much help. Most typically, these are questions not of timing but of motivation. Evidently, even letters that purport to explain motives need not be accurate, since such explanations are as likely to be self-serving, as our memories often are.

In addition, some questions by their nature simply resist being answered. The question I have most frequently been asked is, why did Hayek not get an appointment in the Department of Economics at Chicago instead of the Committee on Social Thought? Hayek had his own opinions about this, and so did on-the-scene contemporaries like John Nef and Milton Friedman. Multiple stories abound. But anyone who has sat in on a contentious tenure case knows that, even for people who witnessed the deliberations, multiple stories end up being constructed, complete with hypotheses about the "stated" versus "real" reasons for whatever decision gets made. In such cases documentary evidence itself, even when it exists, can be challenged. If *Wittgenstein's Poker* (Edmonds and Eidinow 2001) has taught us any thing, it is that reminiscences of events that later come to be viewed as significant are likely to allow multiple reconstructions and hence, in the end, to remain ever mysterious.

On-the-Job Lesson No. 2: Hayek Forces Me toward Thick History

I prepared for writing on Hayek in the usual way. For example, to do the *Contra Keynes and Cambridge* volume, I read what Hayek and Keynes had written, then read lots of secondary sources about what they had written. I did the same thing for the volume on socialism. The literatures in each case were enormous, so I thought I was doing a good, careful academic job. But in the middle of the process I suddenly realized that if I continued on my path I would be guilty of doing thin history.

In the early 1990s (at least this was when I became aware of it) historians of economic thought began talking about thick versus thin history. (I suspect that this distinction will amuse historians.) Thin history limits

6. Of course, such sleuthing may as easily lead one to discover further inconsistencies in a story as to settle on an apparently coherent narrative. But it should at least help one to get the dates right. As Hacohen showed, it can also bring to light episodes that were not part of the person's own narrative.

itself to looking at economic texts when reconstructing an argument or episode in the history of ideas. Thick history aims at contextualizing those arguments, trying to identify the multitude of other factors—political, social, cultural, and what have you—that might have had an effect. For me, the exemplar of thick history was Peter Clarke's ([1988] 1990) book on the lead up to the Keynesian revolution. I still use his and Bradley Bateman's discussions of Keynesian historiography, published in *HOPE* in 1994, in my history of thought class (Clarke 1994; Bateman 1994).

Though I am loath for various reasons to describe myself as a thick historian (a practitioner of thick history at least sounds a little better), it was Hayek who helped me achieve whatever thickness I might claim. He did so by being such a slack, and at times inaccurate, citer of sources.

I found this out while working on the footnotes for the *Collected Works* edition of *The Road to Serfdom*. Part of what we are trying to do with the *Collected Works* is to check Hayek's quotes for accuracy. Well, for *The Road to Serfdom*, a good 50 percent of the quotes were inaccurate, mostly in niggling ways: he would drop words out, or make small changes in phrasing. There were so many of these that I had to change my initial editorial decision to put a note in for each correction, and instead only noted the major discrepancies. These were the cases, again not few, where he would get the page number, or even the name of the source, wrong. An even more maddening habit Hayek had was to directly quote someone but not say whom he was quoting or where the quote could be found. Sometimes he would provide hints: for example, he might say, "as was recently stated in a leading article in *The Economist*." It was my job to try to track all these things down.

I will, for your delectation, mention just a few of the more challenging cases. In chapter 12 he quotes extensively from nationalistic and socialist books published in Germany during and right after World War I, and in the next chapter he quotes extensively from books by the historian E. H. Carr and the natural scientist C. D. Waddington. He provides no page citations for any of the quotes, all of which I had to find myself. In the foreword to the 1956 American paperback edition of the book, he recounted an episode that surrounded a scurrilous passage that was supposed to be found in an obscure book on the book publishing industry. I could not find the passage in the copy I got through interlibrary loan, and almost gave up before discovering after looking at the University of Chicago Press archives that a threatened lawsuit caused the author to excise the passage in subsequent printings of the book. I would have had to have had the first printing of the obscure book to have found the passage. A final example: in chapter 11 Hayek (2007, 177) poses the following challenge:

> I leave it to the reader to guess whether it was in Germany or in Russia that chess-players were officially exhorted that "we must finish once and for all with the neutrality of chess. We must condemn once and for all the formula 'chess for the sake of chess' like the formula 'art for art's sake.'"

If you want to know the answer, you will find it in the *Collected Works* edition.

Anyway, in trying to do my job as the editor of Hayek's books I was forced to at least scan, and sometimes read, and truth be told, sometimes read multiple times, many long-forgotten books. Doing so helped me realize that he was responding to many different contemporary developments and arguments. Especially in *The Road to Serfdom*, many of these did not involve economists.

Working through a person's footnotes, reading those to whom he was responding, slowly but surely allows one to enter into his head and into his times. If I am not yet a thick historian, I am perhaps a little bit broader. I owe it all to Hayek's inability to get his citations right. But it is a policy that may fruitfully be followed by biographers in general, not just those who are checking footnotes for accuracy.

On-the-Job Lesson No. 3: Utilize the Expertise of Your Peers

So far I have said some pretty pedestrian things—all of them, however, have the virtue of being true.

No, I am not crazy enough to get into an extended discussion of the nature of truth. But keeping things on a pedestrian, or perhaps fundamental, level: in at least one respect, for a historian truth simply means trying to get the facts right. Working on Hayek taught me another lesson: getting the facts right is painstaking work.

When I first started out as an academic, my research was in the area of economic methodology. When I did anything that bordered on history, I realize now that what I was actually doing was much closer to a rational reconstruction, or even conjectural history, than to history. In such endeavors, offering a coherent account, or telling a good story, trumps getting the facts right. I got a vivid reminder of the historian's obligation when I received the reader's report from the University of Chicago Press for my editor's introduction to the *Contra Keynes and Cambridge* volume. The reader was Donald Moggridge, and he provided me with four single-spaced pages of nit-picking. And I am eternally grateful for it, for he saved me from many public errors. I got similar reports from two anonymous referees on *The Road to Serfdom*. One of these actually corrected some of my *explanatory* footnotes, which in fact had offered erroneous explanations. All I can say to that particular anonymous referee is—thank you. You get the Moggridge prize.

Even if you think you have gotten the facts right, though, history is, in the end, an interpretive exercise. People can, and will, read the exact same facts differently. We are in the business of interpretation, and we always bring a point of view to our work.

I actually found this out in college when, at home over summer vacation, I was having a phone conversation with my college girlfriend, who lived many states away. I was in the early stages of trying to break up with her. (This is my memory anyway!) Afterward I heard my nosy, eavesdropping mother describe the conversation to my father, telling him how this scamp of a girlfriend was mistreating me! A mother's bias is an understandable thing, but it is not limited to mothers. Bill Bartley was going to be Hayek's biographer, and he conducted an extensive series of interviews in the 1980s to collect information on Hayek's past. Bartley was a philosopher, a student of Popper's, and was also to have been Popper's biographer. When I read the interviews, it was evident that his Popperian philosophical background shaped the questions and follow-up questions he asked. Bartley's approach, from my own biased perception, was clearly biased.

This leads me then to my second piece of advice about making use of the scientific community in which you live: once you think you have gotten the facts right, find someone to read your manuscript who knows the facts as well as you do, but who differs on their interpretation. This will at least serve as a prophylactic against *wildly* biased readings. For me this person is Phil Mirowski. We have similar interests, and often agree on the facts, but we seldom offer similar readings. Phil as prophylactic—I like the sound of that.

Finally, if your project is a really big one, like a book, it is easy to make the mistake of getting the details of each chapter right while forgetting that those chapters are supposed to feed into a larger theme. Readers, like everyone else, want coherent narratives. To the extent that my own book, *Hayek's Challenge*, has any hint of coherence, it is because Mary Morgan did me the wonderful favor of doing an "editor's read" of my first draft. She was kind but firm in her instructions to me, a few of which I reproduce here:

> At the level of chapter subsections and paragraphs, it all goes very smoothly. . . . At the level of the book as a whole, and of the shape and content of some of the chapters, I found myself left with a number of queries.
>
> What role do you want Part I to play in the overall book? What is "the story" or explanatory strategy within Part I? . . . What is the split between Part II and III?
>
> You should keep the history clear: [chapter] 17 should be in Part II, and 18 should be an epilogue to the whole book. But maybe it is not part of this book at all.

And most bluntly:

> How is this held together?

It is never easy to read such things, but their value in helping one draw the threads of a manuscript together is inestimable.

Conclusion: Some Aphorisms to Work By

I have handed out a lot of unsolicited advice here, so I will close by reducing it all to a few on-the-job aphorisms for intellectual historians: Use oral history accounts with caution. Make friends with the archival record. Read not just the footnotes but the stuff referred to in the footnotes. And do not forget the three Ms: find your own counterparts to Moggridge, Mirowski, and Morgan. Your work will be better for it.

References

Bateman, Bradley. 1994. In the Realm of Concept and Circumstance. *HOPE* 26 (Spring): 99–116.

Caldwell, Bruce. 1998. Why Didn't Hayek Review Keynes's *General Theory*? *HOPE* 30 (Winter): 545–69.

——. 2004. *Hayek's Challenge: An Intellectual Biography of F. A. Hayek*. Chicago: University of Chicago Press.

Clarke, Peter. [1988] 1990. *The Keynesian Revolution in the Making, 1924–1936*. Oxford: Clarendon.

——. 1994. Keynes in History. *HOPE* 26 (Spring): 117–35.
Edmonds, David, and John Eidinow. 2001. *Wittgenstein's Poker: The Story of a Ten-Minute Argument between Two Great Philosophers*. New York: Ecco.
Hacohen, Malachi. 2000. *Karl Popper: The Formative Years, 1902–1945*. Cambridge: Cambridge University Press.
Hayek, F. A. 1932. *Prices and Production*. London: Routledge.
——. 1952. *The Sensory Order: An Inquiry into the Foundations of Theoretical Psychology*. Chicago: University of Chicago Press.
——. 1975. Letter to Helmut Wagner, 8 January, box 56, number 42. Hayek Collection, Hoover Institution Archives, Stanford, Calif.
——. 1994. *Hayek on Hayek: An Autobiographical Dialogue*. Edited by Stephen Kresge and Leif Wenar. Chicago: University of Chicago Press.
——. 1997. *Socialism and War: Essays, Documents, and Reviews*. In vol. 10 of *The Collected Works of F. A. Hayek*, edited by Bruce Caldwell. Chicago: University of Chicago Press.
——. 2007. *The Road to Serfdom: Text and Documents*. In vol. 2 of *The Collected Works of F. A. Hayek*, edited by Bruce Caldwell. Chicago: University of Chicago Press.
Howson, Susan. 2001. Why Didn't Hayek Review Keynes's *General Theory*? A Partial Answer. *HOPE* 33 (Summer): 369–74.
Keynes, J. M. 1930. *A Treatise on Money*. 2 vols. London: Macmillan.
——. 1936. *The General Theory of Employment, Interest, and Money*. London: Macmillan.
Moggridge, D. E. 2003. Biography and the History of Economics. In *A Companion to the History of Economic Thought*, edited by Warren Samuels, Jeff Biddle, and John Davis. Oxford: Blackwell.
Pinker, Steven. 2004. How We May Have Become What We Are. In *How a Child Becomes a Scientist*, edited by John Brockman. New York: Pantheon Books.
Weintraub, E. Roy. 1991. *Stabilizing Dynamics: Constructing Economic Knowledge*. Cambridge: Cambridge University Press.

Reflections of a Marshall Biographer

Peter Groenewegen

It is now more than a decade since my biography of Alfred Marshall was published by Elgar, and two decades since I commenced my preliminary work thereon at Cambridge in 1984. Its introduction showed a deliberate stance in writing biography, as concisely summarized in its final paragraph: "It is in Viner's spirit that this first full-length life of Marshall is written. It attempts to present him, insofar as that is possible, warts and all. It is fully concerned with preserving Marshall's social philosophy, linking it with his economics to prevent both being reduced to a period piece and to enable savouring them in their full flavour" (Groenewegen 1995, 16). The following reflections intend to reinterpret the methodological implications for the "scientific biographer" of this brief statement of intent. What is the Jacob Viner stance on intellectual biography with special reference to Marshall? What are the potential constraints on a "warts and all" biography? Why does economic biography need to be aware of the subject's social philosophy and, more generally, the intellectual and other background to the subject's life and work, and what special value is there for the historian of economics in this particular approach? Moreover, it is easy to argue that a biographical study in the case of Marshall assists in understanding the evolution of his economics from the 1860s to the 1920s. It also enables destruction of myths about Marshall and helps place his economics in the appropriate perspective. To address some of these issues, this essay is divided into four sections. Section 1 examines Viner's

History of Political Economy 39 (annual suppl.) DOI 10.1215/00182702-2006-052

remark, quoted at length in my biography (Groenewegen 1995, 16), on Marshall biography as an important part of Marshall studies. Section 2 dwells on the importance of adequate historical context for intellectual biography. Section 3 examines potential problems from the choice open to the biographer between concentrating on the subject's "activities" by type and a more strict chronological treatment. Section 4 draws conclusions and reiterates the author's firm belief in the importance of scientific biography for understanding aspects of the history of economics.

A comment may also be made here on the need for a full-length biography of Marshall. I discussed this at some length in "Marshall Biography after Keynes" (Groenewegen [1996] 2003). Despite the literary brilliance of Keynes's Marshall memoir, praised eloquently by both Virginia Woolf and Lytton Strachey, that memoir is factually defective on crucial points. It therefore could never have served as a life, eliminating the need for a full-length biography as John Neville Keynes suggested to his son when he had completed the Marshall memoir in 1924. However, it remains a delightful personal memoir of Marshall by an author who had known its subject for virtually the whole of his life. However, personal acquaintance is not an essential quality for a biographer, while obituaries, as Viner ([1941] 1991) indicated, have special problems of their own. These are discussed in section 1.

I

In his essay "Marshall's Economics, in Relation to the Man and His Times," Viner made a remark of considerable relevance to modern Marshall biographers. As already indicated, I quoted this extensively in the opening chapter of my biography (Groenewegen 1995, 16) in the context of criticizing aspects of Keynes's Marshall memoir as biography, because it was, after all, first published as an obituary. Viner had made this criticism when he stated,

> But Marshall is now long dead, and the rule "De mortuis non nisi bonum" is a required rule of morals or of good manners only for men very recently dead. There would be no point therefore in treating Marshall, whether the man or his work, with special tenderness or reserve. He had, beyond doubt, his weaknesses on both counts, including some with which he may have infected his followers, so that we may regard them as points of strength. I am sure also that even his virtues are not to

> be admired by us to the point of slavish imitation. Each generation should—and will—work out its own economics, borrowing from, reacting from, improving upon, retrograding from, that of the preceding generation. Marshall's economics is now distinctly that of a generation which is past, and is increasingly *not* that of our own. . . . As a social philosopher, Marshall is not yet merely a period piece. If he should become so in the near future, it would properly be a matter for concern, but not for surprise. (Viner [1941] 1991, 127)

If they are to avoid hagiography or eulogy, biographers should keep Viner's words firmly in mind. When writing my book on Marshall's life and work, I tried to do this explicitly. So, of course, have many other biographers with respect to their subjects. All relevant facts of the subject's behavior should be presented as a matter of course in the biography. Searching for the relevant detail of a person's life is, of course, not a costless exercise. This is well demonstrated by the high research costs entailed in Ronald Coase's 1994 work on Marshall's mother, father, and more distant relatives (see therein chapters 8 and 9, especially the unnumbered footnote on page 130). Biographers need also to have some qualities of the detective to unearth aspects of their subject's life. Examples are diligently following trails left by inadvertent comments in their correspondence or autobiographical comments in their published, or unpublished, writings. Warts and all is the picture of the subject to be drawn by the modern biographer if it is not to be a caricature or an idolatrous tract. This fact alone provides a rationale implicit in Viner's warning that serious biography can be written of those who have been dead only for some time. A striking illustration of the value of Viner's dictum is to compare Roy Harrod's ([1955] 1961) biography of Keynes (which in many respects was premature, in having to leave out reference to Keynes's homosexuality, for example) with those by Donald Moggridge (1992) and by Robert Skidelsky (1983, 1992, 2000).

Two further points might be noted here, even if not directly mentioned by Viner. They are, however, quite relevant to writing biographies of economists. First, "imagined reminiscence" is a frequently used device by biographers to get inside a subject's skin to speculate better on how he or she would have reacted in certain situations. In writing Marshall's biography, I did this quite often. Examples include my evaluation of aspects of Marshall's behavior as a school student, as an undergraduate, and as a graduate in search of a vocation. My supposition that Marshall very much liked to come first, observable both at school and at university, is one example of this. It helped explain his easy abandonment of mathematics when he failed to come in first in the 1865 mathematical tripos. Marshall's vanity, visible in this and in other matters, assisted in making this hypothesis. That vanity was explicitly remarked on by the artist William Rothenstein. As the painter of Marshall's official portrait, Rothenstein described Marshall pertinently as a "vain sitter."

Second, the biographer's task is made more difficult through deliberate distortion of material in an archive. This was noticed occasionally while working on the Marshall papers at Cambridge. Two examples can be given. First, Marshall's sorting, dating, and otherwise annotating his papers late in life was an old-age activity sometimes designed to mislead. Second, the disappearance of Marshall's verses, shown to Keynes by Mary Paley Marshall in 1924 to assist in the writing of Keynes's memoir, is a case where unflattering material was destroyed, this time by Marshall's widow. What other material went missing from the archive in this fashion is impossible to ascertain, but this type of protective action by a friend or relative of the subject, or by the subject himself, enhances the difficulty of writing a warts and all biography.

II

When writing my Marshall biography, I attempted to place the facts of his life and activities in their historical context. The first chapter (Groenewegen 1995, 9–13 especially) did this quite artificially by placing Marshall's early life within a crude résumé of the major "elements of [those] central Victorian decades during which Marshall grew up," that is, the 1840s, 1850s, and 1860s. Quite differently, much of the chapter on Marshall's childhood and school life (chapter 3) is filled with what I considered as relevant historical background, since very little on Marshall's own childhood experiences was preserved for his biographer. Sufficient material survived to address the issue of Marshall's intense dislike of studying the "classics" at school and his equally intense love in his youth for mathematical and, more generally, scientific inquiry. The same can be said for chapter 4 on Marshall's life as an undergraduate student at St John's College, Cambridge. This largely consists of background on the typical life of undergraduates at this time instead of details of Marshall's actual undergraduate experience, because virtually nothing specific about Marshall's student days at St John's is available.

In chapter 5, much intellectual background was supplied to give context to Marshall's loss of religious faith (163–67) and, more important, in connection with his economic apprenticeship, by giving the necessary background to his initial studies of political economy (145–54). In chapter 7 on Marshall's initial work as an academic and teacher, much material is provided on the establishment of Bristol University College (275–76) and on its growth and financial problems during the years when Marshall was its first principal and professor of political economy (279–82). The same applies to chapter 10 on Marshall's work as a professor at Cambridge from 1885. This gives the requisite background on the Cambridge political economy chair and on Marshall's predecessors (302–4) as well as that required for discussing Marshall's official duties as a Cambridge professor over the twenty-three years he held the chair.

The six subsequent chapters, all devoted to specific aspects of Marshall's life and activities as a university professor, provided much material to set these matters in their context. In chapter 11, on the advice Marshall gave to government as a university professor, historical background is systematically provided to explain the nature of the government inquiries in which he participated either as expert witness or as member of a government committee evaluating the evidence in the case of the Labour Commission. With relevance to the discussion of section 3 of this essay, this chapter also explicitly sacrificed chronology by treating Marshall's monetary evidence seriatim (343), while his role with respect to the Aged Poor Commission was examined in the wider context of his, and his wife's, long association with the Charity Organisation Society. This made the chapter very long, unavoidably so, given the importance of this official work in Marshall's life as a practicing academic economist at Cambridge and Bristol. The long chapter on the initial writing and subsequent revisions of Marshall's *Principles of Economics* (chapter 12) interlinks this process with his other writing activities as essential background (e.g., 405–6, 426–27). Adequate historical background was particularly necessary for chapters 13 and 14, devoted respectively to Marshall as advocate of causes and as occasionally strident controversialist, and to his volte-face over feminism and the place of women in the university. Both chapters were designed to highlight aspects of Marshall's character, work, and beliefs not adequately reflected in earlier depictions of Marshall (especially that of Pigou 1925, 81–90). They focused on Marshall, the "austere" scholar, diligently avoiding controversy and simply devoting himself to the search for scientific truth rather than to divisive issues of social reform (Groenewegen 1995, 443). Marshall's quarrels with Cunningham, Eugen von Böhm-Bawerk, Knut Wicksell, and Karl Pearson are striking examples of his deliberate involvement in heated controversy. More generally, this applies to his role in university clubs and societies and, in particular, his very active involvement as a university professor in opposing degrees for women at Cambridge. Subsequent chapters on Marshall's attitudes and activities—chapter 15 on the creation of the economics and politics tripos, chapter 16 on his politics, and chapter 19 on his final volumes—invariably include the essential background to contemporary practice and beliefs on these subjects (pages 581–82 on Henry George in chapter 16 are a good example).

Reviewers of my biography reacted quite differently to the manner in which I added such background to the various chapters. Most appreciated placing Marshall in context, though some reviewers deplored its cost in terms of length of the finished product and the tendency for such detail to swamp key features of the subject of the biography. As Friedman's (1996) review clearly implied, whether background detail in a biography is considered to be too much or too little generally depends on the reader's degree of interest in the subject. For an enthusiastic Marshallian such as Friedman, substantial detail was clearly no problem. Whether the detail could have been more concisely presented if chronological treatment had been consistently adopted in writing the book is briefly pursued in the next section.

III

When I planned the structure of my Marshall biography, the most difficult decision concerned the extent to which it should follow the chronology of Marshall's long life. For the period of Marshall's working life in particular, the alternative was to focus on the material in terms of his major activities. The issue was decided in favor of activities for the chapters at the center of the book (chapters 7–19), comprising two-thirds of its contents. The first six chapters and the final two were essentially constructed on chronological lines. But even this generalization on the division of the text between chronology and activities is somewhat loose. For example, the title of chapter 8 on Marshall's marriage proclaims to cover the years 1877 to 1924. Some of its preliminary material, however, goes back to well before 1850 when discussing the bride and her ancestry (Groenewegen 1995, 225–28) and explicitly includes the years 1872–76 that correspond to Alfred and Mary's courtship and engagement (228–30). Likewise, chapter 12 on the "long haul of the *Principles*" goes from 1881, the year work on that book was started on a Palermo roof, to 1922, the year of the last "reprint" of its eighth edition during Marshall's lifetime, for which Marshall made several minor amendments to the text.

One reviewer (Moggridge 1997, 289) clearly grasped why activities rather than chronology predominated in my story of the greater part of Marshall's active life. There was insufficient material to pursue the Marshall story in strict chronology. That review also argued that even if chronology had been possible, it would probably not have been "all that interesting or helpful." The accuracy of that observation can be demonstrated by chronologically examining a single year from Marshall's "active" academic life as a Cambridge professor on the basis of available sources. For this purpose, 1886 is the year chosen. For much of its chronology, basic data sources include the unpublished diaries of John Neville Keynes and volume 1 of Marshall's published correspondence (Whitaker 1996).

Given that 1886 was the second year of Marshall's professorship at Cambridge, teaching commitments took up a significant part of the year. During Easter term 1886, Marshall lectured on "speculation, Taxation, etc." or, as he alternatively put it, some of the contents of John Stuart Mill's *Principles*, especially books 4 and 5. In Michaelmas term 1886, Marshall lectured on production and value. Both courses involved two lectures per week. In addition, Marshall made himself available to students "at home" during the term for four afternoons per week, that is, between 4:00 p.m. and 7:00 p.m. from Mondays to Thursdays. This teaching schedule left weekends free, hence enabling occasional trips from Cambridge. An example of the last was a visit to Benjamin Jowett at Oxford on the weekend of 22–24 January 1886, to meet with Mr. and Mrs. Humphrey Ward and Mr. Weldon, a new master from Harrow. Alternatively, they were used for extracurricular activities such as giving a speech at the Guildhall on "economic forces," as happened on Saturday, 5 March 1886.

However, on the evidence, the Marshalls spent most of 1886 in Cambridge. For instance, they were there for the whole of August, normally a month when they would have been away in Europe on vacation. This enabled them to take possession of their newly built residence, Balliol Croft, at 6 Madingley Road, completed in July. During 1886, the Marshalls' summer vacation away from Cambridge was probably limited to part of July for that reason. They then stayed at Sherringham, near Cromer in Norfolk, from where Marshall addressed two letters to Foxwell (17 and 26 July 1886; reprinted in Whitaker 1996). These mentioned that Marshall used much of this short summer break to work on his *Principles of Economics*, as he did in fact for most summers of the 1880s. Whether Marshall took a break from that task on 24 July to celebrate his birthday is not recorded.

The Marshalls' move into their new house during early August 1886 must have gone smoothly, since on Wednesday (10 August) Professor and Mrs. Francis Amasa Walker arrived as houseguests and were encountered there by John Neville Keynes for lunch the following Saturday (13 August). The last four months of 1886, as already indicated, were largely spent in Cambridge because of the Marshalls' teaching commitments together with other pressing work. This included giving advice to Charles Booth on the poor law inquiry in October. Earlier in the year (in May), Marshall had been involved in work for the government, answering questions for the Royal Commission on Depression and Trade. Monetary issues continued to occupy Marshall during the first half of 1886, as shown by letters to the *Statist* on 24 May and to Robert Giffen in June, the second of which explained Marshall's "own hobby" of symmetallism in the field of monetary policy.

The Easter term of 1886 also involved Marshall in some academic administrative matters. A Moral Sciences Board meeting, which Marshall dutifully attended as a member, took place in mid-March. A consequence of its deliberations probably includes Marshall's letter to the vice-chancellor on 15 March offering to finance a special prize for political economy students. On 11 May, John Neville Keynes's diary reported a rather stormy Moral Sciences Board meeting with considerable friction between Marshall and Henry Sidgwick, presumably over Sidgwick's right as its chairman to vet Marshall's examination papers in political economy. This matter was not resolved until 29 May. Marshall then informed Keynes in person, and Foxwell by letter, that the political economy papers had been approved after a compromise had been reached between himself and Sidgwick. On 6 June Keynes's diary records a (perhaps celebratory) dinner at the Marshalls attended by Keynes, Foxwell, and Marshall's former Oxford student L. L. Price. A week later (13 June), Keynes's diary noted Marshall's comments in a "confidential letter" to Keynes on the "poor quality" of the moral sciences tripos results. Much of Marshall's 1886 quarrels with Sidgwick related to his staunch opposition to Sidgwick's vetting of his political economy examination papers, which had induced similar quarrels in 1885 (Groenewegen 1995, 307–8).

In short, 1886 was a rather important year for consolidating Marshall's new position as professor of political economy at Cambridge. During 1886 Marshall moved into the Cambridge house that served him and his wife for the remainder of their lives; he continued quarreling with Sidgwick over the extent of his professorial rights in examining political economy students; and he began occasional advice to governments on monetary and associated matters. On another note, his preserved correspondence for 1886 reveals he received copies of their recent books from J. B. Clark (*The Philosophy of Wealth*) in October and from Léon Walras (*Théorie de la monnaie*) in November, that he entertained various visitors at home, and that he worked hard on his own *Principles of Economics* during the summer. He even contributed several letters to the press in 1886 (on 11 February to the *Times* on outdoor relief, on 24 May to the *Statist*). The year seems to have ended with Christmas festivities at St John's College from 27 to 31 December, but the extent of Marshall's active participation is not known. Nothing definite is indicated by the remaining evidence about how the Marshalls spent September 1886. Did they use September to leave Cambridge for another brief holiday at the seaside or, what is in fact far more likely, did they remain in their new home preparing for the new academic year beginning in October?

In describing events in a person's life year by year in this fashion, and even more if the late Victorian practice of strict chronology is followed in writing a "life," many notes would be required to provide context and meaning to the information on activities, classified and ordered by the time they occurred. In particular, much cross-referencing would have to be provided to link these events to their consequences and origins. It may be noted in this context that I did not even follow strict chronology in the three longish paragraphs just devoted to portray Marshall, aged 43–44, anno 1886. The thicket of impenetrable detail (to use Skidelsky's [1996] phrase from his review of my book) would have got even thicker under chronological treatment, since many events in a life are not easily portrayed in chronology if there is to be any continuity to the story at all.

Furthermore, some details for 1886 contained in Marshall's correspondence were not used in these three paragraphs. On 26 February Marshall had written to Arthur H. D. Acland on labor statistics; on 24 March he wrote to Herbert Foxwell on the colonial customs league; on 27 March on the history of the Political Economy Club; on 17 June he wrote Edgeworth on Indian currency and other matters; on 27 October he wrote to Oscar Browning on the transfer of Pryme's pamphlet collection to the gallery of the Philosophical Societies Library; on 13 November he wrote to Macmillan on the planned translation of *Economics of Industry* by an Indian; on 17 November he wrote to Foxwell on the Pryme collection and how it should be bound; and, finally, on 29 November Professor Francis Walker sent Marshall a letter on the history of the second army corps (though this letter was probably not received at Balliol Croft until well into December), while Marshall from Cambridge wrote a letter to Karl Pearson indicating a desire to meet him.

If I were to write my Marshall biography again, I am certain that I would again divide its contents, partly chronologically, partly by activities. The "available material" leaves no other course open, while coherent treatment of the life of an academic economist makes it difficult to avoid writing much of that life in terms of activities. I might note here that Torsten Gardlund's *Life of Knut Wicksell* (1958) was similarly constructed, as were David Weatherall's (1976) biography of Ricardo and Gordon Fletcher's *Understanding Dennis Robertson* (2000). Emphasis on activities appears to be the way to go in biographies of economists.

IV

There are only a few conclusions derivable from my reflections as a Marshall biographer. Viner's demand for a "warts and all" biography is now even less controversial for a prospective biographer of an economist than it was for me when I started writing Marshall's life or when Viner made these remarks in 1940. Likewise, the need to provide the relevant factual background in a biography is rarely questioned. What can be queried is the amount, and type, of detail given, an important matter for judgment by the biographer and one on which there is not always agreement. Finally, blending chronology with a treatment in terms of activities seems the best way to proceed for the economist biographer, since often there is too little material available for a strict chronological account. Moreover, the activities engaged in by the economist subject are generally biographical material of special value to the historian of economics.

The last point is one that needs further emphasis. For the historian of economic ideas, biography is particularly useful because of its ability to provide necessary background on the manner in which the economist in question developed ideas. In Marshall's case, it is not difficult to give examples on this from aspects of his life. His practice of using the summer vacation for extensive travel is one. Marshall's profound knowledge of contemporary industrial practice was greatly sharpened by his visits to industrial towns and factories during many summers, a practice he once described as his "inductions." Their findings color much of the contents of book 4 of his *Principles of Economics* on the theory of production, as indeed they did for substantial parts of the later *Industry and Trade* and earlier *Economics of Industry*. Chapter 7 of my biography attempted to put the fruits of this enduring habit in the context of his writings, sometimes directly linking specific content of some of these writings to observations made during these travels. This aspect of Marshall's regular activities as an economist allows much insight into the empirical nature of some of his theorizing.

I have therefore no doubts about the value of economist biography for the historian of economics, even though the extent of that value is not always easy to generalize. I also confess to enjoy reading biographies of economists or, for that matter, biography in general, including autobiography. My decade of research for the writing of Marshall's biography taught me personally a great deal about Marshall's economics, even if that was not always visible in the biography as published. The biography of an economist, as Bernard Corry (1996, 27) noted in his review of my book, is different from a treatise on that economist's scientific work whether for reinterpretation or initial, critical assessment. It thereby provides an often invaluable input to the work of the historian of economic ideas, on the nature of which it is difficult to generalize. To end these reflections on a personal note, I have absolutely no regrets about devoting a decade or so of my life to writing a biography of Marshall. As a historian of economics, it taught me a great deal, and not only about Marshall. Furthermore, hearing that my volume on Marshall's life has assisted a researcher into his economics continues to give me great pleasure and reinforces my already strong belief in the value of biography for the historian of economics.

References

Coase, R. H. 1994. *Essays on Economics and Economists*. Chicago: University of Chicago Press.

Corry, Bernard A. 1996. The Soaring Eagle: Alfred Marshall, 1842–1924. *History of Economic Thought Newsletter*, no. 56 (Summer): 26–27.

Fletcher, Gordon. 2000. *Understanding Dennis Robertson: The Man and His Work*. Cheltenham, U.K.: Elgar.

Friedman, Milton. 1996. Review of *A Soaring Eagle: Alfred Marshall (1842–1924)*, by Peter Groenewegen. *Journal of Economic Literature* 34.4:1989–91.

Gardlund, Torsten. 1958. *The Life of Knut Wicksell*. Stockholm: Almqvist and Wiksell.

Groenewegen, Peter. 1995. *A Soaring Eagle: Alfred Marshall (1842–1924)*. Cheltenham, U.K.: Elgar.

——. [1996] 2003. Marshall Biography after Keynes. In *Classics and Moderns*, by Peter Groenewegen. London: Routledge.
Harrod, R. F. [1955] 1961. *The Life of John Maynard Keynes*. London: Macmillan.
Keynes, J. M. [1924] 1972. Alfred Marshall. In *Essays in Biography*, vol. 10 of *The Collected Writings of John Maynard Keynes*. London: Macmillan for the Royal Economic Society.
Marshall, Alfred. 1890. *Principles of Economics*. London: Macmillan.
——. 1920. *Principles of Economics*. 8th ed. London: Macmillan.
——. [1893] 1997. Address to the British Economic Association on Economics and Ethics. In vol. 2 of *Alfred Marshall, Collected Essays, 1872–1917*, edited by Peter Groenewegen. Bristol, U.K.: Overstone.
Moggridge, Don. 1992. *Maynard Keynes: An Economist's Biography*. London: Routledge.
——. 1997. Marshall in Context: A Review Essay. *Research in the History of Economic Thought and Methodology* 15:287–94.
Pigou, A. C., ed. 1925. *Memorials of Alfred Marshall*. London: Macmillan.
Skidelsky, Robert. 1983. *Hopes Betrayed, 1883–1920*. Vol. 1 of *John Maynard Keynes*. London: Macmillan.
——. 1992. *The Economist as Saviour, 1920–1937*. Vol. 2 of *John Maynard Keynes*. London: Macmillan.
——. 1996. The Sage Who Was Reluctant to Publish. *Times Literary Supplement*, 26 January, 11–12.
——. 2000. *Fighting for Britain, 1937–1946*. Vol. 3 of *John Maynard Keynes*. London: Macmillan.
Viner, Jacob. [1941] 1991. Marshall's Economics, in Relation to the Man and His Times. In *Essays on the Intellectual History of Economics*, edited by Douglas A. Irwin. Princeton, N.J.: Princeton University Press.
Weatherall, David. 1976. *David Ricardo: A Biography*. The Hague: Martinus Nijhoff.
Whitaker, John K., ed. 1996. *The Correspondence of Alfred Marshall, Economist*. 3 vols. Cambridge: Cambridge University Press for the Royal Economic Society.

A Personal Afterword

E. Roy Weintraub

Timothy Garton Ash's personal history *The File* (1997) tells the story of how Ash, a mature historian and journalist, returned in the mid-1990s to Berlin where he had been a student in the late 1970s and early 1980s. On that visit he gained possession of the file that the Stasi, the East German intelligence service, had kept on him. As he went through that file, he tried to make sense of the life that it recorded and the person, himself, whom the file constructed. Consulting the contemporaneous diary he had kept, and numerous letters he had sent and received in that period, he wrote:

> The galling thing is to discover how much I myself have forgotten of my own life. Even today, when I have this minute documentary record—the file, the diary, the letters—I can still only grope towards an imaginative reconstruction of that past me. For each individual self is built . . . through this continuous remixing of memory and forgetting. But if I can't even work out what I myself was like fifteen years ago, what chance have I of writing anyone else's history? (221)

Ash sought to reconstruct his own personal narrative contextualized, as any historian would wish, by the larger confluence of contingent circumstances in time and place and community. But it is rare that we have the opportunity, as Ash did, to examine such an external record of our

History of Political Economy 39 (annual suppl.) 10.1215/00182702-2006-053

own life to suspend against memory and memorabilia. Moreover, as Jeremy Popkin taught us in *History, Historians, and Autobiography* (2005), historians who attempt autobiographical writing are in the difficult position of having their historian's sensibilities confronted with their own autonarratives, and their personal sensibilities, which are necessarily engaged when recounting their own lives. It is difficult to provide the deeply layered contextualized account that a historian would seek to construct of another when the other is that same historian. As Ludwig Wittgenstein (1984, 34–34e) so properly said, "Nothing is so difficult as not deceiving one's self."

As a therapist works with a client to reconstruct narratives of self that are more useful and productive for living the present life, self-deception must be faced even as the idea unfortunately suggests the existence of a true account with which one is unable to make contact. But even as the therapist helps the client recognize that personal narratives are better characterized as more or less useful rather than true or false, the problem nevertheless remains to bedevil individuals with a historical sensibility.

This difficulty was brought home to me recently when I read Jerome Karabel's study *The Chosen* (2005). Subtitled *The Hidden History of Admission and Exclusion at Harvard, Yale, and Princeton*, the book unsettled me. As the five-year-old son and nephew of academics, I had had my room decorated with pennants from Harvard, Yale, Columbia, and other universities. My father, who had gone to college and graduate school at New York University in the 1930s, was able to become the second Jew in the economics department at the University of Pennsylvania only after achieving a full professorship at St. John's University in New York. Such an uneven path was not to be for me, he insisted. For unlike him, I was to achieve good grades and an impeccable record of activity that would, combined with exceptionally high College Board scores, secure my admission to the best schools and thus ensure my entrance into the best academic jobs (presumably to carry on his own work). With victory in World War II, and with the postwar, post-FDR liberal consensus ascendant, the fullness of American hope was real to my family. From age twelve I constructed my life in school around the idea that academic success would bring its college admission rewards, and I knew exactly what that meant because I had in my possession the college catalogs of Harvard and Yale. Karabel's history is the story of why there was, and I can put it no other way, not a snowball's chance in hell I would have been admitted to Harvard or Yale in 1960. What Karabel uncovers is the exact and precise record of how Harvard, Yale, and Princeton, jointly and separately, excluded most Jews from undergraduate admission to those institutions.

A major thread in the life narrative that I had constructed in 1960, and had maintained over my lifetime since, concerned my failure to gain admission to Harvard and Yale. I had failed in 1960, and that rejection characterized my relative worth along exactly the axes in which I had been taught to define myself, namely, academic success and scholastic aptitude–achievement test scores. Thus in the last few months I have had to reconstruct a portion of my own life narrative. I have had to recontextualize my own experiences to understand the implication of my having had a college admissions profile as "a short and swarthy and recognizably (to an interviewer) Jewish Mid-Atlantic state resident from a suburban public school." My own achievements, although personally satisfying, could never have been instrumental, could never have served as admissions credentials to Harvard or Yale no matter what my father had told me, no matter what my teachers were saying. My own autobiographical account of this episode (Weintraub 2002, 250–51), drafted in ignorance of Karabel's contextualization, appears to me now to be embarrassingly incomplete.

The tensions between autobiographical accounts and the larger frame tales of historians are palpable, though they have hardly drawn the attention of historians of economics, who move comfortably between economists' personal testimony and explications of their texts. Ash's book to the contrary notwithstanding, the connection between history, biography, and autobiography is seldom addressed with any authorial self-consciousness. When I attempted, over the 1990s, to construct a co-joined history of twentieth-century mathematics and economics, a biography of my economist father and his mathematician brother, and my own autobiography as mathematician-economist, I had neither models for such a work in the history of economics nor any discussions by historians of economics alerting me to the difficulties of such a project. In a real sense then, I have been waiting more than a decade to have my subdisciplinary colleagues address such matters. When I found, in Evelyn Forget, a kindred seeker, we were able to organize the conference held at Duke in April 2006 and thus to bring forward for historians of economics the rich complexities of constructing and employing life narratives. The conferees' contributions presented in this volume indeed mark their own serious attention to biography and autobiography in the history of economics and may help all of us discover new ways of thinking about economists' lives.

References

Ash, T. G. 1997. *The File: A Personal History*. London: Flamingo.
Karabel, J. 2005. *The Chosen: The Hidden History of Admission and Exclusion at Harvard, Yale, and Princeton*. Boston: Houghton Mifflin.
Popkin, J. D. 2005. *History, Historians, and Autobiography*. Chicago: University of Chicago Press.
Weintraub, E. R. 2002. *How Economics Became a Mathematical Science*. Durham, N.C.: Duke University Press.
Wittgenstein, L. 1984. *Culture and Value*. Chicago: University of Chicago Press.

Contributors

Roger E. Backhouse is a professor of the history and philosophy of economics at the University of Birmingham (UK) and is author of *The Ordinary Business of Life* (2002).

Bruce Caldwell teaches the history of economic thought at the University of North Carolina at Greensboro. For the past two decades his research has focused on the multifaceted writings of the Nobel Prize–winning economist and social theorist Friedrich A. Hayek. Since 2002 he has been the general editor of *The Collected Works of F. A. Hayek,* which will provide the definitive scholarly collection of Hayek's writings. His intellectual biography of Hayek, titled *Hayek's Challenge*, was published in 2004 by the University of Chicago Press.

Loïc Charles is an associate professor of economics at the University of Paris Panthéon-Assas and a fellow researcher at the National Institute of Demographic Studies in Paris. His main research interest is the history of eighteenth-century French economic thought. He has published articles on the subject in the *European Journal of the History of Economic Thought* and *HOPE.* He is presently preparing a book with Christine Théré on François Quesnay and physiocracy.

William Coleman is a reader in the School of Economics of the Australian National University. He has written extensively on the contested position of economics in society. In 2003 his book *Economics and Its Enemies* won an Outstanding Academic Title Award from the American Libraries Association. In 1997 he won the History of Economics Society prize for best article for a paper that drew on his 1995 book *Rationalism and Anti-Rationalism in the Origins of Economics.*

Robert W. Dimand is a professor of economics at Brock University, St. Catharines, Ontario, Canada. A graduate of McGill and Yale Universities, he has written *The*

Origins of the Keynesian Revolution (1988), co-edited *The Status of Women in Classical Economic Thought* (with C. Nyland; 2003) and *Celebrating Irving Fisher* (with J. Geanakoplos; 2005), and edited *The Origins of International Economics* (2004) and *Irving Fisher: Critical Responses* (2007).

Paul John Eakin has published extensively on autobiography and life writing. His most recent books are *How Our Lives Become Stories: Making Selves* (1999) and an edited collection of essays, *The Ethics of Life Writing* (2004). He has just completed a book on autobiography and narrative identity. Eakin is Ruth N. Halls Professor Emeritus of English at Indiana University.

Ross B. Emmett is an associate professor of political economy and political theory and constitutional democracy, James Madison College, Michigan State University. He has a volume of collected essays, *Frank Knight and the Chicago School in American Economics*, forthcoming from Routledge, and is the editor of the forthcoming *Elgar Companion to the Chicago School of Economics.* He co-edits *Research in the History of Economic Thought and Methodology* with Warren Samuels and Jeff Biddle.

Evelyn L. Forget is a professor of economics in the Faculty of Medicine at the University of Manitoba in Canada. She is particularly interested in the ways in which policy and decision makers understand and use economics, an interest reflected in several of her books and articles including *The Social Economics of Jean-Baptiste Say* (1999) and *A Biographical Dictionary of Women Economists* (with Robert Dimand and Mary Ann Dimand). Current projects include a study of the guaranteed annual income field experiments conducted in North America from the 1960s through the 1980s.

Craufurd D. Goodwin is James B. Duke Professor of Economics at Duke University, where he has served as department chair, vice provost, and dean of the Graduate School. The editor of *History of Political Economy* and of the book series Historical Perspectives on Modern Economics, he has recently published several articles on the Bloomsbury Group and has edited a collection of Roger Fry's essays, *Art and the Market: Roger Fry on Commerce in Art* (1998). His latest research is on the environmental ethic of Aldo Leopold and critical reactions to utilitarian economics.

Peter Groenewegen is emeritus professor of economics at the University of Sydney and has contributed extensively to many aspects of the history of economic thought. He has recently completed an evaluation of Alfred Marshall as economist for Palgrave-Macmillan and is currently completing a history of the Faculty of Economics at the University of Sydney.

Malachi Haim Hacohen is an associate professor of history, political science, and religion and Bass Fellow at Duke University. His *Karl Popper: The Formative Years*

(2000) was awarded the Herbert Baxter Adams Prize of the AHA and the Victor Adler Staatspreis (Austrian state-prize). His research presently focuses on the Central-European Jewish intelligentsia, Jewish-Christian relations, and the multicultural and ethno-national dilemmas of the European nation-state. Recent publications include "From Empire to Cosmopolitanism: The Central-European Jewish Intelligentsia, 1867–1968" (*Simon Dubnow Institute Yearbook*, 2006); "Liberal Dilemmas and Moral Judgment," in *Naming Evil, Judging Evil*, edited by Ruth Grant (2006); and "The Young Popper as a Scholarly Field," in *Proceedings of the Karl Popper Centenary*, edited by Ian Jarvie and David Miller (2005).

Jan-Otmar Hesse is a lecturer of economic and social history at the Johann Wolfgang Goethe-University, Frankfurt am Main. He is preparing a book on the history of German economics between 1945 and 1975. He has recently published articles on the semantics of economic order and competition in economic textbooks of Nazi Germany and on Michel Foucault's perspective of ordo-liberalism and the social market economy.

Patricia Laurence is a professor of English at CUNY, presently teaching at Brooklyn College. She has recently published a monograph, *Julian Bell: The Violent Pacifist* (2006) and a group biography, *Lily Briscoe's Chinese Eyes: Bloomsbury, Modernism, and China* (2003).

Frederic S. Lee is a professor of economics at the University of Missouri–Kansas City. His research is in heterodox economics. He has written a number of papers on the history of heterodox economics that have appeared in various heterodox economics journals.

Robert Leonard is a professor of economics at the Université du Québec à Montréal. He writes on the history of twentieth-century economics in scientific and cultural contexts, and his book, *Von Neumann, Morgenstern, and the Creation of Game Theory, 1900–1960*, will be published by Cambridge University Press in 2008.

Tiago Mata is a postdoctoral fellow at the Technical University of Lisbon, Portugal. In 2005 he concluded a doctoral degree at the London School of Economics with a thesis titled "Dissent in Economics: Making Radical Political Economics and Post Keynesian Economics, 1960–1980." He is currently researching the representation of economic knowledge in the mass media in the United States and Great Britain.

D. E. Moggridge is professor of economics at the University of Toronto. He has been (with Elizabeth Johnson) editor of *The Collected Writings of John Maynard Keynes* (1971–89, for the Royal Economic Society), (with Susan Howson) editor of the diaries of James Meade and Lionel Robbins, and author of *Maynard Keynes: An Economist's Biography* (1992) and *Harry Johnson: A Life in Economics* (2008).

Jeremy D. Popkin is T. Marshall Hahn Jr. Professor of History at the University of Kentucky. In addition to his work on French history, Professor Popkin has published *History, Historians, and Autobiography* (2005) and a number of articles on various aspects of academic autobiography. His most recent book, *Facing Racial Revolution: Eyewitness Accounts of the Haitian Insurrection* (2008), looks at a very different kind of first-person literature: eyewitness accounts of the great slave uprising that led to the independence of Haiti in 1804.

Mike Reay is a visiting assistant professor of sociology at Colorado College. He is interested in economic activity and the authority of experts, especially with respect to patterns of knowledge, ignorance, and misunderstanding between individuals in social locations—such as different occupations—that are somewhat insulated from each other. He is working on these issues not just in the case of American economics, but also more generally in theories of scientific authority, tacit knowledge, the valuation of consumer goods by different subcultures, and the nature of spontaneous laughter.

Christine Théré is a researcher at the National Institute of Demographic Studies (INED) in Paris. She specializes in the history of French political economy and its authors before 1789. She recently coedited *Œuvres économiques complètes et autres textes de François Quesnay* (2005) with Loïc Charles and Jean-Claude Perrot.

E. Roy Weintraub was trained as a mathematician though his professional career has been as an economist. In recent years his research and teaching activities have focused upon the history of the interconnection between mathematics and economics in the twentieth century. This work, in the history of economics, has helped shape the understanding of economists and historians: his *General Equilibrium Theory* (1985), *Stabilizing Dynamics* (1991), *Toward a History of Game Theory* (ed.) (1992), and *How Economics Became a Mathematical Science* (2002) have charted the transformation of economics from a historical to a mathematical discipline. A former president of the History of Economics Society, he is the author of seven books, editor of three others, and has published numerous articles in professional journals and edited volumes. His books have been variously translated into Japanese, Chinese, French, Greek, Spanish, Hungarian, and Italian. Currently he is associate editor of the journals *History of Political Economy* and the *Economics Bulletin*, and co-editor of the book series Science and Cultural Theory.

Index